The International Court of Justice

Facts and documents about the history and work of the Court

The International Court of Justice
Facts and documents about the history and work of the Court
W. van der Wolf, D. de Ruiter (eds.)

ISBN: 978-90-5887-155-8 (Hardcover)
ISBN: 978-90-5887-156-5 (Softcover)

Published by:
International Courts Assocation (ICA)

Distributed by:
Wolf Legal Publishers
6503 CB Nijmegen
the Netherlands
Tel: +31 13 5821 366
Fax: +84 8376 700
E-mail: info@wolfpublishers.nl
www.wolfpublishers.com

TABLE OF CONTENTS

INTRODUCTION V

Organizational matters V
Jurisdiction XI
Ratione personae XI
Ratione materiae XII
Ratione temporis XII
Advisory opinions XII
Procedural law XIII

DOCUMENTS

UN Charter 21
ICJ Statute 57
ICJ Rules 77
1976 Resolution 125
Practice Directions 131
Note concerning the preparation of pleadings 139

CASE LAW

LaGrand Case 143
Wall Case 249

INTRODUCTION

With its seat in The Hague, the International Court of Justice (hereafter 'ICJ' or 'Court') is a permanent international court which is used by virtually all States. The ICJ serves as the principal judicial organ of the United Nations (UN) and its Statute forms an integral part of the UN Charter. On 18 April 1946 the ICJ started its operations and thereby replaced the Permanent Court of International Justice (PCIJ). The powers and procedures of the ICJ looked a lot like those of the PCIJ even though it was a new institution. [1]

The jurisdiction of the ICJ consists of two parts, namely to receive any legal dispute referred to it by States for settlement in accordance with international law, and to render advisory opinions on legal questions presented to it by the General Assembly, Security Council, and other authorized UN organs and special agencies. All 192 members of the UN are also party to the ICJ Statute, which means that they all may bring cases before the Court. Non-members may also join the ICJ Statute at any time, as long as they comply with special conditions. They may even participate in cases before the ICJ without joining the Statute if they meet a distinct set of conditions, this will occur on an ad hoc basis. 103 contentious cases and 24 advisory opinions have been decided by the ICJ since 1946. And as of January 2009, 13 contentious cases and 1 request for an advisory opinion have been pending before the ICJ.[2]

Procedural law with regard to the ICJ can be found in the UN Charter and the ICJ Statute. The former establishes the ICJ and provides the general outline of its powers, while the latter governs the composition and organization of the ICJ, its jurisdiction, and the basic rules of procedure applicable to cases before it. Other sources of procedural law are the Rules of Court (ICJ Rules), the Practice Directions, the 1976 Resolution concerning the internal judicial practice of the Court and the Note Concerning the Preparation of Pleadings.[3]

---

[1] R. Mackenzie, C. Romano, Y. Shany, P. Sands, *The Manual on International Courts and Tribunals, Second Edition*, New York: Oxford University Press, 2010, p. 4.

[2] Ibid., p. 5.

[3] Ibid.

Substantive law with regard to the ICJ can be found in international law such as international treaties, international customary law, and general principles of law. Other sources of substantive law are: judicial decisions, writings of prominent international jurists, unilateral declarations and UN resolutions. Other rules and principles (not being part of existing international law) can be applied upon request of the parties. The ICJ can also decide a case on the basis of equitable considerations as long as the parties agree to authorize the ICJ to do so.[4]

Organizational matters

The organization of the ICJ consists of 15 independent judges which are elected for 9 years by the General Assembly and the Security Council of the UN. Not everyone can be a judge. According to the ICJ Statute and the ICJ Rules an ICJ judge must be a person of high moral character and it should have the qualities to be part of the highest judicial office in their own countries, or they have to be jurists of recognized competence in international law.[5] All judges should have a different nationality and should represent the main forms of civilization and the principal legal systems.[6]

Five judges are in practice chosen from the five permanent members of the Security Council of the UN, and the different other regional groupings of the UN fill up the remaining 10 seats. Former diplomats and legal advisors are commonly nominated as judges.[7] The President and Vice-President are elected by the Court for a renewable period of three years.[8] Current President and Vice-President are respectively Judges Hisashi Owada and Peter Tomka.[9]

---

[4] Ibid., p. 6.

[5] Article 2 of the ICJ Statute.

[6] Article 3(1) and Articel 9 of the ICJ Statute; Article 7(2) of the ICJ Rules.

[7] R. Mackenzie, C. Romano, Y. Shany, P. Sands, *The Manual on International Courts and Tribunals, Second Edition*, New York: Oxford University Press, 2010, p. 7.

[8] Article 21(1) of the ICJ Statute.

[9] R. Mackenzie, C. Romano, Y. Shany, P. Sands, *The Manual on International Courts and Tribunals, Second Edition*, New York: Oxford University Press, 2010, p. 7.

In case a certain nationality of one of the parties is not represented by one of the judges, the party may appoint an ad hoc judge to decide on the case. These ad hoc judges have to meet the same requirements as the permanent judges and are equal to the other judges. Preferably the ad hoc judge should be chosen from those persons who were previously nominated as candidates to serve the ICJ and the ad hoc judges should not have acted as agents, counsels or advocates before the ICJ in the three years before their appointment.[10] Ad hoc judges are used to maintain the confidence of parties in the judicial process before the ICJ.[11]

Cases in which a judge was previously involved as a representative of one of the parties (or involved in any other capacity) may not be decided by that judge.[12] An example of a case where a judge was indirectly involved is the *Wall* case. However, in this case a judge who previously worked in a diplomatic capacity was not disqualified. The court found that the public comments that he offered prior to his appointment to the ICJ and which pertained to some background issues related to the case, did not amount to his having previously taken part in the case and therefore the judge should not be disqualified. The dissenting judge in the *Wall* case criticized this judgment by suggesting that the Court has broad inherent powers to disqualify judges not only upon proof of past participation, but in any case in which their involvement or conduct raises an 'appearance of bias'.[13]

Disqualification cases are brought before the Court by the President. This President may act on his own initiative or upon request of one of the case-parties. In case a judge does not fulfill the required conditions for service,

---

[10] Ibid., pp. 7-8.

[11] S. Rosenne, The *Law and Practice of the International Court 1920-2005* (4th edn, vol III, 2006), pp. 1079-1081; G. Fitzmaurice, 'The Law and Procedure of the International Court of Justice: General Principles and Substantive Law' (1950) 27 *Brit Y B Int'l L*, pp 1-2; S.M. Schwebel, 'National Judges and Judges Ad Hoc of the International Court of Justice' (1999) 48 *ICLQ*, pp. 889-892.

[12] Article 17(2) of the ICJ Statute.

[13] *Legal Consequences of the Construction of a Wall in the Occupied Palestinian Territory*, Order on composition of the bench [2004] ICJ Rep 3.

it can be dismissed by the other judges unanimously who will notify the Secretary-General of the UN of their decision.[14]

There are two ways in which cases can be heard by the Court, namely in plenary or in chambers.[15] Permanent and ad hoc chambers are provided for by the Statute. The procedure before chambers is comparable to the procedure before the full Court. The effects of both procedures are the same.[16]

There are different categories of chambers, namely the Chamber of Summary Procedure, the chambers for particular categories of cases, and the ad hoc chambers.

The Chamber of Summary Procedure has 5 judges. When a party wants to refer a case to a Summary Procedure Chamber it has to make a request in the document instituting proceedings, and the other party must agree with the referral. Until now no cases have been brought before this chamber.[17]

The chambers for particular categories of cases deal with, as the name implies, particular categories of cases. When establishing a permanent chamber, the Court determines the category of cases which will be referred to that chamber, it also determines the number of judges and elects the sitting judges.[18] If the parties to a case agree so, the case will be referred to a chamber for particular categories of cases. The chambers for particular categories of cases have not yet been utilized to today.[19]

---

[14] Article 18 of the ICJ Statute.
[15] Article 25 and 26 of the ICJ Statute.
[16] Article 27 of the ICJ Statute.
[17] Article 91 of the ICJ Rules; R. Mackenzie, C. Romano, Y. Shany, P. Sands, *The Manual on International Courts and Tribunals, Second Edition*, New York: Oxford University Press, 2010, p. 10.
[18] Article 16 of the ICJ Rules.
[19] ICJ Report, 1 August 2007-31 July 2007, GAOR 62nd Sess, Supp No 4 (A/62/4), p. 52.

The third category of chambers, the ad hoc chambers, are formed to deal with particular cases.[20] Parties may request for ad hoc chambers as long as they hand in their request before the end of the written stage of the proceedings.[21] While the parties approve the number of judges sitting in the chamber, they are not authorized to determine the composition of the chamber, this authorization lies only with the Court. Parties choose for ad hoc chambers because in this way they can exclude judges whom they find unsympathetic to their legal positions or national interests.[22]

A Registrar and a Deputy Registrar are appointed by the Court for a renewable period of 7 years.[23] The Court and/or the Registrar appoint the other members of the Registry. Article 26(1) of the ICJ Rules describes the tasks and responsibilities of the Registrar:

'The Registrar, in the discharge of his functions, shall:

(a) be the regular channel of communications to and from the Court, and in particular shall effect all communications, notifications and transmission of documents required by the Statute or by these Rules and ensure that the date of despatch and receipt thereof may be readily verified;

(b) keep, under the supervision of the President, and in such form as may be laid down by the Court, a General List of all cases, entered and numbered in the order in which the documents instituting proceedings or requesting an advisory opinion are received in the Registry;

(c) have the custody of the declarations accepting the jurisdiction of the Court made by States not parties to the Statute in accordance with any resolution adopted by the Security Council under Article 35, paragraph 2, of the Statute, and transmit certified copies thereof to all States parties to the Statute, to such other States as shall have deposited declarations, and to the Secretary-General of the United Nations;

[20] Article 26 of the ICJ Statute.

[21] R. Mackenzie, C. Romano, Y. Shany, P. Sands, *The Manual on International Courts and Tribunals, Second Edition*, New York: Oxford University Press, 2010, p. 10.

[22] Ibid., p. 11.

[23] Article 21(2) of the ICJ Statute; Article 22(1) and 23 of the ICJ Rules.

(d) transmit to the parties copies of all pleadings and documents annexed upon receipt thereof in the Registry;

(e) communicate to the government of the country in which the Court or a Chamber is sitting, and any other governments which may be concerned, the necessary information as to the persons from time to time entitled, under the Statute and relevant agreements, to privileges, immunities, or facilities;

(f) be present, in person or by his deputy, at meetings of the Court, and of the Chambers, and be responsible for the preparation of minutes of such meetings;

(g) make arrangements for such provision or verification of translations and interpretations into the Court's official languages as the Court may require;

(h) sign all judgments, advisory opinions and orders of the Court, and the minutes referred to in subparagraph (f);

(i) be responsible for the printing and publication of the Court's judgments, advisory opinions and orders, the pleadings and statements, and minutes of public sittings in cases, and of such other documents as the Court may direct to be published;

(j) be responsible for all administrative work and in particular for the accounts and financial administration in accordance with the financial procedures of the United Nations;

(k) deal with enquiries concerning the Court and its work;

(l) assist in maintaining relations between the Court and other organs of the United Nations, the specialized agencies, and international bodies and conferences concerned with the codification and progressive development of international law;

(m) ensure that information concerning the Court and its activities is made accessible to governments, the highest national courts of justice, professional and learned societies, legal faculties and schools of law, and public information media;

(n) have custody of the seals and stamps of the Court, of the archives of the Court, and of such other archives as may be entrusted to the Court[1].

---

[1]The Registrar also keeps the Archives of the Permanent Court of International Justice, entrusted to the present Court by decision of the Permanent Court of October 1945 (I.C.J. Yearbook 1946-1947, p. 26).

and the Archives of the Trial of the Major War Criminals before the International Military Tribunal at Nuremberg (1945-1946), entrusted to the Court by decision of that Tribunal of 1 October 1946; the Court authorized the Registrar to accept the latter Archives by decision of 19 November 1949.'[24]

Additional functions may be entrusted by the Court and in case of discharge of his functions, the Registrar is responsible to the Court.[25]

Jurisdiction

Ratione personae

Al 192 States who are party to the UN Charter and to the Statute may bring cases before the ICJ. Non-parties may also ratify the Statute as long as they meet the conditions set by Article 93 of the UN Charter. As mentioned before, non-members of either the Statute or the Charter may participate in cases before the ICJ as long as they meet the special requirements set by the Security Council, namely: the must accept the provisions of the Statute; comply with the ICJ decisions; make an annual contribution to the expenses of the Court.[26]

Both parties to a case must give their consent before the ICJ can exercise its jurisdiction. This consent can be given through different ways. One of them is through special agreements. Parties to a case conclude a special agreement which they notify to the Registry for the purpose of presenting a case to the ICJ. Until now, 16 cases are presented to the ICJ through special agreements.[27]

Parties can also refer cases to the ICJ pursuant to treaties and conventions in force.[28] These are normally cases concerning the interpretation or application of the treaty in question. There have been brought 83 cases before the Court on the basis of treaty clauses.

---

[24] Article 26(1) of the ICJ Rules.

[25] Article 26(2)(3) of the ICJ Rules.

[26] Article 35(2) ICJ Statute.

[27] R. Mackenzie, C. Romano, Y. Shany, P. Sands, *The Manual on International Courts and Tribunals, Second Edition*, New York: Oxford University Press, 2010, p. 14.

[28] Article 36 of the ICJ Statute.

Another way in which the jurisdiction of the ICJ is recognized, is through declarations under the optional clause.[29] There are 66 optional clause declarations in force at this moment and 38 cases have been brought before the ICJ on the basis of optional clause declarations.

Ratione materiae

In principle, parties can refer any legal dispute to the ICJ, however sometimes the subject matter competence of the ICJ might be restricted by the instrument constituting the basis for jurisdiction. For example cases brought before the ICJ through declarations under the optional clause, Article 36(2) of the ICJ Statute states that in these cases the Court may decide about:
'a. the interpretation of a treaty;
b. any question of international law;
c. the existence of any fact which, if established, would constitute a breach of an international obligation;
d. the nature or extent of the reparation to be made for the breach of an international obligation.'[30]

Ratione temporis

No real time limits are set for referring disputes to the ICJ. However, again the instruments constituting the basis of jurisdiction may apply restrictions to the time limit.[31]

Advisory opinions

Next to judgments, the ICJ may also give advisory opinions on the basis of Article 65 of the ICJ Statute. The only requirement is that there is a request for such an opinion made by an authorized body. Examples of authorized bodies are the General Assembly and the Security Council and other UN organs and specialized agencies authorized by the General

---

[29] Ibid.

[30] Ibid.

[31] R. Mackenzie, C. Romano, Y. Shany, P. Sands, *The Manual on International Courts and Tribunals, Second Edition*, New York: Oxford University Press, 2010, p. 17.

Assembly.[32] The request has to be written and the statement of the question on which the opinion is sought has to be included, as well as any relevant documents with regard to the question.[33] The advisory opinion procedure is comparable to the rules of procedure which apply to contentious cases.[34]

Procedural law

English and French are the official languages of the ICJ.[35] In certain circumstances parties may use another language in their submissions, however they do have to provide for translation or interpretation in English or French.[36]

Parties can initiate a case before the ICJ through an application or notification of a special agreement.[37] The requirements for both can be found in Article 40 of the ICJ Statute and Articles 38, 39 and 42 of the ICJ Rules.

Some parties might need financial assistance, therefore the Secretary-General's Trust Fund to Assist States in the Settlement of Disputes through the International Court of Justice has been established on 1 November 1989.[38]

The ICJ may also indicate provisional measures when necessary.[39] Requests for provisional measures can be filed by a party at any time during the proceedings. The request should be written and should include

---

[32] Article 96 of the UN Charter.

[33] R. Mackenzie, C. Romano, Y. Shany, P. Sands, *The Manual on International Courts and Tribunals, Second Edition*, New York: Oxford University Press, 2010, p. 19.

[34] Article 68 of the ICJ Statute.

[35] Article 39 of the ICJ Statute.

[36] Ibid.

[37] Article 40 of the ICJ Statute.

[38] R. Mackenzie, C. Romano, Y. Shany, P. Sands, *The Manual on International Courts and Tribunals, Second Edition*, New York: Oxford University Press, 2010, p. 21.

[39] Article 41 of the ICJ Statute.

the measures requested and the consequences when not granted.[40] Requests for provisional measures have priority over other cases and in the *LaGrand* has been decided that provisional measures orders issued by the ICJ are binding.[41]

When parties object the jurisdiction of the ICJ, they can file a preliminary objection with the Registry. Examples of objections which led to a decline of jurisdiction are: lack of a valid jurisdiction-conferring instrument in force between the parties, invalidity of optional clause declarations, applicability of a reservation to the said agreements or declarations, non-membership of the ICJ Statute, lack of exhaustion of local remedies, lack of right of standing or diplomatic protection, infringement upon rights of third parties, lack or mootness of the dispute or lack of purpose to the proceedings.[42]

Proceedings before the ICJ are divided into a written- and an oral part. The written proceedings start with a memorial which is filed by the applicant and the counter-memorial filed by the respondent. The memorial of the applicant must include a clear statement of the facts and law relevant to the case and the submissions of the relevant party.[43] The counter-memorial contains an admission or denial of the facts given by the applicant in the memorial, any additional facts, and a statement of law in answer to the applicant's statement together with the respondent's submissions.[44] As soon as the written proceedings are closed, the parties cannot submit any documents anymore, except in case of acceptance by the other party or authorization of the Court. Counterclaims can be presented by the respondent party, however these counterclaims should be connected directly to the subject matter of the original claim and of course must fall under the jurisdiction of the ICJ.[45] The applicant may

---

[40] Article 73 of the ICJ Rules; R. Mackenzie, C. Romano, Y. Shany, P. Sands, *The Manual on International Courts and Tribunals, Second Edition*, New York: Oxford University Press, 2010, p. 22.

[41] LaGrand [2001] ICJ Rep 466 at 506.

[42] R. Mackenzie, C. Romano, Y. Shany, P. Sands, *The Manual on International Courts and Tribunals, Second Edition*, New York: Oxford University Press, 2010, pp. 23-24.

[43] Article 49(1) of the ICJ Rules.

[44] Article 49(2) of the ICJ Rules.

[45] Article 80 of the ICJ Rules.

challenge the counter-claim. After hearing both parties, the Court will decide on the case.[46]

The oral part will take place after the written proceedings. During the oral part parties have the opportunity to call witnesses and experts which can testify before the Court. However, the witnesses must be communicated to the Registrar beforehand, witnesses not communicated beforehand may testify only if the other party does not object this or through authorization of the Court. Oral hearings are public, unless otherwise demanded by the parties or otherwise decided by the Court.[47]

Third parties may intervene in proceedings before the ICJ when they have an interest which may be affected by the case. In their request for intervention they must specify their interest, the object of intervention, and any basis of jurisdiction between the intervening state and the parties to the case.[48]

Multiple proceedings can take place as well. For example when several parties to a case are of the same legal interest and appoint *one* ad hoc judge to decide on the case. No formal order is required to join cases.[49]

Parties are represented by agents who must have an address for service at the seat of the Court.[50] Parties can also be assisted by counsel or an advocate.

The final decisions of the ICJ come together in the form of a judgment. The judgment contains:
'the date on which it is read; the names of the judges participating in it; the names of the parties; the names of the agents, counsel and advocates of the

---

[46] R. Mackenzie, C. Romano, Y. Shany, P. Sands, *The Manual on International Courts and Tribunals, Second Edition*, New York: Oxford University Press, 2010, p. 26.
[47] Articles 43, 46, and 51 of the ICJ Statute; Articles 57, 59, 62, 63, and 65 of the ICJ Rules.
[48] Articles 62 and 63 of the ICJ Statute; Article 81 of the ICJ Rules.
[49] R. Mackenzie, C. Romano, Y. Shany, P. Sands, *The Manual on International Courts and Tribunals, Second Edition*, New York: Oxford University Press, 2010, pp. 28-29.
[50] R. Mackenzie, C. Romano, Y. Shany, P. Sands, *The Manual on International Courts and Tribunals, Second Edition*, New York: Oxford University Press, 2010, p. 30.

parties; a summary of the proceedings; the submissions of the parties; a statement of the facts; the reasons in point of law; the operative provisions of the judgment; the decision, if any, in regard to costs; the number and names of the judges constituting the majority; a statement as to the text of the judgment which is authoritative.'[51]

All decisions are made by a majority of the judges, however every judge may append an individual or dissenting opinion. A case may be decided in favor of the other party in case one of the parties withdraws from the proceedings. The judgments issued by the ICJ are read in public and are binding on the parties on the day of reading.[52] Parties cannot appeal a judgment of the ICJ, because they are final and binding.[53] In case of disputes with regard to a judgment, parties may request an interpretation by the ICJ. However, in the *Asylum* case, the Court stated that only requests whose real and sole purpose is to obtain clarification of binding parts of the judgment should be accommodated.[54] The request must relate to the operative part of the judgment and not the reasons for the judgment (unless they cannot be separated).[55]

A party can also file an application for revision of a judgment, however this can only be done in case new facts are discovered which can be decisive in the outcome of the case. The requirements for the application can be found in Article 61 of the ICJ Statute.

Unless otherwise decided, each of the parties to a case before the ICJ bears its own expenses.[56] And both parties should comply with the judgment issued by the ICJ. If a party does not comply with the judgment, the

---

[51] Article 95 of the ICJ Rules.

[52] Articles 94 and 95 of the ICJ Rules.

[53] Article 60 of the ICJ Statute.

[54] Request for Interpretation of the Judgment of 20 November 1950 in the *Asylum* Case (Colombia/Peru) [1950] ICJ Rep 395 at 402.

[55] R. Mackenzie, C. Romano, Y. Shany, P. Sands, *The Manual on International Courts and Tribunals, Second Edition*, New York: Oxford University Press, 2010, p. 32.

[56] Article 64 of the ICJ Statute.

Security Council may adopt recommendations or binding decisions pertaining to the enforcement of judgment.[57]

With the foregoing introduction the 'basics' of the ICJ have been set out. The second part of this book contains the most important documents and case law with regard to the ICJ. This book forms a useful tool for everyone working and studying in the field of international law.

[57] R. Mackenzie, C. Romano, Y. Shany, P. Sands, *The Manual on International Courts and Tribunals, Second Edition*, New York: Oxford University Press, 2010, p. 34.

DOCUMENTS

CHARTER OF THE UNITED NATIONS

INTRODUCTORY NOTE

The Charter of the United Nations was signed on 26 June 1945, in San Francisco, at the conclusion of the United Nations Conference on International Organisation, and came into force on 24 October 1945. The Statute of the International Court of Justice is an integral part of the Charter.

Amendments to Articles 23, 27 and 61 of the Charter were adopted by the General Assembly on 17 December 1963 and came into force on 31 August 1965. A further amendment to Article 61 was adopted by the General Assembly on 20 December 1971, and came into force on 24 September 1973. An amendment to Article 109, adopted by the General Assembly on 20 December 1965, came into force on 12 June 1968.
The amended Article 27 provides that decisions of the Security Council on procedural matters shall be made by an affirmative vote of nine members (formerly seven) and on all other matters by an affirmative vote of nine members (formerly seven), including the concurring votes of the five permanent members of the Security Council.

The amendment to Article 61, which entered into force on 31 August 1965, enlarged the membership of the Economic and Social Council from eighteen to twenty-seven. The subsequent amendment to that Article, which entered into force on 24 September 1973, further increased the membership of the Council from twenty-seven to fifty-four.

The amendment to Article 109, which relates to the 3irst paragraph of that Article, provides that a General Conference of Member States for the purpose of reviewing the Charter may be held at a date and place to be fixed by a two-thirds vote of the members of the General Assembly and by a vote of any nine members (formerly seven) of the Security Council. Paragraph 3 of Article 109, which deals with the consideration of a possible review conference during the tenth regular session of the General Assembly, has been retained in its original form in its reference to a "vote, of any seven members of the Security Council", the paragraph having been acted upon in 1955 by the General Assembly, at its tenth regular session, and by the Security Council.

PREAMBLE TO THE CHARTER OF THE UNITED NATIONS

WE THE PEOPLES OF THE UNITED NATIONS, DETERMINED
to save succeeding generations from the scourge of war, which twice in our lifetime has brought untold sorrow to mankind, and
to reaffirm faith in fundamental human rights, in the dignity and worth of the human person, in the equal rights of men and women and of nations large and small, and
to establish conditions under which justice and respect for the obligations arising from treaties and other sources of international law can be maintained, and
to promote social progress and better standards of life in larger freedom,

AND FOR THESE ENDS
to practice tolerance and live together in peace with one another as good neighbours, and
to unite our strength to maintain international peace and security, and
to ensure, by the acceptance of principles and the institution of methods, that armed force shall not be used, save in the common interest, and
to employ international machinery for the promotion of the economic and social advancement of all peoples,

HAVE RESOLED TO COMBINE OUR EFFORTS TO ACCOMPLISH THESE AIMS
Accordingly, our respective Governments, through representatives assembled in the city of San Francisco, who have exhibited their full powers found to be in good and due form, have agreed to the present Charter of the United Nations and do hereby establish an international organization to be known as the United Nations.

CHAPTER I PURPOSES AND PRINCIPLES

Article 1

The Purposes of the United Nations are: 1. To maintain international peace and security, and to that end: to take effective collective measures for the prevention and removal of threats to the peace, and for the suppression of acts of aggression or other breaches of the peace, and to bring about by peaceful means, and in conformity with the principles of justice and international law, adjustment or settlement of international disputes or situations which might lead to a breach of the peace;
2. To develop friendly relations among nations based on respect for the principle of equal rights and self-determination of peoples, and to take other appropriate measures to strengthen universal peace;
3. To achieve international co-operation in solving international problems of an economic, social, cultural, or humanitarian character, and in promoting and encouraging respect for human rights and for fundamental freedoms for all without distinction as to race, sex, language, or religion; and
4. To be a centre for harmonizing the actions of nations in the attainment of these common ends.

Article 2

The Organization and its Members, in pursuit of the Purposes stated in Article 1, shall act in accordance with the following Principles.
1. The Organization is based on the principle of the sovereign equality of all its Members.
2. All Members, in order to ensure to all of them the rights and benefits resulting from membership, shall fulfil in good faith the obligations assumed by them in accordance with the present Charter.
3. All Members shall settle their international disputes by peaceful means in such a manner that international peace and security, and. justice, are not endangered.
4. All Members shall refrain in their international relations from the threat or use of force against the territorial integrity or political

independence of any state, or in any other manner inconsistent with the Purposes of the United Nations.
5. All Members shall give the United Nations every assistance in any action it takes in accordance with the present Charter, and shall refrain from giving assistance to any state against which the United Nations is taking preventive or enforcement action.
6. The Organization shall ensure that states which are not Members of the United Nations act in accordance with these Principles so far as may be necessary for the maintenance of international peace and security.
7. Nothing contained in the present Charter shall authorize the United Nations to intervene in matters which are essentially within the domestic jurisdiction of any state or shall require the Members to submit such matters to settlement under the present Charter; but this principle shall not prejudice the application of enforcement measures under Chapter VII.

CHAPTER II MEMBERSHIP

Article 3

The original Members of the United Nations shall be the states which, having participated in the United Nations Conference on International Organization at San Francisco, or having previously signed the Declaration by United Nations of 1 January 1942, sign the present Charter and ratify it in accordance with Article 110.

Article 4

1. Membership in the United Nations is open to a other peace-loving states which accept the obligations contained in the present Charter and, in the judgment of the Organization, are able and willing to carry out these obligations.
2. The admission of any such state to membership in the Nations will be effected by a decision of the General Assembly upon the recommendation of the Security Council.

Article 5

A Member of the United Nations against which preventive or enforcement action has been taken by the Security Council may be suspended from the exercise of the rights and privileges of membership by the General Assembly upon the recommendation of the Security Council. The exercise of these rights and privileges may be restored by the Security Council.

Article 6

A Member of the United Nations which has persistently violated the Principles contained in the present Charter may be' expelled from the Organization by the General Assembly upon the recommendation of the Security Council.

CHAPTER III ORGANS

Article 7

1. There are established as the principal organs of the United Nations: a General Assembly, a Security Council, an Economic and Social Council, a Trusteeship Council, an International Court of Justice, and a Secretariat.
2. Such subsidiary organs as may be found necessary may be established in accordance with the present Charter.

Article 8

The United Nations shall place no restrictions on the eligibility of men and women to participate in any capacity and under conditions of equality in its principal and subsidiary organs.

CHAPTER IV THE GENERAL ASSEMBLY

Composition

Article 9

1. The General Assembly shall consist of all the Members of the United Nations. 2. Each Member shall have not more than five representatives in the General Assembly.

Functions and Powers

Article 10

The General Assembly may discuss any questions or any matters within the scope of the present Charter or relating to the powers and functions of any organs provided for in the present Charter, and, except as provided in Article 12, may make recommendations to the Members of the United Nations or to the Security Council or to both on any such questions or matters.

Article 11

1. The General Assembly may consider the general principles of co-operation in the maintenance of international peace and security, including the principles governing disarmament and the regulation of armaments, and may make recommendations with regard to such principles to the Members or to the Security Council or to both.
2. The General Assembly may discuss any questions relating to the maintenance of inter- national peace and security brought before it by any Member of the United Nations, or by the Security Council, or by a state which is not a Member of the United Nations in accordance with Article 35, paragraph 2, and, except as provided in Article 12, may make recommendations with regard to any such questions to the state or states concerned or to the Security Council or to both. Any such question on which action is necessary shall be referred to the Security Council by the General Assembly either before or after discussion.

3. The General Assembly may call the attention of the Security Council to situations which are likely to endanger international peace and security.
4. The powers of the General Assembly set forth in this Article shall not limit the general scope of Article 10.

Article 12

1. While the Security Council is exercising in respect of any dispute or situation the functions assigned to it in the present Charter, the General Assembly shall not make any recommendation with regard to that dispute or situation unless the Security Council so requests.
2. The Secretary-General, with the consent of the Security Council, shall notify the General Assembly at each session of any matters relative to the maintenance of international peace and security which are being dealt with by the Security Council and similarly notify the General Assembly, or the Members of the United Nations if the General Assembly is not in session, immediately the Security Council ceases to deal with such matters.

Article 13

1. The General Assembly shall initiate studies and make recommendations for the purpose of:
a. promoting international co-operation in the political field and encouraging the progressive development of international law and its codification;
b. promoting international co-operation in the economic, social, cultural, educational, and health fields, an assisting in the realization of human rights and fundamental freedoms for all without distinction as to race, sex, language, or religion.
2. The further responsibilities, functions and powers of the General with respect to matters mentioned in paragraph) above are set forth in Chapters IX and X.

Article 14

Subject to the provisions of Article 12, the General Assembly may recommend measures for the peaceful adjustment of any situation, regardless of origin, which it deems likely to impair the general welfare or friendly relations among nations, including situations resulting from a violation of the provisions of the present Charter setting forth the Purposes and Principles of the United Nations.

Article 15

1. The General Assembly shall receive and consider annual and special reports from the Security Council; these reports shall include an account of the measures that the Security Council has decided upon or taken to main- tain international peace and security.
2. The General Assembly shall receive and consider reports from the other organs of the United Nations.

Article 16

The General Assembly shall perform such functions with respect to the international trusteeship system as are assigned to it under Chapters XII and XIII, including the approval of the trusteeship agreements for areas not designated as strategic.

Article 17

1. The Genera Assembly shall consider and approve the budget of the Organization.
2. The expenses of the Organization shall be borne by the Members as apportioned by the General Assembly.
3. The Assembly shall consider and approve any financial and budgetary arrangements with specialize agencies referred to in Article 57 and shall examine the administrative budgets of such specialized agencies with a view to making recommendations to the agencies concerned.

Voting

Article 18

1. Each member of the General Assembly shall have one vote.
2. Decisions of the General Assembly on important questions shall be made by a two- thirds majority of the members present and voting. These questions shall include: recommendations with respect to the maintenance of international peace and security, the election of the non-permanent members of the Security Council, the election of the members of the Economic and Social Council, the election of members of the Trusteeship Council in accordance with paragraph 1 of Article 86, the admission of new Members to the United Nations, the suspension of the rights and privileges of membership, the expulsion of Members, questions relating to the operation of the trusteeship system, and budgetary questions.
3. Decisions on other questions, including the determination of additional categories of questions to be decided by a two-thirds majority, shall be made by a majority of the members present and voting.

Article 19

A Member of the United Nations which is in arrears in the payment of its financial contributions to the Organization shall have no vote in the General Assembly if the amount of its arrears equals or exceeds the amount of the contributions due from it for the preceding two full years. The General Assembly may, nevertheless, permit such a Member to vote if it is satisfied that the failure to pay is due to conditions beyond the of the Member.

Procedure

Article 20

The General Assembly shall meet in regular annual sessions and in such special sessions as occasion may require. Special sessions shall be convoked by the Secretary-General at the request of the Security Council or of a majority of the Members of the United Nations.

Article 21

The General Assembly shall adopt its own rules of procedure. It shall elect its President for each session.

Article 22

The General Assembly may establish such subsidiary organs as it deems necessary for the performance of its functions.

CHAPTER V THE SECURITY COUNCIL

Composition

Article 23

1. The Security Council shall consist of fifteen Members of the United Nations. The Republic of China, France, the Union of Soviet Socialist , the United Kingdom of Great Britain and Northern Ireland, and the United States of America shall be permanent members of the Security Council. The General Assembly shall elect ten other Members of the United Nations to be non-permanent members of the Security Council, due regard being specially paid, in the first in- stance to the contribution of Members of the United Nations to the maintenance of inter- national peace and security and to the other purposes of the Organization, and also to equitable geographical distribution.
2. The non-permanent members of the Security Council shall be elected for a term of two years. In the first election of the non- permanent members after the increase of the membership of the Security Council from eleven to fifteen, two of the four additional members shall be chosen for a term of one year. A retiring member shall not be eligible for immediate re-election.
3. Each member of the Security Council shall have one representative.

Functions and Powers

Article 24

1. In order to ensure prompt and effective action by the United Nations, its Members confer on the Security Council primary responsibility for the maintenance of international peace and security, and agree that in carrying out its duties under this responsibility the Security Council acts on their behalf.
2. In discharging these duties the Security Council shall act in accordance with the Purposes and Principles of the United Nations. The specific powers granted to the Security Council for the discharge of these duties are laid down in Chapters VI, VII, VIII, and XII.
3. The Security Council shall submit annual and, when necessary, special reports to the General Assembly for its consideration.

Article 25

The Members of the United Nations agree to accept and carry out the decisions of the Security Council in accordance with the present Charter.

Article 26

In order to promote the establishment and maintenance of international peace and security with the least diversion for armaments of the world's human and economic resources, the Security Council shall be responsible for formulating, with the assistance of the Military Staff Committee referred to in Article 47, plans to be submitted to the Members of the United-Nations for the establishment of a system for the regulation of armaments.

Voting

Article 27

1. Each member of the Security Council shall have one vote.
2. Decisions of the Security Council on procedural matters shall be made by an affirmative vote of nine members.

3. Decisions of the Security Council on all other matters shall be made by an affirmative vote of nine members including the concurring votes of the permanent members; provided that, in decisions under Chapter VI, and under paragraph 3 of Article 52, a party to a dispute shall abstain from voting.

Procedure

Article 28

1. The Security Council shall be so organized as to be able to function continuously. Each member of the Security Council shall for this purpose be represented at times at the seat of the Organization.
2. The Security Council shall hold meetings at which each of its members may, if it so desires, be represented by a member of the government or by some other specially designated representative.
3. The Security Council may hold meetings at such places other than the seat of the Organization as in its judgment will best facilitate its work.

Article 29

The Security Council may establish such subsidiary organs as it deems necessary for the performance of its functions.

Article 30

The Security Council shall adopt its own rules of procedure, including the method of selecting its President.

Article 31

Any Member of the United Nations which is not a member of the Security Council may participate, without vote, in the discussion of any question brought before the Security Council whenever the latter considers that the interests of that Member are specially affected.

Article 32

Any Member of the United Nations which is not a member of the Security Council or any state which is not a Member of the United Nations, if it is a party to a dispute under consideration by the Security Council, shall be invited to participate, without vote, in the discussion relating to the dispute. The Security Council shall any down such conditions as it deems just for the participation of a state which is not a Member of the United Nations.

CHAPTER VI PACIFIC SETTLEMENT OF DISPUTES

Article 33

1. The parties to any dispute, the continuance of which is likely to endanger the maintenance of international peace and security, shall, first of a, seek a solution by negotiation, enquiry, mediation, conciliation, arbitration, judicial settlement, resort to regional agencies or arrangements, or other peaceful means of their own choice.
2. The Security Council shall, when it deems necessary, call upon the parties to settle their dispute by such means.

Article 34

The Security Council may investigate any dispute, or any situation which might lead to international friction or give rise to a dispute, in order to determine whether the continuance of the dispute or situation is likely to endanger the maintenance of international peace and security.

Article 35

l. Any Member of the United Nations may bring any dispute, ~r any situation of the nature referred to in Article 34, to the attention of the Security Council or of the General Assembly.
2. A state which is not a Member of the United Nations may bring to the attention of the Security Council or of the General Assembly any dispute to which it is a party if it accepts in advance, for the purposes of the

dispute, the obligations of pacific settlement provided in the present Charter.
3. The proceedings of the General Assembly in respect of matters brought to its attention under this Article will be subject to the provisions of Articles 11 and 12.

Article 36

1. The Security Council may, at any stage of a dispute of the nature referred to in Article 33 or of a situation of like nature, recommend appropriate procedures or methods of adjustment.
2. The Security Council should take into consideration any procedures for the settlement of the dispute which have already been adopted by the parties.
3. In making recommendations under this Article the Security Council should also take into consideration that legal disputes should as a general rule be referred by the parties to the International Court of Justice in accordance with the provisions of the Statute of the Court.

Article 37

1. Should the parties to a dispute of the nature referred to in Article 33 fail to settle it by the means indicated in that Article, they shall refer it to the Security Council.
2. If the Security Council deems that the continuance of the dispute is in fact likely to endanger the maintenance of international peace and security, it shall decide whether to take action under Article 36 or to recommend such terms of settlement as it may consider appropriate.

Article 38

Without prejudice to the provisions of Articles 33 to 37, the Security Council may, if all the parties to any dispute so request, make recommendations to the parties with a view to a pacific settlement of the dispute.

CHAPTER VII ACTION WITH RESPECT TO THREATS TO THE PEACE, BREACHES OF THE PEACE, AND ACTS OF AGGRESSION

Article 39

The Security Council shall determine the existence of any threat to the peace, breach of the peace, or act of aggression and shall make recommendations, or decide what measures shall be taken in accordance with Articles 4 and 42, to maintain or restore international peace and security.

Article 40

In order to prevent an aggravation of the situation, the Security Council may, before making the recommendations or deciding upon the measures provided for in Article 39, call upon the parties concerned to comply with such provisional measures as it deems necessary or desirable. Such provisional measures shall be without prejudice to the rights, claims, or position of the parties concerned. The Security Council shall duly take account of failure to comply with such provisional measures.

Article 41

The Security Council may decide what measures not involving the use of armed force are to be employed to give effect to its decisions, and it may call upon the Members of the United Nations to apply such measures. These may include complete or partial interruption of economic relations and of rail, sea, air, postal, telegraphic, radio, and other means of communication, and the severance of diplomatic relations.

Article 42

Should the Security Council consider that measures provided for in Article 41 would be inadequate or have proved to be inadequate, it may take such action by air, sea, or land forces as may be necessary to maintain or restore international peace and security. Such action may include demonstrations, blockade, and other operations by air, sea, or land forces of Members of the United Nations.

Article 43

1. All Members of the United Nations, in order to contribute to the maintenance of international peace and security, undertake to make available to the Security Council, on its and in accordance with a special agreement or agreements, armed forces, assistance, and facilities, including rights of passage, necessary for the purpose of maintaining international peace and security.
2. Such agreement or agreements shall govern the numbers and types of forces, their degree of readiness and general location, and the nature of the facilities and assistance to be provided.
3. The agreement or agreements shall be negotiated as soon as possible on the initiative of the Security Council. They shall be concluded between the Security Council and Members or between the Security Council and groups of Members and shall be subject to ratification by the signatory states in accordance with their respective constitutional processes.

Article 44

When Security Council has decided to use force it shall, before calling upon a Member not represented on it to provide armed forces in fulfilment of the obligations assumed under Article 43, invite that Member, if the Member so desires, to participate in the decisions of the Security Council concerning the employment of contingents of that Member's armed forces.

Article 45

In order to enable the Nations to take urgent military measures, Members shall hold immediately available national air-force contingents for combined international enforcement action. The strength and degree of readiness of these contingents and plans for their combined action shall be determined, within the limits laid down in the special agreement or agreements referred to in Article 43, by the Security Council with the assistance of the Military Committee.

Article 46

Plans for the application of armed force shall be made by the Security Council with the assistance of the Military Staff Committee.

Article 47

1. There shall be established a Military Staff Committee to advise and assist the Security Council on questions relating to the Security Council's military requirements for the maintenance of international peace and security, the employment and command of forces placed at its disposal, the regulation of armaments, and possible disarmament.
2. The Military Staff Committee consist of the Chiefs of Staff of the permanent members of the Security Council or their representatives. Any Member of the United Nations not permanently represented on the Committee shall be invited by the Committee to be associated with it when the efficient discharge of the Committee's responsibilities re- quires the participation of that Member its work.
3. The Military Staff Committee be responsible under the Security Council for the strategic direction of any armed forces paced at the disposal of the Security Council. Questions relating to the command of such forces shall be worked out subsequently.
4. The Military Staff Committee, with the authorization of the security Council and after consultation with appropriate regional agencies, may establish sub-commit- tees.

Article 48

1. The action required to carry out the decisions of the Security Council for the maintenance of international peace and security shall be taken by all the Members of the United Nations or by some of them, as the Security Council may determine.

2. Such decisions shall be carried out by the Members of the United Nations directly and through their action in the appropriate international agencies of which they are members.

Article 49

The Members of the United Nations shall join in affording mutual assistance in carrying out the measures decided upon by the Security Council.

Article 50

If preventive or enforcement measures against any state are taken by the Security Council, any other state, whether a Member of the United Nations or not, which finds itself confronted with special economic problems arising from the carrying out of those measures shall have the right to consult the Security Council with regard to a solution of those problems.
Article 51 Nothing in the present Charter shall impair the inherent right of individual or collective self-defence if an armed attack occurs against a Member of the United Nations, until the Security Council has taken measures necessary to maintain international peace and security. Measures taken by Members in the exercise of this right of self-defence shall be immediately reported to the Security Council and shall not in any way affect the authority and responsibility of the Security Council under the present Charter to take at any time such action as it deems necessary in order to maintain or restore international peace and security.

CHAPTER VIII REGIONAL ARRANGEMENTS

Article 52

1. Nothing in the present Charter the existence of regional arrangements or agencies for dealing with such matters relating to the maintenance of international peace and security as are appropriate fur regional action, provided that such arrangements or agencies and their activities are consistent with the Purposes and Principles of the United Nations.

2. The Members of the United Nations entering into such arrangements or constituting such agencies shall make every effort to achieve pacific settlement of local disputes through such regional arrangements or by such regional agencies before referring them to the Security Council.
3. The Security Council shall encourage the development of pacific settlement of local disputes through such regional arrangements or by such regional agencies either on the initiative of the states concerned or by reference from the Security Council.
4. This Article in no way the application of Articles 34 and 35.

Article 53

1. The Security Council shall, where appropriate, utilize such regional arrangements or agencies for enforcement action under its authority. But no enforcement action shall be taken under regional arrangements or by regional agencies without the authorization of the Security Council, with the exception of measures against any enemy state, as defined in paragraph 2 of this Article, provided for pursuant to Article 107 or in regional arrangements directed against renewal of aggressive policy on the part of any such state, until such time as the Organization may, on request of the Governments concerned, be charged with the responsibility for preventing further aggression by such a state.
2. The term enemy state as used in para- graph 1 of this Article applies to any state which during the Second World War has been an enemy of any signatory of the present Charter.

Article 54

The Security Council shall at all times be kept fully informed of activities undertaken or in contemplation under regional arrangements or by regional agencies for the maintenance of international peace and security.

CHAPTER IX INTERNATIONAL ECONOMIC AND SOCIAL CO-OPERATION

Article 55

With a view to the creation of conditions of stability and well-being which are necessary for peaceful and friendly relations among nations based on respect for the principle of equal rights and self-determination of peoples, the United Nations shall promote:
a. higher standards of living, fu employment, and conditions of economic and social progress and development;
b. solutions of international economic, social, health, and related problems; and international cultural and educational co- operation; and
c. universal respect for, and observance of, human rights and fundamental freedoms for all without distinction as to race, sex, language, or religion.

Article 56

All Members pledge themselves to take joint and separate action in co-operation with the Organization for the achievement of the purposes set forth in Article 55.

Article 57

1. The various specialized agencies, established by intergovernmental agreement and having wide international responsibilities, as defined in their basic instruments, in economic, social, cultural, educational, health, and related fields, shall be brought into relationship with the United Nations in accordance with the provisions of Article 63.
2. Such agencies thus brought into relationship with the United Nations are hereinafter referred to as specialized agencies.

Article 58

The Organization shall make recommendations for the co-ordination of the policies and activities of the specialized agencies.

Article 59

The Organization shall, where appropriate, initiate negotiations among the states concerned for the creation of any new specialized agencies required for the accomplishment of the purposes set forth in Article 55.

Article 60

Responsibility for the discharge of the functions of the Organization set forth in this Chapter shall be vested in the General Assembly and, under the authority of the General Assembly, in the Economic and Social Council, which shall have for this purpose the powers set forth in Chapter X.

CHAPTER X THE ECONOMIC AND SOCIAL COUNCIL

Composition

Article 61

1. The Economic and Social Council shall consist of fifty-four Members of the United Nations elected by the General Assembly.
2. Subject to the provisions of paragraph 3, eighteen members of the Economic and Social Council shall be elected each year for a term of three years. A retiring member shall be eligible for immediate re-election.
3. At the first election after the increase in the membership of the Economic and Social Council from twenty-seven to fifty-four members, in addition to the members elected in place of the nine members whose term of office expires at the end of that year, twenty-seven additional members shall be elected. Of these twenty-seven additional members, the term of office of nine members so elected shall expire at the end of one year, and of nine other members at the end of two years, in accordance with arrangements made by the General Assembly.
4. Each member of the Economic and Social Council shall have one representative.

Functions and Powers

Article 62

1. The Economic and Social Council may make or initiate studies and reports with respect to international economic, social, cultural, educational, health, and related matters and may make recommendations with respect to any such matters to the General Assembly, to the Members of the United Nations, and to the specialized agencies concerned.
2. It may make recommendations for the purpose of promoting respect for, and observance of, human rights and fundamental freedoms for all.
3. It may prepare draft conventions for submission to the General Assembly, with respect to matters falling within its competence.
4. It may call, in accordance with the rules prescribed by the United Nations, international conferences on matters falling within its competence.

Article 63

1. The Economic and Social Council may enter into agreements with any of the agencies referred to in Article 57, defining the terms on which the agency concerned shall be brought into relationship with the United Nations. Such agreements shall be subject to approval by the General Assembly.
2. It may co-ordinate the activities of the specialized agencies through consultation with and recommendations to such agencies and through recommendations to the General Assembly and to the Members of the United Nations.

Article 64

1. The Economic and Social Council may take appropriate steps to obtain regular re- ports from the specialized agencies. may make arrangements with the Members of the United Nations and with the specialized agencies to obtain reports on the steps taken to give effect to its own recommendations and to recommendations on matters falling within its competence made by the General Assembly.

2. It may communicate its observations on these reports to the General Assembly.

Article 65

The Economic and Social Council may furnish information to the Security Council and shall assist the Security Council upon its request.

Article 66

1. The Economic and Social Council shall perform such functions as fall within its competence in connexion with the carrying out of the recommendations of the General Assembly.
2. It may, with the approval of the General Assembly, perform services at the request of Members of the United Nations and at the request of specialized agencies.
3. It shall perform such other functions as are specified elsewhere in the present Charter or as may be assigned to it by the General Assembly.

Voting

Article 67

1. Each member of the Economic and Social Council shall have one vote.
2. Decisions of the Economic and Social Council shall be made by a majority of the members present and voting.

Procedure

Article 68

The Economic and Social Council shall set up commissions in economic and social fields and for the promotion of human rights, and such other commissions as may for the performance of its functions.

Article 69

The Economic and Social Council shall invite any Member of the United Nations to participate, without vote, in its deliberations on any matter of particular concern to that Member.

Article 70

The Economic and Social Council may make arrangements for representatives of the specialized agencies to participate, without vote, in its deliberations and in those of the commissions established by it, and for its representatives to participate in the deliberations of the specialized agencies.

Article 71

The Economic and Social Council may make suitable arrangements for consultation with non-governmental organizations which are concerned with matters within its competence. Such arrangements may be made with international organizations and, where appropriate, with national organizations after consultation with the Member of the United Nations concerned.

Article 72

1. The Economic and Social Council shall adopt its own rules of procedure, including the method of selecting its President.
2. The Economic and Social Council shall meet as required in accordance with its rules, which shall include provision for the convening of meetings on the request of a majority of its members.

CHAPTER XI DECLARATION REGARDING NON-SELF-GOVERNING TERRITORIES

Article 73

Members of the United Nations which have or assume responsibilities for the administration of territories whose peoples have not yet attained a full measure of self-government recognize the principle that the interests of the inhabitants of these territories are paramount, and accept as a sacred trust the obligation to promote to the utmost, within the system of international peace and security established by the present Charter, the well- being of the inhabitants of these territories, and, to this end:

a. to ensure, with due respect for the culture of the peoples concerned, their political, economic, social, and educational advancement, their just treatment, and their protection against abuses;

b. to develop self-government, to take due account of the political aspirations of the peoples, and to assist them in the progressive development of their free political institutions, according to the particular circumstances of each territory and its peoples and their varying stages of advancement;

c. to further international peace and security;

d. to promote constructive measures of development, to encourage research, and to co-operate with one another and, when and where appropriate, with specialized international bodies with a view to the practical achievement of the social, eco- nomic, and scientific purposes set forth in this Article; and

e. to transmit regularly to the Secretary- General for information purposes, subject to such limitation as security and constitutional considerations may require, statistical and other information of a technical nature relating to economic, social, and educational conditions in the territories for which they are respectively responsible other than those territories to which Chapters XII and XIII apply.

Article 74

Members of the United Nations also agree that their policy in respect of the territories to which this Chapter applies, no less than in respect of their metropolitan areas, must be based on the general principle of good-neigh-bourliness, due account being taken of the interests and well-being of the rest of the world, in social, economic, and commercial matters.

CHAPTER XII INTERNATIONAL TRUSTEESHIP SYSTEM

Article 75

The United Nations shall establish under its authority an international trusteeship system for the administration and supervision of such territories as may be placed thereunder by subsequent individual agreements. These territories are hereinafter referred to as trust territories.

Article 76

The basic objectives of the trusteeship system, in accordance with the Purposes of the United Nations laid down in Article 1 of the present Charter, shall be:

a. to further international peace and security;

b. to promote the political, economic, social, and educational advancement of the inhabitants of the trust territories, and their progressive development towards self-government or independence as may be appropriate to the particular circumstances of each territory and its peoples and the freely expressed wishes of the peoples concerned, and as may be provided by the terms of each trusteeship agreement;

c. to encourage respect for human rights and for fundamental freedoms for all with- out : as to race, sex, language, or religion, and to encourage recognition of the interdependence of the peoples of the world; and

d. to ensure equal treatment in social, economic, and commercial matters for all Members of the United Nations and their , and also equal treatment for the latter in the administration of justice, with- out prejudice to the attainment of the fore- going objectives and subject to the provisions of Article 80.

Article 77

1. The trusteeship system shall apply to such territories in the following categories as may be placed thereunder by means of trusteeship agreements:
a. territories now held under mandate;
b. territories which may be detached from enemy states as a result of the Second World War; and
c. territories voluntarily placed under the system by states responsible for their administration.
2. It will be a matter for subsequent agreement as to which territories in the foregoing categories will be brought under the trustee- ship system and upon what terms.

Article 78

The trusteeship system shall not apply to territories which have become Members of the United Nations, relationship among which shall be based on respect for the principle of sovereign equality.

Article 79

The terms of trusteeship for each territory to be placed under the trusteeship system, including any alteration or amendment, shall be agreed upon by the states directly concerned, including the mandatory power in the case of territories held under mandate by a Member of the United Nations, and shall be approved as provided for in Articles 83 and 85.

Article 80

1. Except as may be agreed upon in individual trusteeship agreements, made under Articles 77, 79, and 81, placing each territory under the trusteeship system, and until such agreements have been concluded, nothing in this Chapter shall be construed in or of itself to alter in any manner the rights whatsoever of any states or any peoples or the terms of

existing international instruments to which Members of the United Nations may respectively be parties.
2. Paragraph 1 of this Article shall not be interpreted as giving grounds for delay or postponement of the negotiation and conclusion of agreements for placing mandated and other territories under the trusteeship system as provided for in Article 77.

Article 81

The trusteeship agreement shall in each case include the terms under which the trust territory will be administered and designate the authority which will exercise the administration of the trust territory. Such authority, hereinafter called the administering authority, may be one or more states or the Organization itself.

Article 82

There may be designated, in any trusteeship agreement, a strategic area or areas which may include part or all of the trust territory to which the agreement applies, without prejudice to any special agreement or agreements made under Article 43.

Article 83

1. All functions of the United Nations relating to strategic areas, including the approval of the terms of the trusteeship agreements and of their alteration or amendment, shall be exercised by the Security Council.
2. he basic objectives set forth in Article 76 shall be applicable to the people of each strategic area. 43 3. The Security Council shall, subject to the provisions of the trusteeship agreements and without prejudice to security considerations, avail itself of the assistance of the Trusteeship Council to perform those functions of the United Nations under the trusteeship system relating to political, economic, social, and educational matters in the strategic areas.

Article 84

It shall be the duty of the administering authority to ensure that the trust territory shall play its part in the maintenance of international peace and security. To this end the administering authority may make use of volunteer forces, facilities, and assistance from the trust territory in carrying out the obligations towards the Security Council undertaken in this regard by the administering authority, as well as for local defence and the maintenance of law and order within the trust territory.

Article 85

1. The functions of the United Nations with regard to trusteeship agreements for all areas not designated as strategic, including the approval of the terms of the trusteeship agreements and of their alteration or amendment, shall be exercised by the General Assembly.
2. The Trusteeship Council, operating under the authority of the General Assembly, shall assist the General Assembly in carrying out these functions.

CHAPTER XIII THE TRUSTEESHIP COUNCIL

Composition

Article 86

1. The Trusteeship Council shall consist of the following Members of the United Nations:
a. those Members administering trust territories;
b. such of those Members mentioned by name in Article 23 as are not administering trust territories; and
c. as many other Members elected for three-year terms by the General Assembly as may be necessary to ensure that the total number of members of the Trusteeship Council is equally divided between those Members of the United Nations which ad- minister trust territories and those which do not.
2. Each member of the Trusteeship Council shall designate one specially qualified person to represent it therein.

Functions and Powers

Article 87

The General Assembly and, under its authority, the Trusteeship Council, in carrying out their functions, may:
a. consider reports submitted by the ad- ministering authority;
b. accept petitions and examine them in consultation with the administering authority;
c. provide for periodic visits to the respective trust territories at times agreed upon with the administering authority; and
d. take these and other actions in conformity with the terms of the trusteeship agreements.

Article 88

The Trusteeship Council shall formulate a questionnaire on the political, economic, social, and educational advancement of the inhabitants of each trust territory, and the administering authority for each trust territory within the competence of the General Assembly shall make an annual report to the General Assembly upon the basis of such questionnaire.

Voting

Article 89

1. Each member of the Trusteeship Council shall have one vote.
2. Decisions of the Trusteeship Council shall be made by a majority of the members present and voting.

Procedure

Article 90

1. The Trusteeship Council shall adopt its own rules of procedure, including the method of selecting its President.
2. The Trusteeship Council shall meet as required in accordance with its rules, which shall include provision for the convening of meetings on the request of a majority of its members.

Article 91

The Trusteeship Council shall, when appropriate, avail itself of the assistance of the Economic and Social Council and of the specialized agencies in regard to matters with which they are respectively concerned.

CHAPTER XIV THE INTERNATIONAL COURT OF JUSTICE

Article 92

The International Court of Justice shall be the principal judicial organ of the United Nations. It shall function in accordance with the annexed Statute, which is based upon the Statute of the Permanent Court of International Justice and forms an integral part of the present Charter.

Article 93

1. All Members of the United Nations are facto parties to the Statute of the International Court of Justice.
2. A state which is not ~ of the United Nations may become a party to the Statute of the International Court of Justice on to be determined in each case by the General Assembly upon the recommendation of the Security Council.

Article 94

1. Each Member of the United Nations undertakes to comply with the decision of the International Court of Justice in any case to which it is a party.
2. If any party to a case fails to perform the obligations incumbent upon it under a judgment rendered by the Court, the other party may have recourse to the Security Council, which may, if it deems necessary, make recommendations or decide upon measures to be taken to give to the judgment.

Article 95

Nothing in the present Charter shall prevent Members of the United Nations from entrusting the solution of their differences to other tribunals by virtue of agreements already in existence or which may be concluded in the future.

Article 96

1. The General Assembly or the Security Council may request the International Court of Justice to give an advisory opinion on any legal question.
2. Other organs of the United Nations and specialized agencies, which may at any time be so authorized by the General Assembly, may also request advisory opinions of the Court on legal questions arising within the scope of their activities.

CHAPTER XV THE SECRETARIAT

Article 97

The Secretariat shall comprise a Secretary- General and such staff as the Organization may require. The Secretary-General shall be appointed by the General Assembly upon the recommendation of the Security Council. He shall be the chief administrative officer of the Organization.

Article 98

The Secretary-General shall act in that capacity in all meetings of the General Assembly, of the Security Council, of the Economic and Social Council, and of the Trusteeship Council, and shall perform such other functions as are entrusted to him by these organs. The Secretary-General shall make an annual report to the General Assembly on the work of the Organization.

Article 99

The Secretary-General may bring to the attention of the Security Council any matter which in his opinion may threaten the maintenance of international peace and security.

Article 100

1. In the performance of their duties the Secretary-General and the staff shall not seek or receive instructions from any government or from any other authority externa to the Organization. They shall refrain from any action which might on their position as international officials responsible only to the Organization.
2. Each Member of the United Nations undertakes to respect the exclusively inter- national character of the responsibilities of the Secretary-General and the staff and not to seek to influence them in the discharge of their responsibilities.

Article 101

1. The staff shall be appointed by the Secretary-General under regulations established by the General Assembly.
2. Appropriate staffs shall be permanently assigned to the Economic and Social Council, the Trusteeship Council, and, as required, to other organs of the United Nations. These staffs shall form a part of the Secretariat.
3. The paramount consideration in the employment of the staff and in the determination of the conditions of service shall be the necessity of securing the highest standards of efficiency, competence, and integrity. Due regard shall be paid to the importance of recruiting the staff on as wide a geographical basis as possible.

CHAPTER XVI MISCELLANEOUS PROVISIONS

Article 102

1. Every treaty and every international agreement entered into by any Member of the United Nations after the present Charter comes into force

shall as soon as possible be registered with the Secretariat and published by it.
2. No party to any such treaty or international agreement which has not been registered in accordance with the provisions of paragraph I of this Article may invoke that treaty or agreement before any organ of the United Nations.

Article 103

In the event of a conflict between the obligations of the Members of the United Nations under the present Charter and their obligations under any other international agreement, their obligations under the present Charter shall prevail.

Article 104

The Organization shall enjoy in the territory of each of its Members such legal capacity as may be necessary for the exercise of its functions and the fulfilment of its purposes.

Article 105

1. The Organization shall enjoy in the territory of each of its Members such privileges and immunities as are necessary for the fulfilment of its purposes.
2. Representatives of the Members of the United Nations and officials of the Organization shall similarly enjoy such privileges and immunities as are necessary for the independent exercise of their functions in connexion with the Organization.
3. The General Assembly may make recommendations with a view to determining the details of the application of paragraphs 1 and 2 of this Article or may propose conventions to the Members of the United Nations for this purpose.

CHAPTER XVII TRANSITIONAL SECURITY ARRANGEMENTS

Article 106

Pending the coming into force of such special agreements referred to in Article 43 as in the opinion of the Security Council enable it to begin the exercise of its responsibilities under Article 42, the parties to the Four-Nation Declaration, signed at Moscow, 30 October 1943, and France, shall, in accordance with the provisions of paragraph 5 of that Declaration, consult with one another and as occasion requires with other Members of the United Nations with a view to such joint action on behalf of the Organization as may be necessary for the purpose of maintaining international peace and security.
Article 107 Nothing in the present Charter shall in- validate or preclude action, in relation to any state which during the Second World War has been an enemy of any signatory to the present Charter, taken or authorized as a result of that war by the Governments having responsibility for such action.

CHAPTER XVIII AMENDMENTS

Article 108

Amendments to the present Charter shall come into force for all Members of the United Nations when they have been adopted by a vote of two thirds of the members of the General Assembly and ratified in accordance with their respective constitutional processes by two thirds of the Members of the United Nations, including all the permanent members of the Security Council.

Article 109

1. A General Conference of the Members of the United Nations for the purpose of reviewing the present Charter may be held at a date and place to be fixed by a two-thirds vote of the members of the General Assembly and by a vote of any nine members of the Security Council. Each Member of the United Nations shall have one vote in the conference.

2. Any alteration of the present Charter recommended by a two-thirds vote of the conference shall take effect when ratified in accordance with their respective constitutional processes by two thirds of the Members of the United Nations including the permanent members of the Security Council.
3. If such a conference has not been held before the tenth annual session of the General Assembly following the coming into force of the present Charter, the proposal to call such a conference shall be placed on the agenda of that session of the General Assembly, and the conference shall be held if so decided by a majority vote of the members of the General Assembly and by a vote of any seven members of the Security Council.

CHAPTER XIX RATIFICATION AND SIGNATURE

Article 110

1. The present Charter shall be ratified by the signatory states in accordance with their respective constitutional processes.
2. The shall be deposited with the Government of the Unite States of America, which shall notify a the signatory states of each deposit as well as the Secretary-General of the Organization when he has been appointed.
3. The present Charter shall come into force upon the deposit of by the Republic of China, France, the Union of Soviet Socialist, the United Kingdom of Great Britain and Northern Ireland, and the United States of America, and by a majority of the other signatory states. A protocol of the deposited shall thereupon be drawn up by the Government of the United States of America which shall communicate copies thereof to all the signa- tory states.
4. The states signatory to the present Char- tear which ratify it after it has come into force will become original Members of the United Nations on the date of the deposit of their respective ratifications.

Article 111

The present Charter, of which the Chinese, French, Russian, English, and Spanish texts are equally authentic, shall remain deposited in the archives of the Government of -the United States of America. Duly certified copies

thereof shall be transmitted by that Government to the Governments of the other signatory states.
IN FAITH WHEREOF the representatives of the Governments of the United Nations have signed the present Charter.
DONE at the city of San Francisco the twenty-sixth day of June, one thousand nine hundred and forty-five.

STATUTE OF THE INTERNATIONAL COURT OF JUSTICE

Article 1

The International Court of Justice established by the Charter of the United Nations as the principal judicial organ of the United Nations shall be constituted and shall function in accordance with the provisions of the present Statute.

CHAPTER I - ORGANIZATION OF THE COURT

Article 2

The Court shall be composed of a body of independent judges, elected regardless of their nationality from among persons of high moral character, who possess the qualifications required in their respective countries for appointment to the highest judicial offices, or are jurisconsults of recognized competence in international law.

Article 3

1. The Court shall consist of fifteen members, no two of whom may be nationals of the same state.
2. A person who for the purposes of membership in the Court could be regarded as a national of more than one state shall be deemed to be a national of the one in which he ordinarily exercises civil and political rights.

Article 4

1. The members of the Court shall be elected by the General Assembly and by the Security Council from a list of persons nominated by the national groups in the Permanent Court of Arbitration, in accordance with the following provisions.
2. In the case of Members of the United Nations not represented in the Permanent Court of Arbitration, candidates shall be nominated by national groups appointed for this purpose by their governments under the same conditions as those prescribed for members of the Permanent Court of Arbitration by Article 44 of the Convention of The Hague of 1907 for the pacific settlement of international disputes.
3. The conditions under which a state which is a party to the present Statute but is not a Member of the United Nations may participate in electing the members of the Court shall, in the absence of a special agreement, be laid down by the General Assembly upon recommendation of the Security Council.

Article 5

1. At least three months before the date of the election, the Secretary-General of the United Nations shall address a written request to the members of the Permanent Court of Arbitration belonging to the states which are parties to the present Statute, and to the members of the national groups appointed under Article 4, paragraph 2, inviting them to undertake, within a given time, by national groups, the nomination of persons in a position to accept the duties of a member of the Court.
2. No group may nominate more than four persons, not more than two of whom shall be of their own nationality. In no case may the number of candidates nominated by a group be more than double the number of seats to be filled.

Article 6

Before making these nominations, each national group is recommended to consult its highest court of justice, its legal faculties and schools of law, and its national academies and national sections of international academies devoted to the study of law.

Article 7

1. The Secretary-General shall prepare a list in alphabetical order of all the persons thus nominated. Save as provided in Article 12, paragraph 2, these shall be the only persons eligible.
2. The Secretary-General shall submit this list to the General Assembly and to the Security Council.

Article 8

The General Assembly and the Security Council shall proceed independently of one another to elect the members of the Court.

Article 9

At every election, the electors shall bear in mind not only that the persons to be elected should individually possess the qualifications required, but also that in the body as a whole the representation of the main forms of civilization and of the principal legal systems of the world should be assured.

Article 10

1. Those candidates who obtain an absolute majority of votes in the General Assembly and in the Security Council shall be considered as elected.
2. Any vote of the Security Council, whether for the election of judges or for the appointment of members of the conference envisaged in Article 12, shall be taken without any distinction between permanent and non-permanent members of the Security Council.
3. In the event of more than one national of the same state obtaining an absolute majority of the votes both of the General Assembly and of the Security Council, the eldest of these only shall be considered as elected.

Article 11

If, after the first meeting held for the purpose of the election, one or more seats remain to be filled, a second and, if necessary, a third meeting shall take place.

Article 12

1. If, after the third meeting, one or more seats still remain unfilled, a joint conference consisting of six members, three appointed by the General Assembly and three by the Security Council, may be formed at any time at the request of either the General Assembly or the Security Council, for the purpose of choosing by the vote of an absolute majority one name for each seat still vacant, to submit to the General Assembly and the Security Council for their respective acceptance.
2. If the joint conference is unanimously agreed upon any person who fulfills the required conditions, he may be included in its list, even though he was not included in the list of nominations referred to in Article 7.
3. If the joint conference is satisfied that it will not be successful in procuring an election, those members of the Court who have already been elected shall, within a period to be fixed by the Security Council, proceed to fill the vacant seats by selection from among those candidates who have obtained votes either in the General Assembly or in the Security Council.
4. In the event of an equality of votes among the judges, the eldest judge shall have a casting vote.

Article 13

1. The members of the Court shall be elected for nine years and may be re-elected; provided, however, that of the judges elected at the first election, the terms of five judges shall expire at the end of three years and the terms of five more judges shall expire at the end of six years.
2. The judges whose terms are to expire at the end of the above-mentioned initial periods of three and six years shall be chosen by lot to be drawn by the Secretary-General immediately after the first election has been completed.

3. The members of the Court shall continue to discharge their duties until their places have been filled. Though replaced, they shall finish any cases which they may have begun.
4. In the case of the resignation of a member of the Court, the resignation shall be addressed to the President of the Court for transmission to the Secretary-General. This last notification makes the place vacant.

Article 14

Vacancies shall be filled by the same method as that laid down for the first election, subject to the following provision: the Secretary-General shall, within one month of the occurrence of the vacancy, proceed to issue the invitations provided for in Article 5, and the date of the election shall be fixed by the Security Council.

Article 15

A member of the Court elected to replace a member whose term of office has not expired shall hold office for the remainder of his predecessor's term.

Article 16

1. No member of the Court may exercise any political or administrative function, or engage in any other occupation of a professional nature.
2. Any doubt on this point shall be settled by the decision of the Court.

Article 17

1. No member of the Court may act as agent, counsel, or advocate in any case.
2. No member may participate in the decision of any case in which he has previously taken part as agent, counsel, or advocate for one of the parties, or as a member of a national or international court, or of a commission of enquiry, or in any other capacity.
3. Any doubt on this point shall be settled by the decision of the Court.

Article 18

1. No member of the Court can be dismissed unless, in the unanimous opinion of the other members, he has ceased to fulfill the required conditions.
2. Formal notification thereof shall be made to the Secretary-General by the Registrar.
3. This notification makes the place vacant.

Article 19

The members of the Court, when engaged on the business of the Court, shall enjoy diplomatic privileges and immunities.

Article 20

Every member of the Court shall, before taking up his duties, make a solemn declaration in open court that he will exercise his powers impartially and conscientiously.

Article 21

1. The Court shall elect its President and Vice-President for three years; they may be re-elected.
2. The Court shall appoint its Registrar and may provide for the appointment of such other officers as may be necessary.

Article 22

1. The seat of the Court shall be established at The Hague. This, however, shall not prevent the Court from sitting and exercising its functions elsewhere whenever the Court considers it desirable.
2. The President and the Registrar shall reside at the seat of the Court.

Article 23

1. The Court shall remain permanently in session, except during the judicial vacations, the dates and duration of which shall be fixed by the Court.
2. Members of the Court are entitled to periodic leave, the dates and duration of which shall be fixed by the Court, having in mind the distance between The Hague and the home of each judge.
3. Members of the Court shall be bound, unless they are on leave or prevented from attending by illness or other serious reasons duly explained to the President, to hold themselves permanently at the disposal of the Court.

Article 24

1. If, for some special reason, a member of the Court considers that he should not take part in the decision of a particular case, he shall so inform the President.
2. If the President considers that for some special reason one of the members of the Court should not sit in a particular case, he shall give him notice accordingly.
3. If in any such case the member of the Court and the President disagree, the matter shall be settled by the decision of the Court.

Article 25

1. The full Court shall sit except when it is expressly provided otherwise in the present Statute.
2. Subject to the condition that the number of judges available to constitute the Court is not thereby reduced below eleven, the Rules of the Court may provide for allowing one or more judges, according to circumstances and in rotation, to be dispensed from sitting.
3. A quorum of nine judges shall suffice to constitute the Court.

Article 26

1. The Court may from time to time form one or more chambers, composed of three or more judges as the Court may determine, for dealing with particular categories of cases; for example, labour cases and cases relating to transit and communications.
2. The Court may at any time form a chamber for dealing with a particular case. The number of judges to constitute such a chamber shall be determined by the Court with the approval of the parties.
3. Cases shall be heard and determined by the chambers provided for in this article if the parties so request.

Article 27

A judgment given by any of the chambers provided for in Articles 26 and 29 shall be considered as rendered by the Court.

Article 28

The chambers provided for in Articles 26 and 29 may, with the consent of the parties, sit and exercise their functions elsewhere than at The Hague.

Article 29

With a view to the speedy dispatch of business, the Court shall form annually a chamber composed of five judges which, at the request of the parties, may hear and determine cases by summary procedure. In addition, two judges shall be selected for the purpose of replacing judges who find it impossible to sit.

Article 30

1. The Court shall frame rules for carrying out its functions. In particular, it shall lay down rules of procedure.
2. The Rules of the Court may provide for assessors to sit with the Court or with any of its chambers, without the right to vote.

Article 31

1. Judges of the nationality of each of the parties shall retain their right to sit in the case before the Court.
2. If the Court includes upon the Bench a judge of the nationality of one of the parties, any other party may choose a person to sit as judge. Such person shall be chosen preferably from among those persons who have been nominated as candidates as provided in Articles 4 and 5.
3. If the Court includes upon the Bench no judge of the nationality of the parties, each of these parties may proceed to choose a judge as provided in paragraph 2 of this Article.
4. The provisions of this Article shall apply to the case of Articles 26 and 29. In such cases, the President shall request one or, if necessary, two of the members of the Court forming the chamber to give place to the members of the Court of the nationality of the parties concerned, and, failing such, or if they are unable to be present, to the judges specially chosen by the parties.
5. Should there be several parties in the same interest, they shall, for the purpose of the preceding provisions, be reckoned as one party only. Any doubt upon this point shall be settled by the decision of the Court.
6. Judges chosen as laid down in paragraphs 2, 3, and 4 of this Article shall fulfill the conditions required by Articles 2, 17 (paragraph 2), 20, and 24 of the present Statute. They shall take part in the decision on terms of complete equality with their colleagues.

Article 32

1. Each member of the Court shall receive an annual salary.
2. The President shall receive a special annual allowance.
3. The Vice-President shall receive a special allowance for every day on which he acts as President.
4. The judges chosen under Article 31, other than members of the Court, shall receive compensation for each day on which they exercise their functions.
5. These salaries, allowances, and compensation shall be fixed by the General Assembly. They may not be decreased during the term of office.

6. The salary of the Registrar shall be fixed by the General Assembly on the proposal of the Court.
7. Regulations made by the General Assembly shall fix the conditions under which retirement pensions may be given to members of the Court and to the Registrar, and the conditions under which members of the Court and the Registrar shall have their travelling expenses refunded.
8. The above salaries, allowances, and compensation shall be free of all taxation.

Article 33

The expenses of the Court shall be borne by the United Nations in such a manner as shall be decided by the General Assembly.

CHAPTER II - COMPETENCE OF THE COURT

Article 34

1. Only states may be parties in cases before the Court.
2. The Court, subject to and in conformity with its Rules, may request of public international organizations information relevant to cases before it, and shall receive such information presented by such organizations on their own initiative.
3. Whenever the construction of the constituent instrument of a public international organization or of an international convention adopted thereunder is in question in a case before the Court, the Registrar shall so notify the public international organization concerned and shall communicate to it copies of all the written proceedings.

Article 35

1. The Court shall be open to the states parties to the present Statute.
2. The conditions under which the Court shall be open to other states shall, subject to the special provisions contained in treaties in force, be laid down by the Security Council, but in no case shall such conditions place the parties in a position of inequality before the Court.

3. When a state which is not a Member of the United Nations is a party to a case, the Court shall fix the amount which that party is to contribute towards the expenses of the Court. This provision shall not apply if such state is bearing a share of the expenses of the Court

Article 36

1. The jurisdiction of the Court comprises all cases which the parties refer to it and all matters specially provided for in the Charter of the United Nations or in treaties and conventions in force.
2. The states parties to the present Statute may at any time declare that they recognize as compulsory ipso facto and without special agreement, in relation to any other state accepting the same obligation, the jurisdiction of the Court in all legal disputes concerning:
a. the interpretation of a treaty;
b. any question of international law;
c. the existence of any fact which, if established, would constitute a breach of an international obligation;
d. the nature or extent of the reparation to be made for the breach of an international obligation.
3. The declarations referred to above may be made unconditionally or on condition of reciprocity on the part of several or certain states, or for a certain time.
4. Such declarations shall be deposited with the Secretary-General of the United Nations, who shall transmit copies thereof to the parties to the Statute and to the Registrar of the Court.
5. Declarations made under Article 36 of the Statute of the Permanent Court of International Justice and which are still in force shall be deemed, as between the parties to the present Statute, to be acceptances of the compulsory jurisdiction of the International Court of Justice for the period which they still have to run and in accordance with their terms.
6. In the event of a dispute as to whether the Court has jurisdiction, the matter shall be settled by the decision of the Court.

Article 37

Whenever a treaty or convention in force provides for reference of a matter to a tribunal to have been instituted by the League of Nations, or to the Permanent Court of International Justice, the matter shall, as between the parties to the present Statute, be referred to the International Court of Justice.

Article 38

1. The Court, whose function is to decide in accordance with international law such disputes as are submitted to it, shall apply:
a. international conventions, whether general or particular, establishing rules expressly recognized by the contesting states;
b. international custom, as evidence of a general practice accepted as law;
c. the general principles of law recognized by civilized nations;
d. subject to the provisions of Article 59, judicial decisions and the teachings of the most highly qualified publicists of the various nations, as subsidiary means for the determination of rules of law.
2. This provision shall not prejudice the power of the Court to decide a case ex aequo et bono, if the parties agree thereto.

CHAPTER III - PROCEDURE

Article 39

1. The official languages of the Court shall be French and English. If the parties agree that the case shall be conducted in French, the judgment shall be delivered in French. If the parties agree that the case shall be conducted in English, the judgment shall be delivered in English.
2. In the absence of an agreement as to which language shall be employed, each party may, in the pleadings, use the language which it prefers; the decision of the Court shall be given in French and English. In this case the Court shall at the same time determine which of the two texts shall be considered as authoritative.
3. The Court shall, at the request of any party, authorize a language other than French or English to be used by that party.

Article 40

1. Cases are brought before the Court, as the case may be, either by the notification of the special agreement or by a written application addressed to the Registrar. In either case the subject of the dispute and the parties shall be indicated.

2. The Registrar shall forthwith communicate the application to all concerned.
3. He shall also notify the Members of the United Nations through the Secretary-General, and also any other states entitled to appear before the Court.

Article 41

1. The Court shall have the power to indicate, if it considers that circumstances so require, any provisional measures which ought to be taken to preserve the respective rights of either party.
2. Pending the final decision, notice of the measures suggested shall forthwith be given to the parties and to the Security Council.

Article 42

1. The parties shall be represented by agents.
2. They may have the assistance of counsel or advocates before the Court.
3. The agents, counsel, and advocates of parties before the Court shall enjoy the privileges and immunities necessary to the independent exercise of their duties.

Article 43

1. The procedure shall consist of two parts: written and oral.
2. The written proceedings shall consist of the communication to the Court and to the parties of memorials, counter-memorials and, if necessary, replies; also all papers and documents in support.
3. These communications shall be made through the Registrar, in the order and within the time fixed by the Court.

4. A certified copy of every document produced by one party shall be communicated to the other party.
5. The oral proceedings shall consist of the hearing by the Court of witnesses, experts, agents, counsel, and advocates.

Article 44

1. For the service of all notices upon persons other than the agents, counsel, and advocates, the Court shall apply direct to the government of the state upon whose territory the notice has to be served.
2. The same provision shall apply whenever steps are to be taken to procure evidence on the spot.

Article 45

The hearing shall be under the control of the President or, if he is unable to preside, of the Vice-President; if neither is able to preside, the senior judge present shall preside.

Article 46

The hearing in Court shall be public, unless the Court shall decide otherwise, or unless the parties demand that the public be not admitted .

Article 47

1. Minutes shall be made at each hearing and signed by the Registrar and the President.
2. These minutes alone shall be authentic.

Article 48

The Court shall make orders for the conduct of the case, shall decide the form and time in which each party must conclude its arguments, and make all arrangements connected with the taking of evidence.

Article 49

The Court may, even before the hearing begins, call upon the agents to produce any document or to supply any explanations. Formal note shall be taken of any refusal.

Article 50

The Court may, at any time, entrust any individual, body, bureau, commission, or other organization that it may select, with the task of carrying out an enquiry or giving an expert opinion.

Article 51

During the hearing any relevant questions are to be put to the witnesses and experts under the conditions laid down by the Court in the rules of procedure referred to in Article 30.

Article 52

After the Court has received the proofs and evidence within the time specified for the purpose, it may refuse to accept any further oral or written evidence that one party may desire to present unless the other side consents.

Article 53

1. Whenever one of the parties does not appear before the Court, or fails to defend its case, the other party may call upon the Court to decide in favour of its claim.
2. The Court must, before doing so, satisfy itself, not only that it has jurisdiction in accordance with Articles 36 and 37, but also that the claim is well founded in fact and law.

Article 54

1. When, subject to the control of the Court, the agents, counsel, and advocates have completed their presentation of the case, the President shall declare the hearing closed.
2. The Court shall withdraw to consider the judgment.
3. The deliberations of the Court shall take place in private and remain secret.

Article 55

1. All questions shall be decided by a majority of the judges present.
2. In the event of an equality of votes, the President or the judge who acts in his place shall have a casting vote.

Article 56

1. The judgment shall state the reasons on which it is based.
2. It shall contain the names of the judges who have taken part in the decision.

Article 57

If the judgment does not represent in whole or in part the unanimous opinion of the judges, any judge shall be entitled to deliver a separate opinion.

Article 58

The judgment shall be signed by the President and by the Registrar. It shall be read in open court, due notice having been given to the agents.

Article 59

The decision of the Court has no binding force except between the parties and in respect of that particular case.

Article 60

The judgment is final and without appeal. In the event of dispute as to the meaning or scope of the judgment, the Court shall construe it upon the request of any party.

Article 61

1. An application for revision of a judgment may be made only when it is based upon the discovery of some fact of such a nature as to be a decisive factor, which fact was, when the judgment was given, unknown to the Court and also to the party claiming revision, always provided that such ignorance was not due to negligence.
2. The proceedings for revision shall be opened by a judgment of the Court expressly recording the existence of the new fact, recognizing that it has such a character as to lay the case open to revision, and declaring the application admissible on this ground.
3. The Court may require previous compliance with the terms of the judgment before it admits proceedings in revision.
4. The application for revision must be made at latest within six months of the discovery of the new fact.
5. No application for revision may be made after the lapse of ten years from the date of the judgment.

Article 62

l. Should a state consider that it has an interest of a legal nature which may be affected by the decision in the case, it may submit a request to the Court to be permitted to intervene.
2 It shall be for the Court to decide upon this request.

Article 63

1. Whenever the construction of a convention to which states other than those concerned in the case are parties is in question, the Registrar shall notify all such states forthwith.

2. Every state so notified has the right to intervene in the proceedings; but if it uses this right, the construction given by the judgment will be equally binding upon it.

Article 64

Unless otherwise decided by the Court, each party shall bear its own costs.

CHAPTER IV - ADVISORY OPINIONS

Article 65

1. The Court may give an advisory opinion on any legal question at the request of whatever body may be authorized by or in accordance with the Charter of the United Nations to make such a request.
2. Questions upon which the advisory opinion of the Court is asked shall be laid before the Court by means of a written request containing an exact statement of the question upon which an opinion is required, and accompanied by all documents likely to throw light upon the question.

Article 66

1. The Registrar shall forthwith give notice of the request for an advisory opinion to all states entitled to appear before the Court.
2. The Registrar shall also, by means of a special and direct communication, notify any state entitled to appear before the Court or international organization considered by the Court, or, should it not be sitting, by the President, as likely to be able to furnish information on the question, that the Court will be prepared to receive, within a time-limit to be fixed by the President, written statements, or to hear, at a public sitting to be held for the purpose, oral statements relating to the question.
3. Should any such state entitled to appear before the Court have failed to receive the special communication referred to in paragraph 2 of this Article, such state may express a desire to submit a written statement or to be heard; and the Court will decide.
4. States and organizations having presented written or oral statements or both shall be permitted to comment on the statements made by other

states or organizations in the form, to the extent, and within the time-limits which the Court, or, should it not be sitting, the President, shall decide in each particular case. Accordingly, the Registrar shall in due time communicate any such written statements to states and organizations having submitted similar statements.

Article 67

The Court shall deliver its advisory opinions in open court, notice having been given to the Secretary-General and to the representatives of Members of the United Nations, of other states and of international organizations immediately concerned.

Article 68

In the exercise of its advisory functions the Court shall further be guided by the provisions of the present Statute which apply in contentious cases to the extent to which it recognizes them to be applicable.

CHAPTER V - AMENDMENT

Article 69

Amendments to the present Statute shall be effected by the same procedure as is provided by the Charter of the United Nations for amendments to that Charter, subject however to any provisions which the General Assembly upon recommendation of the Security Council may adopt concerning the participation of states which are parties to the present Statute but are not Members of the United Nations.

Article 70

The Court shall have power to propose such amendments to the present Statute as it may deem necessary, through written communications to the Secretary-General, for consideration in conformity with the provisions of Article 69.

RULES OF COURT (1978)

ADOPTED ON 14 APRIL 1978 AND ENTERED INTO FORCE ON 1 JULY 1978[1]

PREAMBLE*

The Court, Having regard to Chapter XIV of the Charter of the United Nations;

Having regard to the Statute of the Court annexed thereto; Acting in pursuance of Article 30 of the Statute; Adopts the following Rules.

---

*Amendment entered into force on 14 April 2005.

[1]Any amendments to the Rules of Court, following their adoption by the Court, are now posted on the Court's website, with an indication of the date of their entry into force and a note of any temporal reservations relating to their applicability (for example, whether the application of the amended rule is limited to cases instituted after the date of entry into force of the amendment); they are also published in the Court's *Yearbook*. Articles amended since 1 July 1978 are marked with an asterisk and appear in their amended form.

PART I
THE COURT

SECTION A. JUDGES AND ASSESSORS

Subsection 1. The Members of the Court

Article 1

1. The Members of the Court are the judges elected in accordance with Articles 2 to 15 of the Statute.
2. For the purposes of a particular case, the Court may also include upon the Bench one or more persons chosen under Article 31 of the Statute to sit as judges *ad hoc*.

3. In the following Rules, the term "Member of the Court" denotes any elected judge; the term "judge" denotes any Member of the Court, and any judge *ad hoc*.

Article 2

1. The term of office of Members of the Court elected at a triennial election shall begin to run from the sixth of February[1] in the year in which the vacancies to which they are elected occur.
2. The term of office of a Member of the Court elected to replace a Member whose term of office has not expired shall begin to run from the date of the election.

[1]This is the date on which the terms of office of the Members of the Court elected at the first election began in 1946.

Article 3

1. The Members of the Court, in the exercise of their functions, are of equal status, irrespective of age, priority of election or length of service.
2. The Members of the Court shall, except as provided in paragraphs 4 and 5 of this Article, take precedence according to the date on which their terms of office respectively began, as provided for by Article 2 of these Rules.
3. Members of the Court whose terms of office began on the same date shall take precedence in relation to one another according to seniority of age.
4. A Member of the Court who is re-elected to a new term of office which is continuous with his previous term shall retain his precedence.
5. The President and the Vice-President of the Court, while holding these offices, shall take precedence before all other Members of the Court.
6. The Member of the Court who, in accordance with the foregoing paragraphs, takes precedence next after the President and the Vice-President is in these Rules designated the "senior judge". If that Member is unable to act, the Member of the Court who is next after him in precedence and able to act is considered as senior judge.

Article 4

1. The declaration to be made by every Member of the Court in accordance with Article 20 of the Statute shall be as follows:
"I solemnly declare that I will perform my duties and exercise my powers as judge honourably, faithfully, impartially and conscientiously."
2. This declaration shall be made at the first public sitting at which the Member of the Court is present. Such sitting shall be held as soon as practicable after his term of office begins and, if necessary, a special sitting shall be held for the purpose.
3. A Member of the Court who is re-elected shall make a new declaration only if his new term is not continuous with his previous one.

Article 5

1. A Member of the Court deciding to resign shall communicate his decision to the President, and the resignation shall take effect as provided in Article 13, paragraph 4, of the Statute.
2. If the Member of the Court deciding to resign from the Court is the President, he shall communicate his decision to the Court, and the resignation shall take effect as provided in Article 13, paragraph 4, of the Statute.

Article 6

In any case in which the application of Article 18 of the Statute is under consideration, the Member of the Court concerned shall be so informed by the President or, if the circumstances so require, by the Vice-President, in a written statement which shall include the grounds therefor and any relevant evidence. He shall subsequently, at a private meeting of the Court specially convened for the purpose, be afforded an opportunity of making a statement, of furnishing any information or explanations he wishes to give, and of supplying answers, orally or in writing, to any questions put to him. At a further private meeting, at which the Member of the Court concerned shall not be present, the matter shall be discussed; each Member of the Court shall state his opinion, and if requested a vote shall be taken.

Subsection 2. Judges ad hoc

Article 7

1. Judges *ad hoc*, chosen under Article 31 of the Statute for the purposes of particular cases, shall be admitted to sit on the Bench of the Court in the circumstances and according to the procedure indicated in Article 17, paragraph 2, Articles 35, 36, 37, Article 91, paragraph 2, and Article 102, paragraph 3, of these Rules.
2. They shall participate in the case in which they sit on terms of complete equality with the other judges on the Bench.
3. Judges *ad hoc* shall take precedence after the Members of the Court and in order of seniority of age.

Article 8

1. The solemn declaration to be made by every judge *ad hoc* in accordance with Articles 20 and 31, paragraph 6, of the Statute shall be as set out in Article 4, paragraph 1, of these Rules.
2. This declaration shall be made at a public sitting in the case in which the judge *ad hoc* is participating. If the case is being dealt with by a chamber of the Court, the declaration shall be made in the same manner in that chamber.
3. Judges *ad hoc* shall make the declaration in relation to any case in which they are participating, even if they have already done so in a previous case, but shall not make a new declaration for a later phase of the same case.

Subsection 3. Assessors

Article 9

1. The Court may, either *proprio motu* or upon a request made not later than the closure of the written proceedings, decide, for the purpose of a contentious case or request for advisory opinion, to appoint assessors to sit with it without the right to vote.

2. When the Court so decides, the President shall take steps to obtain all the information relevant to the choice of the assessors.
3. The assessors shall be appointed by secret ballot and by a majority of the votes of the judges composing the Court for the case.
4. The same powers shall belong to the chambers provided for by Articles 26 and 29 of the Statute and to the presidents thereof, and may be exercised in the same manner.
5. Before entering upon their duties, assessors shall make the following declaration at a public sitting:
"I solemnly declare that I will perform my duties as an assessor honourably, impartially and conscientiously, and that I will faithfully observe all the provisions of the Statute and of the Rules of the Court."

SECTION B. THE PRESIDENCY

Article 10

1. The term of office of the President and that of the Vice-President shall begin to run from the date on which the terms of office of the Members of the Court elected at a triennial election begin in accordance with Article 2 of these Rules.
2. The elections to the presidency and vice-presidency shall be held on that date or shortly thereafter. The former President, if still a Member of the Court, shall continue to exercise his functions until the election to the presidency has taken place.

Article 11

1. If, on the date of the election to the presidency, the former President is still a Member of the Court, he shall conduct the election. If he has ceased to be a Member of the Court, or is unable to act, the election shall be conducted by the Member of the Court exercising the functions of the presidency by virtue of Article 13, paragraph 1, of these Rules.
2. The election shall take place by secret ballot, after the presiding Member of the Court has declared the number of affirmative votes necessary for election; there shall be no nominations. The Member of the Court obtaining the votes of a majority of the Members composing it at

the time of the election shall be declared elected, and shall enter forthwith upon his functions.
3. The new President shall conduct the election of the Vice-President either at the same or at the following meeting. The provisions of paragraph 2 of this Article shall apply equally to this election.

Article 12

The President shall preside at all meetings of the Court; he shall direct the work and supervise the administration of the Court.

Article 13

1. In the event of a vacancy in the presidency or of the inability of the President to exercise the functions of the presidency, these shall be exercised by the Vice-President, or failing him, by the senior judge.
2. When the President is precluded by a provision of the Statute or of these Rules either from sitting or from presiding in a particular case, he shall continue to exercise the functions of the presidency for all purposes save in respect of that case.
3. The President shall take the measures necessary in order to ensure the continuous exercise of the functions of the presidency at the seat of the Court. In the event of his absence, he may, so far as is compatible with the Statute and these Rules, arrange for these functions to be exercised by the Vice-President, or failing him, by the senior judge.
4. If the President decides to resign the presidency, he shall communicate his decision in writing to the Court through the Vice-President, or failing him, the senior judge. If the Vice-President decides to resign his office, he shall communicate his decision to the President.

Article 14

If a vacancy in the presidency or the vice-presidency occurs before the date when the current term is due to expire under Article 21, paragraph 1, of the Statute and Article 10, paragraph 1, of these Rules, the Court shall decide whether or not the vacancy shall be filled during the remainder of the term.

SECTION C. THE CHAMBERS

Article 15

1. The Chamber of Summary Procedure to be formed annually under Article 29 of the Statute shall be composed of five Members of the Court, comprising the President and Vice-President of the Court, acting ex officio, and three other members elected in accordance with Article 18, paragraph 1, of these Rules. In addition, two Members of the Court shall be elected annually to act as substitutes.
2. The election referred to in paragraph 1 of this Article shall be held as soon as possible after the sixth of February in each year. The members of the Chamber shall enter upon their functions on election and continue to serve until the next election; they may be re-elected.
3. If a member of the Chamber is unable, for whatever reason, to sit in a given case, he shall be replaced for the purposes of that case by the senior in precedence of the two substitutes.
4. If a member of the Chamber resigns or otherwise ceases to be a member, his place shall be taken by the senior in precedence of the two substitutes, who shall thereupon become a full member of the Chamber and be replaced by the election of another substitute. Should vacancies exceed the number of available substitutes, elections shall be held as soon as possible in respect of the vacancies still existing after the substitutes have assumed full membership and in respect of the vacancies in the substitutes.

Article 16

1. When the Court decides to form one or more of the Chambers provided for in Article 26, paragraph 1, of the Statute, it shall determine the particular category of cases for which each Chamber is formed, the number of its members, the period for which they will serve, and the date at which they will enter upon their duties.
2. The members of the Chamber shall be elected in accordance with Article 18, paragraph 1, of these Rules from among the Members of the Court, having regard to any special knowledge, expertise or previous

experience which any of the Members of the Court may have in relation to the category of case the Chamber is being formed to deal with.
3. The Court may decide upon the dissolution of a Chamber, but without prejudice to the duty of the Chamber concerned to finish any cases pending before it.

Article 17

1. A request for the formation of a Chamber to deal with a particular case, as provided for in Article 26, paragraph 2, of the Statute, may be filed at any time until the closure of the written proceedings. Upon receipt of a request made by one party, the President shall ascertain whether the other party assents.
2. When the parties have agreed, the President shall ascertain their views regarding the composition of the Chamber, and shall report to the Court accordingly. He shall also take such steps as may be necessary to give effect to the provisions of Article 31, paragraph 4, of the Statute.
3. When the Court has determined, with the approval of the parties, the number of its Members who are to constitute the Chamber, it shall proceed to their election, in accordance with the provisions of Article 18, paragraph 1, of these Rules. The same procedure shall be followed as regards the filling of any vacancy that may occur on the Chamber.
4. Members of a Chamber formed under this Article who have been replaced, in accordance with Article 13 of the Statute following the expiration of their terms of office, shall continue to sit in all phases of the case, whatever the stage it has then reached.

Article 18

1. Elections to all Chambers shall take place by secret ballot. The Members of the Court obtaining the largest number of votes constituting a majority of the Members of the Court composing it at the time of the election shall be declared elected. If necessary to fill vacancies, more than one ballot shall take place, such ballot being limited to the number of vacancies that remain to be filled.
2. If a Chamber when formed includes the President or Vice-President of the Court, or both of them, the President or Vice-President, as the case

may be, shall preside over that Chamber. In any other event, the Chamber shall elect its own president by secret ballot and by a majority of votes of its members. The Member of the Court who, under this paragraph, presides over the Chamber at the time of its formation shall continue to preside so long as he remains a member of that Chamber.
3. The president of a Chamber shall exercise, in relation to cases being dealt with by that Chamber, all the functions of the President of the Court in relation to cases before the Court.
4. If the president of a Chamber is prevented from sitting or from acting as president, the functions of the presidency shall be assumed by the member of the Chamber who is the senior in precedence and able to act.

SECTION D. INTERNAL FUNCTIONING OF THE COURT

Article 19

The internal judicial practice of the Court shall, subject to the provisions of the Statute and these Rules, be governed by any resolutions on the subject adopted by the Court[1].

[1]The resolution now in force was adopted on 12 April 1976.

Article 20

1. The quorum specified by Article 25, paragraph 3, of the Statute applies to all meetings of the Court.
2. The obligation of Members of the Court under Article 23, paragraph 3, of the Statute, to hold themselves permanently at the disposal of the Court, entails attendance at all such meetings, unless they are prevented from attending by illness or for other serious reasons duly explained to the President, who shall inform the Court.
3. Judges *ad hoc* are likewise bound to hold themselves at the disposal of the Court and to attend all meetings held in the case in which they are participating. They shall not be taken into account for the calculation of the quorum.
4. The Court shall fix the dates and duration of the judicial vacations and the periods and conditions of leave to be accorded to individual Members

of the Court under Article 23, paragraph 2, of the Statute, having regard in both cases to the state of its General List and to the requirements of its current work.
5. Subject to the same considerations, the Court shall observe the public holidays customary at the place where the Court is sitting.
6. In case of urgency the President may convene the Court at any time.

Article 21

1. The deliberations of the Court shall take place in private and remain secret. The Court may however at any time decide in respect of its deliberations on other than judicial matters to publish or allow publication of any part of them.
2. Only judges, and the assessors, if any, take part in the Court's judicial deliberations. The Registrar, or his deputy, and other members of the staff of the Registry as may be required shall be present. No other person shall be present except by permission of the Court.
3. The minutes of the Court's judicial deliberations shall record only the title or nature of the subjects or matters discussed, and the results of any vote taken. They shall not record any details of the discussions nor the views expressed, provided however that any judge is entitled to require that a statement made by him be inserted in the minutes.

PART II
THE REGISTRY

Article 22

1. The Court shall elect its Registrar by secret ballot from amongst candidates proposed by Members of the Court. The Registrar shall be elected for a term of seven years. He may be re-elected.
2. The President shall give notice of a vacancy or impending vacancy to Members of the Court, either forthwith upon the vacancy arising, or, where the vacancy will arise on the expiration of the term of office of the Registrar, not less than three months prior thereto. The President shall fix a date for the closure of the list of candidates so as to enable

nominations and information concerning the candidates to be received in sufficient time.
3. Nominations shall indicate the relevant information concerning the candidate, and in particular information as to his age, nationality, and present occupation, university qualifications, knowledge of languages, and any previous experience in law, diplomacy or the work of international organizations.
4. The candidate obtaining the votes of the majority of the Members of the Court composing it at the time of the election shall be declared elected.

Article 23

The Court shall elect a Deputy-Registrar: the provisions of Article 22 of these Rules shall apply to his election and term of office.

Article 24

1. Before taking up his duties, the Registrar shall make the following declaration at a meeting of the Court:
"I solemnly declare that I will perform the duties incumbent upon me as Registrar of the International Court of Justice in all loyalty, discretion and good conscience, and that I will faithfully observe all the provisions of the Statute and of the Rules of the Court."
2. The Deputy-Registrar shall make a similar declaration at a meeting of the Court before taking up his duties.

Article 25

1. The staff-members of the Registry shall be appointed by the Court on proposals submitted by the Registrar. Appointments to such posts as the Court shall determine may however be made by the Registrar with the approval of the President.
2. Before taking up his duties, every staff-member shall make the following declaration before the President, the Registrar being present:
"I solemnly declare that I will perform the duties incumbent upon me as an official of the International Court of Justice in all loyalty, discretion

and good conscience, and that I will faithfully observe all the provisions of the Statute and of the Rules of the Court."

Article 26

1. The Registrar, in the discharge of his functions, shall:

(a) be the regular channel of communications to and from the Court, and in particular shall effect all communications, notifications and transmission of documents required by the Statute or by these Rules and ensure that the date of despatch and receipt thereof may be readily verified;

(b) keep, under the supervision of the President, and in such form as may be laid down by the Court, a General List of all cases, entered and numbered in the order in which the documents instituting proceedings or requesting an advisory opinion are received in the Registry;

(c) have the custody of the declarations accepting the jurisdiction of the Court made by States not parties to the Statute in accordance with any resolution adopted by the Security Council under Article 35, paragraph 2, of the Statute, and transmit certified copies thereof to all States parties to the Statute, to such other States as shall have deposited declarations, and to the Secretary-General of the United Nations;

(d) transmit to the parties copies of all pleadings and documents annexed upon receipt thereof in the Registry;

(e) communicate to the government of the country in which the Court or a Chamber is sitting, and any other governments which may be concerned, the necessary information as to the persons from time to time entitled, under the Statute and relevant agreements, to privileges, immunities, or facilities;

(f) be present, in person or by his deputy, at meetings of the Court, and of the Chambers, and be responsible for the preparation of minutes of such meetings;

(g) make arrangements for such provision or verification of translations and interpretations into the Court's official languages as the Court may require;

(h) sign all judgments, advisory opinions and orders of the Court, and the minutes referred to in subparagraph *(f)*;

(i) be responsible for the printing and publication of the Court's judgments, advisory opinions and orders, the pleadings and statements, and minutes of public sittings in cases, and of such other documents as the Court may direct to be published;

(j) be responsible for all administrative work and in particular for the accounts and financial administration in accordance with the financial procedures of the United Nations;

(k) deal with enquiries concerning the Court and its work;

(l) assist in maintaining relations between the Court and other organs of the United Nations, the specialized agencies, and international bodies and conferences concerned with the codification and progressive development of international law;

(m) ensure that information concerning the Court and its activities is made accessible to governments, the highest national courts of justice, professional and learned societies, legal faculties and schools of law, and public information media;

(n) have custody of the seals and stamps of the Court, of the archives of the Court, and of such other archives as may be entrusted to the Court[1].

2. The Court may at any time entrust additional functions to the Registrar.

3. In the discharge of his functions the Registrar shall be responsible to the Court.

---

[1]The Registrar also keeps the Archives of the Permanent Court of International Justice, entrusted to the present Court by decision of the Permanent Court of October 1945 (*I.C.J. Yearbook 1946-1947*, p. 26). and the Archives of the Trial of the Major War Criminals before the International Military Tribunal at Nuremberg (1945-1946), entrusted to the Court by decision of that Tribunal of 1 October 1946; the Court authorized the Registrar to accept the latter Archives by decision of 19 November 1949.

Article 27

1. The Deputy-Registrar shall assist the Registrar, act as Registrar in the latter's absence and, in the event of the office becoming vacant, exercise the functions of Registrar until the office has been filled.
2. If both the Registrar and the Deputy-Registrar are unable to carry out the duties of Registrar, the President shall appoint an official of the Registry to discharge those duties for such time as may be necessary. If both offices are vacant at the same time, the President, after consulting the Members of the Court, shall appoint an official of the Registry to discharge the duties of Registrar pending an election to that office.

Article 28

1. The Registry shall comprise the Registrar, the Deputy-Registrar, and such other staff as the Registrar shall require for the efficient discharge of his functions.
2. The Court shall prescribe the organization of the Registry, and shall for this purpose request the Registrar to make proposals.
3. Instructions for the Registry shall be drawn up by the Registrar and approved by the Court.
4. The staff of the Registry shall be subject to Staff Regulations drawn up by the Registrar, so far as possible in conformity with the United Nations Staff Regulations and Staff Rules, and approved by the Court.

Article 29

1. The Registrar may be removed from office only if, in the opinion of two-thirds of the Members of the Court, he has either become permanently incapacitated from exercising his functions, or has committed a serious breach of his duties.
2. Before a decision is taken under this Article, the Registrar shall be informed by the President of the action contemplated, in a written statement which shall include the grounds therefor and any relevant evidence. He shall subsequently, at a private meeting of the Court, be afforded an opportunity of making a statement, of furnishing any

information or explanations he wishes to give, and of supplying answers, orally or in writing, to any questions put to him.
3. The Deputy-Registrar may be removed from office only on the same grounds and by the same procedure.

PART III
PROCEEDINGS IN CONTENTIOUS CASES

SECTION A. COMMUNICATIONS TO THE COURT AND CONSULTATIONS

Article 30

All communications to the Court under these Rules shall be addressed to the Registrar unless otherwise stated. Any request made by a party shall likewise be addressed to the Registrar unless made in open court in the course of the oral proceedings.

Article 31

In every case submitted to the Court, the President shall ascertain the views of the parties with regard to questions of procedure. For this purpose he shall summon the agents of the parties to meet him as soon as possible after their appointment, and whenever necessary thereafter.

SECTION B. THE COMPOSITION OF THE COURT FOR PARTICULAR CASES

Article 32

1. If the President of the Court is a national of one of the parties in a case he shall not exercise the functions of the presidency in respect of that case. The same rule applies to the Vice-President, or to the senior judge, when called on to act as President.
2. The Member of the Court who is presiding in a case on the date on which the Court convenes for the oral proceedings shall continue to preside in that case until completion of the current phase of the case,

notwithstanding the election in the meantime of a new President or Vice-President. If he should become unable to act, the presidency for the case shall be determined in accordance with Article 13 of these Rules, and on the basis of the composition of the Court on the date on which it convened for the oral proceedings.

Article 33

Except as provided in Article 17 of these Rules, Members of the Court who have been replaced, in accordance with Article 13, paragraph 3, of the Statute following the expiration of their terms of office, shall discharge the duty imposed upon them by that paragraph by continuing to sit until the completion of any phase of a case in respect of which the Court convenes for the oral proceedings prior to the date of such replacement.

Article 34

1. In case of any doubt arising as to the application of Article 17, paragraph 2, of the Statute or in case of a disagreement as to the application of Article 24 of the Statute, the President shall inform the Members of the Court, with whom the decision lies.
2. If a party desires to bring to the attention of the Court facts which it considers to be of possible relevance to the application of the provisions of the Statute mentioned in the previous paragraph, but which it believes may not be known to the Court, that party shall communicate confidentially such facts to the President in writing.

Article 35

1. If a party proposes to exercise the power conferred by Article 31 of the Statute to choose a judge *ad hoc* in a case, it shall notify the Court of its intention as soon as possible. If the name and nationality of the judge selected are not indicated at the same time, the party shall, not later than two months before the time-limit fixed for the filing of the Counter-Memorial, inform the Court of the name and nationality of the person chosen and supply brief biographical details. The judge *ad hoc* may be of a nationality other than that of the party which chooses him.

2. If a party proposes to abstain from choosing a judge *ad hoc*, on condition of a like abstention by the other party, it shall so notify the Court which shall inform the other party. If the other party thereafter gives notice of its intention to choose, or chooses, a judge *ad hoc*, the time-limit for the party which has previously abstained from choosing a judge may be extended by the President.
3. A copy of any notification relating to the choice of a judge *ad hoc* shall be communicated by the Registrar to the other party, which shall be requested to furnish, within a time-limit to be fixed by the President, such observations as it may wish to make. If within the said time-limit no objection is raised by the other party, and if none appears to the Court itself, the parties shall be so informed.
4. In the event of any objection or doubt, the matter shall be decided by the Court, if necessary after hearing the parties.
5. A judge *ad hoc* who has accepted appointment but who becomes unable to sit may be replaced.
6. If and when the reasons for the participation of a judge *ad hoc* are found no longer to exist, he shall cease to sit on the Bench.

Article 36

1. If the Court finds that two or more parties are in the same interest, and therefore are to be reckoned as one party only, and that there is no Member of the Court of the nationality of any one of those parties upon the Bench, the Court shall fix a time-limit within which they may jointly choose a judge *ad hoc*.
2. Should any party amongst those found by the Court to be in the same interest allege the existence of a separate interest of its own, or put forward any other objection, the matter shall be decided by the Court, if necessary after hearing the parties.

Article 37

1. If a Member of the Court having the nationality of one of the parties is or becomes unable to sit in any phase of a case, that party shall thereupon become entitled to choose a judge *ad hoc* within a time-limit to be fixed by the Court, or by the President if the Court is not sitting.

2. Parties in the same interest shall be deemed not to have a judge of one of their nationalities upon the Bench if the Member of the Court having one of their nationalities is or becomes unable to sit in any phase of the case.
3. If the Member of the Court having the nationality of a party becomes able to sit not later than the closure of the written proceedings in that phase of the case, that Member of the Court shall resume his seat on the Bench in the case.

SECTION C. PROCEEDINGS BEFORE THE COURT

Subsection 1. Institution of Proceedings

Article 38

1. When proceedings before the Court are instituted by means of an application addressed as specified in Article 40, paragraph 1, of the Statute, the application shall indicate the party making it, the State against which the claim is brought, and the subject of the dispute.
2. The application shall specify as far as possible the legal grounds upon which the jurisdiction of the Court is said to be based; it shall also specify the precise nature of the claim, together with a succinct statement of the facts and grounds on which the claim is based.
3. The original of the application shall be signed either by the agent of the party submitting it, or by the diplomatic representative of that party in the country in which the Court has its seat, or by some other duly authorized person. If the application bears the signature of someone other than such diplomatic representative, the signature must be authenticated by the latter or by the competent authority of the applicant's foreign ministry.
4. The Registrar shall forthwith transmit to the respondent a certified copy of the application.
5. When the applicant State proposes to found the jurisdiction of the Court upon a consent thereto yet to be given or manifested by the State against which such application is made, the application shall be transmitted to that State. It shall not however be entered in the General List, nor any action be taken in the proceedings, unless and until the State

against which such application is made consents to the Court's jurisdiction for the purposes of the case.

Article 39

1. When proceedings are brought before the Court by the notification of a special agreement, in conformity with Article 40, paragraph 1, of the Statute, the notification may be effected by the parties jointly or by any one or more of them. If the notification is not a joint one, a certified copy of it shall forthwith be communicated by the Registrar to the other party.
2. In each case the notification shall be accompanied by an original or certified copy of the special agreement. The notification shall also, in so far as this is not already apparent from the agreement, indicate the precise subject of the dispute and identify the parties to it.

Article 40

1. Except in the circumstances contemplated by Article 38, paragraph 5, of these Rules, all steps on behalf of the parties after proceedings have been instituted shall be taken by agents. Agents shall have an address for service at the seat of the Court to which all communications concerning the case are to be sent. Communications addressed to the agents of the parties shall be considered as having been addressed to the parties themselves.
2. When proceedings are instituted by means of an application, the name of the agent for the applicant shall be stated. The respondent, upon receipt of the certified copy of the application, or as soon as possible thereafter, shall inform the Court of the name of its agent.
3. When proceedings are brought by notification of a special agreement, the party making the notification shall state the name of its agent. Any other party to the special agreement, upon receiving from the Registrar a certified copy of such notification, or as soon as possible thereafter, shall inform the Court of the name of its agent if it has not already done so.

Article 41

The institution of proceedings by a State which is not a party to the Statute but which, under Article 35, paragraph 2, thereof, has accepted the jurisdiction of the Court by a declaration made in accordance with any resolution adopted by the Security Council under that Article[1], shall be accompanied by a deposit of the declaration in question, unless the latter has previously been deposited with the Registrar. If any question of the validity or effect of such declaration arises, the Court shall decide.

---

[1]The resolution now in force was adopted on 15 October 1946.

Article 42

The Registrar shall transmit copies of any application or notification of a special agreement instituting proceedings before the Court to: *(a)* the Secretary-General of the United Nations; *(b)* the Members of the United Nations; *(c)* other States entitled to appear before the Court.

Article 43[*1]

1. Whenever the construction of a convention to which States other than those concerned in the case are parties may be in question within the meaning of Article 63, paragraph 1, of the Statute, the Court shall consider what directions shall be given to the Registrar in the matter.
2. Whenever the construction of a convention to which a public international organization is a party may be in question in a case before the Court, the Court shall consider whether the Registrar shall so notify the public international organization concerned. Every public international organization notified by the Registrar may submit its observations on the particular provisions of the convention the construction of which is in question in the case.
3. If a public international organization sees fit to furnish its observations under paragraph 2 of this Article, the procedure to be followed shall be that provided for in Article 69, paragraph 2, of these Rules.

---

[*]Amendment entered into force on 29 September 2005.

[1]Article 43, paragraph 1, as amended, repeats unchanged the text of Article 43, as adopted on 14 April 1978.
Paragraphs 2 and 3 of the amended Article 43 are new.

Subsection 2. The Written Proceedings

Article 44

1. In the light of the information obtained by the President under Article 31 of these Rules, the Court shall make the necessary orders to determine, *inter alia*, the number and the order of filing of the pleadings and the time-limits within which they must be filed.
2. In making an order under paragraph 1 of this Article, any agreement between the parties which does not cause unjustified delay shall be taken into account.
3. The Court may, at the request of the party concerned, extend any time-limit, or decide that any step taken after the expiration of the time-limit fixed therefor shall be considered as valid, if it is satisfied that there is adequate justification for the request. In either case the other party shall be given an opportunity to state its views.
4. If the Court is not sitting, its powers under this Article shall be exercised by the President, but without prejudice to any subsequent decision of the Court. If the consultation referred to in Article 31 reveals persistent disagreement between the parties as to the application of Article 45, paragraph 2, or Article 46, paragraph 2, of these Rules, the Court shall be convened to decide the matter.

Article 45

1. The pleadings in a case begun by means of an application shall consist, in the following order, of: a Memorial by the applicant; a Counter-Memorial by the respondent.
2. The Court may authorize or direct that there shall be a Reply by the applicant and a Rejoinder by the respondent if the parties are so agreed, or if the Court decides, *proprio motu* or at the request of one of the parties, that these pleadings are necessary.

Article 46

1. In a case begun by the notification of a special agreement, the number and order of the pleadings shall be governed by the provisions of the agreement, unless the Court, after ascertaining the views of the parties, decides otherwise.
2. If the special agreement contains no such provision, and if the parties have not subsequently agreed on the number and order of pleadings, they shall each file a Memorial and Counter-Memorial, within the same time-limits. The Court shall not authorize the presentation of Replies unless it finds them to be necessary.

Article 47

The Court may at any time direct that the proceedings in two or more cases be joined. It may also direct that the written or oral proceedings, including the calling of witnesses, be in common; or the Court may, without effecting any formal joinder, direct common action in any of these respects.

Article 48

Time-limits for the completion of steps in the proceedings may be fixed by assigning a specified period but shall always indicate definite dates. Such time-limits shall be as short as the character of the case permits.

Article 49

1. A Memorial shall contain a statement of the relevant facts, a statement of law, and the submissions.
2. A Counter-Memorial shall contain: an admission or denial of the facts stated in the Memorial; any additional facts, if necessary; observations concerning the statement of law in the Memorial; a statement of law in answer thereto; and the submissions.
3. The Reply and Rejoinder, whenever authorized by the Court, shall not merely repeat the parties' contentions, but shall be directed to bringing out the issues that still divide them.

4. Every pleading shall set out the party's submissions at the relevant stage of the case, distinctly from the arguments presented, or shall confirm the submissions previously made.

Article 50

1. There shall be annexed to the original of every pleading certified copies of any relevant documents adduced in support of the contentions contained in the pleading.
2. If only parts of a document are relevant, only such extracts as are necessary for the purpose of the pleading in question need be annexed. A copy of the whole document shall be deposited in the Registry, unless it has been published and is readily available.
3. A list of all documents annexed to a pleading shall be furnished at the time the pleading is filed.

Article 51

1. If the parties are agreed that the written proceedings shall be conducted wholly in one of the two official languages of the Court, the pleadings shall be submitted only in that language. If the parties are not so agreed, any pleading or any part of a pleading shall be submitted in one or other of the official languages.
2. If in pursuance of Article 39, paragraph 3, of the Statute a language other than French or English is used, a translation into French or English certified as accurate by the party submitting it, shall be attached to the original of each pleading.
3. When a document annexed to a pleading is not in one of the official languages of the Court, it shall be accompanied by a translation into one of these languages certified by the party submitting it as accurate. The translation may be confined to part of an annex, or to extracts therefrom, but in this case it must be accompanied by an explanatory note indicating what passages are translated. The Court may however require a more extensive or a complete translation to be furnished.

Article 52*[1][2]

1. The original of every pleading shall be signed by the agent and filed in the Registry. It shall be accompanied by a certified copy of the pleading, documents annexed, and any translations, for communication to the other party in accordance with Article 43, paragraph 4, of the Statute, and by the number of additional copies required by the Registry, but without prejudice to an increase in that number should the need arise later.
2. All pleadings shall be dated. When a pleading has to be filed by a certain date, it is the date of the receipt of the pleading in the Registry which will be regarded by the Court as the material date.
3. The correction of a slip or error in any document which has been filed may be made at any time with the consent of the other party or by leave of the President. Any correction so effected shall be notified to the other party in the same manner as the pleading to which it relates.

---

*Amendment entered into force on 14 April 2005.

1The agents of the parties are requested to ascertain from the Registry the usual format of the pleadings.

2The text of Article 52, as adopted on 14 April 1978, contained a paragraph 3 concerning the procedure to be followed where the Registrar arranges for the printing of a pleading; this paragraph has been deleted and the footnote to the Article has been amended. Former paragraph 4 has been renumbered and is now paragraph 3.

Article 53

1. The Court, or the President if the Court is not sitting, may at any time decide, after ascertaining the views of the parties, that copies of the pleadings and documents annexed shall be made available to a State entitled to appear before it which has asked to be furnished with such copies.
2. The Court may, after ascertaining the views of the parties, decide that copies of the pleadings and documents annexed shall be made accessible to the public on or after the opening of the oral proceedings.

Subsection 3. The Oral Proceedings

Article 54

1. Upon the closure of the written proceedings, the case is ready for hearing. The date for the opening of the oral proceedings shall be fixed by the Court, which may also decide, if occasion should arise, that the opening or the continuance of the oral proceedings be postponed.
2. When fixing the date for, or postponing, the opening of the oral proceedings the Court shall have regard to the priority required by Article 74 of these Rules and to any other special circumstances, including the urgency of a particular case.
3. When the Court is not sitting, its powers under this Article shall be exercised by the President.

Article 55

The Court may, if it considers it desirable, decide pursuant to Article 22, paragraph 1, of the Statute that all or part of the further proceedings in a case shall be held at a place other than the seat of the Court. Before so deciding, it shall ascertain the views of the parties.

Article 56

1. After the closure of the written proceedings, no further documents may be submitted to the Court by either party except with the consent of the other party or as provided in paragraph 2 of this Article. The party desiring to produce a new document shall file the original or a certified copy thereof, together with the number of copies required by the Registry, which shall be responsible for communicating it to the other party and shall inform the Court. The other party shall be held to have given its consent if it does not lodge an objection to the production of the document.
2. In the absence of consent, the Court, after hearing the parties, may, if it considers the document necessary, authorize its production.

3. If a new document is produced under paragraph 1 or paragraph 2 of this Article, the other party shall have an opportunity of commenting upon it and of submitting documents in support of its comments.
4. No reference may be made during the oral proceedings to the contents of any document which has not been produced in accordance with Article 43 of the Statute or this Article, unless the document is part of a publication readily available.
5. The application of the provisions of this Article shall not in itself constitute a ground for delaying the opening or the course of the oral proceedings.

Article 57

Without prejudice to the provisions of the Rules concerning the production of documents, each party shall communicate to the Registrar, in sufficient time before the opening of the oral proceedings, information regarding any evidence which it intends to produce or which it intends to request the Court to obtain. This communication shall contain a list of the surnames, first names, nationalities, descriptions and places of residence of the witnesses and experts whom the party intends to call, with indications in general terms of the point or points to which their evidence will be directed. A copy of the communication shall also be furnished for transmission to the other party.

Article 58

1. The Court shall determine whether the parties should present their arguments before or after the production of the evidence; the parties shall, however, retain the right to comment on the evidence given.
2. The order in which the parties will be heard, the method of handling the evidence and of examining any witnesses and experts, and the number of counsel and advocates to be heard on behalf of each party, shall be settled by the Court after the views of the parties have been ascertained in accordance with Article 31 of these Rules.

Article 59

The hearing in Court shall be public, unless the Court shall decide otherwise, or unless the parties demand that the public be not admitted. Such a decision or demand may concern either the whole or part of the hearing, and may be made at any time.

Article 60

1. The oral statements made on behalf of each party shall be as succinct as possible within the limits of what is requisite for the adequate presentation of that party's contentions at the hearing. Accordingly, they shall be directed to the issues that still divide the parties, and shall not go over the whole ground covered by the pleadings, or merely repeat the facts and arguments these contain.
2. At the conclusion of the last statement made by a party at the hearing, its agent, without recapitulation of the arguments, shall read that party's final submissions. A copy of the written text of these, signed by the agent, shall be communicated to the Court and transmitted to the other party.

Article 61

1. The Court may at any time prior to or during the hearing indicate any points or issues to which it would like the parties specially to address themselves, or on which it considers that there has been sufficient argument.
2. The Court may, during the hearing, put questions to the agents, counsel and advocates, and may ask them for explanations.
3. Each judge has a similar right to put questions, but before exercising it he should make his intention known to the President, who is made responsible by Article 45 of the Statute for the control of the hearing.
4. The agents, counsel and advocates may answer either immediately or within a time-limit fixed by the President.

Article 62

1. The Court may at any time call upon the parties to produce such evidence or to give such explanations as the Court may consider to be necessary for the elucidation of any aspect of the matters in issue, or may itself seek other information for this purpose.
2. The Court may, if necessary, arrange for the attendance of a witness or expert to give evidence in the proceedings.

Article 63

1. The parties may call any witnesses or experts appearing on the list communicated to the Court pursuant to Article 57 of these Rules. If at any time during the hearing a party wishes to call a witness or expert whose name was not included in that list, it shall so inform the Court and the other party, and shall supply the information required by Article 57. The witness or expert may be called either if the other party makes no objection or if the Court is satisfied that his evidence seems likely to prove relevant.
2. The Court, or the President if the Court is not sitting, shall, at the request of one of the parties or *proprio motu*, take the necessary steps for the examination of witnesses otherwise than before the Court itself.

Article 64

Unless on account of special circumstances the Court decides on a different form of words,

(a) every witness shall make the following declaration before giving any evidence:

"I solemnly declare upon my honour and conscience that I will speak the truth, the whole truth and nothing but the truth";

(b) every expert shall make the following declaration before making any statement:

"I solemnly declare upon my honour and conscience that I will speak the truth, the whole truth and nothing but the truth, and that my statement will be in accordance with my sincere belief."

Article 65

Witnesses and experts shall be examined by the agents, counsel or advocates of the parties under the control of the President. Questions may be put to them by the President and by the judges. Before testifying, witnesses shall remain out of court.

Article 66

The Court may at any time decide, either *proprio motu* or at the request of a party, to exercise its functions with regard to the obtaining of evidence at a place or locality to which the case relates, subject to such conditions as the Court may decide upon after ascertaining the views of the parties. The necessary arrangements shall be made in accordance with Article 44 of the Statute.

Article 67

1. If the Court considers it necessary to arrange for an enquiry or an expert opinion, it shall, after hearing the parties, issue an order to this effect, defining the subject of the enquiry or expert opinion, stating the number and mode of appointment of the persons to hold the enquiry or of the experts, and laying down the procedure to be followed. Where appropriate, the Court shall require persons appointed to carry out an enquiry, or to give an expert opinion, to make a solemn declaration.
2. Every report or record of an enquiry and every expert opinion shall be communicated to the parties, which shall be given the opportunity of commenting upon it.

Article 68

Witnesses and experts who appear at the instance of the Court under Article 62, paragraph 2, and persons appointed under Article 67, paragraph 1, of these Rules, to carry out an enquiry or to give an expert opinion, shall, where appropriate, be paid out of the funds of the Court.

Article 69

1. The Court may, at any time prior to the closure of the oral proceedings, either *proprio motu* or at the request of one of the parties communicated as provided in Article 57 of these Rules, request a public international organization, pursuant to Article 34 of the Statute, to furnish information relevant to a case before it. The Court, after consulting the chief administrative officer of the organization concerned, shall decide whether such information shall be presented to it orally or in writing, and the time-limits for its presentation.
2. When a public international organization sees fit to furnish, on its own initiative, information relevant to a case before the Court, it shall do so in the form of a Memorial to be filed in the Registry before the closure of the written proceedings. The Court shall retain the right to require such information to be supplemented, either orally or in writing, in the form of answers to any questions which it may see fit to formulate, and also to authorize the parties to comment, either orally or in writing, on the information thus furnished.
3. In the circumstances contemplated by Article 34, paragraph 3, of the Statute, the Registrar, on the instructions of the Court, or of the President if the Court is not sitting, shall proceed as prescribed in that paragraph. The Court, or the President if the Court is not sitting, may, as from the date on which the Registrar has communicated copies of the written proceedings and after consulting the chief administrative officer of the public international organization concerned, fix a time-limit within which the organization may submit to the Court its observations in writing. These observations shall be communicated to the parties and may be discussed by them and by the representative of the said organization during the oral proceedings.
4. In the foregoing paragraph, the term "public international organization" denotes an international organization of States.

Article 70

1. In the absence of any decision to the contrary by the Court, all speeches and statements made and evidence given at the hearing in one of the official languages of the Court shall be interpreted into the other official

language. If they are made or given in any other language, they shall be interpreted into the two official languages of the Court.
2. Whenever, in accordance with Article 39, paragraph 3, of the Statute, a language other than French or English is used, the necessary arrangements for interpretation into one of the two official languages shall be made by the party concerned; however, the Registrar shall make arrangements for the verification of the interpretation provided by a party of evidence given on the party's behalf. In the case of witnesses or experts who appear at the instance of the Court, arrangements for interpretation shall be made by the Registry.
3. A party on behalf of which speeches or statements are to be made, or evidence given, in a language which is not one of the official languages of the Court, shall so notify the Registrar in sufficient time for him to make the necessary arrangements.
4. Before first interpreting in the case, interpreters provided by a party shall make the following declaration in open court:
"I solemnly declare upon my honour and conscience that my interpretation will be faithful and complete."

Article 71

1. A verbatim record shall be made by the Registrar of every hearing, in the official language of the Court which has been used. When the language used is not one of the two official languages of the Court, the verbatim record shall be prepared in one of the Court's official languages.
2. When speeches or statements are made in a language which is not one of the official languages of the Court, the party on behalf of which they are made shall supply to the Registry in advance a text thereof in one of the official languages, and this text shall constitute the relevant part of the verbatim record.
3. The transcript of the verbatim record shall be preceded by the names of the judges present, and those of the agents, counsel and advocates of the parties.
4. Copies of the transcript shall be circulated to the judges sitting in the case, and to the parties. The latter may, under the supervision of the Court, correct the transcripts of speeches and statements made on their behalf, but in no case may such corrections affect the sense and bearing

thereof. The judges may likewise make corrections in the transcript of anything they may have said.
5. Witnesses and experts shall be shown that part of the transcript which relates to the evidence given, or the statements made by them, and may correct it in like manner as the parties.
6. One certified true copy of the eventual corrected transcript, signed by the President and the Registrar, shall constitute the authentic minutes of the sitting for the purpose of Article 47 of the Statute. The minutes of public hearings shall be printed and published by the Court.

Article 72

Any written reply by a party to a question put under Article 61, or any evidence or explanation supplied by a party under Article 62 of these Rules, received by the Court after the closure of the oral proceedings, shall be communicated to the other party, which shall be given the opportunity of commenting upon it. If necessary the oral proceedings may be reopened for that purpose.

SECTION D. INCIDENTAL PROCEEDINGS

Subsection 1. Interim Protection

Article 73

1. A written request for the indication of provisional measures may be made by a party at any time during the course of the proceedings in the case in connection with which the request is made.
2. The request shall specify the reasons therefor, the possible consequences if it is not granted, and the measures requested. A certified copy shall forthwith be transmitted by the Registrar to the other party.

Article 74

1. A request for the indication of provisional measures shall have priority over all other cases.

2. The Court, if it is not sitting when the request is made, shall be convened forthwith for the purpose of proceeding to a decision on the request as a matter of urgency.
3. The Court, or the President if the Court is not sitting, shall fix a date for a hearing which will afford the parties an opportunity of being represented at it. The Court shall receive and take into account any observations that may be presented to it before the closure of the oral proceedings.
4. Pending the meeting of the Court, the President may call upon the parties to act in such a way as will enable any order the Court may make on the request for provisional measures to have its appropriate effects.

Article 75

1. The Court may at any time decide to examine *proprio motu* whether the circumstances of the case require the indication of provisional measures which ought to be taken or complied with by any or all of the parties.
2. When a request for provisional measures has been made, the Court may indicate measures that are in whole or in part other than those requested, or that ought to be taken or complied with by the party which has itself made the request.
3. The rejection of a request for the indication of provisional measures shall not prevent the party which made it from making a fresh request in the same case based on new facts.

Article 76

1. At the request of a party the Court may, at any time before the final judgment in the case, revoke or modify any decision concerning provisional measures if, in its opinion, some change in the situation justifies such revocation or modification.
2. Any application by a party proposing such a revocation or modification shall specify the change in the situation considered to be relevant.
3. Before taking any decision under paragraph 1 of this Article the Court shall afford the parties an opportunity of presenting their observations on the subject.

Article 77

Any measures indicated by the Court under Articles 73 and 75 of these Rules, and any decision taken by the Court under Article 76, paragraph 1, of these Rules, shall forthwith be communicated to the Secretary-General of the United Nations for transmission to the Security Council in pursuance of Article 41, paragraph 2, of the Statute.

Article 78

The Court may request information from the parties on any matter connected with the implementation of any provisional measures it has indicated.

Subsection 2. Preliminary Objections

Article 79[*][1]

1. Any objection by the respondent to the jurisdiction of the Court or to the admissibility of the application, or other objection the decision upon which is requested before any further proceedings on the merits, shall be made in writing as soon as possible, and not later than three months after the delivery of the Memorial. Any such objection made by a party other than the respondent shall be filed within the time-limit fixed for the delivery of that party's first pleading.
2. Notwithstanding paragraph 1 above, following the submission of the application and after the President has met and consulted with the parties, the Court may decide that any questions of jurisdiction and admissibility shall be determined separately.
3. Where the Court so decides, the parties shall submit any pleadings as to jurisdiction and admissibility within the time-limits fixed by the Court and in the order determined by it, notwithstanding Article 45, paragraph 1.
4. The preliminary objection shall set out the facts and the law on which the objection is based, the submissions and a list of the documents in support; it shall mention any evidence which the party may desire to produce. Copies of the supporting documents shall be attached.

5. Upon receipt by the Registry of a preliminary objection, the proceedings on the merits shall be suspended and the Court, or the President if the Court is not sitting, shall fix the time-limit within which the other party may present a written statement of its observations and submissions; documents in support shall be attached and evidence which it is proposed to produce shall be mentioned.
6. Unless otherwise decided by the Court, the further proceedings shall be oral.
7. The statements of facts and law in the pleadings referred to in paragraphs 4 and 5 of this Article, and the statements and evidence presented at the hearings contemplated by paragraph 6, shall be confined to those matters that are relevant to the objection.
8. In order to enable the Court to determine its jurisdiction at the preliminary stage of the proceedings, the Court, whenever necessary, may request the parties to argue all questions of law and fact, and to adduce all evidence, which bear on the issue.
9. After hearing the parties, the Court shall give its decision in the form of a judgment, by which it shall either uphold the objection, reject it, or declare that the objection does not possess, in the circumstances of the case, an exclusively preliminary character. If the Court rejects the objection or declares that it does not possess an exclusively preliminary character, it shall fix time-limits for the further proceedings.
10. Any agreement between the parties that an objection submitted under paragraph 1 of this Article be heard and determined within the framework of the merits shall be given effect by the Court.

---

*Amendment entered into force on 1 February 2001. Article 79 of the Rules of Court as adopted on 14 April 1978 has continued to apply to all cases submitted to the Court prior to 1 February 2001.
[1]In Article 79, paragraph 1, as amended, the words "as soon as possible, and not later than three months after the delivery of the Memorial" have been substituted for the words "within the time-limit fixed for the delivery of the Counter-Memorial" contained in the text of this paragraph as adopted on 14 April 1978.
Paragraphs 2 and 3 of the amended Article 79 are new.
The former paragraphs 2 to 8 have been renumbered, respectively, as paragraphs 4 to 10.

Subsection 3. Counter-Claims

Article 80*[1]

1. The Court may entertain a counter-claim only if it comes within the jurisdiction of the Court and is directly connected with the subject-matter of the claim of the other party.
2. A counter-claim shall be made in the Counter-Memorial and shall appear as part of the submissions contained therein. The right of the other party to present its views in writing on the counter-claim, in an additional pleading, shall be preserved, irrespective of any decision of the Court, in accordance with Article 45, paragraph 2, of these Rules, concerning the filing of further written pleadings.
3. Where an objection is raised concerning the application of paragraph 1 or whenever the Court deems necessary, the Court shall take its decision thereon after hearing the parties.

---

*Amendment entered into force on 1 February 2001. Article 80 of the Rules of Court as adopted on 14 April 1978 has continued to apply to all cases submitted to the Court prior to 1 February 2001.

[1]Article 80 of the Rules of Court as adopted on 14 April 1978 read as follows:

"*Article 80*

1. A counter-claim may be presented provided that it is directly connected with the subject-matter of the claim of the other party and that it comes within the jurisdiction of the Court.
2. A counter-claim shall be made in the Counter-Memorial of the party presenting it, and shall appear as part of the submissions of that party.
3. In the event of doubt as to the connection between the question presented by way of counter-claim and the subject-matter of the claim of the other party the Court shall, after hearing the parties, decide whether or not the question thus presented shall be joined to the original proceedings."

Subsection 4. Intervention

Article 81

1. An application for permission to intervene under the terms of Article 62 of the Statute, signed in the manner provided for in Article 38, paragraph 3, of these Rules, shall be filed as soon as possible, and not later than the closure of the written proceedings. In exceptional circumstances, an application submitted at a later stage may however be admitted.
2. The application shall state the name of an agent. It shall specify the case to which it relates, and shall set out:
(a) the interest of a legal nature which the State applying to intervene considers may be affected by the decision in that case;
(b) the precise object of the intervention;
(c) any basis of jurisdiction which is claimed to exist as between the State applying to intervene and the parties to the case.
3. The application shall contain a list of the documents in support, which documents shall be attached.

Article 82

1. A State which desires to avail itself of the right of intervention conferred upon it by Article 63 of the Statute shall file a declaration to that effect, signed in the manner provided for in Article 38, paragraph 3, of these Rules. Such a declaration shall be filed as soon as possible, and not later than the date fixed for the opening of the oral proceedings. In exceptional circumstances a declaration submitted at a later stage may however be admitted.
2. The declaration shall state the name of an agent. It shall specify the case and the convention to which it relates and shall contain:
(a) particulars of the basis on which the declarant State considers itself a party to the convention;
(b) identification of the particular provisions of the convention the construction of which it considers to be in question;
(c) a statement of the construction of those provisions for which it contends;

(d) a list of the documents in support, which documents shall be attached.
3. Such a declaration may be filed by a State that considers itself a party to the convention the construction of which is in question but has not received the notification referred to in Article 63 of the Statute.

Article 83

1. Certified copies of the application for permission to intervene under Article 62 of the Statute, or of the declaration of intervention under Article 63 of the Statute, shall be communicated forthwith to the parties to the case, which shall be invited to furnish their written observations within a time-limit to be fixed by the Court or by the President if the Court is not sitting.
2. The Registrar shall also transmit copies to: *(a)* the Secretary-General of the United Nations; *(b)* the Members of the United Nations; *(c)* other States entitled to appear before the Court; *(d)* any other States which have been notified under Article 63 of the Statute.

Article 84

1. The Court shall decide whether an application for permission to intervene under Article 62 of the Statute should be granted, and whether an intervention under Article 63 of the Statute is admissible, as a matter of priority unless in view of the circumstances of the case the Court shall otherwise determine.
2. If, within the time-limit fixed under Article 83 of these Rules, an objection is filed to an application for permission to intervene, or to the admissibility of a declaration of intervention, the Court shall hear the State seeking to intervene and the parties before deciding.

Article 85

1. If an application for permission to intervene under Article 62 of the Statute is granted, the intervening State shall be supplied with copies of the pleadings and documents annexed and shall be entitled to submit a written statement within a time-limit to be fixed by the Court. A further

time-limit shall be fixed within which the parties may, if they so desire, furnish their written observations on that statement prior to the oral proceedings. If the Court is not sitting, these time-limits shall be fixed by the President.
2. The time-limits fixed according to the preceding paragraph shall, so far as possible, coincide with those already fixed for the pleadings in the case.
3. The intervening State shall be entitled, in the course of the oral proceedings, to submit its observations with respect to the subject-matter of the intervention.

Article 86

1. If an intervention under Article 63 of the Statute is admitted, the intervening State shall be furnished with copies of the pleadings and documents annexed, and shall be entitled, within a time-limit to be fixed by the Court, or by the President if the Court is not sitting, to submit its written observations on the subject-matter of the intervention.
2. These observations shall be communicated to the parties and to any other State admitted to intervene. The intervening State shall be entitled, in the course of the oral proceedings, to submit its observations with respect to the subject-matter of the intervention.

Subsection 5. Special Reference to the Court

Article 87

1. When in accordance with a treaty or convention in force a contentious case is brought before the Court concerning a matter which has been the subject of proceedings before some other international body, the provisions of the Statute and of the Rules governing contentious cases shall apply.
2. The application instituting proceedings shall identify the decision or other act of the international body concerned and a copy thereof shall be annexed; it shall contain a precise statement of the questions raised in regard to that decision or act, which constitute the subject of the dispute referred to the Court.

Subsection 6. Discontinuance

Article 88

1. If at any time before the final judgment on the merits has been delivered the parties, either jointly or separately, notify the Court in writing that they have agreed to discontinue the proceedings, the Court shall make an order recording the discontinuance and directing that the case be removed from the list.
2. If the parties have agreed to discontinue the proceedings in consequence of having reached a settlement of the dispute and if they so desire, the Court may record this fact in the order for the removal of the case from the list, or indicate in, or annex to, the order, the terms of the settlement.
3. If the Court is not sitting, any order under this Article may be made by the President.

Article 89

1. If in the course of proceedings instituted by means of an application, the applicant informs the Court in writing that it is not going on with the proceedings, and if, at the date on which this communication is received by the Registry, the respondent has not yet taken any step in the proceedings, the Court shall make an order officially recording the discontinuance of the proceedings and directing the removal of the case from the list. A copy of this order shall be sent by the Registrar to the respondent.
2. If, at the time when the notice of discontinuance is received, the respondent has already taken some step in the proceedings, the Court shall fix a time-limit within which the respondent may state whether it opposes the discontinuance of the proceedings. If no objection is made to the discontinuance before the expiration of the time-limit, acquiescence will be presumed and the Court shall make an order officially recording the discontinuance of the proceedings and directing the removal of the case from the list. If objection is made, the proceedings shall continue.
3. If the Court is not sitting, its powers under this Article may be exercised by the President.

SECTION E. PROCEEDINGS BEFORE THE CHAMBERS

Article 90

Proceedings before the Chambers mentioned in Articles 26 and 29 of the Statute shall, subject to the provisions of the Statute and of these Rules relating specifically to the Chambers, be governed by the provisions of Parts I to III of these Rules applicable in contentious cases before the Court.

Article 91

1. When it is desired that a case should be dealt with by one of the Chambers which has been formed in pursuance of Article 26, paragraph 1, or Article 29 of the Statute, a request to this effect shall either be made in the document instituting the proceedings or accompany it. Effect will be given to the request if the parties are in agreement.
2. Upon receipt by the Registry of this request, the President of the Court shall communicate it to the members of the Chamber concerned. He shall take such steps as may be necessary to give effect to the provisions of Article 31, paragraph 4, of the Statute.
3. The President of the Court shall convene the Chamber at the earliest date compatible with the requirements of the procedure.

Article 92

1. Written proceedings in a case before a Chamber shall consist of a single pleading by each side. In proceedings begun by means of an application, the pleadings shall be delivered within successive time-limits. In proceedings begun by the notification of a special agreement, the pleadings shall be delivered within the same time-limits, unless the parties have agreed on successive delivery of their pleadings. The time-limits referred to in this paragraph shall be fixed by the Court, or by the President if the Court is not sitting, in consultation with the Chamber concerned if it is already constituted.

2. The Chamber may authorize or direct that further pleadings be filed if the parties are so agreed, or if the Chamber decides, *proprio motu* or at the request of one of the parties, that such pleadings are necessary.
3. Oral proceedings shall take place unless the parties agree to dispense with them, and the Chamber consents. Even when no oral proceedings take place, the Chamber may call upon the parties to supply information or furnish explanations orally.

Article 93

Judgments given by a Chamber shall be read at a public sitting of that Chamber.

SECTION F. JUDGMENTS, INTERPRETATION AND REVISION

Subsection 1. Judgments

Article 94

1. When the Court has completed its deliberations and adopted its judgment, the parties shall be notified of the date on which it will be read.
2. The judgment shall be read at a public sitting of the Court and shall become binding on the parties on the day of the reading.

Article 95

1. The judgment, which shall state whether it is given by the Court or by a Chamber, shall contain:

the date on which it is read;
the names of the judges participating in it;
the names of the parties;
the names of the agents, counsel and advocates of the parties;
a summary of the proceedings;
the submissions of the parties;
a statement of the facts;
the reasons in point of law;
the operative provisions of the judgment;

the decision, if any, in regard to costs;
the number and names of the judges constituting the majority;
a statement as to the text of the judgment which is authoritative.

2. Any judge may, if he so desires, attach his individual opinion to the judgment, whether he dissents from the majority or not; a judge who wishes to record his concurrence or dissent without stating his reasons may do so in the form of a declaration. The same shall also apply to orders made by the Court.

3. One copy of the judgment duly signed and sealed, shall be placed in the archives of the Court and another shall be transmitted to each of the parties. Copies shall be sent by the Registrar to: *(a)* the Secretary-General of the United Nations; *(b)* the Members of the United Nations; *(c)* other Sates entitled to appear before the Court.

Article 96

When by reason of an agreement reached between the parties, the written and oral proceedings have been conducted in one of the Court's two official languages, and pursuant to Article 39, paragraph 1, of the Statute the judgment is to be delivered in that language, the text of the judgment in that language shall be the authoritative text.

Article 97

If the Court, under Article 64 of the Statute, decides that all or part of a party's costs shall be paid by the other party, it may make an order for the purpose of giving effect to that decision.

Subsection 2. Requests for the Interpretation or Revision of a Judgment

Article 98

1. In the event of dispute as to the meaning or scope of a judgment any party may make a request for its interpretation, whether the original proceedings were begun by an application or by the notification of a special agreement.

2. A request for the interpretation of a judgment may be made either by an application or by the notification of a special agreement to that effect between the parties; the precise point or points in dispute as to the meaning or scope of the judgment shall be indicated.
3. If the request for interpretation is made by an application, the requesting party's contentions shall be set out therein, and the other party shall be entitled to file written observations thereon within a time-limit fixed by the Court, or by the President if the Court is not sitting.
4. Whether the request is made by an application or by notification of a special agreement, the Court may, if necessary, afford the parties the opportunity of furnishing further written or oral explanations.

Article 99

1. A request for the revision of a judgment shall be made by an application containing the particulars necessary to show that the conditions specified in Article 61 of the Statute are fulfilled. Any documents in support of the application shall be annexed to it.
2. The other party shall be entitled to file written observations on the admissibility of the application within a time-limit fixed by the Court, or by the President if the Court is not sitting. These observations shall be communicated to the party making the application.
3. The Court, before giving its judgment on the admissibility of the application may afford the parties a further opportunity of presenting their views thereon.
4. If the Court finds that the application is admissible it shall fix time-limits for such further proceedings on the merits of the application as, after ascertaining the views of the parties, it considers necessary.
5. If the Court decides to make the admission of the proceedings in revision conditional on previous compliance with the judgment, it shall make an order accordingly.

Article 100

1. If the judgment to be revised or to be interpreted was given by the Court, the request for its revision or interpretation shall be dealt with by

the Court. If the judgment was given by a Chamber, the request for its revision or interpretation shall be dealt with by that Chamber.
2. The decision of the Court, or of the Chamber, on a request for interpretation or revision of a judgment shall itself be given in the form of a judgment.

SECTION G. MODIFICATIONS PROPOSED BY THE PARTIES

Article 101

The parties to a case may jointly propose particular modifications or additions to the rules contained in the present Part (with the exception of Articles 93 to 97 inclusive), which may be applied by the Court or by a Chamber if the Court or the Chamber considers them appropriate in the circumstances of the case.

PART IV
ADVISORY PROCEEDINGS

Article 102

1. In the exercise of its advisory functions under Article 65 of the Statute, the Court shall apply, in addition to the provisions of Article 96 of the Charter and Chapter IV of the Statute, the provisions of the present Part of the Rules.
2. The Court shall also be guided by the provisions of the Statute and of these Rules which apply in contentious cases to the extent to which it recognizes them to be applicable. For this purpose, it shall above all consider whether the request for the advisory opinion relates to a legal question actually pending between two or more States.
3. When an advisory opinion is requested upon a legal question actually pending between two or more States, Article 31 of the Statute shall apply, as also the provisions of these Rules concerning the application of that Article.

Article 103

When the body authorized by or in accordance with the Charter of the United Nations to request an advisory opinion informs the Court that its request necessitates an urgent answer, or the Court finds that an early answer would be desirable, the Court shall take all necessary steps to accelerate the procedure, and it shall convene as early as possible for the purpose of proceeding to a hearing and deliberation on the request.

Article 104

All requests for advisory opinions shall be transmitted to the Court by the Secretary-General of the United Nations or, as the case may be, the chief administrative officer of the body authorized to make the request. The documents referred to in Article 65, paragraph 2, of the Statute shall be transmitted to the Court at the same time as the request or as soon as possible thereafter, in the number of copies required by the Registry.

Article 105

1. Written statements submitted to the Court shall be communicated by the Registrar to any States and organizations which have submitted such statements.
2. The Court, or the President if the Court is not sitting, shall:
(a) determine the form in which, and the extent to which, comments permitted under Article 66, paragraph 4, of the Statute shall be received, and fix the time-limit for the submission of any such comments in writing;
(b) decide whether oral proceedings shall take place at which statements and comments may be submitted to the Court under the provisions of Article 66 of the Statute, and fix the date for the opening of such oral proceedings.

Article 106

The Court, or the President if the Court is not sitting, may decide that the written statements and annexed documents shall be made accessible to the public on or after the opening of the oral proceedings. If the request for advisory opinion relates to a legal question actually pending between two or more States, the views of those States shall first be ascertained.

Article 107

1. When the Court has completed its deliberations and adopted its advisory opinion, the opinion shall be read at a public sitting of the Court.
2. The advisory opinion shall contain:
   the date on which it is delivered;
   the names of the judges participating;
   a summary of the proceedings;
   a statement of the facts;
   the reasons in point of law;
   the reply to the question put to the Court;
   the number and names of the judges constituting the majority;
   a statement as to the text of the opinion which is authoritative.
3. Any judge may, if he so desires, attach his individual opinion to the advisory opinion of the Court, whether he dissents from the majority or not; a judge who wishes to record his concurrence or dissent without stating his reasons may do so in the form of a declaration.

Article 108

The Registrar shall inform the Secretary-General of the United Nations, and, where appropriate, the chief administrative officer of the body which requested the advisory opinion, as to the date and the hour fixed for the public sitting to be held for the reading of the opinion. He shall also inform the representatives of the Members of the United Nations and other States, specialized agencies and public international organizations immediately concerned.

Article 109

One copy of the advisory opinion, duly signed and sealed, shall be placed in the archives of the Court, another shall be sent to the Secretary-General of the United Nations and, where appropriate, a third to the chief administrative officer of the body which requested the opinion of the Court. Copies shall be sent by the Registrar to the Members of the United

Nations and to any other States, specialized agencies and public international organizations immediately concerned.

(*Signed*) Rosalyn HIGGINS, President.
(Signed) Ph. COUVREUR, Registrar.

RESOLUTION CONCERNING THE INTERNAL JUDICIAL PRACTICE OF THE COURT

(RULES OF COURT, ARTICLE 19)

ADOPTED ON 12 APRIL 1976

The Court decides to revise its Resolution concerning the Internal Judicial Practice of the Court of 5 July 1968[1] and to adopt the articles concerning its internal judicial practice which are set out in the present Resolution. The Court remains entirely free to depart from the present Resolution, or any part of it, in a given case, if it considers that the circumstances justify that course.

Article 1

(i) After the termination of the written proceedings and before the beginning of the oral proceedings, a deliberation is held at which the judges exchange views concerning the case, and bring to the notice of the Court any point in regard to which they consider it may be necessary to call for explanations during the course of the oral proceedings.
(ii) In cases where two exchanges of oral arguments take place, after the first such exchange has been concluded, a further deliberation is held having the same objects.
(iii) The Court also meets in private from time to time during the oral proceedings to enable judges to exchange views concerning the case and to inform each other of possible questions which they may intend to put in the exercise of their right under Article 61, paragraph 3, of the Rules.

Article 2

After the termination of the oral proceedings, an appropriate period is allowed to the judges in order that they may study the arguments presented to the Court.

Article 3

(i) At the expiration of this period a deliberation is held at which the President outlines the issues which in his opinion will require discussion and decision by the Court. Any judge may then comment on the statement or call attention to any other issue or question which he considers relevant, and may at any time during or at the close of the deliberation cause to be distributed a text formulating a new question or reformulating a question already brought to notice.
(ii) During this deliberation any judge may comment on the pertinence of any issues or questions arising in the case. The President also invites judges to indicate their preliminary impressions regarding any issue or question.
(iii) Judges will be called on by the President in the order in which they signify their desire to speak.

Article 4

(i) At a suitable interval of time after this deliberation, each judge prepares a written note which is distributed to the other judges.
(ii) The written note expresses the judge's views on the case, indicating, inter alia:
(a) whether any questions which have been called to notice should be eliminated from further consideration or should not, or need not, be decided by the Court;
(b) the precise questions which should be answered by the Court;
(c) his tentative opinion as to the answers to be given to the questions in (b) and his reasons therefor;
(d) his tentative conclusion as to the correct disposal of the case.

Article 5

(i) After the judges have had an opportunity to examine the written notes, a further deliberation is held, in the course of which all the judges, called upon by the President as a rule in inverse order of seniority, must declare their views. Any judge may address comments to or ask for further

explanations from a judge concerning the latter's statement declaring his views.
(ii) During this deliberation any judge may circulate an additional question or a reformulation of a question already brought to notice.
(iii) On the request of any judge the President shall ask the Court to decide whether a vote shall be taken on any question.

Article 6

(i) On the basis of the views expressed in the deliberations and in the written notes, the Court proceeds to choose a drafting committee by secret ballot and by an absolute majority of votes of the judges present. Two members are elected who should be chosen from among those judges whose oral statements and written notes have most closely and effectively reflected the opinion of the majority of the Court as it appears then to exist.
(ii) The President shall ex officio be a member of the drafting com mittee unless he does not share the majority opinion of the Court as it appears then to exist, in which case his place shall be taken by the Vice-President. If the Vice-President is ineligible for the same reason, the Court shall proceed, by the process already employed, to the election of a third member, in which case the senior of the elected judges shall preside in the drafting committee.
(iii) If the President is not a member of the drafting committee, the committee shall discuss its draft with him before submitting it to the Court. If the President proposes amendments which the committee does not find it possible to adopt, it shall submit the President's proposals to the Court together with its own draft.

Article 7

(i) A preliminary draft of the decision is circulated to the judges, who may submit amendments in writing. The drafting committee, having considered these amendments, submits a revised draft for discussion by the Court in first reading.

(ii) Judges who wish to deliver separate or dissenting opinions make the text thereof available to the Court after the first reading is concluded and within a time-limit fixed by the Court.
(iii) The drafting committee circulates an amended draft of the decision for the second reading, at which the President enquires whether any judge wishes to propose further amendments.
(iv) Judges who are delivering separate or dissenting opinions may make changes in or additions to their opinions only to the extent that changes have been made in the draft decision. During the second reading they inform the Court of any changes in or additions to their opinions which they propose to make for that reason. A time-limit is fixed by the Court for the filing of the revised texts of separate or dissenting opinions, copies of which are distributed to the Court.

Article 8

(i) At or after a suitable interval following upon the termination of the second reading, the President calls upon the judges to give their final vote on the decision or conclusion concerned in inverse order of seniority, and in the manner provided for by paragraph (v) of this Article.
(ii) Where the decision deals with issues that are separable, the Court shall in principle, and unless the exigencies of the particular case require a different course, proceed on the following basis, namely that:
(a) any judge may request a separate vote on any such issue;
(b) wherever the question before the Court is whether the Court is competent or the claim admissible, any separate vote on particular issues of competence or admissibility shall (unless such vote has shown some preliminary objection to be well-founded under the Statute and the Rules of Court) be followed by a vote on the question of whether the Court may proceed to entertain the merits of the case or, if that stage has already been reached, on the global question of whether, finally, the Court is competent or the claim admissible.
(iii) In any case coming under paragraph (ii) of this Article, or in any other case in which a judge so requests, the final vote shall take place only after a discussion on the need for separate voting, and whenever possible after a suitable interval following upon such discussion.

(iv) Any question whether separate votes as envisaged in paragraph (ii) of this Article should be recorded in the decision shall be decided by the Court.
(v) Every judge, when called upon by the President to record his final vote in any phase of the proceedings, or to vote upon any question relative to the putting to the vote of the decision or conclusion concerned, shall do so only by means of an affirmative or negative.

Article 9

(i) Although because of illness or other reason deemed adequate by the President, a judge may have failed to attend part of the public hearing or of the Court's internal proceedings under Articles 1 to 7 inclusive of this Resolution, he may nevertheless participate in the final vote provided that:
(a) during most of the proceedings, he shall have been, or remained, at the seat of the Court or other locality in which the Court is sitting and exercising its functions for the purposes of the case under paragraph 1 of Article 22 of the Statute;
(b) as regards the public hearing, he shall have been able to read the official transcript of the proceedings;
(c) as regards the internal proceedings under Articles 1 to 7 inclusive, he shall have been able at least to submit his own written note, read those of the other judges, and study the drafts of the drafting committee; and
(d) as regards the proceedings as a whole, he shall have taken a sufficient part in the public hearing and in the internal proceedings under Articles 1 to 7 inclusive to enable him to arrive at a judicial determina tion of all issues of fact and law material to the decision of the case.
(ii) A judge who is qualified to participate in the final vote must record his vote in person. In the event of a judge who is otherwise in a fit condition to record his vote being unable because of physical incapacity or other compelling reason to attend the meeting at which the vote is to be taken, the vote shall, if the circumstances permit, be postponed until he can attend. If, in the opinion of the Court, the circumstances do not permit of such a postponement, or render it inadvisable, the Court may, for the purpose of enabling the judge to record his vote, decide to convene elsewhere than at its normal meeting place. If neither of these alternatives

is practicable, the judge may be permitted to record his vote in any other manner which the Court decides to be compatible with the Statute.
(iii) In the event of any doubt arising as to whether a judge may vote in the circumstances contemplated by paragraphs (i) and (ii) hereof - and if this doubt cannot be resolved in the course of discussion - the matter shall, upon the proposal of the President, or at the request of any other Member of the Court, be decided by the Court.
(iv) When a judge casts his final vote in the circumstances contem plated by paragraphs (i) and (ii) of the present Article, paragraph (v) of Article 8 shall apply.

Article 10

The foregoing provisions shall apply whether the proceedings before the Court are contentious or advisory.

PRACTICE DIRECTIONS

As amended on 20 January 2009

Practice Direction I

The Court wishes to discourage the practice of simultaneous deposit of pleadings in cases brought by special agreement.

The Court would expect future special agreements to contain provisions as to the number and order of pleadings, in accordance with Article 46, paragraph 1, of the Rules of Court. Such provisions shall be without prejudice to any issue in the case, including the issue of burden of proof.

If the special agreement contains no provisions on the number and order of pleadings, the Court will expect the parties to reach agreement to that effect, in accordance with Article 46, paragraph 2, of the Rules of Court.

Practice Direction II

Each of the parties is, in drawing up its written pleadings, to bear in mind the fact that these pleadings are intended not only to reply to the submissions and arguments of the other party, but also, and above all, to present clearly the submissions and arguments of the party which is filing the proceedings.

In the light of this, at the conclusion of the written pleadings of each party, there is to appear a short summary of its reasoning.

Practice Direction III

The parties are strongly urged to keep the written pleadings as concise as possible, in a manner compatible with the full presentation of their positions.

In view of an excessive tendency towards the proliferation and protraction of annexes to written pleadings, the parties are also urged to append to their pleadings only strictly selected documents.

Practice Direction IV

Where one of the parties has a full or partial translation of its own pleadings or of those of the other party in the other official language of the Court, these translations should as a matter of course be passed to the Registry of the Court. The same applies to the annexes.

These translations will be examined by the Registry and communicated to the other party. The latter will also be informed of the manner in which they were prepared.

Practice Direction V

With the aim of accelerating proceedings on preliminary objections made by one party under Article 79, paragraph 1, of the Rules of Court, the time-limit for the presentation by the other party of a written statement of its observations and submissions under Article 79, paragraph 5, shall generally not exceed four months from the date of the filing of the preliminary objections.

Practice Direction VI

The Court requires full compliance with Article 60, paragraph 1, of the Rules of Court and observation of the requisite degree of brevity in oral pleadings. In that context, the Court will find it very helpful if the parties focus in the first round of the oral proceedings on those points which have been raised by one party at the stage of written proceedings but which have not so far been adequately addressed by the other, as well as on those which each party wishes to emphasize by way of winding up its arguments. Where objections of lack of jurisdiction or of inadmissibility are being considered, oral proceedings are to be limited to statements on the objections.

Practice Direction VII*

The Court considers that it is not in the interest of the sound administration of justice that a person sit as judge *ad hoc* in one case who is also acting or has recently acted as agent, counsel or advocate in another case before the Court. Accordingly, parties, when choosing a judge *ad hoc* pursuant to Article 31 of the Statute and Article 35 of the Rules of Court, should refrain from nominating persons who are acting as agent, counsel or advocate in another case before the Court or have acted in that capacity in the three years preceding the date of the nomination. Furthermore, parties should likewise refrain from designating as agent, counsel or advocate in a case before the Court a person who sits as judge *ad hoc* in another case before the Court.

Practice Direction VIII*

The Court considers that it is not in the interest of the sound administration of justice that a person who until recently was a Member of the Court, judge *ad hoc*, Registrar, Deputy-Registrar or higher official of the Court (principal legal secretary, first secretary or secretary), appear as agent, counsel or advocate in a case before the Court. Accordingly, parties should refrain from designating as agent, counsel or advocate in a case before the Court a person who in the three years preceding the date of the designation was a Member of the Court, judge *ad hoc*, Registrar, Deputy-Registrar or higher official of the Court.

Practice Direction IX

1. The parties to proceedings before the Court should refrain from submitting new documents after the closure of the written proceedings.

2. A party nevertheless desiring to submit a new document after the closure of the written proceedings, including during the oral proceedings, pursuant to Article 56, paragraphs 1 and 2, of the Rules, shall explain why it considers it necessary to include the document in the case file and shall indicate the reasons preventing the production of the document at an earlier stage.

3. In the absence of consent of the other party, the Court will authorize the production of the new document only in exceptional circumstances, if it considers it necessary and if the production of the document at this stage of the proceedings appears justified to the Court.

4. If a new document has been added to the case file under Article 56 of the Rules of Court, the other party, when commenting upon it, shall confine the introduction of any further documents to what is strictly necessary and relevant to its comments on what is contained in this new document.

Practice Direction IX*bis*

1. Any recourse to Article 56, paragraph 4, of the Rules of Court, is not to be made in such a manner as to undermine the general rule that all documents in support of a party's contentions shall be annexed to its written pleadings or produced in accordance with Article 56, paragraphs 1 and 2, of the Rules of Court.

2. While the Court will determine, in the context of a particular case, whether a document referred to under Article 56, paragraph 4, of the Rules of Court, can be considered "part of a publication readily available", it wishes to make it clear to the parties that both of the following two criteria must be met whenever that provision is applied.
(i) First, the document should form "part of a publication", i.e. should be available in the public domain. The publication may be in any format (printed or electronic), form (physical or on-line, such as posted on the internet) or on any data medium (on paper, on digital or any other media).
(ii) Second, the requirement of a publication being "readily available" shall be assessed by reference to its accessibility to the Court as well as to the other party. Thus the publication or its relevant parts should be accessible in either of the official languages of the Court, and it should be possible to consult the publication within a reasonably short period of time. This means that a party wishing to make reference during the oral proceedings to a new document emanating from a publication which is not accessible in one of the official languages of the Court should produce

a translation of that document into one of these languages certified as accurate.

3. In order to demonstrate that a document is part of a publication readily available in conformity with paragraph 2 above and to ensure the proper administration of the judicial process, a party when referring to the contents of a document under Article 56, paragraph 4, of the Rules of Court, should give the necessary reference for the rapid consultation of the document, unless the source of the publication is well known (e.g. United Nations documents, collections of international treaties, major monographs on international law, established reference works, etc.).

4. If during the oral proceedings a party objects to the reference by the other party to a document under Article 56, paragraph 4, of the Rules of Court, the matter shall be settled by the Court.

5. If during the oral proceedings a party refers to a document which is part of a publication readily available, the other party shall have an opportunity of commenting upon it.

Practice Direction IX*ter*

The Court has noted the practice by the parties of preparing folders of documents for the convenience of the judges during the oral proceedings. The Court invites parties to exercise restraint in this regard and recalls that the documents included in a judge's folder should be produced in accordance with Article 43 of the Statute or Article 56, paragraphs 1 and 2, of the Rules of Court. No other documents may be included in the folder except for any document which is part of a publication readily available in conformity with Practice Direction IX*bis* and under the conditions specified therein. In addition, parties should indicate from which annex to the written pleadings or which document produced under Article 56, paragraphs 1 and 2, of the Rules, the documents included in a judge's folder originate.

Practice Direction X

Whenever a decision on a procedural issue needs to be made in a case and the President deems it necessary to call a meeting of the agents to ascertain the views of the parties in this regard pursuant to Article 31 of the Rules of Court, agents are expected to attend that meeting as early as possible.

Practice Direction XI

In the oral pleadings on requests for the indication of provisional measures parties should limit themselves to what is relevant to the criteria for the indication of provisional measures as stipulated in the Statute, Rules and jurisprudence of the Court. They should not enter into the merits of the case beyond what is strictly necessary for that purpose.

Practice Direction XII

1. Where an international non-governmental organization submits a written statement and/or document in an advisory opinion case on its own initiative, such statement and/or document is not to be considered as part of the case file.

2. Such statements and/or documents shall be treated as publications readily available and may accordingly be referred to by States and intergovernmental organizations presenting written and oral statements in the case in the same manner as publications in the public domain.

3. Written statements and/or documents submitted by international non-governmental organizations will be placed in a designated location in the Peace Palace. All States as well as intergovernmental organizations presenting written or oral statements under Article 66 of the Statute will be informed as to the location where statements and/or documents submitted by international non-governmental organizations may be consulted.

Practice Direction XIII

The reference in Article 31 of the Rules of Court to ascertaining the views of the parties with regard to questions of procedure is to be understood as follows:

After the initial meeting with the President, and in the context of any further ascertainment of the parties' views relating to questions of procedure, the parties may, should they agree on the procedure to be followed, inform the President by letter accordingly.

The views of the parties as to the future procedure may also, should they agree, be ascertained by means of a video or telephone conference.

---

*Practice Directions VII and VIII do not affect a choice or designation made by the parties prior to 7 February 2002, the date of the adoption by the Court of those Directions.

NOTE FOR THE PARTIES CONCERNING THE PREPARATION OF PLEADINGS

1.The original of every pleading shall be signed by the agent and filed in the Registry, preferably in two copies, or accompanied by a certified copy, for communication to the other party; it must include the documents annexed and any translations (Art. 52, para. 1, of the Rules of Court). A signed list of all documents annexed must also be furnished at the time the pleading is filed (Art. 50, para. 3, of the Rules of Court). Lastly, the original of the pleading shall be accompanied by the number of additional copies required by the Registry (Art. 52, para. 1, of the Rules of Court).

*

2.The documents annexed to the pleading must be certified by the agent as true copies of the originals (Art. 50, para. 1, of the Rules of Court). It should be remembered that it may well not be necessary to annex to a pleading the complete text of a document produced in support of the contentions advanced and that it may be possible to annex only the relevant extracts (Art. 50, para. 2, of the Rules of Court). In that event, however, at least two certified copies of the whole document must be deposited with the pleading, unless it has been published and is readily available (ibid.), one of which will be transmitted to the other party. Further, if the reproduction in large numbers of a particular annex (e.g., a large map) presents technical problems, the matter should be raised with the Registrar at the earliest opportunity, so that other arrangements can be made.

3.Documents which are not in English or French must be translated into one of those languages and the translation certified as accurate by the agent (Art. 51, para. 3, of the Rules of Court). For practical convenience, it is acceptable for such a translation to constitute the relevant annex to a pleading; but if this is done, at least two certified copies of the original-language text of the document must be filed with the pleading, one of which will be transmitted to the other party.

4.In the present case, the number of copies of the pleadings to be filed in the first instance, including annexes, is 125. The parties may choose to file all 125 copies of the pleadings in paper form, or 75 copies in paper form and 50 on CD-ROM or DVD-ROM (using MS-Word or PDF-text for the electronic format). If a party chooses to file all 125 copies of a pleading in paper form, it should nevertheless provide the Registry with an electronic version of that pleading.

5.In a footnote to Article 52 of the Rules of Court, the agents of the parties are requested to ascertain from the Registry the usual format of the pleadings. The format to be respected, irrespective of whether the document is printed or not, is 19 cm x 26 cm, so as to ensure some degree of uniformity in the presentation of the pleadings. These must in addition be readily legible and easy to handle.

The Hague, 1 June 2010.

CASE LAW

INTERNATIONAL COURT OF JUSTICE

REPORTS OF JUDGMENTS,
ADVISORY OPINIONS AND ORDERS

LaGrand Case

(GERMANY *v.* UNITED STATES OF AMERICA)

JUDGMENT OF 27 JUNE 2001

2001

COUR INTERNATIONALE DE JUSTICE

RECUEIL DES ARRÊTS,
AVIS CONSULTATIFS ET ORDONNANCES

Affaire LaGrand

(ALLEMAGNE c. ÉTATS-UNIS D'AMÉRIQUE)

ARRÊT DU 27 JUIN 2001

INTERNATIONAL COURT OF JUSTICE

YEAR 2001

27 June 2001

LAGRAND CASE

(GERMANY *v.* UNITED STATES OF AMERICA)

Facts of the case.

* *

Jurisdiction of the Court — Article I of Optional Protocol concerning Compulsory Settlement of Disputes to Vienna Convention on Consular Relations of 24 April 1963.

Jurisdiction of Court in respect of Germany's first submission — Recognition by United States of existence of dispute arising out of breach of subparagraph (b) *of Article 36, paragraph 1, of Vienna Convention on Consular Relations — Recognition by United States of Court's jurisdiction to hear this dispute in so far as concerns Germany's own rights — Objection by United States to Court's jurisdiction over Germany's claim founded on diplomatic protection — Objection by United States to Court's jurisdiction over alleged breach of subparagraphs* (a) *and* (c) *of Article 36, paragraph 1, of Convention.*

Jurisdiction of Court in respect of Germany's third submission concerning implementation of Order of 3 March 1999 indicating provisional measures.

Jurisdiction of Court in respect of Germany's fourth submission — Objection by United States — United States argument that submission seeking guarantees of non-repetition falls outside terms of Optional Protocol.

* *

Admissibility of Germany's submissions.

United States objection to admissibility of Germany's second, third and fourth submissions — United States argument that Court cannot be turned into ultimate court of appeal in criminal proceedings before its own domestic courts.

United States objection to admissibility of Germany's third submission —

COUR INTERNATIONALE DE JUSTICE

ANNÉE 2001

27 juin 2001

AFFAIRE LAGRAND

(ALLEMAGNE c. ÉTATS-UNIS D'AMÉRIQUE)

Faits à l'origine de l'affaire.

* *

Compétence de la Cour — Article premier du protocole de signature facultative concernant le règlement obligatoire des différends à la convention de Vienne sur les relations consulaires du 24 avril 1963.

Compétence de la Cour pour connaître de la première conclusion de l'Allemagne — Reconnaissance par les Etats-Unis de l'existence d'un différend résultant de la violation de l'alinéa b) *du paragraphe 1 de l'article 36 de la convention de Vienne sur les relations consulaires — Reconnaissance par les Etats-Unis de la compétence de la Cour pour connaître de ce différend quant aux droits propres de l'Allemagne — Objection des Etats-Unis à la compétence de la Cour pour connaître de la prétention de l'Allemagne fondée sur la protection diplomatique — Objection des Etats-Unis à la compétence de la Cour pour connaître de la violation alléguée des alinéas* a) *et* c) *du paragraphe 1 de l'article 36 de la convention.*

Compétence de la Cour pour connaître de la troisième conclusion de l'Allemagne relative à l'application de l'ordonnance en indication de mesures conservatoires du 3 mars 1999.

Compétence de la Cour pour connaître de la quatrième conclusion de l'Allemagne — Objection des Etats-Unis — Conclusion tendant à l'obtention de garanties de non-répétition n'entrant pas, selon les Etats-Unis, dans les prévisions du protocole de signature facultative.

* *

Recevabilité des conclusions de l'Allemagne.

Objection des Etats-Unis à la recevabilité des deuxième, troisième et quatrième conclusions de l'Allemagne — La Cour ne pouvant s'ériger, selon les Etats-Unis, en juridiction statuant en dernier degré d'appel sur des questions pénales soumises à leurs tribunaux internes.

Objection des Etats-Unis à la recevabilité de la troisième conclusion de l'Alle-

United States challenging manner of Germany's institution of present proceedings before the Court.

United States objection to admissibility of Germany's first submission — Allegation of failure to exhaust local remedies.

United States objection to Germany's submissions — Allegation that Germany seeking to apply standard to United States different from own practice.

* *

Germany's first submission — Question of disregard by United States of its legal obligations to Germany under Articles 5 and 36, paragraph 1, of Convention.

Submission advanced by Germany in own right — Recognition by United States of breach of Article 36, paragraph 1 (b), *of Convention — Article 36, paragraph 1, establishing interrelated régime designed to facilitate implementation of system of consular protection.*

Submission by Germany based on diplomatic protection — Article 36, paragraph 1 (b), *of Convention and obligations of receiving State to detained person and to sending State.*

* *

Germany's second submission — Question of disregard by United States of its legal obligation under Article 36, paragraph 2, of Convention.

Argument of United States that Article 36, paragraph 2, applicable only to rights of sending State.

"Procedural default" rule — Distinction to be drawn between rule as such and application in present case.

* *

Germany's third submission — Question of disregard by United States of its legal obligation to comply with Order indicating provisional measures of 3 March 1999.

Court called upon to rule expressly on question of legal effects of orders under Article 41 of Statute — Interpretation of that provision — Comparison of French and English texts — French and English versions of Statute "equally authentic" by virtue of Article 111 of United Nations Charter — Article 33, paragraph 4, of Vienna Convention on Law of Treaties — Object and purpose of Statute — Context — Principle that party to legal proceedings must abstain from any measure which might aggravate or extend the dispute — Preparatory work of Article 41 — Article 94 of United Nations Charter.

Question of binding nature of Order of 3 March 1999 — Measures taken by United States to give effect to Order — No request for reparation in Germany's third submission — Time pressure due to circumstances in which proceedings were instituted.

* *

Germany's fourth submission — Question of obligation to provide certain assurances of non-repetition.

magne — Circonstances dans lesquelles, selon les Etats-Unis, cette dernière a introduit la présente instance devant la Cour.

Objection des Etats-Unis à la recevabilité de la première conclusion de l'Allemagne — Allégation de non-épuisement des voies de recours internes.

Objection des Etats-Unis à la recevabilité des conclusions de l'Allemagne — Allégation selon laquelle l'Allemagne chercherait à faire appliquer aux Etats-Unis une norme différente de celle qui prévaut dans la pratique allemande.

* *

Première conclusion de l'Allemagne — Question de la méconnaissance par les Etats-Unis de leurs obligations juridiques vis-à-vis de l'Allemagne au titre de l'article 5 et du paragraphe 1 de l'article 36 de la convention.

Conclusion de l'Allemagne en son nom propre — Reconnaissance par les Etats-Unis de la violation de l'alinéa b) *du paragraphe 1 de l'article 36 de la convention — Paragraphe 1 de l'article 36 instituant un régime aux éléments interdépendants conçu pour faciliter la mise en œuvre du système de protection consulaire.*

Conclusion de l'Allemagne fondée sur la protection diplomatique — Alinéa b) *du paragraphe 1 de l'article 36 de la convention et obligations de l'Etat de résidence vis-à-vis d'une personne détenue et de l'Etat d'envoi.*

* *

Deuxième conclusion de l'Allemagne — Question de la méconnaissance par les Etats-Unis de leur obligation juridique en vertu du paragraphe 2 de l'article 36 de la convention.

Paragraphe 2 de l'article 36 ne s'appliquant, selon les Etats-Unis, qu'aux droits de l'Etat d'envoi.

Règle de la «carence procédurale» — Distinction à établir entre cette règle en tant que telle et son application en l'espèce.

* *

Troisième conclusion de l'Allemagne — Question de la méconnaissance par les Etats-Unis de leur obligation juridique de se conformer à l'ordonnance en indication de mesures conservatoires du 3 mars 1999.

Cour appelée à se prononcer expressément sur la question des effets juridiques des ordonnances rendues en vertu de l'article 41 du Statut — Interprétation de cette disposition — Comparaison entre les textes français et anglais — Versions française et anglaise du Statut faisant «également foi» en vertu de l'article 111 de la Charte des Nations Unies — Paragraphe 4 de l'article 33 de la convention de Vienne sur le droit des traités — Objet et but du Statut — Contexte — Principe interdisant à une partie à une instance judiciaire de procéder à aucun acte susceptible d'aggraver ou d'étendre le différend — Travaux préparatoires de l'article 41 — Article 94 de la Charte des Nations Unies.

Question du caractère obligatoire de l'ordonnance du 3 mars 1999 — Mesures prises par les Etats-Unis pour donner effet à cette ordonnance — Absence de demande en réparation dans la troisième conclusion de l'Allemagne — Contraintes de temps résultant des conditions de l'introduction de l'instance.

* *

Quatrième conclusion de l'Allemagne — Question de l'obligation de fournir certaines assurances de non-répétition.

General request for assurance of non-repetition — Measures taken by United States to prevent recurrence of violation of Article 36, paragraph 1 (b) — *Commitment undertaken by United States to ensure implementation of specific measures adopted in performance of obligations under that provision.*

Consideration of other assurances requested by Germany — Germany's characterization of individual right provided for in Article 36, paragraph 1, as human right — Court's power to determine existence of violation of international obligation and, if necessary, to hold that domestic law has caused violation — United States having apologized to Germany for breach of Article 36, paragraph 1, of Convention — Germany not having requested material reparation for injury to itself and to LaGrand brothers — Question of review and reconsideration of certain sentences.

JUDGMENT

Present: *President* GUILLAUME; *Vice-President* SHI; *Judges* ODA, BEDJAOUI, RANJEVA, HERCZEGH, FLEISCHHAUER, KOROMA, VERESHCHETIN, HIGGINS, PARRA-ARANGUREN, KOOIJMANS, REZEK, AL-KHASAWNEH, BUERGENTHAL; *Registrar* COUVREUR.

In the LaGrand case,

between

the Federal Republic of Germany,

represented by

Mr. Gerhard Westdickenberg, Director General for Legal Affairs and Legal Adviser, Federal Foreign Office of the Federal Republic of Germany,

H.E. Mr. Eberhard U. B. von Puttkamer, Ambassador of the Federal Republic of Germany to the Kingdom of the Netherlands,

as Agents;

Mr. Bruno Simma, Professor of Public International Law at the University of Munich,

as Co-Agent and Counsel;

Mr. Pierre-Marie Dupuy, Professor of Public International Law at the University of Paris (Panthéon-Assas) and at the European University Institute in Florence,

Mr. Donald Francis Donovan, Debevoise & Plimpton, New York,

Mr. Hans-Peter Kaul, Head of the Public International Law Division, Federal Foreign Office of the Federal Republic of Germany,

Mr. Daniel Khan, University of Munich,

Mr. Andreas Paulus, University of Munich,

as Counsel;

Demande de caractère général visant l'obtention d'une assurance de non-répétition — Mesures prises par les Etats-Unis en vue d'empêcher la répétition de la violation de l'alinéa b) *du paragraphe 1 de l'article 36 — Engagement pris par les Etats-Unis d'assurer la mise en œuvre des mesures spécifiques adoptées en exécution de leurs obligations au titre de cette disposition.*

Examen des autres assurances demandées par l'Allemagne — Qualification par l'Allemagne du droit individuel prévu au paragraphe 1 de l'article 36 comme un droit de l'homme — Pouvoir de la Cour d'établir la violation d'une obligation internationale et, si nécessaire, de constater aussi qu'une loi interne a été la cause de cette violation — Excuses présentées par les Etats-Unis pour la violation du paragraphe 1 de l'article 36 de la convention — Absence de demande de l'Allemagne en réparation matérielle de son préjudice et de celui des frères LaGrand — Question du réexamen et de la revision de certaines condamnations.

ARRÊT

Présents: M. GUILLAUME, *président*; M. SHI, *vice-président*; MM. ODA, BEDJAOUI, RANJEVA, HERCZEGH, FLEISCHHAUER, KOROMA, VERESHCHETIN, Mme HIGGINS, MM. PARRA-ARANGUREN, KOOIJMANS, REZEK, AL-KHASAWNEH, BUERGENTHAL, *juges*; M. COUVREUR, *greffier*.

En l'affaire LaGrand,

entre

la République fédérale d'Allemagne,

représentée par

M. Gerhard Westdickenberg, directeur général des affaires juridiques et conseiller juridique du ministère fédéral des affaires étrangères de la République fédérale d'Allemagne,

S. Exc. M. Eberhard U. B. von Puttkamer, ambassadeur de la République fédérale d'Allemagne auprès du Royaume des Pays-Bas,

comme agents;

M. Bruno Simma, professeur de droit international public à l'Université de Munich,

comme coagent et conseil;

M. Pierre-Marie Dupuy, professeur de droit international public à l'Université de Paris (Panthéon-Assas) et à l'Institut universitaire européen de Florence,

M. Donald Francis Donovan, du cabinet Debevoise & Plimpton, New York,

M. Hans-Peter Kaul, chef de la division du droit international public du ministère fédéral des affaires étrangères de la République fédérale d'Allemagne,

M. Daniel Khan, de l'Université de Munich,

M. Andreas Paulus, de l'Université de Munich,

comme conseils;

Mr. Eberhard Desch, Federal Ministry of Justice of the Federal Republic of Germany,

Mr. S. Johannes Trommer, Embassy of the Federal Republic of Germany in the Netherlands,

Mr. Andreas Götze, Federal Foreign Office of the Federal Republic of Germany,

as Advisers;

Ms Fiona Sneddon,

as Assistant,

and

the United States of America,

represented by

Mr. James H. Thessin, Acting Legal Adviser, United States Department of State,

as Agent;

Ms Catherine W. Brown, Assistant Legal Adviser for Consular Affairs, United States Department of State,

Mr. D. Stephen Mathias, Assistant Legal Adviser for United Nations Affairs, United States Department of State,

as Deputy Agents;

The Honourable Janet Napolitano, Attorney General, State of Arizona,

Mr. Michael J. Matheson, Professor of International Law, School of Advanced International Studies, Johns Hopkins University; former Acting Legal Adviser, United States Department of State,

Mr. Theodor Meron, Counsellor on International Law, United States Department of State; Charles L. Denison Professor of International Law, New York University; Associate Member of the Institute of International Law,

Mr. Stefan Trechsel, Professor of Criminal Law and Procedure, University of Zurich Faculty of Law,

as Counsel and Advocates;

Mr. Shabtai Rosenne, Member of the Israel Bar; Honorary Member of the American Society of International Law; Member of the Institute of International Law,

Ms Norma B. Martens, Assistant Attorney General, State of Arizona,

Mr. Paul J. McMurdie, Assistant Attorney General, State of Arizona,

Mr. Robert J. Erickson, Principal Deputy Chief, Appellate Section, Criminal Division, United States Department of Justice,

Mr. Allen S. Weiner, Counsellor for Legal Affairs, Embassy of the United States of America in the Netherlands,

Ms Jessica R. Holmes, Attaché, Office of the Counsellor for Legal Affairs, Embassy of the United States of America in the Netherlands,

as Counsel,

M. Eberhard Desch, du ministère fédéral de la justice de la République fédérale d'Allemagne,
M. S. Johannes Trommer, de l'ambassade de la République fédérale d'Allemagne aux Pays-Bas,
M. Andreas Götze, du ministère fédéral des affaires étrangères de la République fédérale d'Allemagne,

comme conseillers:

Mme Fiona Sneddon,

comme assistante,

et

les Etats-Unis d'Amérique,

représentés par

M. James H. Thessin, conseiller juridique par intérim du département d'Etat des Etats-Unis d'Amérique,

comme agent;

Mme Catherine W. Brown, conseiller juridique adjoint chargé des affaires consulaires au département d'Etat des Etats-Unis d'Amérique,
M. D. Stephen Mathias, conseiller juridique adjoint chargé des questions concernant les Nations Unies au département d'Etat des Etats-Unis d'Amérique,

comme agents adjoints;

l'honorable Janet Napolitano, *Attorney General* de l'Etat de l'Arizona,
M. Michael J. Matheson, professeur de droit international à la School of Advanced International Studies de la Johns Hopkins University, ancien conseiller juridique par intérim du département d'Etat des Etats-Unis d'Amérique,
M. Theodor Meron, conseiller en droit international au département d'Etat des Etats-Unis d'Amérique, titulaire de la chaire Charles L. Denison de droit international à la New York University, membre associé de l'Institut de droit international,
M. Stefan Trechsel, professeur de droit pénal et de procédure pénale à la faculté de droit de l'Université de Zurich,

comme conseils et avocats;

M. Shabtai Rosenne, membre du barreau israélien, membre honoraire de l'American Society of International Law, membre de l'Institut de droit international,
Mme Norma B. Martens, *Attorney General* adjoint de l'Etat de l'Arizona,
M. Paul J. McMurdie, *Attorney General* adjoint de l'Etat de l'Arizona,
M. Robert J. Erickson, chef principal adjoint à la section des recours de la division du droit pénal du département de la justice des Etats-Unis d'Amérique,
M. Allen S. Weiner, conseiller aux affaires juridiques à l'ambassade des Etats-Unis d'Amérique aux Pays-Bas,
Mme Jessica R. Holmes, attachée, bureau du conseiller aux affaires juridiques à l'ambassade des Etats-Unis d'Amérique aux Pays-Bas,

comme conseils,

The Court,

composed as above,

after deliberation,

delivers the following Judgment:

1. On 2 March 1999 the Federal Republic of Germany (hereinafter referred to as "Germany") filed in the Registry of the Court an Application instituting proceedings against the United States of America (hereinafter referred to as the "United States") for "violations of the Vienna Convention on Consular Relations [of 24 April 1963]" (hereinafter referred to as the "Vienna Convention").

In its Application, Germany based the jurisdiction of the Court on Article 36, paragraph 1, of the Statute of the Court and on Article I of the Optional Protocol concerning the Compulsory Settlement of Disputes, which accompanies the Vienna Convention (hereinafter referred to as the "Optional Protocol").

2. Pursuant to Article 40, paragraph 2, of the Statute, the Application was forthwith communicated to the Government of the United States; and, in accordance with paragraph 3 of that Article, all States entitled to appear before the Court were notified of the Application.

3. On 2 March 1999, the day on which the Application was filed, the German Government also filed in the Registry of the Court a request for the indication of provisional measures based on Article 41 of the Statute and Articles 73, 74 and 75 of the Rules of Court.

By a letter dated 2 March 1999, the Vice-President of the Court, acting President in the case, addressed the Government of the United States in the following terms:

> "Exercising the functions of the presidency in terms of Articles 13 and 32 of the Rules of Court, and acting in conformity with Article 74, paragraph 4, of the said Rules, I hereby draw the attention of [the] Government [of the United States] to the need to act in such a way as to enable any Order the Court will make on the request for provisional measures to have its appropriate effects."

By an Order of 3 March 1999, the Court indicated certain provisional measures (see paragraph 32 below).

4. In accordance with Article 43 of the Rules of Court, the Registrar sent the notification referred to in Article 63, paragraph 1, of the Statute to all States parties to the Vienna Convention or to that Convention and the Optional Protocol.

5. By an Order of 5 March 1999, the Court, taking account of the views of the Parties, fixed 16 September 1999 and 27 March 2000, respectively, as the time-limits for the filing of a Memorial by Germany and of a Counter-Memorial by the United States.

The Memorial and Counter-Memorial were duly filed within the time-limits so prescribed.

6. By letter of 26 October 2000, the Agent of Germany expressed his Government's desire to produce five new documents in accordance with Article 56 of the Rules.

By letter of 6 November 2000, the Agent of the United States informed the Court that his Government consented to the production of the first and second documents, but not to that of the third, fourth and fifth documents.

LA COUR,

ainsi composée,

après délibéré en chambre du conseil,

rend l'arrêt suivant:

1. Le 2 mars 1999, la République fédérale d'Allemagne (dénommée ci-après l'«Allemagne») a déposé au Greffe de la Cour une requête introduisant une instance contre les Etats-Unis d'Amérique (dénommés ci-après les «Etats-Unis») pour «violations de la convention de Vienne [du 24 avril 1963] sur les relations consulaires» (dénommée ci-après la «convention de Vienne»).

Dans sa requête, l'Allemagne fonde la compétence de la Cour sur le paragraphe 1 de l'article 36 du Statut de la Cour et l'article premier du protocole de signature facultative concernant le règlement obligatoire des différends qui accompagne la convention de Vienne (dénommé ci-après le «protocole de signature facultative»).

2. Conformément au paragraphe 2 de l'article 40 du Statut, la requête a été immédiatement communiquée au Gouvernement des Etats-Unis; et, conformément au paragraphe 3 de cet article, tous les Etats admis à ester devant la Cour ont été informés de la requête.

3. Le 2 mars 1999, jour du dépôt de la requête, le Gouvernement allemand a également déposé au Greffe de la Cour une demande en indication de mesures conservatoires fondée sur l'article 41 du Statut et les articles 73, 74 et 75 du Règlement.

Par lettre du 2 mars 1999, le vice-président de la Cour, faisant fonction de président en l'affaire, s'est adressé au Gouvernement des Etats-Unis dans les termes suivants:

> «Exerçant la présidence de la Cour en vertu des articles 13 et 32 du Règlement de la Cour, et agissant conformément aux dispositions du paragraphe 4 de l'article 74 dudit Règlement, j'appelle par la présente l'attention [du] Gouvernement [des Etats-Unis] sur la nécessité d'agir de manière que toute ordonnance de la Cour sur la demande en indication de mesures conservatoires puisse avoir les effets voulus.»

Par ordonnance du 3 mars 1999, la Cour a indiqué certaines mesures conservatoires (voir paragraphe 32 ci-après).

4. Conformément à l'article 43 du Règlement, le greffier a adressé la notification prévue au paragraphe 1 de l'article 63 du Statut à tous les Etats parties soit à la convention de Vienne, soit à ladite convention et à son protocole de signature facultative.

5. Par ordonnance du 5 mars 1999, la Cour, compte tenu des vues des Parties, a fixé au 16 septembre 1999 et au 27 mars 2000, respectivement, les dates d'expiration des délais pour le dépôt d'un mémoire de l'Allemagne et d'un contre-mémoire des Etats-Unis d'Amérique.

Le mémoire et le contre-mémoire ont été dûment déposés dans les délais ainsi prescrits.

6. Par lettre du 26 octobre 2000, l'agent de l'Allemagne a exprimé le vœu de son gouvernement de produire cinq documents nouveaux conformément aux dispositions de l'article 56 du Règlement.

Par lettre du 6 novembre 2000, l'agent des Etats-Unis a fait savoir à la Cour que son gouvernement acceptait la production des premier et deuxième documents, mais non celle des troisième, quatrième et cinquième documents.

The Court decided, pursuant to Article 56, paragraph 2, of the Rules, to authorize the production of the latter group of documents by Germany, it being understood that the United States would have the opportunity, in accordance with paragraph 3 of that Article, to comment subsequently thereon and to submit documents in support of those comments. That decision was duly communicated to the Parties by letters from the Registrar dated 9 November 2000.

7. Pursuant to Article 53, paragraph 2, of the Rules, the Court, after ascertaining the views of the Parties, decided that copies of the pleadings and documents annexed would be made available to the public at the opening of the oral proceedings.

8. Public hearings were held from 13 to 17 November 2000, at which the Court heard the oral arguments and replies of:

For Germany:	Mr. Gerhard Westdickenberg, Mr. Bruno Simma, Mr. Daniel Khan, Mr. Hans-Peter Kaul, Mr. Andreas Paulus, Mr. Donald Francis Donovan, Mr. Pierre-Marie Dupuy.
For the United States:	Mr. James H. Thessin, The Honourable Janet Napolitano, Mr. Theodor Meron, Ms Catherine W. Brown, Mr. D. Stephen Mathias, Mr. Stefan Trechsel, Mr. Michael J. Matheson.

9. At the hearings, Members of the Court put questions to Germany, to which replies were given in writing, in accordance with Article 61, paragraph 4, of the Rules of Court.

In addition, the United States, acting within the time-limit accorded it for this purpose, commented on the new documents filed by Germany on 26 October 2000 (see paragraph 6 above) and produced documents in support of those comments.

*

10. In its Application, Germany formulated the decision requested in the following terms:

"Accordingly the Federal Republic of Germany asks the Court to adjudge and declare

(1) that the United States, in arresting, detaining, trying, convicting and sentencing Karl and Walter LaGrand, as described in the preceding statement of facts, violated its international legal obligations to Germany, in its own right and in its right of diplomatic protection of its nationals, as provided by Articles 5 and 36 of the Vienna Convention,

(2) that Germany is therefore entitled to reparation,

(3) that the United States is under an international legal obligation not to

La Cour a décidé, en application du paragraphe 2 de l'article 56 de son Règlement, d'autoriser la production par l'Allemagne de ce second groupe de documents, étant entendu que les Etats-Unis auraient, conformément au paragraphe 3 dudit article, la possibilité de présenter ultérieurement des observations à ce sujet et de soumettre des documents à l'appui de ces observations. Cette décision a été dûment communiquée aux Parties par lettres du greffier en date du 9 novembre 2000.

7. Conformément au paragraphe 2 de l'article 53 de son Règlement, la Cour, après s'être renseignée auprès des Parties, a décidé que des exemplaires des pièces de procédure et des documents annexés seraient rendus accessibles au public à l'ouverture de la procédure orale.

8. Des audiences publiques ont été tenues du 13 au 17 novembre 2000, au cours desquelles ont été entendus en leurs plaidoiries et réponses:

Pour l'Allemagne: M. Gerhard Westdickenberg,
M. Bruno Simma,
M. Daniel Khan,
M. Hans-Peter Kaul,
M. Andreas Paulus,
M. Donald Francis Donovan,
M. Pierre-Marie Dupuy.

Pour les Etats-Unis: M. James H. Thessin,
l'honorable Janet Napolitano,
M. Theodor Meron,
Mme Catherine W. Brown,
M. D. Stephen Mathias,
M. Stefan Trechsel,
M. Michael J. Matheson.

9. A l'audience, des membres de la Cour ont posé à l'Allemagne des questions auxquelles il a été répondu par écrit, conformément au paragraphe 4 de l'article 61 du Règlement.

Dans le délai qui leur avait été fixé à cet effet, les Etats-Unis ont par ailleurs présenté des observations au sujet des documents nouveaux déposés par l'Allemagne le 26 octobre 2000 (voir paragraphe 6 ci-dessus), et ont eux-mêmes produit des documents à l'appui de ces observations.

*

10. Dans la requête, la décision demandée par l'Allemagne a été ainsi formulée:

«En conséquence, la République fédérale d'Allemagne prie la Cour de dire et juger que:

1) en arrêtant, détenant, jugeant, déclarant coupables et condamnant Karl et Walter LaGrand dans les conditions indiquées dans l'exposé des faits qui précède, les Etats-Unis ont violé leurs obligations juridiques internationales envers l'Allemagne, en son nom propre et dans l'exercice du droit qu'elle a d'assurer la protection diplomatique de ses ressortissants, ainsi qu'il est prévu aux articles 5 et 36 de la convention de Vienne;
2) l'Allemagne a en conséquence droit à réparation;
3) les Etats-Unis ont l'obligation juridique internationale de ne pas appli-

apply the doctrine of 'procedural default' or any other doctrine of national law, so as to preclude the exercise of the rights accorded under Article 36 of the Vienna Convention; and

(4) that the United States is under an international obligation to carry out in conformity with the foregoing international legal obligations any future detention of or criminal proceedings against any other German national in its territory, whether by a constituent, legislative, executive, judicial or other power, whether that power holds a superior or subordinate position in the organization of the United States, and whether that power's functions are of an international or internal character;

and that, pursuant to the foregoing international legal obligations,

(1) the criminal liability imposed on Karl and Walter LaGrand in violation of international legal obligations is void, and should be recognized as void by the legal authorities of the United States;
(2) the United States should provide reparation, in the form of compensation and satisfaction, for the execution of Karl LaGrand on 24 February 1999;
(3) the United States should restore the *status quo ante* in the case of Walter LaGrand, that is re-establish the situation that existed before the detention of, proceedings against, and conviction and sentencing of that German national in violation of the United States' international legal obligation took place; and
(4) the United States should provide Germany a guarantee of the non-repetition of the illegal acts."

11. In the course of the written proceedings, the following submissions were presented by the Parties:

On behalf of the Government of Germany,

in the Memorial:

"Having regard to the facts and points of law set forth in the present Memorial, and without prejudice to such elements of fact and law and to such evidence as may be submitted at a later time, and likewise without prejudice to the right to supplement and amend the present Submissions, the Federal Republic of Germany respectfully requests the Court to adjudge and declare

(1) that the United States, by not informing Karl and Walter LaGrand without delay following their arrest of their rights under Article 36 subparagraph 1 *(b)* of the Vienna Convention on Consular Relations, and by depriving Germany of the possibility of rendering consular assistance, which ultimately resulted in the execution of Karl and Walter LaGrand, violated its international legal obligations to Germany, in its own right and in its right of diplomatic protection of its nationals, under Articles 5 and 36 paragraph 1 of the said Convention;

(2) that the United States, by applying rules of its domestic law, in par-

quer la doctrine dite de la «carence procédurale» *(procedural default)*, ni aucune autre doctrine de leur droit interne, d'une manière qui fasse obstacle à l'exercice des droits conférés par l'article 36 de la convention de Vienne; et

4) les Etats-Unis ont l'obligation internationale d'agir conformément aux obligations juridiques internationales susmentionnées dans le cas où ils placeraient en détention tout autre ressortissant allemand sur leur territoire ou engageraient une action pénale à son encontre à l'avenir, que cet acte soit accompli par un pouvoir constitué, qu'il soit législatif, exécutif, judiciaire ou autre, que ce pouvoir occupe une place supérieure ou subordonnée dans l'organisation des Etats-Unis ou que les fonctions de ce pouvoir présentent un caractère international ou interne;

et que, conformément aux obligations juridiques internationales susmentionnées:

1) toute responsabilité pénale qui ait été attribuée à Karl et Walter LaGrand en violation d'obligations juridiques internationales est nulle et doit être reconnue comme nulle par les autorités légales des Etats-Unis;
2) les Etats-Unis devraient accorder réparation, sous la forme d'une indemnisation ou de satisfaction, pour l'exécution de Karl LaGrand le 24 février 1999;
3) les Etats-Unis doivent restaurer le *statu quo ante* dans le cas de Walter LaGrand, c'est-à-dire rétablir la situation qui existait avant les actes de détention, de poursuite, de déclaration de culpabilité et de condamnation de ce ressortissant allemand commis en violation des obligations juridiques internationales des Etats-Unis;
4) les Etats-Unis doivent donner à l'Allemagne la garantie que de tels actes illicites ne se reproduiront pas.»

11. Dans la procédure écrite, les conclusions ci-après ont été présentées par les Parties:

Au nom du Gouvernement de l'Allemagne,

dans le mémoire:

«Au vu des points de fait et de droit exposés dans le présent mémoire, et sans préjudice des éléments de fait et de droit et des éléments de preuve qui pourront être ultérieurement produits, ainsi que du droit de compléter et d'amender les présentes conclusions, la République fédérale d'Allemagne prie respectueusement la Cour de dire et juger que:

1) en n'informant pas sans retard Karl et Walter LaGrand après leur arrestation de leurs droits en vertu de l'alinéa *b)* du paragraphe 1 de l'article 36 de la convention de Vienne sur les relations consulaires, et en privant l'Allemagne de la possibilité de fournir son assistance consulaire, ce qui a finalement conduit à l'exécution de Karl et Walter LaGrand, les Etats-Unis ont violé leurs obligations juridiques internationales vis-à-vis de l'Allemagne au titre de l'article 5 et du paragraphe 1 de l'article 36 de ladite convention, tant en ce qui concerne les droits propres de l'Allemagne que le droit de cette dernière d'exercer sa protection diplomatique à l'égard de ses ressortissants;
2) en appliquant des règles de leur droit interne, notamment la doctrine

ticular the doctrine of procedural default, which barred Karl and Walter LaGrand from raising their claims under the Vienna Convention on Consular Relations, and by ultimately executing them, violated its international legal obligation to Germany under Article 36 paragraph 2 of the Vienna Convention to give full effect to the purposes for which the rights accorded under Article 36 of the said Convention are intended;

(3) that the United States, by failing to take all measures at its disposal to ensure that Walter LaGrand was not executed pending the final decision of the International Court of Justice on the matter, violated its international legal obligation to comply with the Order on provisional measures issued by the Court on 3 March 1999, and to refrain from any action which might interfere with the subject matter of a dispute while judicial proceedings are pending;

and, pursuant to the foregoing international legal obligations,

(4) that the United States shall provide Germany a guarantee that it will not repeat its illegal acts and ensure that, in any future cases of detention of or criminal proceedings against German nationals, United States domestic law and practice will not constitute a bar to the effective exercise of the rights under Article 36 of the Vienna Convention on Consular Relations."

On behalf of the Government of the United States,

in the Counter-Memorial:

"Accordingly, on the basis of the facts and arguments set forth in this Counter-Memorial, and without prejudice to the right further to amend and supplement these submissions in the future, the United States asks the Court to adjudge and declare that:

(1) There was a breach of the United States obligation to Germany under Article 36 (1) *(b)* of the Vienna Convention on Consular Relations, in that the competent authorities of the United States did not promptly give to Karl and Walter LaGrand the notification required by that Article, and that the United States has apologized to Germany for this breach, and is taking substantial measures aimed at preventing any recurrence; and

(2) That all other claims and submissions of the Federal Republic of Germany are dismissed."

12. At the oral proceedings, the following submissions were presented by the Parties:

On behalf of the Government of Germany,

"The Federal Republic of Germany respectfully requests the Court to adjudge and declare

(1) that the United States, by not informing Karl and Walter LaGrand without delay following their arrest of their rights under Article 36, subparagraph 1 *(b)*, of the Vienna Convention on Consular Relations, and by depriving Germany of the possibility of rendering con-

dite de la «carence procédurale», qui ont empêché Karl et Walter LaGrand de faire valoir leurs réclamations au titre de la convention de Vienne sur les relations consulaires, et en procédant finalement à leur exécution, les Etats-Unis ont violé l'obligation juridique internationale, dont ils étaient tenus à l'égard de l'Allemagne en vertu du paragraphe 2 de l'article 36 de la convention de Vienne, de permettre la pleine réalisation des fins pour lesquelles sont prévus les droits énoncés à l'article 36 de ladite convention;

3) en ne prenant pas toutes les mesures dont ils disposaient pour que Walter LaGrand ne soit pas exécuté tant que la Cour internationale de Justice n'aurait pas rendu sa décision définitive en l'affaire, les Etats-Unis ont violé leur obligation juridique internationale de se conformer à l'ordonnance en indication de mesures conservatoires rendue par la Cour le 3 mars 1999 et de s'abstenir de tout acte pouvant interférer avec l'objet d'un différend tant que l'instance est en cours:

et que, conformément aux obligations juridiques internationales susmentionnées,

4) les Etats-Unis devront donner à l'Allemagne la garantie qu'ils ne répéteront pas de tels actes illicites et qu'ils feront en sorte que, dans tous les cas futurs de détention de ressortissants allemands ou d'actions pénales à l'encontre de tels ressortissants, le droit et la pratique internes des Etats-Unis ne feront pas obstacle à l'exercice effectif des droits énoncés à l'article 36 de la convention de Vienne sur les relations consulaires.»

Au nom du Gouvernement des Etats-Unis,

dans le contre-mémoire:

«Partant, sur la base des faits et moyens exposés dans le présent contre-mémoire et sans préjudice de leur droit de modifier et de compléter à l'avenir les présentes conclusions, les Etats-Unis prient la Cour de dire et juger:

1) qu'ils ont violé l'obligation dont ils étaient tenus envers l'Allemagne en vertu de l'alinéa *b)* du paragraphe 1 de l'article 36 de la convention de Vienne sur les relations consulaires en ce que les autorités compétentes des Etats-Unis n'ont pas informé sans retard de leurs droits Karl et Walter LaGrand ainsi que l'exigeait cet article et que les Etats-Unis ont présenté leurs excuses à l'Allemagne pour cette violation et prennent des mesures concrètes visant à empêcher qu'elle ne se reproduise; et
2) que toutes les autres demandes et conclusions de la République fédérale d'Allemagne sont rejetées.»

12. Dans la procédure orale, les conclusions ci-après ont été présentées par les Parties:

Au nom du Gouvernement de l'Allemagne,

«[L]a République fédérale d'Allemagne prie respectueusement la Cour de dire et juger que:

1) en n'informant pas sans retard Karl et Walter LaGrand après leur arrestation de leurs droits en vertu de l'alinéa *b)* du paragraphe 1 de l'article 36 de la convention de Vienne sur les relations consulaires, et en privant l'Allemagne de la possibilité de fournir son assistance consu-

sular assistance, which ultimately resulted in the execution of Karl and Walter LaGrand, violated its international legal obligations to Germany, in its own right and in its right of diplomatic protection of its nationals, under Articles 5 and 36, paragraph 1, of the said Convention;

(2) that the United States, by applying rules of its domestic law, in particular the doctrine of procedural default, which barred Karl and Walter LaGrand from raising their claims under the Vienna Convention on Consular Relations, and by ultimately executing them, violated its international legal obligation to Germany under Article 36, paragraph 2, of the Vienna Convention to give full effect to the purposes for which the rights accorded under Article 36 of the said Convention are intended;

(3) that the United States, by failing to take all measures at its disposal to ensure that Walter LaGrand was not executed pending the final decision of the International Court of Justice on the matter, violated its international legal obligation to comply with the Order on provisional measures issued by the Court on 3 March 1999, and to refrain from any action which might interfere with the subject-matter of a dispute while judicial proceedings are pending;

and, pursuant to the foregoing international legal obligations,

(4) that the United States shall provide Germany an assurance that it will not repeat its unlawful acts and that, in any future cases of detention of or criminal proceedings against German nationals, the United States will ensure in law and practice the effective exercise of the rights under Article 36 of the Vienna Convention on Consular Relations. In particular in cases involving the death penalty, this requires the United States to provide effective review of and remedies for criminal convictions impaired by a violation of the rights under Article 36."

On behalf of the Government of the United States,

"The United States of America respectfully requests the Court to adjudge and declare that:

(1) There was a breach of the United States obligation to Germany under Article 36, paragraph 1 *(b)*, of the Vienna Convention on Consular Relations, in that the competent authorities of the United States did not promptly give to Karl and Walter LaGrand the notification required by that Article, and that the United States has apologized to Germany for this breach, and is taking substantial measures aimed at preventing any recurrence; and
(2) All other claims and submissions of the Federal Republic of Germany are dismissed."

* * *

13. Walter LaGrand and Karl LaGrand were born in Germany in

laire, ce qui a finalement conduit à l'exécution de Karl et Walter LaGrand, les Etats-Unis ont violé leurs obligations juridiques internationales vis-à-vis de l'Allemagne au titre de l'article 5 et du paragraphe 1 de l'article 36 de ladite convention, tant en ce qui concerne les droits propres de l'Allemagne que le droit de cette dernière d'exercer sa protection diplomatique à l'égard de ses ressortissants;

2) en appliquant des règles de leur droit interne, notamment la doctrine dite de la «carence procédurale», qui ont empêché Karl et Walter LaGrand de faire valoir leurs réclamations au titre de la convention de Vienne sur les relations consulaires, et en procédant finalement à leur exécution, les Etats-Unis ont violé l'obligation juridique internationale, dont ils étaient tenus à l'égard de l'Allemagne en vertu du paragraphe 2 de l'article 36 de la convention de Vienne, de permettre la pleine réalisation des fins pour lesquelles sont prévus les droits énoncés à l'article 36 de ladite convention;

3) en ne prenant pas toutes les mesures dont ils disposaient pour que Walter LaGrand ne soit pas exécuté tant que la Cour internationale de Justice n'aurait pas rendu sa décision définitive en l'affaire, les Etats-Unis ont violé leur obligation juridique internationale de se conformer à l'ordonnance en indication de mesures conservatoires rendue par la Cour le 3 mars 1999 et de s'abstenir de tout acte pouvant interférer avec l'objet d'un différend tant que l'instance est en cours;

et que, conformément aux obligations juridiques internationales susmentionnées,

4) les Etats-Unis devront donner à l'Allemagne l'assurance qu'ils ne répéteront pas de tels actes illicites et que, dans tous les cas futurs de détention de ressortissants allemands ou d'actions pénales à l'encontre de tels ressortissants, les Etats-Unis veilleront à assurer en droit et en pratique l'exercice effectif des droits visés à l'article 36 de la convention de Vienne sur les relations consulaires. En particulier dans les cas où un accusé est passible de la peine de mort, cela entraîne pour les Etats-Unis l'obligation de prévoir le réexamen effectif des condamnations pénales entachées d'une violation des droits énoncés à l'article 36 de la convention, ainsi que les moyens pour y porter remède.»

Au nom du Gouvernement des Etats-Unis,

«Les Etats-Unis d'Amérique prient respectueusement la Cour de dire et juger:

1) qu'ils ont violé l'obligation dont ils étaient tenus envers l'Allemagne en vertu de l'alinéa *b)* du paragraphe 1 de l'article 36 de la convention de Vienne sur les relations consulaires en ce que les autorités compétentes des Etats-Unis n'ont pas informé sans retard de leurs droits Karl et Walter LaGrand ainsi que l'exigeait cet article et que les Etats-Unis ont présenté leurs excuses à l'Allemagne pour cette violation et prennent des mesures concrètes visant à empêcher qu'elle ne se reproduise; et

2) que toutes les autres demandes et conclusions de la République fédérale d'Allemagne sont rejetées.»

* * *

13. Walter LaGrand et Karl LaGrand étaient nés en Allemagne res-

1962 and 1963 respectively, and were German nationals. In 1967, when they were still young children, they moved with their mother to take up permanent residence in the United States. They returned to Germany only once, for a period of about six months in 1974. Although they lived in the United States for most of their lives, and became the adoptive children of a United States national, they remained at all times German nationals, and never acquired the nationality of the United States. However, the United States has emphasized that both had the demeanour and speech of Americans rather than Germans, that neither was known to have spoken German, and that they appeared in all respects to be native citizens of the United States.

14. On 7 January 1982, Karl LaGrand and Walter LaGrand were arrested in the United States by law enforcement officers on suspicion of having been involved earlier the same day in an attempted armed bank robbery in Marana, Arizona, in the course of which the bank manager was murdered and another bank employee seriously injured. They were subsequently tried before the Superior Court of Pima County, Arizona, which, on 17 February 1984, convicted them both of murder in the first degree, attempted murder in the first degree, attempted armed robbery and two counts of kidnapping. On 14 December 1984, each was sentenced to death for first degree murder and to concurrent sentences of imprisonment for the other charges.

15. At all material times, Germany as well as the United States were parties to both the Vienna Convention on Consular Relations and the Optional Protocol to that Convention. Article 36, paragraph 1 *(b)*, of the Vienna Convention provides that:

> "if he so requests, the competent authorities of the receiving State shall, without delay, inform the consular post of the sending State if, within its consular district, a national of that State is arrested or committed to prison or to custody pending trial or is detained in any other manner. Any communication addressed to the consular post by the person arrested, in prison, custody or detention shall be forwarded by the said authorities without delay. The said authorities shall inform the person concerned without delay of his rights under this subparagraph."

It is not disputed that at the time the LaGrands were convicted and sentenced, the competent United States authorities had failed to provide the LaGrands with the information required by this provision of the Vienna Convention, and had not informed the relevant German consular post of the LaGrands' arrest. The United States concedes that the competent authorities failed to do so, even after becoming aware that the LaGrands were German nationals and not United States nationals, and admits that pectivement en 1962 et 1963 et étaient ressortissants allemands. En 1967, alors qu'ils étaient encore très jeunes, ils sont partis avec leur mère aux Etats-Unis pour y résider à titre permanent. Ils ne sont revenus en Allemagne qu'une seule fois, pour une durée d'environ six mois, en 1974. Bien qu'ils aient passé la plus grande partie de leur existence aux Etats-Unis et qu'ils aient été adoptés par un ressortissant des Etats-Unis, ils ont toujours conservé leur nationalité allemande et n'ont jamais acquis la nationalité américaine. Toutefois, les Etats-Unis ont souligné le fait que l'un comme l'autre avaient l'allure et la manière de parler d'Américains plutôt que d'Allemands, qu'à la connaissance générale ni l'un ni l'autre ne parlaient allemand et qu'ils semblaient à tous égards être des citoyens natifs des Etats-Unis.

14. Le 7 janvier 1982, Karl LaGrand et Walter LaGrand ont été arrêtés aux Etats-Unis par des officiers de police, qui les soupçonnaient d'avoir pris part plus tôt dans la journée à une tentative de vol à main armée dans une banque de Marana en Arizona, au cours de laquelle le directeur de la banque avait été tué et une autre employée grièvement blessée. Ils ont par la suite été traduits en justice devant la cour supérieure du comté de Pima en Arizona, qui, le 17 février 1984, les a reconnus tous deux coupables de meurtre aggravé, de tentative de meurtre aggravé, de tentative de vol à main armée et de deux chefs d'enlèvement de personne. Le 14 décembre 1984, ils ont été l'un et l'autre condamnés à mort pour meurtre aggravé et à des peines confondues d'emprisonnement pour les autres chefs d'accusation.

15. Lors des faits à prendre en considération, tant l'Allemagne que les Etats-Unis étaient parties à la fois à la convention de Vienne sur les relations consulaires et au protocole de signature facultative à ladite convention. L'alinéa *b)* du paragraphe 1 de l'article 36 de la convention de Vienne dispose:

> «si l'intéressé en fait la demande, les autorités compétentes de l'Etat de résidence doivent avertir sans retard le poste consulaire de l'Etat d'envoi lorsque, dans sa circonscription consulaire, un ressortissant de cet Etat est arrêté, incarcéré ou mis en état de détention préventive ou toute autre forme de détention. Toute communication adressée au poste consulaire par la personne arrêtée, incarcérée ou mise en état de détention préventive ou toute autre forme de détention doit également être transmise sans retard par lesdites autorités. Celles-ci doivent sans retard informer l'intéressé de ses droits aux termes du présent alinéa.»

Il n'est pas contesté que, lorsque les LaGrand ont été reconnus coupables et condamnés, les autorités compétentes des Etats-Unis avaient omis de leur fournir les informations requises conformément à cette disposition de la convention de Vienne et n'avaient pas averti le poste consulaire allemand compétent de l'arrestation des LaGrand. Les Etats-Unis reconnaissent que les autorités compétentes ne se sont pas acquittées de cette obligation, même après avoir eu connaissance du fait que les LaGrand the United States has therefore violated its obligations under this provision of the Vienna Convention.

16. However, there is some dispute between the Parties as to the time at which the competent authorities in the United States became aware of the fact that the LaGrands were German nationals. Germany argues that the authorities of Arizona were aware of this from the very beginning, and in particular that probation officers knew by April 1982. The United States argues that at the time of their arrest, neither of the LaGrands identified himself to the arresting authorities as a German national, and that Walter LaGrand affirmatively stated that he was a United States citizen. The United States position is that its "competent authorities" for the purposes of Article 36, paragraph 1 *(b)*, of the Vienna Convention were the arresting and detaining authorities, and that these became aware of the German nationality of the LaGrands by late 1984, and possibly by mid-1983 or earlier, but in any event not at the time of their arrest in 1982. Although other authorities, such as immigration authorities or probation officers, may have known this even earlier, the United States argues that these were not "competent authorities" for the purposes of this provision of the Vienna Convention. The United States has also suggested that at the time of their arrest, the LaGrands may themselves have been unaware that they were not nationals of the United States.

17. At their trial, the LaGrands were represented by counsel assigned by the court, as they were unable to afford legal counsel of their own choice. Their counsel at trial did not raise the issue of non-compliance with the Vienna Convention, and did not themselves contact the German consular authorities.

18. The convictions and sentences pronounced by the Superior Court of Pima County, Arizona, were subsequently challenged by the LaGrands in three principal sets of legal proceedings.

19. The first set of proceedings consisted of appeals against the convictions and sentences to the Supreme Court of Arizona, which were rejected by that court on 30 January 1987. The United States Supreme Court, in the exercise of its discretion, denied applications by the LaGrands for further review of these judgments on 5 October 1987.

20. The second set of proceedings involved petitions by the LaGrands for post-conviction relief, which were denied by an Arizona state court in 1989. Review of this decision was denied by the Supreme Court of Arizona in 1990, and by the United States Supreme Court in 1991.

21. At the time of these two sets of proceedings, the LaGrands had

étaient des ressortissants allemands et non des ressortissants des Etats-Unis, et ils admettent donc avoir manqué à leurs obligations au titre de cette disposition de la convention de Vienne.

16. Toutefois, la question de savoir à quel moment les autorités compétentes des Etats-Unis ont eu connaissance du fait que les LaGrand étaient des ressortissants allemands demeure un point litigieux entre les Parties. Selon l'Allemagne, les autorités de l'Arizona ont été informées de ce fait dès l'origine, et les agents de mise à l'épreuve étaient en particulier au courant de ce fait dès avril 1982. Les Etats-Unis allèguent que, au moment de leur arrestation, ni l'un ni l'autre des LaGrand ne se sont présentés aux autorités qui ont procédé à celle-ci comme des ressortissants allemands et que Walter LaGrand a déclaré qu'il était citoyen des Etats-Unis. La position des Etats-Unis est que leurs «autorités compétentes» au sens de l'alinéa *b)* du paragraphe 1 de l'article 36 de la convention de Vienne étaient les autorités ayant procédé à l'arrestation et à la mise en détention, et que ces dernières ont eu connaissance de la nationalité allemande des LaGrand à la fin de 1984, ou peut-être vers le milieu de l'année 1983, voire plus tôt, mais qu'en tout état de cause elles ignoraient ce fait lors de leur arrestation en 1982. Bien que d'autres autorités, telles que les services de l'immigration ou les agents de mise à l'épreuve, aient pu en avoir eu connaissance à une date encore antérieure, les Etats-Unis allèguent qu'il ne s'agissait pas là d'«autorités compétentes» au sens de cette disposition de la convention de Vienne. Les Etats-Unis ont également laissé entendre que, au moment de leur arrestation, les LaGrand n'avaient peut-être pas eux-mêmes conscience qu'ils n'étaient pas des ressortissants des Etats-Unis.

17. Lors de leur procès, les LaGrand étaient représentés par des avocats commis d'office, car ils n'avaient pas les moyens de s'attacher les services de défenseurs de leur choix. Au cours du procès, ces avocats n'ont pas soulevé la question du non-respect de la convention de Vienne et n'ont pas pris eux-mêmes contact avec les autorités consulaires allemandes.

18. Les LaGrand ont par la suite contesté les verdicts de culpabilité et les peines prononcés par la cour supérieure du comté de Pima en Arizona dans le cadre de trois séries principales de procédures judiciaires.

19. La première série de procédures a concerné les appels interjetés devant la cour suprême de l'Arizona contre les verdicts de culpabilité et les peines prononcés; cette cour les a rejetés le 30 janvier 1987. La Cour suprême des Etats-Unis, exerçant son pouvoir discrétionnaire, a opposé, le 5 octobre 1987, une fin de non-recevoir aux recours en revision de ces décisions formés par les LaGrand.

20. La deuxième série de procédures a porté sur des recours ouverts après condamnation, rejetés par une juridiction de l'Etat de l'Arizona en 1989. La cour suprême de l'Arizona a refusé en 1990 de réexaminer cette décision et la Cour suprême des Etats-Unis a fait de même en 1991.

21. A l'époque où ont été engagées ces deux séries de procédures, les

still not been informed by the competent United States authorities of their rights under Article 36, paragraph 1 *(b)*, of the Vienna Convention, and the German consular post had still not been informed of their arrest. The issue of the lack of consular notification, which had not been raised at trial, was also not raised in these two sets of proceedings.

22. The relevant German consular post was only made aware of the case in June 1992 by the LaGrands themselves, who had learnt of their rights from other sources, and not from the Arizona authorities. In December 1992, and on a number of subsequent occasions between then and February 1999, an official of the Consulate-General of Germany in Los Angeles visited the LaGrands in prison. Germany claims that it subsequently helped the LaGrands' attorneys to investigate the LaGrands' childhood in Germany, and to raise the issue of the omission of consular advice in further proceedings before the federal courts.

23. The LaGrands commenced a third set of legal proceedings by filing applications for writs of *habeas corpus* in the United States District Court for the District of Arizona, seeking to have their convictions — or at least their death sentences — set aside. In these proceedings they raised a number of different claims, which were rejected by that court in orders dated 24 January 1995 and 16 February 1995. One of these claims was that the United States authorities had failed to notify the German consulate of their arrest, as required by the Vienna Convention. This claim was rejected on the basis of the "procedural default" rule. According to the United States, this rule:

> "is a federal rule that, before a state criminal defendant can obtain relief in federal court, the claim must be presented to a state court. If a state defendant attempts to raise a new issue in a federal *habeas corpus* proceeding, the defendant can only do so by showing cause and prejudice. Cause is an external impediment that prevents a defendant from raising a claim and prejudice must be obvious on its face. One important purpose of this rule is to ensure that the state courts have an opportunity to address issues going to the validity of state convictions before the federal courts intervene."

The United States District Court held that the LaGrands had not shown an objective external factor that prevented them from raising the issue of the lack of consular notification earlier. On 16 January 1998, this judgment was affirmed on appeal by the United States Court of Appeals,

LaGrand n'avaient toujours pas été informés par les autorités compétentes des Etats-Unis des droits que leur conférait l'alinéa *b)* du paragraphe 1 de l'article 36 de la convention de Vienne et le poste consulaire allemand n'avait toujours pas été informé de leur arrestation. La question du défaut de notification consulaire, qui n'avait pas été soulevée lors du procès initial, ne l'a pas été davantage lors de ces deux séries de procédures.

22. Le poste consulaire allemand compétent n'a été informé de cette affaire qu'en juin 1992 par les LaGrand eux-mêmes, qui avaient eu connaissance de leurs droits par d'autres sources et non par les autorités de l'Arizona. En décembre 1992, et à plusieurs reprises entre cette date et le mois de février 1999, un fonctionnaire du consulat général d'Allemagne à Los Angeles a rendu visite aux LaGrand dans leur prison. L'Allemagne allègue qu'elle a par la suite aidé les avocats des LaGrand à enquêter sur leur enfance en Allemagne et à soulever la question de l'omission de la notification consulaire lors de procédures ultérieures devant les juridictions fédérales.

23. Les LaGrand ont entamé une troisième série de procédures judiciaires en introduisant des actions d'*habeas corpus* devant le tribunal fédéral de première instance *(United States District Court)* pour le district de l'Arizona, aux fins de faire annuler leurs condamnations — du moins leur condamnation à mort. Lors de ces procédures, ils ont soulevé différents moyens qui ont été rejetés par des décisions de ce tribunal en date du 24 janvier et du 16 février 1995. L'un de ces moyens était fondé sur le fait que les autorités des Etats-Unis avaient manqué à leur obligation de notifier leur arrestation au consulat d'Allemagne, comme le prescrit la convention de Vienne. Ce moyen a été rejeté par application de la règle de la «carence procédurale». D'après les Etats-Unis, cette règle

> «[est] une règle fédérale qui oblige l'accusé traduit devant les tribunaux d'un Etat à soumettre ses moyens à un tribunal de cet Etat avant de pouvoir exercer un recours devant un tribunal fédéral. Si cet accusé veut soulever une question nouvelle lors d'une procédure d'*habeas corpus* devant un tribunal fédéral, il ne pourra le faire qu'en justifiant sa carence antérieure et en démontrant le préjudice porté par cette carence à sa cause. La justification doit être un élément extérieur qui a empêché l'accusé de faire valoir un moyen et le préjudice, lui, doit être à priori manifeste. L'une des fonctions importantes de cette règle est de garantir que les tribunaux des Etats auront eu l'occasion d'examiner les points concernant la validité des verdicts de culpabilité prononcés au niveau de l'Etat avant que les tribunaux fédéraux n'interviennent.»

Le tribunal fédéral de première instance a conclu que les LaGrand n'avaient pas démontré l'existence d'un élément extérieur objectif les ayant empêché de soulever plus tôt la question du défaut de notification consulaire. Le 16 janvier 1998, cette décision a été confirmée en appel par

Ninth Circuit, which also held that the LaGrands' claim relating to the Vienna Convention was "procedurally defaulted", as it had not been raised in any of the earlier proceedings in state courts. On 2 November 1998, the United States Supreme Court denied further review of this judgment.

24. On 21 December 1998, the LaGrands were formally notified by the United States authorities of their right to consular access.

25. On 15 January 1999, the Supreme Court of Arizona decided that Karl LaGrand was to be executed on 24 February 1999, and that Walter LaGrand was to be executed on 3 March 1999. Germany claims that the German Consulate learned of these dates on 19 January 1999.

26. In January and early February 1999, various interventions were made by Germany seeking to prevent the execution of the LaGrands. In particular, the German Foreign Minister and German Minister of Justice wrote to their respective United States counterparts on 27 January 1999; the German Foreign Minister wrote to the Governor of Arizona on the same day; the German Chancellor wrote to the President of the United States and to the Governor of Arizona on 2 February 1999; and the President of the Federal Republic of Germany wrote to the President of the United States on 5 February 1999. These letters referred to German opposition to capital punishment generally, but did not raise the issue of the absence of consular notification in the case of the LaGrands. The latter issue was, however, raised in a further letter, dated 22 February 1999, two days before the scheduled date of execution of Karl LaGrand, from the German Foreign Minister to the United States Secretary of State.

27. On 23 February 1999, the Arizona Board of Executive Clemency rejected an appeal for clemency by Karl LaGrand. Under the law of Arizona, this meant that the Governor of Arizona was prevented from granting clemency.

28. On the same day, the Arizona Superior Court in Pima County rejected a further petition by Walter LaGrand, based *inter alia* on the absence of consular notification, on the ground that these claims were "procedurally precluded".

29. On 24 February 1999, certain last-minute federal court proceedings brought by Karl LaGrand ultimately proved to be unsuccessful. In the course of these proceedings the United States Court of Appeals, Ninth Circuit, again held the issue of failure of consular notification to be procedurally defaulted. Karl LaGrand was executed later that same day.

30. On 2 March 1999, the day before the scheduled date of execution of Walter LaGrand, at 7.30 p.m. (The Hague time), Germany filed in the Registry of this Court the Application instituting the present proceedings against the United States (see paragraph 1 above), accompanied by a request for the following provisional measures:

la cour d'appel des Etats-Unis pour le neuvième circuit, qui a également jugé que le moyen soulevé par les LaGrand concernant la convention de Vienne était entaché de «carence procédurale», car il n'avait été soulevé dans aucune des procédures introduites auparavant devant les juridictions de l'Etat. Le 2 novembre 1998, la Cour suprême des Etats-Unis a refusé de réexaminer cette décision.

24. Le 21 décembre 1998, les LaGrand ont été officiellement informés par les autorités des Etats-Unis de leur droit de communiquer avec leurs autorités consulaires.

25. Le 15 janvier 1999, la cour suprême de l'Arizona a décidé que Karl LaGrand devait être exécuté le 24 février 1999, et que Walter LaGrand le serait le 3 mars 1999. L'Allemagne allègue que le consulat d'Allemagne a eu connaissance de ces dates le 19 janvier 1999.

26. En janvier et au début du mois de février 1999, l'Allemagne a effectué plusieurs démarches pour tenter d'empêcher l'exécution des LaGrand. Les ministres allemands des affaires étrangères et de la justice ont ainsi saisi leurs homologues respectifs aux Etats-Unis le 27 janvier 1999; le ministre allemand des affaires étrangères a écrit le même jour au gouverneur de l'Arizona; le chancelier de la République fédérale d'Allemagne s'est adressé au président des Etats-Unis et au gouverneur de l'Arizona le 2 février 1999; le président de la République fédérale d'Allemagne a écrit au président des Etats-Unis le 5 février 1999. Ces lettres faisaient état de l'opposition de l'Allemagne à la peine capitale d'une manière générale, mais ne soulevaient pas la question du défaut de notification consulaire dans le cas des LaGrand. Cette dernière question a été toutefois évoquée dans une lettre ultérieure, adressée le 22 février 1999, deux jours avant la date fixée pour l'exécution de Karl LaGrand, par le ministre allemand des affaires étrangères au secrétaire d'Etat des Etats-Unis.

27. Le 23 février 1999, la commission des grâces de l'Arizona a rejeté l'appel de Karl LaGrand à la clémence. En vertu de la législation de l'Arizona, cette décision signifiait que le gouverneur de l'Arizona n'avait plus la possibilité d'accorder une mesure de grâce.

28. Ce même jour, la cour supérieure du comté de Pima en Arizona a rejeté une autre demande de Walter LaGrand fondée notamment sur le défaut de notification consulaire, au motif que ce moyen était entaché de «carence procédurale».

29. Le 24 février 1999, certaines procédures judiciaires de dernière minute engagées au niveau fédéral par Karl LaGrand se sont avérées infructueuses. Au cours de ces procédures, la cour d'appel des Etats-Unis pour le neuvième circuit a de nouveau jugé que le moyen tiré du défaut de notification consulaire était entaché de carence procédurale. Karl LaGrand a été exécuté plus tard le même jour.

30. Le 2 mars 1999, la veille du jour fixé pour l'exécution de Walter LaGrand, à 19 h 30 (heure de La Haye), l'Allemagne a déposé au Greffe de la Cour la requête qui a introduit la présente instance contre les Etats-Unis (voir paragraphe 1 ci-dessus), accompagnée d'une demande en indication de mesures conservatoires tendant à ce que:

> "The United States should take all measures at its disposal to ensure that Walter LaGrand is not executed pending the final decision in these proceedings, and should inform the Court of all the measures which it has taken in implementation of that Order."

By a letter of the same date, the German Foreign Minister requested the Secretary of State of the United States "to urge [the] Governor [of Arizona] for a suspension of Walter LaGrand's execution pending a ruling by the International Court of Justice".

31. On the same day, the Arizona Board of Executive Clemency met to consider the case of Walter LaGrand. It recommended against a commutation of his death sentence, but recommended that the Governor of Arizona grant a 60-day reprieve having regard to the Application filed by Germany in the International Court of Justice. Nevertheless, the Governor of Arizona decided, "in the interest of justice and with the victims in mind", to allow the execution of Walter LaGrand to go forward as scheduled.

32. In an Order of 3 March 1999, this Court found that the circumstances required it to indicate, as a matter of the greatest urgency and without any other proceedings, provisional measures in accordance with Article 41 of its Statute and with Article 75, paragraph 1, of its Rules (*I.C.J. Reports 1999 (I)*, p. 15, para. 26); it indicated provisional measures in the following terms:

> "*(a)* The United States of America should take all measures at its disposal to ensure that Walter LaGrand is not executed pending the final decision in these proceedings, and should inform the Court of all the measures which it has taken in implementation of this Order;
>
> *(b)* The Government of the United States of America should transmit this Order to the Governor of the State of Arizona."

33. On the same day, proceedings were brought by Germany in the United States Supreme Court against the United States and the Governor of Arizona, seeking *inter alia* to enforce compliance with this Court's Order indicating provisional measures. In the course of these proceedings, the United States Solicitor General as counsel of record took the position, *inter alia*, that "an order of the International Court of Justice indicating provisional measures is not binding and does not furnish a basis for judicial relief". On the same date, the United States Supreme Court dismissed the motion by Germany, on the ground of the tardiness of Germany's application and of jurisdictional barriers under United States domestic law.

34. On that same day, proceedings were also instituted in the United

« Les Etats-Unis prennent toutes les mesures en leur pouvoir pour que Walter LaGrand ne soit pas exécuté en attendant la décision finale en la présente instance, et qu'ils informent la Cour de toutes les mesures qu'ils ont prises pour donner effet à cette ordonnance. »

Par lettre datée du même jour, le ministre allemand des affaires étrangères a demandé au secrétaire d'Etat des Etats-Unis de « prier instamment le gouverneur [de l'Arizona] de surseoir à l'exécution de Walter LaGrand tant que la Cour internationale de Justice n'aura pas pris sa décision ».

31. Le même jour, la commission des grâces de l'Arizona s'est réunie pour examiner le cas de Walter LaGrand. Elle s'est prononcée contre une commutation de sa condamnation à mort, mais a recommandé au gouverneur de l'Arizona d'accorder un sursis de soixante jours, compte tenu de la requête déposée par l'Allemagne devant la Cour internationale de Justice. Le gouverneur de l'Arizona a néanmoins décidé, « dans l'intérêt de la justice et eu égard aux victimes », d'autoriser l'exécution de Walter LaGrand, comme cela avait été prévu.

32. Par une ordonnance datée du 3 mars 1999, la Cour a jugé que les circonstances exigeaient qu'elle indiquât, de toute urgence et sans autre procédure, des mesures conservatoires, conformément à l'article 41 de son Statut et au paragraphe 1 de l'article 75 de son Règlement (*C.I.J. Recueil 1999 (I)*, p. 15, par. 26); les mesures conservatoires indiquées étaient libellées de la manière suivante:

« *a)* les Etats-Unis d'Amérique doivent prendre toutes les mesures dont ils disposent pour que M. Walter LaGrand ne soit pas exécuté tant que la décision définitive en la présente instance n'aura pas été rendue, et doivent porter à la connaissance de la Cour toutes les mesures qui auront été prises en application de la présente ordonnance;

b) le Gouvernement des Etats-Unis d'Amérique doit transmettre la présente ordonnance au gouverneur de l'Etat d'Arizona. »

33. Ce même jour, l'Allemagne a introduit une action contre les Etats-Unis et le gouverneur de l'Arizona devant la Cour suprême des Etats-Unis aux fins, entre autres, de faire respecter l'ordonnance de la Cour portant indication de mesures conservatoires. Au cours de cette procédure, le *Solicitor General* des Etats-Unis, agissant en tant que conseil de l'autorité fédérale, a émis notamment l'avis qu'« une ordonnance de la Cour internationale de Justice en indication de mesures conservatoires ne revêt pas un caractère obligatoire et ne peut fonder un recours susceptible d'être exercé en justice ». Le même jour, la Cour suprême des Etats-Unis a rejeté l'action introduite par l'Allemagne pour tardiveté et en raison d'obstacles en matière de compétence résultant du droit interne des Etats-Unis.

34. Ce même jour, des procédures ont aussi été engagées par Walter

States Supreme Court by Walter LaGrand. These proceedings were decided against him. Later that day, Walter LaGrand was executed.

* * *

35. The Court must as a preliminary matter deal with certain issues, which were raised by the Parties in these proceedings, concerning the jurisdiction of the Court in relation to Germany's Application, and the admissibility of its submissions.

* *

36. In relation to the jurisdiction of the Court, the United States, without having raised preliminary objections under Article 79 of the Rules of Court, nevertheless presented certain objections thereto.

Germany bases the jurisdiction of the Court on Article I of the Optional Protocol, which reads as follows:

> "Disputes arising out of the interpretation or application of the Convention shall lie within the compulsory jurisdiction of the International Court of Justice and may accordingly be brought before the Court by an application made by any party to the dispute being a Party to the present Protocol."

Germany contends that the

> "proceedings instituted by [it] in the present case raise questions of the interpretation and application of the Vienna Convention on Consular Relations and of the legal consequences arising from the non-observance on the part of the United States of certain of its provisions vis-à-vis Germany and two of its nationals".

Accordingly, Germany states that all four of its submissions

> "are covered by one and the same jurisdictional basis, namely Art. I of the Optional Protocol to the Vienna Convention on Consular Relations concerning the Compulsory Settlement of Disputes of 24 April 1963".

*

37. The Court will first examine the question of its jurisdiction with respect to the first submission of Germany. Germany relies on paragraph 1 of Article 36 of the Vienna Convention, which provides:

> "With a view to facilitating the exercise of consular functions relating to nationals of the sending State:

LaGrand devant la Cour suprême des Etats-Unis. Ces procédures ont échoué. Walter LaGrand a été exécuté plus tard dans la journée.

* * *

35. La Cour doit à titre préliminaire examiner certaines questions soulevées par les Parties à l'instance concernant sa compétence pour connaître de la requête de l'Allemagne et la recevabilité des conclusions de celle-ci.

* *

36. S'agissant de la compétence de la Cour, les Etats-Unis, sans soulever d'exceptions préliminaires en vertu de l'article 79 du Règlement, ont cependant fait valoir certaines objections à cet égard.

L'Allemagne fonde la compétence de la Cour sur l'article premier du protocole de signature facultative, qui se lit ainsi:

> «Les différends relatifs à l'interprétation ou à l'application de la convention relèvent de la compétence obligatoire de la Cour internationale de Justice, qui, à ce titre, pourra être saisie par une requête de toute partie au différend qui sera elle-même partie au présent protocole.»

Elle fait valoir que

> «[l]'instance introduite par [elle] en l'espèce soulève des questions relatives à l'interprétation et à l'application de la convention de Vienne sur les relations consulaires et aux conséquences juridiques découlant du non-respect par les Etats-Unis de certaines des dispositions de cet instrument à l'égard de l'Allemagne et de deux de ses ressortissants».

En conséquence, l'Allemagne affirme que les quatre conclusions qu'elle a présentées

> «relèvent [toutes] d'une seule et même base de compétence, à savoir l'article premier du protocole de signature facultative concernant le règlement obligatoire des différends qui accompagne la convention de Vienne sur les relations consulaires du 24 avril 1963».

*

37. La Cour examinera tout d'abord la question de sa compétence pour connaître de la première conclusion de l'Allemagne. Celle-ci se prévaut du paragraphe 1 de l'article 36 de la convention de Vienne selon lequel:

> «Afin que l'exercice des fonctions consulaires relatives aux ressortissants de l'Etat d'envoi soit facilité:

(a) consular officers shall be free to communicate with nationals of the sending State and to have access to them. Nationals of the sending State shall have the same freedom with respect to communication with and access to consular officers of the sending State;

(b) if he so requests, the competent authorities of the receiving State shall, without delay, inform the consular post of the sending State if, within its consular district, a national of that State is arrested or committed to prison or to custody pending trial or is detained in any other manner. Any communication addressed to the consular post by the person arrested, in prison, custody or detention shall be forwarded by the said authorities without delay. The said authorities shall inform the person concerned without delay of his rights under this subparagraph;

(c) consular officers shall have the right to visit a national of the sending State who is in prison, custody or detention, to converse and correspond with him and to arrange for his legal representation. They shall also have the right to visit any national of the sending State who is in prison, custody or detention in their district in pursuance of a judgement. Nevertheless, consular officers shall refrain from taking action on behalf of a national who is in prison, custody or detention if he expressly opposes such action."

38. Germany alleges that the failure of the United States to inform the LaGrand brothers of their right to contact the German authorities "prevented Germany from exercising its rights under Art. 36 (1) *(a)* and *(c)* of the Convention" and violated "the various rights conferred upon the sending State vis-à-vis its nationals in prison, custody or detention as provided for in Art. 36 (1) *(b)* of the Convention". Germany further alleges that by breaching its obligations to inform, the United States also violated individual rights conferred on the detainees by Article 36, paragraph 1 *(a)*, second sentence, and by Article 36, paragraph 1 *(b)*. Germany accordingly claims that it "was injured in the person of its two nationals", a claim which Germany raises "as a matter of diplomatic protection on behalf of Walter and Karl LaGrand".

39. The United States acknowledges that "there was a breach of the U.S. obligation . . . to inform the LaGrand brothers that they could ask that a German consular post be notified of their arrest and detention". It does not deny that this violation of Article 36, paragraph 1 *(b)*, has given rise to a dispute between the two States and recognizes that the Court has

a) les fonctionnaires consulaires doivent avoir la liberté de communiquer avec les ressortissants de l'Etat d'envoi et de se rendre auprès d'eux. Les ressortissants de l'Etat d'envoi doivent avoir la même liberté de communiquer avec les fonctionnaires consulaires et de se rendre auprès d'eux;

b) si l'intéressé en fait la demande, les autorités compétentes de l'Etat de résidence doivent avertir sans retard le poste consulaire de l'Etat d'envoi lorsque, dans sa circonscription consulaire, un ressortissant de cet Etat est arrêté, incarcéré ou mis en état de détention préventive ou toute autre forme de détention. Toute communication adressée au poste consulaire par la personne arrêtée, incarcérée ou mise en état de détention préventive ou toute autre forme de détention doit également être transmise sans retard par lesdites autorités. Celles-ci doivent sans retard informer l'intéressé de ses droits aux termes du présent alinéa;

c) les fonctionnaires consulaires ont le droit de se rendre auprès d'un ressortissant de l'Etat d'envoi qui est incarcéré, en état de détention préventive ou toute autre forme de détention, de s'entretenir et de correspondre avec lui et de pourvoir à sa représentation en justice. Ils ont également le droit de se rendre auprès d'un ressortissant de l'Etat d'envoi qui, dans leur circonscription, est incarcéré ou détenu en exécution d'un jugement. Néanmoins, les fonctionnaires consulaires doivent s'abstenir d'intervenir en faveur d'un ressortissant incarcéré ou mis en état de détention préventive ou toute autre forme de détention lorsque l'intéressé s'y oppose expressément.»

38. L'Allemagne prétend que, en n'informant pas les frères LaGrand de leur droit de communiquer avec les autorités allemandes, les Etats-Unis l'«ont empêché[e] ... d'exercer les droits que lui confèrent les alinéas *a)* et *c)* du paragraphe 1 de l'article 36 de la convention» et ont violé «les différents droits conférés à l'Etat d'envoi vis-à-vis de ses ressortissants en prison, en détention préventive ou en garde à vue, tels que prévus par l'alinéa *b)* du paragraphe 1 de l'article 36 de la convention». Elle soutient en outre que, en méconnaissant leur obligation d'information, les Etats-Unis ont également violé les droits individuels que l'alinéa *a)* du paragraphe 1 de l'article 36, deuxième phrase, et l'alinéa *b)* du paragraphe 1 de l'article 36 confèrent aux personnes détenues. L'Allemagne affirme qu'en conséquence elle «a subi un préjudice en la personne de ses deux ressortissants», grief qu'elle invoque «au titre de la procédure de protection diplomatique engagée au nom de Karl et Walter LaGrand».

39. Les Etats-Unis reconnaissent «avoir méconnu l'obligation ... d'informer ... les frères LaGrand de leur droit à demander qu'un poste consulaire allemand soit averti de leur arrestation et mise en détention». Ils ne contestent pas que cette violation de l'alinéa *b)* du paragraphe 1 de l'article 36 a donné naissance à un différend entre les deux Etats et recon-

jurisdiction under the Optional Protocol to hear this dispute in so far as it concerns Germany's own rights.

40. Concerning Germany's claims of violation of Article 36, paragraph 1 *(a)* and *(c)*, the United States however calls these claims "particularly misplaced" on the grounds that the "underlying conduct complained of is the same" as the claim of the violation of Article 36, paragraph 1 *(b)*. It contends, moreover, that "to the extent that this claim by Germany is based on the general law of diplomatic protection, it is not within the Court's jurisdiction" under the Optional Protocol because it "does not concern the interpretation or application of the Vienna Convention". The United States points to the distinction between jurisdiction over treaties and jurisdiction over customary law and observes that "[e]ven if a treaty norm and a customary norm were to have exactly the same content", each would have its "separate applicability". It contests the German assertion that diplomatic protection "enters through the intermediary of the Vienna Convention" and submits:

> "the Vienna Convention deals with consular assistance . . . it does not deal with diplomatic protection. Legally, a world of difference exists between the right of the consul to assist an incarcerated national of his country, and the wholly different question whether the State can espouse the claims of its national through diplomatic protection. The former is within the jurisdiction of the Court under the Optional Protocol; the latter is not . . . Germany based its right of diplomatic protection on customary law . . . [T]his case comes before this Court not under Article 36, paragraph 2, of its Statute, but under Article 36, paragraph 1. Is it not obvious . . . that whatever rights Germany has under customary law, they do not fall within the jurisdiction of this Court under the Optional Protocol?"

41. Germany responds that the breach of paragraph 1 *(a)* and *(c)* of Article 36 must be distinguished from that of paragraph 1 *(b)*, and that as a result, the Court should not only rule on the latter breach, but also on the violation of paragraph 1 *(a)* and *(c)*. Germany further asserts "that 'application of the Convention' in the sense of the Optional Protocol very well encompasses the consequences of a violation of individual rights under the Convention, including the espousal of respective claims by the State of nationality".

42. The Court cannot accept the United States objections. The dispute between the Parties as to whether Article 36, paragraph 1 *(a)* and *(c)*, of the Vienna Convention have been violated in this case in consequence of the breach of paragraph 1 *(b)* does relate to the interpretation and appli-

naissent que la Cour a compétence en vertu du protocole de signature facultative pour connaître de ce différend dans la mesure où ce dernier concerne les droits propres de l'Allemagne.

40. Les Etats-Unis en revanche jugent «particulièrement mal fondé» l'argument de l'Allemagne selon lequel il y aurait eu violation des alinéas *a)* et *c)* du paragraphe 1 de l'article 36, au motif que «le comportement critiqué est le même» que celui visé par l'allégation de violation de l'alinéa *b)* du paragraphe 1 de l'article 36. Ils font en outre valoir que la prétention allemande, fondée sur le droit général de la protection diplomatique, ne relève pas de la compétence de la Cour en vertu du protocole de signature facultative, parce que cette prétention «ne concerne pas l'interprétation ou l'application de la convention de Vienne». Les Etats-Unis soulignent à cet égard la distinction qu'il faut opérer entre la compétence en matière conventionnelle et la compétence relative au droit coutumier, et font observer que, «[m]ême si une norme conventionnelle et une norme coutumière avaient exactement le même contenu», chacune aurait une «applicabilité distincte». Les Etats-Unis contestent l'affirmation selon laquelle le moyen tiré de la protection diplomatique invoqué par l'Allemagne «entre en ligne de compte par le truchement de la convention de Vienne» et soutiennent:

> «la convention de Vienne traite de l'assistance consulaire ... et non de la protection diplomatique. Juridiquement un monde sépare le droit du consul d'assister un ressortissant de son pays incarcéré et la question totalement différente de savoir si l'Etat peut endosser les réclamations de ses ressortissants au titre de la protection diplomatique. Le premier entre dans le champ de la compétence de la Cour, en vertu du protocole de signature facultative, non la seconde... L'Allemagne fonde son droit de protection diplomatique sur le droit coutumier ... la Cour est saisie de la présente affaire au titre non pas du paragraphe 2 mais du paragraphe 1 de l'article 36 de son Statut. N'est-il pas évident ... que quelques droits qu'ait l'Allemagne en vertu du droit coutumier, ils ne ressortissent pas à la compétence conférée à la Cour par le protocole de signature facultative?»

41. En réponse, l'Allemagne soutient que la violation des alinéas *a)* et *c)* du paragraphe 1 de l'article 36 doit être distinguée de la violation de l'alinéa *b)* du même paragraphe et qu'en conséquence la Cour doit se prononcer non seulement sur cette dernière violation, mais encore sur celle des alinéas *a)* et *c)*. L'Allemagne estime en outre «que «l'application de la convention», au sens du protocole de signature facultative, englobe bien les conséquences de la violation des droits que la convention reconnaît aux individus, y compris le fait pour l'Etat d'envoi de faire siennes les demandes y relatives».

42. La Cour ne saurait retenir les objections formulées par les Etats-Unis. En effet, le différend qui oppose les Parties sur le point de savoir si les alinéas *a)* et *c)* du paragraphe 1 de l'article 36 de la convention de Vienne ont été violés en l'espèce du fait de la violation de l'alinéa *b)* a

cation of the Convention. This is also true of the dispute as to whether paragraph 1 *(b)* creates individual rights and whether Germany has standing to assert those rights on behalf of its nationals. These are consequently disputes within the meaning of Article I of the Optional Protocol. Moreover, the Court cannot accept the contention of the United States that Germany's claim based on the individual rights of the LaGrand brothers is beyond the Court's jurisdiction because diplomatic protection is a concept of customary international law. This fact does not prevent a State party to a treaty, which creates individual rights, from taking up the case of one of its nationals and instituting international judicial proceedings on behalf of that national, on the basis of a general jurisdictional clause in such a treaty. Therefore the Court concludes that it has jurisdiction with respect to the whole of Germany's first submission.

*

43. The United States does not challenge the Court's jurisdiction in regard to Germany's second submission. Nor does it as such address the issue of the jurisdiction of the Court over the third submission concerning the binding nature of the Order of the Court of 3 March 1999 indicating provisional measures. It argues, however, that this submission is inadmissible (see paragraphs 50 and 53-55 below), and that the Court can fully and adequately dispose of the merits of this case without having to rule on the submission.

44. Germany asserts that the Court's Order of 3 March 1999 was intended to "enforce" the rights enjoyed by Germany under the Vienna Convention and "preserve those rights pending its decision on the merits". Germany claims that a dispute as to "whether the United States were obliged to comply and did comply with the Order" necessarily arises out of the interpretation or application of the Convention and thus falls within the jurisdiction of the Court. Germany argues further that questions "relating to the non-compliance with a decision of the Court under Article 41, para. 1, of the Statute, e.g. Provisional Measures, are an integral component of the entire original dispute between the parties". Moreover, Germany contends that its third submission also implicates "in an auxiliary and subsidiary manner . . . the inherent jurisdiction of the Court for claims as closely interrelated with each other as the ones before the Court in the present case".

45. The third submission of Germany concerns issues that arise directly out of the dispute between the Parties before the Court over which the Court has already held that it has jurisdiction (see paragraph 42 above), and which are thus covered by Article I of the Optional Protocol. The Court reaffirms, in this connection, what it said in its Judgment in the

trait à l'interprétation et à l'application de la convention. Il en est de même du différend sur le point de savoir si l'alinéa *b)* crée des droits pour les particuliers et si l'Allemagne a qualité pour faire valoir ces droits au nom de ses ressortissants. Ces différends entrent par suite dans les prévisions de l'article premier du protocole de signature facultative. Par ailleurs, la Cour ne peut accepter la thèse des Etats-Unis selon laquelle la demande de l'Allemagne fondée sur les droits individuels des frères LaGrand ne relève pas de sa compétence, au motif que la protection diplomatique serait une notion de droit international coutumier. Cela ne fait pas obstacle à ce qu'un Etat partie à un traité qui crée des droits pour les individus puisse prendre fait et cause pour l'un de ses ressortissants et mettre en mouvement l'action judiciaire internationale en faveur de ce ressortissant sur la base d'une clause attributive de compétence figurant dans un tel traité. La Cour en conclut qu'elle a dès lors compétence pour connaître dans son ensemble de la première conclusion de l'Allemagne.

*

43. Les Etats-Unis ne contestent pas la compétence de la Cour pour connaître de la deuxième conclusion de l'Allemagne. En outre, ils ne traitent pas en tant que telle de la question de la compétence de la Cour pour connaître de la troisième conclusion concernant le caractère obligatoire de l'ordonnance de la Cour du 3 mars 1999 en indication de mesures conservatoires. Ils affirment cependant que cette conclusion est irrecevable (voir paragraphes 50 et 53-55 ci-après), et que la Cour peut statuer pleinement et de manière adéquate sur le fond de l'affaire sans avoir à se prononcer sur ladite conclusion.

44. L'Allemagne affirme que l'ordonnance du 3 mars 1999 avait pour but d'« assurer le respect » des droits que la convention de Vienne confère à l'Allemagne et de « préserver ces droits dans l'attente d'une décision sur le fond ». L'Allemagne prétend que le différend relatif à la question de savoir « si les Etats-Unis étaient tenus de se conformer à l'ordonnance, et s'ils s'y sont effectivement conformés », constitue donc bien un différend relatif à l'interprétation et à l'application de la convention et, partant, un différend qui relève de la compétence de la Cour. Elle avance en outre que des questions « relatives au non-respect d'une décision de la Cour prise aux termes du paragraphe 1 de l'article 41 du Statut, c'est-à-dire les mesures conservatoires, font partie intégrante de l'ensemble du différend initial entre les Parties ». Enfin, l'Allemagne soutient que sa troisième conclusion relève aussi, « de manière accessoire et subsidiaire, de la compétence inhérente de la Cour pour connaître de demandes aussi étroitement liées les unes aux autres que celles dont elle est saisie en l'espèce ».

45. La troisième conclusion de l'Allemagne porte sur des questions qui découlent directement du différend opposant les Parties devant la Cour, à l'égard desquelles la Cour a déjà conclu qu'elle était compétente (voir paragraphe 42 ci-dessus), et qui relèvent dès lors de l'article premier du protocole de signature facultative. A cet égard, la Cour réaffirme ce

Fisheries Jurisdiction case, where it declared that in order to consider the dispute in all its aspects it may also deal with a submission that "is one based on facts subsequent to the filing of the Application, but arising directly out of the question which is the subject-matter of that Application. As such it falls within the scope of the Court's jurisdiction . . ." (*Fisheries Jurisdiction (Federal Republic of Germany* v. *Iceland), Merits, Judgment, I.C.J. Reports 1974*, p. 203, para. 72). Where the Court has jurisdiction to decide a case, it also has jurisdiction to deal with submissions requesting it to determine that an order indicating measures which seeks to preserve the rights of the Parties to this dispute has not been complied with.

*

46. The United States objects to the jurisdiction of the Court over the fourth submission in so far as it concerns a request for assurances and guarantees of non-repetition. The United States submits that its "jurisdictional argument [does] not apply to jurisdiction to order cessation of a breach or to order reparation, but is limited to the question of assurances and guarantees . . . [which] are conceptually distinct from reparation". It contends that Germany's fourth submission

> "goes beyond any remedy that the Court can or should grant, and should be rejected. The Court's power to decide cases . . . does not extend to the power to order a State to provide any 'guarantee' intended to confer additional legal rights on the Applicant State . . . The United States does not believe that it can be the role of the Court . . . to impose any obligations that are additional to or that differ in character from those to which the United States consented when it ratified the Vienna Convention."

47. Germany counters this argument by asserting that

> "a dispute whether or not the violation of a provision of the Vienna Convention gives rise to a certain remedy is a dispute concerning 'the application and interpretation' of the aforesaid Convention, and thus falls within the scope of Art. I of the Optional Protocol".

Germany notes in this regard that the Court, in its Order of 9 April 1998 in the case concerning the *Vienna Convention on Consular Relations (Paraguay* v. *United States of America)*, held that

> "there exists a dispute as to whether the relief sought by Paraguay is a remedy available under the Vienna Convention, in particular in relation to Articles 5 and 36 thereof; and . . . this is a dispute arising out of the application of the Convention within the meaning of Article I of the Optional Protocol concerning the Compulsory Settlement of Disputes of 24 April 1963" (*I.C.J. Reports 1998*, p. 256, para. 31).

qu'elle a dit dans l'affaire de la *Compétence en matière de pêcheries*, lorsqu'elle a estimé que, afin de considérer le différend sous tous ses aspects, elle pouvait aussi connaître d'une conclusion qui «se fonde sur des faits postérieurs au dépôt de la requête mais découlant directement de la question qui fait l'objet de cette requête. A ce titre, elle relève de la compétence de la Cour...» (*Compétence en matière de pêcheries (République fédérale d'Allemagne c. Islande), fond, arrêt, C.I.J. Recueil 1974*, p. 203, par. 72.) Lorsque la Cour a compétence pour trancher un différend, elle a également compétence pour se prononcer sur des conclusions la priant de constater qu'une ordonnance en indication de mesures rendue aux fins de préserver les droits des Parties à ce différend n'a pas été exécutée.

*

46. Les Etats-Unis contestent que la Cour soit compétente pour statuer sur la quatrième conclusion de l'Allemagne, dans la mesure où cette conclusion tend à l'obtention d'assurances et de garanties de non-répétition. Ils affirment que «la compétence qu'aurait la Cour d'ordonner la cessation d'une violation ou d'ordonner une réparation n'englobe pas la question des assurances et des garanties ... [lesquelles] sont conceptuellement différentes de la réparation». Ils soulignent que la quatrième conclusion de l'Allemagne

> «va bien au-delà de toute mesure de réparation que la Cour peut ou devrait accorder, et qu'elle devrait par conséquent être rejetée. Le pouvoir qu'a la Cour de trancher des affaires ... n'englobe pas celui d'ordonner à un Etat de fournir une «garantie» visant à conférer des droits additionnels à l'Etat requérant... [L]es Etats-Unis ne croient pas qu'il appartienne à la Cour ... d'imposer des obligations qui viennent s'ajouter à celles qu'ils ont acceptées lorsqu'ils ont ratifié la convention de Vienne ou qui diffèrent de celles-ci.»

47. A l'encontre de cet argument, l'Allemagne fait valoir

> «qu'un différend portant sur la question de savoir si une disposition de la convention de Vienne donne droit à certains remèdes est un différend relatif à «l'application et à l'interprétation» de la convention susmentionnée, et entre ainsi dans les prévisions de l'article premier du protocole de signature facultative».

L'Allemagne relève à ce sujet que, dans l'ordonnance qu'elle a rendue le 9 avril 1998 en l'affaire relative à la *Convention de Vienne sur les relations consulaires (Paraguay c. Etats-Unis d'Amérique)*, la Cour a déclaré:

> «il existe un différend sur la question de savoir si la solution recherchée par le Paraguay figure parmi les mesures possibles en vertu de la convention de Vienne, en particulier au regard des dispositions des articles 5 et 36 de cette convention; et ... il s'agit là d'un différend relatif à l'application de la convention au sens de l'article premier du protocole de signature facultative concernant le règlement obligatoire des différends du 24 avril 1963» (*C.I.J. Recueil 1998*, p. 256, par. 31).

Germany asserts also that its fourth submission arises under principles of State responsibility, according to which Germany is entitled to a "whole range of remedies" as a consequence of the particular violations alleged in this case and that these questions of State responsibility "are clearly within the ambit of the Optional Protocol".

48. The Court considers that a dispute regarding the appropriate remedies for the violation of the Convention alleged by Germany is a dispute that arises out of the interpretation or application of the Convention and thus is within the Court's jurisdiction. Where jurisdiction exists over a dispute on a particular matter, no separate basis for jurisdiction is required by the Court to consider the remedies a party has requested for the breach of the obligation (*Factory at Chorzów, P.C.I.J., Series A, No. 9*, p. 22). Consequently, the Court has jurisdiction in the present case with respect to the fourth submission of Germany.

* *

49. The United States has argued that the submissions of Germany are inadmissible on various grounds. The Court will consider these objections in the order presented by the United States.

*

50. The United States objects first to Germany's second, third and fourth submissions. According to the United States, these submissions are inadmissible because Germany seeks to have this Court "play the role of ultimate court of appeal in national criminal proceedings", a role which it is not empowered to perform. The United States maintains that many of Germany's arguments, in particular those regarding the rule of "procedural default", ask the Court "to address and correct . . . asserted violations of US law and errors of judgment by US judges" in criminal proceedings in national courts.

51. Germany denies that it requests the Court to act as an appellate criminal court, or that Germany's requests are in any way aimed at interfering with the administration of justice within the United States judicial system. It maintains that it is merely asking the Court to adjudge and declare that the conduct of the United States was inconsistent with its international legal obligations towards Germany under the Vienna Convention, and to draw from this failure certain legal consequences provided for in the international law of State responsibility.

52. The Court does not agree with these arguments of the United

L'Allemagne soutient en outre que sa quatrième conclusion relève des principes de la responsabilité des Etats, selon lesquels elle est en droit de faire valoir «toute la gamme des voies de droit» disponibles au titre des violations particulières alléguées en l'espèce, et que ces questions de responsabilité de l'Etat «entrent clairement dans le cadre du protocole de signature facultative».

48. La Cour considère qu'un différend portant sur les voies de droit à mettre en œuvre au titre d'une violation de la convention qu'invoque l'Allemagne est un différend concernant l'interprétation ou l'application de la convention et qui de ce fait relève de la compétence de la Cour. S'il est établi que la Cour a compétence pour connaître d'un différend portant sur une question déterminée, elle n'a pas besoin d'une base de compétence distincte pour examiner les remèdes demandés par une partie pour la violation en cause (*Usine de Chorzów, C.P.J.I. série A n° 9*, p. 22). La Cour a par suite compétence en l'espèce pour connaître de la quatrième conclusion de l'Allemagne.

* *

49. Les Etats-Unis font valoir que les conclusions de l'Allemagne sont irrecevables pour diverses raisons. La Cour examinera ces objections en suivant la présentation qui en a été faite par les Etats-Unis.

*

50. La première objection présentée par les Etats-Unis est dirigée contre les deuxième, troisième et quatrième conclusions de l'Allemagne. Selon les Etats-Unis, ces conclusions seraient irrecevables, motif pris de ce que l'Allemagne cherche à faire jouer à la Cour «le rôle d'une juridiction statuant en dernier degré d'appel sur des questions pénales soumises aux tribunaux internes», rôle qu'elle n'est pas habilitée à jouer. Ils font valoir que de nombreux arguments développés par l'Allemagne, en particulier ceux relatifs à la règle de la «carence procédurale», reviennent à demander à la Cour d'«examiner et de réparer ... de prétendues violations du droit des Etats-Unis et des erreurs d'appréciation qui auraient été le fait de juges des Etats-Unis» à l'occasion d'affaires pénales portées devant des juridictions internes.

51. L'Allemagne nie, pour sa part, qu'elle demande à la Cour d'agir comme une juridiction d'appel en matière pénale, ou que ses demandes visent d'une quelconque manière à s'immiscer dans l'administration de la justice des Etats-Unis. Elle prierait simplement la Cour de dire et juger que la conduite des Etats-Unis a méconnu les obligations juridiques internationales dont ils étaient tenus à son endroit en vertu de la convention de Vienne, et de tirer de cette méconnaissance certaines conséquences juridiques prévues par le droit international de la responsabilité des Etats.

52. La Cour ne souscrit pas à l'argumentation des Etats-Unis relative

States concerning the admissibility of the second, third and fourth German submissions. In the second submission, Germany asks the Court to interpret the scope of Article 36, paragraph 2, of the Vienna Convention; the third submission seeks a finding that the United States violated an Order issued by this Court pursuant to Article 41 of its Statute; and in Germany's fourth submission, the Court is asked to determine the applicable remedies for the alleged violations of the Convention. Although Germany deals extensively with the practice of American courts as it bears on the application of the Convention, all three submissions seek to require the Court to do no more than apply the relevant rules of international law to the issues in dispute between the Parties to this case. The exercise of this function, expressly mandated by Article 38 of its Statute, does not convert this Court into a court of appeal of national criminal proceedings.

*

53. The United States also argues that Germany's third submission is inadmissible because of the manner in which these proceedings were brought before the Court by Germany. It notes that German consular officials became aware of the LaGrands' cases in 1992, but that the German Government did not express concern or protest to the United States authorities for some six and a half years. It maintains that the issue of the absence of consular notification was not raised by Germany until 22 February 1999, two days before the date scheduled for Karl LaGrand's execution, in a letter from the German Foreign Minister to the Secretary of State of the United States (see paragraph 26 above). Germany then filed the Application instituting these proceedings, together with a request for provisional measures, after normal business hours in the Registry in the evening of 2 March 1999, some 27 hours before the execution of Walter LaGrand (see paragraph 30 above).

54. The United States rejects the contention that Germany found out only seven days before the filing of its Application that the authorities of Arizona knew as early as 1982 that the LaGrands were German nationals; according to the United States, their German nationality was referred to in pre-sentence reports prepared in 1984, which should have been familiar to German consular officers much earlier than 1999, given Germany's claims regarding the vigour and effectiveness of its consular assistance.

55. According to the United States, Germany's late filing compelled the Court to respond to its request for provisional measures by acting *ex parte*, without full information. The United States claims that the procedure followed was inconsistent with the principles of "equality of the

à la recevabilité des deuxième, troisième et quatrième conclusions de l'Allemagne. Par sa deuxième conclusion, l'Allemagne demande à la Cour d'interpréter la portée du paragraphe 2 de l'article 36 de la convention de Vienne; par sa troisième conclusion, elle prie la Cour de dire que les Etats-Unis ont violé une ordonnance qu'elle a rendue conformément à l'article 41 de son Statut; et, par sa quatrième conclusion, l'Allemagne demande à la Cour de déterminer quels sont les remèdes à apporter aux violations alléguées de la convention. Même si l'Allemagne s'est longuement étendue sur la pratique des tribunaux américains relative à l'application de la convention, ces trois conclusions visent exclusivement à prier la Cour d'appliquer les règles pertinentes de droit international aux questions litigieuses opposant les Parties à l'instance. L'exercice de cette fonction, expressément prévue par l'article 38 de son Statut, ne fait pas de cette Cour une juridiction statuant en appel sur des questions pénales soumises aux tribunaux internes.

*

53. Les Etats-Unis soutiennent également que la troisième conclusion de l'Allemagne est irrecevable compte tenu des circonstances dans lesquelles celle-ci a introduit la présente instance devant la Cour. Ils font valoir que les agents consulaires allemands ont pris connaissance en 1992 des affaires relatives aux LaGrand, mais que, pendant six ans et demi environ, le Gouvernement allemand n'a pas fait part de ses préoccupations aux autorités des Etats-Unis et n'a pas élevé de protestations à ce sujet. Ils font observer que c'est seulement le 22 février 1999, soit deux jours avant la date prévue pour l'exécution de Karl LaGrand, que l'Allemagne a soulevé la question du défaut de notification consulaire, dans une lettre adressée au secrétaire d'Etat des Etats-Unis par le ministre allemand des affaires étrangères (voir paragraphe 26 ci-dessus). L'Allemagne a ensuite saisi la Cour d'une requête introductive d'instance ainsi que d'une demande en indication de mesures conservatoires, dans la soirée du 2 mars 1999, après les heures normales de travail au Greffe, soit environ vingt-sept heures avant l'heure fixée pour l'exécution de Walter LaGrand (voir paragraphe 30 ci-dessus).

54. Les Etats-Unis rejettent l'argument selon lequel l'Allemagne n'aurait découvert que sept jours avant le dépôt de sa requête que les autorités de l'Arizona avaient été au courant dès 1982 de la nationalité allemande des frères LaGrand; selon les Etats-Unis, celle-ci avait été mentionnée dans des rapports de 1984 préalables au prononcé de la peine, dont les agents consulaires allemands auraient dû avoir connaissance bien avant 1999, à en croire les affirmations de l'Allemagne relatives au sérieux et à l'efficacité de son assistance consulaire.

55. Selon les Etats-Unis, le fait que l'Allemagne ait déposé sa requête aussi tardivement a contraint la Cour à répondre à la demande en indication de mesures conservatoires sans que le défendeur ait pu être entendu et sans qu'elle dispose de toutes les informations voulues. Les Etats-Unis

Parties" and of giving each Party a sufficient opportunity to be heard, and that this would justify the Court in not addressing Germany's third submission which is predicated wholly upon the Order of 3 March 1999.

56. Germany acknowledges that delay on the part of a claimant State may render an application inadmissible, but maintains that international law does not lay down any specific time-limit in that regard. It contends that it was only seven days before it filed its Application that it became aware of all the relevant facts underlying its claim, in particular, the fact that the authorities of Arizona knew of the German nationality of the LaGrands since 1982. According to Germany, it cannot be accused of negligence in failing to obtain the 1984 pre-sentence reports earlier. It also maintains that in the period between 1992, when it learned of the LaGrands' cases, and the filing of its Application, it engaged in a variety of activities at the diplomatic and consular level. It adds that it had been confident for much of this period that the United States would ultimately rectify the violations of international law involved.

57. The Court recognizes that Germany may be criticized for the manner in which these proceedings were filed and for their timing. The Court recalls, however, that notwithstanding its awareness of the consequences of Germany's filing at such a late date it nevertheless considered it appropriate to enter the Order of 3 March 1999, given that an irreparable prejudice appeared to be imminent. In view of these considerations, the Court considers that Germany is now entitled to challenge the alleged failure of the United States to comply with the Order. Accordingly, the Court finds that Germany's third submission is admissible.

*

58. The United States argues further that Germany's first submission, as far as it concerns its right to exercise diplomatic protection with respect to its nationals, is inadmissible on the ground that the LaGrands did not exhaust local remedies. The United States maintains that the alleged breach concerned the duty to inform the LaGrands of their right to consular access, and that such a breach could have been remedied at the trial stage, provided it was raised in a timely fashion. The United States contends that when a person fails, for example, to sue in a national court before a statute of limitations has expired, the claim is both procedurally barred in national courts and inadmissible in international tribunals for failure to exhaust local remedies. It adds that the failure of counsel for the LaGrands to raise the breach of the Vienna Convention at the appropriate stage and time of the proceedings does not excuse the non-exhaustion of local remedies. According to the United States, this

font valoir que la procédure suivie n'a pas respecté le principe de «l'égalité des Parties», ni le droit de chaque Partie à être entendue dans des conditions satisfaisantes, et que par conséquent la Cour ne devrait pas examiner la troisième conclusion de l'Allemagne, qui repose entièrement sur l'ordonnance du 3 mars 1999.

56. L'Allemagne reconnaît pour sa part que le retard d'un Etat demandeur peut rendre une requête irrecevable, mais soutient que le droit international ne fixe aucun délai spécifique en la matière. Elle fait valoir que c'est sept jours seulement avant le dépôt de sa requête qu'elle a eu connaissance de tous les faits pertinents sur lesquels elle fonde son action, et en particulier du fait que les autorités de l'Arizona avaient été au courant dès 1982 de la nationalité allemande des frères LaGrand. L'Allemagne ne saurait, estime-t-elle, être accusée de négligence pour ne pas avoir obtenu plus tôt les rapports de 1984 préalables au prononcé de la peine. Elle soutient également qu'entre 1992, année où elle a eu connaissance des affaires relatives aux LaGrand, et le dépôt de sa requête, elle a effectué diverses démarches aux niveaux diplomatique et consulaire. Elle ajoute que pendant une grande partie de cette période elle était persuadée que les Etats-Unis finiraient par remédier aux violations du droit international en cause.

57. La Cour reconnaît que l'Allemagne peut être critiquée pour la manière dont l'instance a été introduite et pour le moment choisi pour l'introduire. La Cour rappelle toutefois que, tout en étant consciente des conséquences de l'introduction de l'instance par l'Allemagne à une date si avancée, elle n'en a pas moins estimé approprié de rendre son ordonnance du 3 mars 1999, un préjudice irréparable semblant imminent. Dans ces conditions, la Cour estime que l'Allemagne est en droit de se plaindre aujourd'hui de la non-application, alléguée par elle, de ladite ordonnance par les Etats-Unis. En conséquence, la Cour conclut que la troisième conclusion de l'Allemagne est recevable.

*

58. Les Etats-Unis soutiennent aussi que la première conclusion de l'Allemagne, en tant qu'elle concerne son droit à exercer sa protection diplomatique à l'égard de ses ressortissants, est irrecevable parce que les frères LaGrand n'avaient pas épuisé les voies de recours internes. Les Etats-Unis font valoir que le manquement allégué concernait l'obligation d'informer les frères LaGrand de leur droit de communiquer avec leur consulat et qu'un tel manquement aurait pu facilement être réparé au stade du procès si la question avait été soulevée en temps opportun. Selon les Etats-Unis, quand, par exemple, une personne omet d'agir devant un tribunal national avant l'expiration des délais de forclusion, sa demande ne peut plus être examinée devant les juridictions nationales et elle est irrecevable devant les juridictions internationales pour non-épuisement des voies de recours internes. Ils ajoutent que le fait que les avocats des LaGrand n'avaient pas soulevé en temps opportun le moyen tiré de la

failure of counsel is imputable to their clients because the law treats defendants and their lawyers as a single entity in terms of their legal positions. Moreover, the State is not accountable for the errors or mistaken strategy by lawyers.

59. Germany responds that international law requires the exhaustion of only those remedies which are legally and practically available. Germany claims that in this case there was no remedy which the LaGrands failed to invoke that would have been available in the specific context of their case. This is so because, prior to 1992, the LaGrands could not resort to the available remedies, since they were unaware of their rights due to failure of the United States authorities to comply with the requirements of the Vienna Convention; thereafter, the "procedural default" rule prevented them from seeking any remedy.

60. The Court notes that it is not disputed that the LaGrands sought to plead the Vienna Convention in United States courts after they learned in 1992 of their rights under the Convention; it is also not disputed that by that date the procedural default rule barred the LaGrands from obtaining any remedy in respect of the violation of those rights. Counsel assigned to the LaGrands failed to raise this point earlier in a timely fashion. However, the United States may not now rely before this Court on this fact in order to preclude the admissibility of Germany's first submission, as it was the United States itself which had failed to carry our its obligation under the Convention to inform the LaGrand brothers.

*

61. The United States also contends that Germany's submissions are inadmissible on the ground that Germany seeks to have a standard applied to the United States that is different from its own practice. According to the United States, Germany has not shown that its system of criminal justice requires the annulment of criminal convictions where there has been a breach of the duty of consular notification; and that the practice of Germany in similar cases has been to do no more than offer an apology. The United States maintains that it would be contrary to basic principles of administration of justice and equality of the Parties to apply against the United States alleged rules that Germany appears not to accept for itself.

62. Germany denies that it is asking the United States to adhere to standards which Germany itself does not abide by; it maintains that its law and practice is fully in compliance with the standards which it invokes. In this regard, it explains that the German Code of Criminal

violation de la convention de Vienne n'excuse pas le non-épuisement des voies de recours internes. Selon les Etats-Unis, cette carence des avocats est imputable à leurs clients, puisqu'il est de règle qu'un accusé et son avocat constituent une seule et même entité au regard des positions juridiques qu'ils adoptent. De plus, un Etat ne saurait être tenu responsable des erreurs commises par des avocats, ni des stratégies inappropriées adoptées par eux.

59. L'Allemagne répond que le droit international exige seulement l'épuisement de celles des voies de recours qu'il est juridiquement et matériellement possible de mettre en œuvre. Selon elle, il n'existait en l'espèce aucun recours que les LaGrand pouvaient invoquer dans le contexte particulier de l'instance les concernant et qu'ils auraient négligé d'exercer. En effet, avant 1992, ils n'étaient pas en mesure d'exercer les recours qui leur étaient ouverts puisqu'ils n'étaient pas au courant de leurs droits, du fait que les autorités des Etats-Unis avaient manqué de se conformer aux prescriptions de la convention de Vienne; par la suite, la règle de la «carence procédurale» les a empêchés d'exercer tout recours.

60. La Cour note qu'il n'est pas contesté que les frères LaGrand ont cherché à se prévaloir des dispositions de la convention de Vienne devant les tribunaux américains après avoir pris connaissance en 1992 du droit qu'ils tenaient de ladite convention; il n'est pas davantage contesté qu'à cette époque la règle de la carence procédurale a fait que les LaGrand n'ont pu obtenir qu'il soit remédié à la violation de ce droit. Les avocats commis d'office pour les défendre n'ont pas soulevé cette question en temps voulu. Cependant les Etats-Unis ne sauraient se prévaloir aujourd'hui devant la Cour de cette circonstance pour faire obstacle à la recevabilité de la première conclusion de l'Allemagne, dès lors qu'ils avaient eux-mêmes failli à l'exécution de leur obligation, en vertu de la convention, d'informer les frères LaGrand.

*

61. Les Etats-Unis soutiennent également que les conclusions de l'Allemagne sont irrecevables au motif qu'elle cherche à faire appliquer par les Etats-Unis une norme différente de celle qui prévaut dans la pratique allemande. Aux dires des Etats-Unis, l'Allemagne n'a pas montré que son système judiciaire exigeait l'annulation de condamnations pénales en cas de manquement à l'obligation de notification consulaire et, confrontée à des affaires de ce genre, elle s'est bornée dans la pratique à présenter des excuses. Pour les Etats-Unis, il serait contraire aux principes fondamentaux de bonne administration de la justice et d'égalité entre les Parties d'appliquer à l'encontre des Etats-Unis des règles que l'Allemagne elle-même, en apparence, ne suivrait pas.

62. L'Allemagne se défend de demander aux Etats-Unis d'appliquer des normes qu'elle ne respecterait pas elle-même et soutient que, dans son droit comme dans sa pratique, elle respecte pleinement les normes qu'elle invoque. Elle précise à cet égard que le code de procédure pénale alle-

Procedure provides a ground of appeal where a legal norm, including a norm of international law, is not applied or incorrectly applied and where there is a possibility that the decision was impaired by this fact.

63. The Court need not decide whether this argument of the United States, if true, would result in the inadmissibility of Germany's submissions. Here the evidence adduced by the United States does not justify the conclusion that Germany's own practice fails to conform to the standards it demands from the United States in this litigation. The United States relies on certain German cases to demonstrate that Germany has itself proffered only an apology for violating Article 36 of the Vienna Convention, and that State practice shows that this is the appropriate remedy for such a violation. But the cases concerned entailed relatively light criminal penalties and are not evidence as to German practice where an arrested person, who has not been informed without delay of his or her rights, is facing a severe penalty as in the present case. It is no doubt the case, as the United States points out, that Article 36 of the Vienna Convention imposes identical obligations on States, irrespective of the gravity of the offence a person may be charged with and of the penalties that may be imposed. However, it does not follow therefrom that the remedies for a violation of this Article must be identical in all situations. While an apology may be an appropriate remedy in some cases, it may in others be insufficient. The Court accordingly finds that this claim of inadmissibility must be rejected.

* * *

64. Having determined that the Court has jurisdiction, and that the submissions of Germany are admissible, the Court now turns to the merits of each of these four submissions.

* *

65. Germany's first submission requests the Court to adjudge and declare:

> "that the United States, by not informing Karl and Walter LaGrand without delay following their arrest of their rights under Article 36 subparagraph 1 *(b)* of the Vienna Convention on Consular Relations, and by depriving Germany of the possibility of rendering consular assistance, which ultimately resulted in the execution of Karl and Walter LaGrand, violated its international legal obligations to Germany, in its own right and in its right of diplomatic protection of its nationals, under Articles 5 and 36 paragraph 1 of the said Convention".

mand prévoit un recours dans les cas où une norme juridique, y compris une norme de droit international, n'a pas été ou a été mal appliquée, et où il existe une possibilité que la décision en ait été altérée.

63. Point n'est besoin pour la Cour de décider si l'argument en question des Etats-Unis, à supposer qu'il fût exact, rendrait les conclusions de l'Allemagne irrecevables. En l'occurrence, les éléments produits par les Etats-Unis ne permettent pas de conclure que la pratique de l'Allemagne s'écarte des normes dont elle demande l'application en l'espèce de la part des Etats-Unis. Les Etats-Unis se sont fondés sur certaines affaires allemandes pour démontrer que l'Allemagne elle-même s'était contentée d'offrir des excuses lorsqu'elle avait violé l'article 36 de la convention de Vienne et que la pratique des Etats fait apparaître qu'il s'agit là d'un remède approprié en cas de violation. Les affaires citées concernaient toutefois des peines relativement légères et ne constituent pas des preuves de la pratique que suit l'Allemagne lorsqu'une personne arrêtée, qui n'a pas été informée sans retard de ses droits, risque une peine sévère, comme cela a été le cas en l'espèce. Sans doute l'article 36 de la convention de Vienne impose-t-il aux Etats des obligations identiques quelle que soit la gravité de l'infraction imputée à une personne et de la peine qui peut lui être infligée, comme le soulignent à juste titre les Etats-Unis. Mais il n'en résulte pas que les remèdes à retenir en cas de violation de cet article dussent être identiques dans toutes les situations. Si de simples excuses peuvent constituer un remède approprié dans certains cas, elles pourraient se révéler insuffisantes dans d'autres. Aussi la Cour estime-t-elle que ce motif d'irrecevabilité doit être rejeté.

* * *

64. Ayant établi qu'elle était compétente et que les conclusions de l'Allemagne étaient recevables, la Cour examinera maintenant au fond chacune des quatre conclusions en question.

* *

65. Dans sa première conclusion, l'Allemagne demande à la Cour de dire et juger que:

> «en n'informant pas sans retard Karl et Walter LaGrand après leur arrestation de leurs droits en vertu de l'alinéa *b)* du paragraphe 1 de l'article 36 de la convention de Vienne sur les relations consulaires, et en privant l'Allemagne de la possibilité de fournir son assistance consulaire, ce qui a finalement conduit à l'exécution de Karl et Walter LaGrand, les Etats-Unis ont violé leurs obligations juridiques internationales vis-à-vis de l'Allemagne au titre de l'article 5 et du paragraphe 1 de l'article 36 de ladite convention, tant en ce qui concerne les droits propres de l'Allemagne que le droit de cette dernière d'exercer sa protection diplomatique à l'égard de ses ressortissants».

66. Germany claims that the United States violated its obligation under Article 36, paragraph 1 *(b)*, to "inform a national of the sending State without delay of his or her right to inform the consular post of his home State of his arrest or detention". Specifically, Germany maintains that the United States violated its international legal obligation to Germany under Article 36, paragraph 1 *(b)*, by failing to inform the German nationals Karl and Walter LaGrand "without delay" of their rights under that subparagraph.

67. The United States acknowledges, and does not contest Germany's basic claim, that there was a breach of its obligation under Article 36, paragraph 1 *(b)*, of the Convention "promptly to inform the LaGrand brothers that they could ask that a German consular post be notified of their arrest and detention".

68. Germany also claims that the violation by the United States of Article 36, paragraph 1 *(b)*, led to consequential violations of Article 36, paragraph 1 *(a)* and *(c)*. It points out that, when the obligation to inform the arrested person without delay of his or her right to contact the consulate is disregarded, "the other rights contained in Article 36, paragraph 1, become in practice irrelevant, indeed meaningless". Germany maintains that, "[b]y informing the LaGrand brothers of their right to inform the consulate more than 16 years after their arrest, the United States . . . clearly failed to meet the standard of Article 36 [(1) *(c)*]". It concludes that, by not preventing the execution of Karl and Walter LaGrand, and by "making irreversible its earlier breaches of Art. 5 and 36 (1) and (2) and causing irreparable harm, the United States violated its obligations under international law".

69. The United States argues that the underlying conduct complained of by Germany is one and the same, namely, the failure to inform the LaGrand brothers as required by Article 36, paragraph 1 *(b)*. Therefore, it disputes any other basis for Germany's claims that other provisions, such as subparagraphs *(a)* and *(c)* of Article 36, paragraph 1, of the Convention, were also violated. The United States asserts that Germany's claims regarding Article 36, paragraph 1 *(a)* and *(c)*, are "particularly misplaced" in that the LaGrands were able to and did communicate freely with consular officials after 1992. There was, in the view of the United States, "no deprivation of Germany's right to provide consular assistance, under Article 5 or Article 36, to Karl or Walter LaGrand" and "Germany's attempt to transform a breach of one obligation into an additional breach of a wholly separate and distinct obligation should be rejected by the Court."

70. In response, Germany asserts that it is "commonplace that one

66. L'Allemagne soutient que les Etats-Unis ont violé l'obligation que leur imposait l'alinéa *b)* du paragraphe 1 de l'article 36 «d'avertir sans retard un ressortissant de l'Etat d'envoi de son droit d'informer le poste consulaire de son Etat d'origine de son arrestation ou de sa détention». Plus précisément, elle fait valoir que, en n'avertissant pas «sans retard» les ressortissants allemands Karl et Walter LaGrand des droits qu'ils tenaient de cette disposition, les Etats-Unis ont méconnu l'obligation juridique internationale dont ils étaient tenus envers elle, au titre de l'alinéa *b)* du paragraphe 1 de l'article 36.

67. Les Etats-Unis ne contestent pas la principale demande de l'Allemagne et reconnaissent qu'ils ont violé l'obligation découlant de l'alinéa *b)* du paragraphe 1 de l'article 36 de la convention «d'informer sans retard les frères LaGrand de leur droit de demander à ce que leurs arrestations et mises en détention soient notifiées à un poste consulaire allemand».

68. L'Allemagne prétend aussi que la violation par les Etats-Unis de l'alinéa *b)* du paragraphe 1 de l'article 36 a entraîné par voie de conséquence celle des alinéas *a)* et *c)* du paragraphe 1 de l'article 36. Selon l'Allemagne, dès lors que l'obligation d'informer sans retard la personne arrêtée de son droit de contacter le consulat est méconnue, il s'ensuit que «les autres droits qu'énonce le paragraphe 1 de l'article 36 perdent en pratique toute pertinence, voire toute signification». Elle soutient que, «[e]n informant, plus de seize ans après leur arrestation, les frères LaGrand de leur droit d'aviser le consulat, les Etats-Unis ne se sont manifestement ... pas conformés à la norme prescrite par [l'alinéa *c)* du paragraphe 1 de] l'article 36». Elle conclut que, en n'empêchant pas l'exécution de Karl et de Walter LaGrand, et en «rendant ... irréversibles leurs violations antérieures de l'article 5 et des paragraphes 1 et 2 de l'article 36, causant de ce fait un préjudice irréparable, les Etats-Unis ont violé les obligations qui sont les leurs en vertu du droit international».

69. Les Etats-Unis font valoir que, fondamentalement, l'Allemagne se plaint d'un seul et même comportement, à savoir le fait qu'ils n'ont pas informé les frères LaGrand, comme le prescrit l'alinéa *b)* du paragraphe 1 de l'article 36. Ils contestent donc tout autre fondement aux demandes de l'Allemagne, selon lesquelles d'autres dispositions, telles que les alinéas *a)* et *c)* du paragraphe 1 de l'article 36 de la convention, auraient aussi été violées. Ils affirment que les allégations de l'Allemagne concernant les alinéas *a)* et *c)* du paragraphe 1 de l'article 36 sont «particulièrement mal fondées», étant donné que les LaGrand ont pu communiquer librement avec les fonctionnaires consulaires après 1992 et l'ont effectivement fait. Ils considèrent que l'Allemagne n'a pas «été privée de son droit de fournir son assistance consulaire à Karl et Walter LaGrand, en vertu de l'article 5 ou de l'article 36» de la convention, et que «la tentative que fait l'Allemagne de transformer la violation d'une obligation en une violation supplémentaire d'une obligation totalement distincte doit être rejetée par la Cour».

70. En réponse, l'Allemagne affirme qu'il est «courant qu'un seul et

and the same conduct may result in several violations of distinct obligations". Hence, when a detainee's right to notification without delay is violated, he or she cannot establish contact with the consulate, receive visits from consular officers, nor be supported by adequate counsel. "Therefore, violation of this right is bound to imply violation of the other rights . . . [and] later observance of the rights of Article 36, paragraph 1 *(a)* and *(c)*, could not remedy the previous violation of those provisions."

71. Germany further contends that there is a causal relationship between the breach of Article 36 and the ultimate execution of the LaGrand brothers. Germany's inability to render prompt assistance was, in its view, a "direct result of the United States' breach of its Vienna Convention obligations". It is claimed that, had Germany been properly afforded its rights under the Vienna Convention, it would have been able to intervene in time and present a "persuasive mitigation case" which "likely would have saved" the lives of the brothers. Germany believes that, "[h]ad proper notification been given under the Vienna Convention, competent trial counsel certainly would have looked to Germany for assistance in developing this line of mitigating evidence". Moreover, Germany argues that, due to the doctrine of procedural default and the high post-conviction threshold for proving ineffective counsel under United States law, Germany's intervention at a stage later than the trial phase could not "remedy the extreme prejudice created by the counsel appointed to represent the LaGrands".

72. The United States terms these arguments as "suppositions about what might have occurred had the LaGrand brothers been properly informed of the possibility of consular notification". It calls into question Germany's assumption that German consular officials from Los Angeles would rapidly have given extensive assistance to the LaGrands' defence counsel before the 1984 sentencing, and contests that such consular assistance would have affected the outcome of the sentencing proceedings. According to the United States, these arguments "rest on speculation" and do not withstand analysis. Finally, the United States finds it extremely doubtful that the early childhood "mitigating evidence" mentioned by Germany, if introduced at the trial, would have persuaded the sentencing judge to be lenient, as the brothers' subsequent 17 years of experiences in the United States would have been given at least equal weight. The United States points out, moreover, that such evidence was in fact presented at trial.

73. The Court will first examine the submission Germany advances in its own right. The Court observes, in this connection, that the United States does not deny that it violated paragraph 1 *(b)* in relation to Ger-

même comportement se traduise par plusieurs manquements à des obligations différentes». Ainsi, lorsque le droit à notification sans retard d'un détenu est violé, ce dernier ne peut ni entrer en communication avec le consulat, ni recevoir la visite des fonctionnaires du consulat, ni être assisté par un avocat compétent. «En conséquence, la violation de ce droit implique fatalement la violation des autres droits ... [et] respecter par la suite les droits conférés par les alinéas *a)* et *c)* du paragraphe 1 de l'article 36 ne pouvait remédier au fait que ces dispositions avaient été précédemment violées.»

71. L'Allemagne soutient également qu'il y a un lien de causalité entre la violation de l'article 36 et l'exécution finale des frères LaGrand. Selon elle, l'incapacité où elle s'est trouvée de leur fournir promptement une assistance est une «conséquence directe du manquement des Etats-Unis aux obligations qui sont les leurs en vertu de la convention de Vienne». Elle fait valoir que, si elle avait pu exercer correctement ses droits en vertu de cette convention, elle aurait été en mesure d'intervenir à temps et de présenter, «de manière convaincante, un dossier de circonstances atténuantes», de sorte qu'il est «probable» que les frères LaGrand «auraient eu la vie sauve». Elle est convaincue que, «si la notification appropriée, prévue par la convention de Vienne, avait été effectuée, des avocats compétents auraient certainement sollicité l'assistance de l'Allemagne pour exposer l'argument tiré des circonstances atténuantes». De plus, elle soutient que, en raison de la doctrine de la carence procédurale et des conditions rigoureuses qu'impose le droit des Etats-Unis à celui qui cherche à prouver, après le verdict de culpabilité, que l'avocat était incompétent, son intervention à un stade postérieur à celui du procès ne pouvait pas «réparer le préjudice grave causé par les avocats commis d'office des LaGrand».

72. Les Etats-Unis qualifient ces arguments de «suppositions ... au sujet de ce qui aurait pu se passer si les frères LaGrand avaient été dûment informés de la possibilité de communiquer avec leur consulat». Ils mettent en doute la thèse de l'Allemagne selon laquelle les fonctionnaires du poste consulaire allemand de Los Angeles auraient apporté rapidement une assistance importante aux avocats des LaGrand avant les verdicts de culpabilité de 1984 et contestent que cette assistance consulaire aurait influé sur le résultat des procédures pénales. Selon eux, ces arguments «relèvent de la spéculation» et ne résistent pas à l'analyse. Enfin, il leur paraît extrêmement douteux que les «preuves de circonstances atténuantes» relatives à la prime enfance des frères LaGrand, qu'invoque l'Allemagne, auraient, si elles avaient été produites au procès, persuadé le juge de faire preuve d'indulgence; un poids au moins égal aurait en effet été donné aux dix-sept années qu'ils avaient passées ultérieurement aux Etats-Unis. De plus, les Etats-Unis notent que de telles preuves ont en fait été présentées au procès.

73. La Cour examinera tout d'abord la conclusion présentée par l'Allemagne en son nom propre. La Cour note à ce propos que les Etats-Unis ne nient pas avoir violé, à l'encontre de l'Allemagne, l'alinéa *b)* du para-

many. The Court also notes that as a result of this breach, Germany did not learn until 1992 of the detention, trial and sentencing of the LaGrand brothers. The Court concludes therefrom that on the facts of this case, the breach of the United States had the consequence of depriving Germany of the exercise of the rights accorded it under Article 36, paragraph 1 *(a)* and paragraph 1 *(c)*, and thus violated these provisions of the Convention. Although the violation of paragraph 1 *(b)* of Article 36 will not necessarily always result in the breach of the other provisions of this Article, the Court finds that the circumstances of this case compel the opposite conclusion, for the reasons indicated below. In view of this finding, it is not necessary for the Court to deal with Germany's further claim under Article 5 of the Convention.

74. Article 36, paragraph 1, establishes an interrelated régime designed to facilitate the implementation of the system of consular protection. It begins with the basic principle governing consular protection: the right of communication and access (Art. 36, para. 1 *(a)*). This clause is followed by the provision which spells out the modalities of consular notification (Art. 36, para. 1 *(b)*). Finally Article 36, paragraph 1 *(c)*, sets out the measures consular officers may take in rendering consular assistance to their nationals in the custody of the receiving State. It follows that when the sending State is unaware of the detention of its nationals due to the failure of the receiving State to provide the requisite consular notification without delay, which was true in the present case during the period between 1982 and 1992, the sending State has been prevented for all practical purposes from exercising its rights under Article 36, paragraph 1. It is immaterial for the purposes of the present case whether the LaGrands would have sought consular assistance from Germany, whether Germany would have rendered such assistance, or whether a different verdict would have been rendered. It is sufficient that the Convention conferred these rights, and that Germany and the LaGrands were in effect prevented by the breach of the United States from exercising them, had they so chosen.

*

75. Germany further contends that "the breach of Article 36 by the United States did not only infringe upon the rights of Germany as a State party to the [Vienna] Convention but also entailed a violation of the individual rights of the LaGrand brothers". Invoking its right of diplomatic protection, Germany also seeks relief against the United States on this ground.

Germany maintains that the right to be informed of the rights under Article 36, paragraph 1 *(b)*, of the Vienna Convention, is an individual right of every national of a State party to the Convention who enters the graphe 1 de l'article 36 de la convention de Vienne. La Cour relève en outre que, par suite de cette violation, l'Allemagne a appris seulement en 1992 la détention, le jugement et la condamnation des frères LaGrand. La Cour en conclut que, au vu des faits de l'espèce, le manquement des Etats-Unis a eu pour conséquence d'interdire à l'Allemagne d'exercer les droits que lui confèrent les alinéas *a)* et *c)* du paragraphe 1 de l'article 36 et, partant, qu'il y a bien eu violation de ces dispositions de la convention. Bien que la violation du seul alinéa *b)* du paragraphe 1 de l'article 36 n'entraîne pas toujours nécessairement la violation des autres dispositions de cet article, la Cour est amenée à conclure que tel est le cas en l'espèce pour les raisons exposées ci-après. Compte tenu de cette conclusion, point n'est besoin pour la Cour d'examiner le grief additionnel de l'Allemagne concernant l'article 5 de la convention.

74. Le paragraphe 1 de l'article 36 institue un régime dont les divers éléments sont interdépendants et qui est conçu pour faciliter la mise en œuvre du système de protection consulaire. Le principe de base régissant la protection consulaire est énoncé dès l'abord: le droit de communication et d'accès (alinéa *a)* du paragraphe 1 de l'article 36). La disposition suivante précise les modalités selon lesquelles doit s'effectuer la notification consulaire (alinéa *b)* du paragraphe 1 de l'article 36). Enfin, l'alinéa *c)* du paragraphe 1 de l'article 36 énonce les mesures que les agents consulaires peuvent prendre pour fournir leur assistance aux ressortissants de leur pays détenus dans l'Etat de résidence. Il s'ensuit que, lorsque l'Etat d'envoi n'a pas connaissance de la détention de l'un de ses ressortissants, parce que l'Etat de résidence n'a pas effectué sans retard la notification consulaire requise, ce qui fut le cas en l'espèce entre 1982 et 1992, l'Etat d'envoi se trouve dans l'impossibilité pratique d'exercer, à toutes fins utiles, les droits que lui confère le paragraphe 1 de l'article 36. Peu importe à cet égard de savoir, aux fins de la présente instance, si les LaGrand auraient sollicité l'assistance consulaire de l'Allemagne, si l'Allemagne leur aurait apporté une telle assistance et si un verdict différent aurait alors été prononcé. Il suffit de constater que la convention conférait ces droits, et que l'Allemagne et les LaGrand, eussent-ils souhaité s'en prévaloir, ont en fait été empêchés de le faire en raison de la violation commise par les Etats-Unis.

*

75. L'Allemagne soutient ensuite que «la violation de l'article 36 par les Etats-Unis ne porte pas seulement atteinte [à ses] droits ... en tant qu'Etat partie à la convention, mais constitue également une violation des droits individuels des frères LaGrand». Agissant au titre de la protection diplomatique, elle demande également la condamnation des Etats-Unis sur ce terrain.

Pour l'Allemagne. le droit d'être informé au moment de son arrestation des droits conférés par l'alinéa *b)* du paragraphe 1 de l'article 36 de la convention de Vienne est un droit qui appartient à tout ressortissant d'un territory of another State party. It submits that this view is supported by the ordinary meaning of the terms of Article 36, paragraph 1 *(b)*, of the Vienna Convention, since the last sentence of that provision speaks of the "rights" under this subparagraph of "the person concerned", i.e., of the foreign national arrested or detained. Germany adds that the provision in Article 36, paragraph 1 *(b)*, according to which it is for the arrested person to decide whether consular notification is to be provided, has the effect of conferring an individual right upon the foreign national concerned. In its view, the context of Article 36 supports this conclusion since it relates to both the concerns of the sending and receiving States and to those of individuals. According to Germany, the *travaux préparatoires* of the Vienna Convention lend further support to this interpretation. In addition, Germany submits that the "United Nations Declaration on the human rights of individuals who are not nationals of the country in which they live", adopted by General Assembly resolution 40/144 on 13 December 1985, confirms the view that the right of access to the consulate of the home State, as well as the information on this right, constitute individual rights of foreign nationals and are to be regarded as human rights of aliens.

76. The United States questions what this additional claim of diplomatic protection contributes to the case and argues that there are no parallels between the present case and cases of diplomatic protection involving the espousal by a State of economic claims of its nationals. The United States maintains that the right of a State to provide consular assistance to nationals detained in another country, and the right of a State to espouse the claims of its nationals through diplomatic protection, are legally different concepts.

The United States contends, furthermore, that rights of consular notification and access under the Vienna Convention are rights of States, and not of individuals, even though these rights may benefit individuals by permitting States to offer them consular assistance. It maintains that the treatment due to individuals under the Convention is inextricably linked to and derived from the right of the State, acting through its consular officer, to communicate with its nationals, and does not constitute a fundamental right or a human right. The United States argues that the fact that Article 36 by its terms recognizes the rights of individuals does not determine the nature of those rights or the remedies required under the Vienna Convention for breaches of that Article. It points out that Article 36 begins with the words "[w]ith a view to facilitating the exercise of consular functions relating to nationals of the sending State", and that this wording gives no support to the notion that the rights and obligations enumerated in paragraph 1 of that Article are intended to ensure that nationals of the sending State have any particular rights or

Etat partie à la convention de Vienne, lorsqu'il pénètre sur le territoire d'un autre Etat partie. Cette interprétation serait corroborée par les termes de l'alinéa *b)* du paragraphe 1 de l'article 36 de la convention de Vienne pris dans leur sens ordinaire, car la dernière phrase de cette disposition fait état des «droits», au titre dudit alinéa, de «l'intéressé», c'est-à-dire du ressortissant étranger arrêté ou détenu. L'Allemagne ajoute que l'alinéa *b)* du paragraphe 1 de l'article 36, qui stipule qu'il appartient à la personne arrêtée de décider si son consulat doit être averti, a pour effet de conférer un droit individuel au ressortissant étranger concerné. Elle considère que le contexte de l'article 36 conforte cette conclusion puisqu'il vise tant les intérêts de l'Etat d'envoi et de l'Etat de résidence que les intérêts des particuliers. Elle affirme que les travaux préparatoires de la convention de Vienne étayent cette interprétation. Elle soutient en outre que la «Déclaration sur les droits de l'homme des personnes qui ne possèdent pas la nationalité du pays dans lequel elles vivent», adoptée par l'Assemblée générale des Nations Unies par sa résolution n° 40/144 du 13 décembre 1985, confirme que le droit de se mettre en rapport avec le consulat de l'Etat de nationalité, de même que le droit d'être informé de ce droit, sont des droits que possède tout individu en sa qualité de ressortissant étranger et qui doivent être considérés comme des droits de la personne humaine reconnus aux étrangers.

76. Les Etats-Unis, pour leur part, s'interrogent sur ce que cette prétention supplémentaire relative à la protection diplomatique apporte au cas d'espèce et ils soutiennent qu'il n'y a rien de commun entre la présente affaire et les cas de protection diplomatique portant sur la défense par un Etat de réclamations d'ordre économique de ses ressortissants. Pour les Etats-Unis, le droit pour un Etat d'apporter une assistance consulaire à des ressortissants détenus dans un pays étranger et le droit pour un Etat d'endosser les revendications de ses ressortissants par la voie de la protection diplomatique sont des concepts juridiquement différents.

Les Etats-Unis soutiennent en outre que ce sont les Etats et non les individus qui sont titulaires des droits que reconnaît la convention de Vienne en matière de notification consulaire, même si les individus peuvent bénéficier de ces droits, du fait que les Etats sont autorisés à leur offrir une assistance consulaire. Ils affirment que le traitement qui doit être réservé aux individus aux termes de la convention est indissociablement lié au droit de l'Etat, agissant par l'intermédiaire de ses agents consulaires, de communiquer avec ses ressortissants — et découle de ce droit — et qu'il ne constitue ni un droit fondamental ni un droit de l'homme. A leur avis, le fait qu'aux termes de l'article 36 les droits des individus soient reconnus ne détermine pas la nature de ces droits ni les voies de droit dont la convention de Vienne appelle l'existence en cas de violation de cette disposition. Ils soulignent que l'article 36 débute ainsi «[a]fin que l'exercice des fonctions consulaires relatives aux ressortissants de l'Etat d'envoi soit facilité», et que ce libellé ne conforte pas l'idée selon laquelle les droits et obligations visés au paragraphe 1 de cet article ont treatment in the context of a criminal prosecution. The *travaux préparatoires* of the Vienna Convention according to the United States do not reflect a consensus that Article 36 was addressing immutable individual rights, as opposed to individual rights derivative of the rights of States.

77. The Court notes that Article 36, paragraph 1 *(b)*, spells out the obligations the receiving State has towards the detained person and the sending State. It provides that, at the request of the detained person, the receiving State must inform the consular post of the sending State of the individual's detention "without delay". It provides further that any communication by the detained person addressed to the consular post of the sending State must be forwarded to it by authorities of the receiving State "without delay". Significantly, this subparagraph ends with the following language: "The said authorities shall inform the person concerned without delay of *his rights* under this subparagraph" (emphasis added). Moreover, under Article 36, paragraph 1 *(c)*, the sending State's right to provide consular assistance to the detained person may not be exercised "if he expressly opposes such action". The clarity of these provisions, viewed in their context, admits of no doubt. It follows, as has been held on a number of occasions, that the Court must apply these as they stand (see *Acquisition of Polish Nationality, Advisory Opinion, 1923, P.C.I.J., Series B, No. 7*, p. 20; *Competence of the General Assembly for the Admission of a State to the United Nations, Advisory Opinion, I.C.J. Reports 1950*, p. 8; *Arbitral Award of 31 July 1989, Judgment, I.C.J. Reports 1991*, pp. 69-70, para. 48; *Territorial Dispute (Libyan Arab Jamahiriya/Chad), Judgment, I.C.J. Reports 1994*, p. 25, para. 51). Based on the text of these provisions, the Court concludes that Article 36, paragraph 1, creates individual rights, which, by virtue of Article I of the Optional Protocol, may be invoked in this Court by the national State of the detained person. These rights were violated in the present case.

78. At the hearings, Germany further contended that the right of the individual to be informed without delay under Article 36, paragraph 1, of the Vienna Convention was not only an individual right but has today assumed the character of a human right. In consequence, Germany added, "the character of the right under Article 36 as a human right renders the effectiveness of this provision even more imperative". The Court having found that the United States violated the rights accorded by Article 36, paragraph 1, to the LaGrand brothers, it does not appear necessary to it to consider the additional argument developed by Germany in this regard.

* *

pour fonction de garantir aux ressortissants de l'Etat d'envoi des droits ou un traitement particuliers dans le cadre d'une procédure pénale. Les Etats-Unis estiment que les travaux préparatoires de la convention de Vienne ne font pas apparaître qu'il y ait eu consensus sur le fait que l'article 36 vise des droits intransgressibles de l'individu par opposition à des droits individuels dérivés des droits des Etats.

77. La Cour constate que l'alinéa *b)* du paragraphe 1 de l'article 36 énonce les obligations que l'Etat de résidence a vis-à-vis d'une personne détenue et de l'Etat d'envoi. Il dispose que, à la demande de la personne mise en détention, l'Etat de résidence doit informer «sans retard» le poste consulaire de l'Etat d'envoi de la détention de l'individu. Il dispose en outre que toute communication par la personne détenue adressée au poste consulaire de l'Etat d'envoi doit lui être transmise par les autorités de l'Etat de résidence «sans retard». Il est significatif que cet alinéa se termine par la disposition suivante: lesdites autorités «doivent sans retard informer l'intéressé de *ses droits* aux termes du présent alinéa» (les italiques sont de la Cour). En outre, en vertu de l'alinéa *c)* du paragraphe 1 de l'article 36, le droit de l'Etat d'envoi de prêter son assistance consulaire à la personne en détention ne peut s'exercer si celle-ci «s'y oppose expressément». La clarté de ces dispositions, lues dans leur contexte, ne laisse en rien à désirer. De ce fait, et comme il a été jugé à plusieurs reprises, la Cour est tenue de les appliquer telles qu'elles sont (voir *Acquisition de la nationalité polonaise, avis consultatif, 1923, C.P.J.I. série B n° 7*, p. 20; *Compétence de l'Assemblée générale pour l'admission d'un Etat aux Nations Unies, avis consultatif, C.I.J. Recueil 1950*, p. 8; *Sentence arbitrale du 31 juillet 1989, arrêt, C.I.J. Recueil 1991*, p. 69-70, par. 48; *Différend territorial (Jamahiriya arabe libyenne/Tchad), arrêt, C.I.J. Recueil 1994*, p. 25, par. 51). Compte tenu du libellé de ces dispositions, la Cour conclut que le paragraphe 1 de l'article 36 crée des droits individuels qui, en vertu de l'article premier du protocole de signature facultative, peuvent être invoqués devant la Cour par l'Etat dont la personne détenue a la nationalité. En l'espèce, ces droits ont été violés.

78. A l'audience, l'Allemagne a en outre soutenu que le droit de l'intéressé d'être informé sans retard aux termes du paragraphe 1 de l'article 36 de la convention de Vienne sur les relations consulaires n'était pas seulement un droit individuel, mais avait aujourd'hui acquis le caractère d'un droit de l'homme. De ce fait, elle ajoute que «le caractère de droit de l'homme que revêt le droit prévu à l'article 36 rend l'effectivité de cette disposition plus impérieuse encore». La Cour ayant conclu à la violation par les Etats-Unis des droits que les frères LaGrand tiraient du paragraphe 1 de l'article 36, il ne lui paraît pas nécessaire d'examiner l'argumentation supplémentaire développée par l'Allemagne à cet égard.

* *

79. The Court will now consider Germany's second submission, which it asks the Court to adjudge and declare:

> "that the United States, by applying rules of its domestic law, particular the doctrine of procedural default, which barred Ka and Walter LaGrand from raising their claims under the Vien Convention on Consular Relations, and by ultimately executi them, violated its international legal obligation to Germany und Article 36 paragraph 2 of the Vienna Convention to give full effe to the purposes for which the rights accorded under Article 36 the said Convention are intended".

80. Germany argues that, under Article 36, paragraph 2, of the Vien Convention

> "the United States is under an obligation to ensure that its municip 'laws and regulations . . . enable full effect to be given to the pu poses for which the rights accorded under this article are intende [and that it] is in breach of this obligation by upholding rules domestic law which make it impossible to successfully raise a vio tion of the right to consular notification in proceedings subseque to a conviction of a defendant by a jury".

81. Germany points out that the "procedural default" rule is amo the rules of United States domestic law whose application make it impo sible to invoke a breach of the notification requirement. According Germany, this rule "is closely connected with the division of labo between federal and state jurisdiction in the United States . . . [whe [c]riminal jurisdiction belongs to the states except in cases provided for the Constitution". This rule, Germany explains, requires "exhaustion remedies at the state level before a *habeas corpus* motion can be filed wi federal Courts".

Germany emphasizes that it is not the "procedural default" rule such that is at issue in the present proceedings, but the manner in whi it was applied in that it "deprived the brothers of the possibility to ra the violations of their right to consular notification in US crimir proceedings".

82. Furthermore, having examined the relevant United States jurispr dence, Germany contends that the procedural default rule had "made impossible for the LaGrand brothers to effectively raise the issue of t lack of consular notification after they had at last learned of their rigl and established contact with the German consulate in Los Angeles 1992".

79. La Cour passera maintenant à l'examen de la deuxième conclusion de l'Allemagne, par laquelle cette dernière demande à la Cour de dire et juger que:

> «en appliquant des règles de leur droit interne, notamment la doctrine dite de la «carence procédurale», qui ont empêché Karl et Walter LaGrand de faire valoir leurs réclamations au titre de la convention de Vienne sur les relations consulaires, et en procédant finalement à leur exécution, les Etats-Unis ont violé l'obligation juridique internationale, dont ils étaient tenus à l'égard de l'Allemagne en vertu du paragraphe 2 de l'article 36 de la convention de Vienne, de permettre la pleine réalisation des fins pour lesquelles sont prévus les droits énoncés à l'article 36 de ladite convention».

80. L'Allemagne soutient que, aux termes du paragraphe 2 de l'article 36 de la convention de Vienne,

> «les Etats-Unis ont l'obligation de faire en sorte que leurs «lois et règlements [internes] ... permet[tent] la pleine réalisation des fins pour lesquelles les droits sont accordés en vertu du présent article» [et qu'ils] manquent à cette obligation en faisant observer des règles de droit interne qui rendent impossible l'invocation d'un moyen tiré de la violation du droit à la notification au consulat lors de la procédure consécutive à la déclaration de culpabilité d'un accusé ou d'un prévenu par un jury».

81. L'Allemagne souligne que la règle de la «carence procédurale» est l'une des règles du droit interne des Etats-Unis dont l'application rend impossible l'invocation d'un moyen tiré de la violation du droit à la notification. Selon l'Allemagne, cette règle «est étroitement liée à la séparation des compétences entre les juridictions fédérales et les juridictions des Etats qui prévaut aux Etats-Unis ... [où la] compétence pénale revient aux Etats fédérés, sauf dans les cas prévus par la constitution». Ladite règle, expose l'Allemagne, exige «l'épuisement des voies de recours internes au niveau de l'Etat fédéré avant qu'un recours tendant à l'obtention d'une ordonnance d'*habeas corpus* ne puisse être introduit devant les juridictions fédérales».

L'Allemagne souligne que ce n'est pas la règle de la «carence procédurale» en tant que telle qui est en question dans la présente instance mais la manière dont elle a été appliquée en ce sens qu'elle «a privé les frères LaGrand de la possibilité de soulever, dans le cadre de procédures pénales devant les instances judiciaires des Etats-Unis, les moyens tirés de la violation de leur droit d'avertir leur consulat».

82. Par ailleurs, ayant examiné la jurisprudence pertinente des Etats-Unis, l'Allemagne soutient que la règle de la carence procédurale «a empêché les frères LaGrand de soulever la question de l'absence de notification adressée au consulat après avoir enfin eu connaissance de leurs droits et pris contact avec le consulat d'Allemagne à Los Angeles en 1992».

83. Finally, Germany states that it seeks

> "[n]othing . . . more than compliance, or, at least, a system in place which does not automatically reproduce violation after violation of the Vienna Convention, only interrupted by the apologies of the United States Government".

84. The United States objects to Germany's second submission, since it considers that "Germany's position goes far beyond the wording of the Convention, the intentions of the parties when it was negotiated, and the practice of States, including Germany's practice".

85. In the view of the United States:

> "[t]he Vienna Convention does not require States Party to create a national law remedy permitting individuals to assert claims involving the Convention in criminal proceedings. If there is no such requirement, it cannot violate the Convention to require that efforts to assert such claims be presented to the first court capable of adjudicating them".

According to the United States,

> "[i]f there is no obligation under the Convention to create such individual remedies in criminal proceedings, the rule of procedural default — requiring that claims seeking such remedies be asserted at an appropriately early stage — cannot violate the Convention".

86. The United States believes that Article 36, paragraph 2, "has a very clear meaning" and

> "means, as it says, that the rights referred to in paragraph 1 shall be exercised in conformity with the laws and regulations of the receiving State, subject to the proviso that said laws and regulations must enable full effect to be given to the purposes for which the rights accorded under the Article are intended".

In the view of the United States,

> "[i]n the context of a foreign national in detention, the relevant laws and regulations contemplated by Article 36 (2) are those that may affect the exercise of specific rights under Article 36 (1), such as those addressing the timing of communications, visiting hours, and security in a detention facility. There is no suggestion in the text of Article 36 (2) that the rules of criminal law and procedure under which a defendant would be tried or have his conviction and sentence reviewed by appellate courts are also within the scope of this provision."

83. L'Allemagne indique enfin qu'elle ne demande

> «rien de plus que le respect de la convention de Vienne ou du moins la mise en place d'un régime qui ne permette pas la violation automatique et répétée de la convention, avec, pour seule interruption, les excuses du Gouvernement des Etats-Unis».

84. Les Etats-Unis s'opposent à la deuxième conclusion de l'Allemagne, car ils estiment que «la prétention de l'Allemagne va bien au-delà du texte de la convention, de l'intention des parties lorsqu'elles l'ont négociée et de la pratique des Etats, y compris celle de l'Allemagne».

85. De l'avis des Etats-Unis, en effet,

> «[l]a convention de Vienne n'oblige pas les Etats qui y sont parties à instituer dans leur droit interne un recours permettant aux particuliers d'invoquer dans des procédures pénales des griefs fondés sur la convention [, et, à] défaut d'une telle obligation, exiger de faire valoir ces griefs devant la première juridiction susceptible d'en connaître ne saurait emporter violation de la convention».

Selon les Etats-Unis,

> «[s]i la convention n'impose aucune obligation d'accorder de telles mesures de réparation à des individus dans des poursuites pénales, la règle de la carence procédurale — qui exige de faire valoir le plus tôt possible et au moment approprié les moyens visant à obtenir de telles mesures de réparation — ne saurait par conséquent violer la convention».

86. Les Etats-Unis considèrent que le paragraphe 2 de l'article 36 «a un sens très clair» et qu'il

> «signifie, comme dit le texte lui-même, que les droits visés au paragraphe 1 doivent s'exercer dans le cadre des lois et règlements de l'Etat de résidence, étant entendu, toutefois, que ces lois et règlements doivent permettre la pleine réalisation des fins pour lesquelles les droits sont accordés en vertu de l'article».

De leur point de vue,

> «[d]ans le cas d'un ressortissant étranger détenu, les lois et règlements applicables visés au paragraphe 2 de l'article 36 sont ceux qui peuvent avoir une incidence sur l'exercice des droits expressément reconnus au paragraphe 1 de cette disposition, par exemple les lois et règlements concernant le moment choisi pour procéder aux communications, les heures de visite et la sécurité dans l'établissement de détention. Rien n'indique dans le texte du paragraphe 2 de l'article 36 que les règles de droit pénal et de procédure pénale en vertu desquelles un accusé serait jugé ou ferait réexaminer par les juridictions d'appel la déclaration de culpabilité et la peine prononcées à son encontre entrent également dans les prévisions de cette disposition.»

87. The United States concludes that Germany's second submission must be rejected "because it is premised on a misinterpretation of Article 36, paragraph 2, which reads the context of the provision — the exercise of a right under paragraph 1 — out of existence".

88. Article 36, paragraph 2, of the Vienna Convention reads as follows:

> "The rights referred to in paragraph 1 of this article shall be exercised in conformity with the laws and regulations of the receiving State, subject to the proviso, however, that the said laws and regulations must enable full effect to be given to the purposes for which the rights accorded under this article are intended."

89. The Court cannot accept the argument of the United States which proceeds, in part, on the assumption that paragraph 2 of Article 36 applies only to the rights of the sending State and not also to those of the detained individual. The Court has already determined that Article 36, paragraph 1, creates individual rights for the detained person in addition to the rights accorded the sending State, and that consequently the reference to "rights" in paragraph 2 must be read as applying not only to the rights of the sending State, but also to the rights of the detained individual (see paragraph 77 above).

90. Turning now to the "procedural default" rule, the application of which in the present case Germany alleges violated Article 36, paragraph 2, the Court emphasizes that a distinction must be drawn between that rule as such and its specific application in the present case. In itself, the rule does not violate Article 36 of the Vienna Convention. The problem arises when the procedural default rule does not allow the detained individual to challenge a conviction and sentence by claiming, in reliance on Article 36, paragraph 1, of the Convention, that the competent national authorities failed to comply with their obligation to provide the requisite consular information "without delay", thus preventing the person from seeking and obtaining consular assistance from the sending State.

91. In this case, Germany had the right at the request of the LaGrands "to arrange for [their] legal representation" and was eventually able to provide some assistance to that effect. By that time, however, because of the failure of the American authorities to comply with their obligation under Article 36, paragraph 1 *(b)*, the procedural default rule prevented counsel for the LaGrands to effectively challenge their convictions and sentences other than on United States constitutional grounds. As a result, although United States courts could and did examine the professional competence of counsel assigned to the indigent LaGrands by reference to United States constitutional standards, the procedural default rule prevented them from attaching any legal significance to the fact, *inter alia*, that the violation of the rights set forth in Article 36, paragraph 1, prevented Germany, in a timely fashion, from retaining private counsel for

87. Les Etats-Unis concluent que la deuxième conclusion de l'Allemagne doit être rejetée «parce qu'elle se fonde sur une interprétation erronée du paragraphe 2 de l'article 36, qui ferait complètement abstraction du contexte de cette disposition — l'exercice d'un droit en application du paragraphe 1».

88. Le paragraphe 2 de l'article 36 de la convention de Vienne est ainsi libellé:

> «Les droits visés au paragraphe 1 du présent article doivent s'exercer dans le cadre des lois et règlements de l'Etat de résidence, étant entendu, toutefois, que ces lois et règlements doivent permettre la pleine réalisation des fins pour lesquelles les droits sont accordés en vertu du présent article.»

89. La Cour ne saurait retenir l'argument des Etats-Unis qui repose en partie sur l'hypothèse que le paragraphe 2 de l'article 36 ne s'applique qu'aux droits de l'Etat d'envoi et non à ceux de la personne mise en détention. La Cour a déjà établi que le paragraphe 1 de l'article 36 crée des droits individuels pour les personnes détenues, en sus des droits accordés à l'Etat d'envoi, et que, par voie de conséquence, les «droits» visés au paragraphe 2 désignent non seulement les droits de l'Etat d'envoi, mais aussi ceux des personnes détenues (voir paragraphe 77 ci-dessus).

90. S'agissant de la règle de la «carence procédurale», dont l'application dans la présente affaire a constitué, selon l'Allemagne, une violation du paragraphe 2 de l'article 36, la Cour tient à souligner qu'il y a lieu d'établir une distinction entre cette règle en tant que telle et son application en l'espèce. En elle-même, cette règle ne viole pas l'article 36 de la convention de Vienne. Le problème se pose lorsque la règle de la carence procédurale ne permet pas à une personne détenue de faire recours contre sa condamnation et sa peine en prétendant, sur la base du paragraphe 1 de l'article 36 de la convention, que les autorités nationales compétentes ne se seraient pas acquittées de leur obligation d'informer «sans retard» les autorités consulaires compétentes, empêchant par là même cette personne de solliciter et d'obtenir l'assistance consulaire de l'Etat d'envoi.

91. En l'espèce, l'Allemagne avait le droit, à la demande des frères LaGrand, «de pourvoir à [leur] représentation en justice» et elle a été finalement en mesure de le faire. Toutefois, à l'époque, du fait du manquement des autorités américaines à leurs obligations aux termes de l'alinéa *b)* du paragraphe 1 de l'article 36, la règle de la carence procédurale a empêché les avocats des LaGrand de remettre en cause de façon efficace, si ce n'est sur la base du droit constitutionnel des Etats-Unis, leurs condamnations et leurs peines. En conséquence, bien que les tribunaux américains fussent habilités à examiner, au regard des normes constitutionnelles des Etats-Unis, la compétence professionnelle des avocats des frères LaGrand commis d'office en raison de l'indigence de ces derniers, et bien qu'ils eussent procédé à cet examen, la règle de la carence procédurale les empêchait d'attacher des conséquences juridiques au fait,

them and otherwise assisting in their defence as provided for by the Convention. Under these circumstances, the procedural default rule had the effect of preventing "full effect [from being] given to the purposes for which the rights accorded under this article are intended", and thus violated paragraph 2 of Article 36.

* *

92. The Court will now consider Germany's third submission, in which it asks the Court to adjudge and declare:

> "that the United States, by failing to take all measures at its disposal to ensure that Walter LaGrand was not executed pending the final decision of the International Court of Justice on the matter, violated its international legal obligation to comply with the Order on provisional measures issued by the Court on 3 March 1999, and to refrain from any action which might interfere with the subject matter of a dispute while judicial proceedings are pending".

93. In its Memorial, Germany contended that "[p]rovisional [m]easures indicated by the International Court of Justice [were] binding by virtue of the law of the United Nations Charter and the Statute of the Court". In support of its position, Germany developed a number of arguments in which it referred to the "principle of effectiveness", to the "procedural prerequisites" for the adoption of provisional measures, to the binding nature of provisional measures as a "necessary consequence of the bindingness of the final decision", to "Article 94 (1), of the United Nations Charter", to "Article 41 (1), of the Statute of the Court" and to the "practice of the Court".

Referring to the duty of the "parties to a dispute before the Court . . . to preserve its subject-matter", Germany added that:

> "[a]part from having violated its duties under Art. 94 (1) of the United Nations Charter and Art. 41 (1) of the Statute, the United States has also violated the obligation to refrain from any action which might interfere with the subject-matter of a dispute while judicial proceedings are pending".

At the hearings, Germany further stated the following:

> "A judgment by the Court on jurisdiction or merits cannot be treated on exactly the same footing as a provisional measure . . . Article 59 and Article 60 [of the Statute] do not apply to provisional measures or, to be more exact, apply to them only by implication; that is to say, to the extent that such measures, being both incidental

notamment, que la violation des droits prévus au paragraphe 1 de l'article 36 n'avait pas permis à l'Allemagne d'assurer en temps opportun aux frères LaGrand le concours d'avocats privés et de les assister, de manière générale, dans leur défense, comme le prévoit la convention. Dans ces conditions, la règle de la carence procédurale a eu pour effet d'empêcher «la pleine réalisation des fins pour lesquelles les droits sont accordés en vertu du présent article» et a ainsi violé les dispositions du paragraphe 2 de l'article 36.

* *

92. La Cour passera maintenant à l'examen de la troisième conclusion de l'Allemagne, par laquelle cette dernière prie la Cour de dire et juger que:

> «en ne prenant pas toutes les mesures dont ils disposaient pour que Walter LaGrand ne soit pas exécuté tant que la Cour internationale de Justice n'aurait pas rendu sa décision définitive en l'affaire, les Etats-Unis ont violé leur obligation juridique internationale de se conformer à l'ordonnance en indication de mesures conservatoires rendue par la Cour le 3 mars 1999 et de s'abstenir de tout acte pouvant interférer avec l'objet d'un différend tant que l'instance est en cours».

93. Dans son mémoire, l'Allemagne a soutenu que «[l]es mesures conservatoires indiquées par la Cour internationale de Justice [avaient] force obligatoire en vertu du droit établi par la Charte des Nations Unies et le Statut de la Cour». A l'appui de sa thèse, l'Allemagne a développé plusieurs arguments en se référant au «principe de l'effet utile», aux «conditions de procédure pour l'adoption des mesures conservatoires», au caractère obligatoire des mesures conservatoires comme «conséquence nécessaire du caractère obligatoire de l'arrêt définitif», au «paragraphe 1 de l'article 94 de la Charte des Nations Unies», au «paragraphe 1 de l'article 41 du Statut de la Cour», ainsi qu'à la «pratique de la Cour».

Mentionnant l'obligation qu'auraient les «parties à un différend devant la Cour ... de préserver son objet», l'Allemagne a ajouté que:

> «[m]is à part le manquement aux obligations qui leur incombent en vertu du paragraphe 1 de l'article 94 de la Charte des Nations Unies et du paragraphe 1 de l'article 41 du Statut, les Etats-Unis ont également manqué à leur obligation de s'abstenir de tout acte pouvant interférer avec l'objet d'un différend tant que l'instance est en cours».

A l'audience, l'Allemagne a en outre précisé ce qui suit:

> «On ne peut pas mettre totalement sur le même pied un jugement de la Cour intervenant sur sa compétence ou sur le fond et une mesure conservatoire ... l'article 59 et l'article 60 [du Statut] ne s'appliquent pas aux mesures conservatoires ou plus exactement ... ne s'y appliquent que par implication; c'est-à-dire dans la mesure, à la

and provisional, contribute to the exercise of a judicial function whose end-result is, by definition, the delivery of a judicial decision. There is here an inherent logic in the judicial procedure, and to disregard it would be tantamount, as far as the Parties are concerned, to deviating from the principle of good faith and from what the German pleadings call 'the principle of institutional effectiveness' . . . [P]rovisional measures . . . are indeed legal decisions, but they are decisions of procedure . . . Since their decisional nature is, however, implied by the logic of urgency and by the need to safeguard the effectiveness of the proceedings, they accordingly create genuine legal obligations on the part of those to whom they are addressed."

94. Germany claims that the United States committed a threefold violation of the Court's Order of 3 March 1999:

"(1) Immediately after the International Court of Justice had rendered its Order on Provisional Measures, Germany appealed to the US Supreme Court in order to reach a stay of the execution of Walter LaGrand, in accordance with the International Court's Order to the same effect. In the course of these proceedings — and in full knowledge of the Order of the International Court — the Office of the Solicitor General, a section of the US Department of Justice — in a letter to the Supreme Court argued once again that: 'an order of the International Court of Justice indicating provisional measures is not binding and does not furnish a basis for judicial relief'.

This statement of a high-ranking official of the Federal Government . . . had a direct influence on the decision of the Supreme Court.

. . . .

(2) In the following, the US Supreme Court — an agency of the United States — refused by a majority vote to order that the execution be stayed. In doing so, it rejected the German arguments based essentially on the Order of the International Court of Justice on Provisional Measures . . .

(3) Finally, the Governor of Arizona did not order a stay of the execution of Walter LaGrand although she was vested with the right to do so by the laws of the State of Arizona. Moreover, in the present case, the Arizona Executive Board of Clemency — for the first time in the history of this institution — had issued a recommendation for a temporary stay, not least in light of the international legal issues involved in the case . . ."

95. The United States argues that it "did what was called for by the Court's 3 March Order, given the extraordinary and unprecedented cir-

fois incidente et provisoire, où elles contribuent à l'exercice d'une fonction judiciaire dont le résultat final est, par définition, le prononcé d'une décision de justice. C'est là qu'il y a une logique inhérente à la procédure judiciaire dont la méconnaissance équivaudrait pour les Parties à s'écarter de la bonne foi et de ce que les écritures allemandes appellent *« the principle of institutional effectiveness »*... [L]es mesures conservatoires ... sont bien des décisions juridiques, mais des décisions de procédure... Leur caractère décisoire étant cependant impliqué par la logique de l'urgence et la nécessité de sauvegarder l'efficacité de la procédure, elles créent par conséquent des obligations proprement juridiques à la charge de leurs destinataires. »

94. L'Allemagne prétend que les Etats-Unis ont commis une triple violation de l'ordonnance de la Cour du 3 mars 1999:

« 1) Immédiatement après que la Cour internationale de Justice a rendu son ordonnance en indication de mesures conservatoires, l'Allemagne s'est adressée à la Cour suprême des Etats-Unis afin d'obtenir un sursis à l'exécution de Walter LaGrand, conformément à l'ordonnance de la Cour internationale de Justice qui tendait à la même fin. Au cours de cette procédure, et en parfaite connaissance de l'ordonnance de la Cour, le bureau du *Solicitor General*, un service relevant du département de la justice des Etats-Unis, a avancé une nouvelle fois, dans une lettre adressée à la Cour suprême, qu'« une ordonnance en indication de mesures conservatoires émanant de la Cour internationale de Justice n'a pas force obligatoire et n'ouvre pas de recours susceptible d'être exercé en justice ».

Cette déclaration émanant d'un haut fonctionnaire du gouvernement fédéral ... a exercé une influence directe sur la décision de la Cour suprême.

. . . .

2) Par la suite, la Cour suprême des Etats-Unis (organe institutionnel des Etats-Unis) a refusé, par un vote à la majorité, d'ordonner un sursis à l'exécution. Ce faisant, elle a rejeté les arguments de l'Allemagne qui étaient fondés essentiellement sur l'ordonnance en indication de mesures conservatoires de la Cour internationale de Justice...

3) Enfin, le gouverneur de l'Arizona n'a pas ordonné le sursis à l'exécution de Walter LaGrand bien qu'il ait été en droit de le faire en vertu de la loi de l'Etat d'Arizona. Par ailleurs, en la présente affaire, la commission des grâces de l'Arizona a, pour la première fois dans son histoire, recommandé le sursis à titre temporaire, en particulier au vu des questions de droit international soulevées en l'espèce... »

95. Les Etats-Unis soutiennent qu'ils « se sont conformés à l'ordonnance de la Cour du 3 mars compte tenu des circonstances extraordi-

cumstances in which it was forced to act". It points out in this connection that the United States Government "immediately transmitt[ed] the Order to the Governor of Arizona", that "the United States placed the Order in the hands of the one official who, at that stage, might have had legal authority to stop the execution" and that by a letter from the Legal Counsellor of the United States Embassy in The Hague dated 8 March 1999, it informed the International Court of Justice of all the measures which had been taken in implementation of the Order.

The United States further states that:

> "[t]wo central factors constrained the United States ability to act. The first was the extraordinarily short time between issuance of the Court's Order and the time set for the execution of Walter LaGrand . . .
>
> . . . .
>
> The second constraining factor was the character of the United States of America as a federal republic of divided powers."

96. The United States also alleges that the "terms of the Court's 3 March Order did not create legal obligations binding on [it]". It argues in this respect that "[t]he language used by the Court in the key portions of its Order is not the language used to create binding legal obligations" and that

> "the Court does not need here to decide the difficult and controversial legal question of whether its orders indicating provisional measures would be capable of creating international legal obligations if worded in mandatory . . . terms".

It nevertheless maintains that those orders cannot have such effects and, in support of that view, develops arguments concerning "the language and history of Article 41 (1) of the Court's Statute and Article 94 of the Charter of the United Nations", the "Court's and State practice under these provisions", and the "weight of publicists' commentary".

Concerning Germany's argument based on the "principle of effectiveness", the United States contends that

> "[i]n an arena where the concerns and sensitivities of States, and not abstract logic, have informed the drafting of the Court's constitutive documents, it is perfectly understandable that the Court might have the power to issue binding final judgments, but a more circumscribed authority with respect to provisional measures".

Referring to Germany's argument that the United States "violated the obligation to refrain from any action which might interfere with the subnaires et inédites dans lesquelles ils ont été contraints d'agir». Ils soulignent à cet égard que le Gouvernement des Etats-Unis a transmis «immédiatement l'ordonnance au gouverneur de l'Arizona»; que «les Etats-Unis ont remis celle-ci entre les mains du seul responsable qui, à ce stade, aurait pu encore avoir légalement le pouvoir d'empêcher l'exécution»; et que, par une lettre du 8 mars 1999 émanant du conseiller juridique de l'ambassade des Etats-Unis à La Haye, ils ont porté à la connaissance de la Cour internationale de Justice toutes les mesures qui avaient été prises en application de l'ordonnance.

Les Etats-Unis précisent en outre ce qui suit:

> «[d]eux éléments principaux réduisaient la capacité d'agir des Etats-Unis. Il y avait tout d'abord le délai extrêmement bref entre le prononcé de l'ordonnance de la Cour et l'heure fixée pour l'exécution de Walter LaGrand...
>
> . . . .
>
> Le deuxième obstacle était la nature même des Etats-Unis d'Amérique en tant que république fédérale au sein de laquelle les pouvoirs sont partagés.»

96. Les Etats-Unis avancent également que le «libellé de l'ordonnance de la Cour du 3 mars n'a pas créé d'obligations juridiques contraignantes pour [eux]». Ils font valoir à cet égard que «[l]es termes employés par la Cour dans les passages clés de son ordonnance ne sont pas de ceux qui sont utilisés pour créer des obligations juridiques contraignantes» et que

> «[p]oint n'est ... besoin en l'espèce pour la Cour de trancher la question juridique difficile et controversée de savoir si ses ordonnances en indication de mesures conservatoires sont susceptibles de donner naissance à des obligations juridiques internationales si elles sont exprimées en des termes impératifs...».

Ils n'en soutiennent pas moins que ces ordonnances ne peuvent avoir de tels effets et, à l'appui de cette thèse, développent des arguments portant sur «le libellé et la genèse du paragraphe 1 de l'article 41 du Statut de la Cour et de l'article 94 de la Charte des Nations Unies», la «pratique de la Cour et des Etats au regard de ces dispositions» ainsi que sur l'«autorité de la doctrine des publicistes».

Concernant l'argument de l'Allemagne tiré du «principe de l'effet utile», les Etats-Unis prétendent que

> «[d]ans un domaine où ce sont les préoccupations et les susceptibilités des Etats et non la logique abstraite qui ont guidé la rédaction des actes constitutifs de la Cour, il est parfaitement compréhensible que celle-ci puisse avoir le pouvoir de rendre des arrêts définitifs obligatoires, mais ait un pouvoir plus restreint en ce qui concerne l'indication de mesures conservatoires».

Se référant à l'argument de l'Allemagne selon lequel ils auraient «manqué à leur obligation de s'abstenir de tout acte pouvant interférer avec ject matter of a dispute while judicial proceedings are pending", the United States further asserts that:

> "The implications of the rule as presented by Germany are potentially quite dramatic, however. Germany appears to contend that by merely filing a case with the Court, an Applicant can force a Respondent to refrain from continuing any action that the Applicant deems to affect the subject of the dispute. If the law were as Germany contends, the entirety of the Court's rules and practices relating to provisional measures would be surplussage. This is not the law, and this is not how States or this Court have acted in practice."

97. Lastly, the United States states that in any case, "[b]ecause of the press of time stemming from Germany's last-minute filing of the case, basic principles fundamental to the judicial process were not observed in connection with the Court's 3 March Order" and that

> "[t]hus, whatever one might conclude regarding a general rule for provisional measures, it would be anomalous — to say the least — for the Court to construe this Order as a source of binding legal obligations".

98. Neither the Permanent Court of International Justice, nor the present Court to date, has been called upon to determine the legal effects of orders made under Article 41 of the Statute. As Germany's third submission refers expressly to an international legal obligation "to comply with the Order on Provisional Measures issued by the Court on 3 March 1999", and as the United States disputes the existence of such an obligation, the Court is now called upon to rule expressly on this question.

99. The dispute which exists between the Parties with regard to this point essentially concerns the interpretation of Article 41, which is worded in identical terms in the Statute of each Court (apart from the respective references to the Council of the League of Nations and the Security Council). This interpretation has been the subject of extensive controversy in the literature. The Court will therefore now proceed to the interpretation of Article 41 of the Statute. It will do so in accordance with customary international law, reflected in Article 31 of the 1969 Vienna Convention on the Law of Treaties. According to paragraph 1 of Article 31, a treaty must be interpreted in good faith in accordance with the ordinary meaning to be given to its terms in their context and in the light of the treaty's object and purpose.

100. The French text of Article 41 reads as follows:

> "1. La Cour a le pouvoir d'*indiquer*, si elle estime que les circons-

l'objet d'un différend tant que l'instance est en cours», les Etats-Unis font en outre valoir ce qui suit:

> «Les conséquences découlant de la règle formulée par l'Allemagne peuvent être tout à fait extraordinaires. Celle-ci semble affirmer qu'un requérant pourrait, par la simple saisine de la Cour, forcer un défendeur à s'abstenir dans le futur de tout acte qui, selon le demandeur, serait susceptible d'affecter l'objet du différend. Si tel était l'état du droit, l'ensemble des règles et pratiques de la Cour relatives aux mesures conservatoires seraient surabondantes. Telle n'est pas la règle de droit et telle n'est pas davantage l'attitude que les Etats ou la Cour ont adoptée en pratique.»

97. Enfin, les Etats-Unis exposent qu'en tout état de cause «[l]e dépôt au dernier moment de la requête par l'Allemagne, qui n'a laissé aucun temps pour réagir, a fait que les principes fondamentaux du règlement judiciaire n'ont pu être respectés dans le cas de l'ordonnance rendue le 3 mars par la Cour» et que

> «[d]ès lors, quelle que soit la conclusion à laquelle on puisse parvenir au sujet d'un principe général applicable aux mesures conservatoires, il serait à tout le moins anormal pour la Cour de voir dans l'ordonnance qui nous occupe en l'espèce une source d'obligations juridiques contraignantes».

98. A ce jour, ni la Cour permanente de Justice internationale ni la présente Cour n'ont été appelées à se prononcer sur les effets juridiques des ordonnances qu'elles ont rendues en vertu de l'article 41 du Statut. Etant donné que la troisième conclusion de l'Allemagne se réfère expressément à une obligation juridique internationale «de se conformer à l'ordonnance en indication de mesures conservatoires rendue par la Cour le 3 mars 1999» et que les Etats-Unis contestent l'existence d'une telle obligation, la Cour est maintenant appelée à se prononcer expressément sur cette question.

99. Le différend existant à cet égard entre les Parties concerne essentiellement l'interprétation de l'article 41, qui est libellé en termes identiques dans le Statut des deux Cours (sous réserve de la référence faite respectivement au Conseil de la Société des Nations et au Conseil de sécurité). Cette interprétation a fait l'objet d'abondantes controverses doctrinales. La Cour passera donc maintenant à l'interprétation de l'article 41 du Statut. Elle procédera à cette interprétation conformément au droit international coutumier qui a trouvé son expression dans l'article 31 de la convention de Vienne de 1969 sur le droit des traités. Selon le paragraphe 1 de l'article 31, un traité doit être interprété de bonne foi suivant le sens ordinaire à attribuer à ses termes dans leur contexte et à la lumière de son objet et de son but.

100. Le texte français de l'article 41 se lit comme suit:

> «1. La Cour a le pouvoir d'*indiquer*, si elle estime que les circons-

tances l'exigent, quelles mesures conservatoires du droit de chacun *doivent* être prises à titre provisoire.

2. En attendant l'arrêt définitif, l'*indication* de ces mesures est immédiatement notifiée aux parties et au Conseil de sécurité." (Emphasis added.)

In this text, the terms "indiquer" and "l'indication" may be deemed to be neutral as to the mandatory character of the measure concerned; by contrast the words "doivent être prises" have an imperative character.

For its part, the English version of Article 41 reads as follows:

"1. The Court shall have the power to *indicate*, if it considers that circumstances so require, any provisional measures which *ought* to be taken to preserve the respective rights of either party.

2. Pending the final decision, notice of the measures *suggested* shall forthwith be given to the parties and to the Security Council." (Emphasis added.)

According to the United States, the use in the English version of "indicate" instead of "order", of "ought" instead of "must" or "shall", and of "suggested" instead of "ordered", is to be understood as implying that decisions under Article 41 lack mandatory effect. It might however be argued, having regard to the fact that in 1920 the French text was the original version, that such terms as "indicate" and "ought" have a meaning equivalent to "order" and "must" or "shall".

101. Finding itself faced with two texts which are not in total harmony, the Court will first of all note that according to Article 92 of the Charter, the Statute "forms an integral part of the present Charter". Under Article 111 of the Charter, the French and English texts of the latter are "equally authentic". The same is equally true of the Statute.

In cases of divergence between the equally authentic versions of the Statute, neither it nor the Charter indicates how to proceed. In the absence of agreement between the parties in this respect, it is appropriate to refer to paragraph 4 of Article 33 of the Vienna Convention on the Law of Treaties, which in the view of the Court again reflects customary international law. This provision reads "when a comparison of the authentic texts discloses a difference of meaning which the application of Articles 31 and 32 does not remove the meaning which best reconciles the texts, having regard to the object and purpose of the treaty, shall be adopted".

The Court will therefore now consider the object and purpose of the Statute together with the context of Article 41.

102. The object and purpose of the Statute is to enable the Court to fulfil the functions provided for therein, and, in particular, the basic function of judicial settlement of international disputes by binding decisions in accordance with Article 59 of the Statute. The context in which Article 41 has to be seen within the Statute is to prevent the Court from

tances l'exigent, quelles mesures conservatoires du droit de chacun *doivent* être prises à titre provisoire.

2. En attendant l'arrêt définitif, l'*indication* de ces mesures est immédiatement notifiée aux parties et au Conseil de sécurité.» (Les italiques sont de la Cour.)

Dans ce texte les termes «indiquer» et «l'indication» peuvent être considérés comme neutres au regard du caractère obligatoire des mesures en question; en revanche les mots «doivent être prises» ont un caractère impératif.

Quant à elle, la version anglaise de l'article 41 se lit comme suit:

«1. The Court shall have the power to *indicate*, if it considers that circumstances so require, any provisional measures which *ought* to be taken, to preserve the respective rights of either party.

2. Pending the final decision, notice of the measures *suggested* shall forthwith be given to the parties and to the Security Council.» (Les italiques sont de la Cour.)

Selon les Etats-Unis, l'emploi dans la version anglaise des verbes «indicate» au lieu de «order», «ought» au lieu de «must» ou «shall», et «suggested» au lieu de «ordered» impliquerait que les décisions prises au titre de l'article 41 ne revêtent pas un caractère obligatoire. On pourrait cependant faire valoir, compte tenu du fait que la version française a été en 1920 la version originelle, que des verbes tels que «indicate» et «ought» ont un sens qui est équivalent à «order» et «must» ou «shall».

101. Se trouvant en présence de deux textes qui ne sont pas en totale harmonie, la Cour notera tout d'abord que, selon l'article 92 de la Charte, le Statut «fait partie intégrante» de la Charte. En vertu de l'article 111 de la Charte, les versions française et anglaise de celle-ci font «également foi». Il en va donc de même pour le Statut.

En cas de divergence entre des versions faisant foi du Statut, ni celui-ci ni la Charte n'indiquent la manière de procéder. En l'absence d'accord entre les parties à cet égard, il convient donc de se référer aux dispositions du paragraphe 4 de l'article 33 de la convention de Vienne sur le droit des traités qui, de l'avis de la Cour, reflète là encore le droit international coutumier. Aux termes de cette disposition, «lorsque la comparaison des textes authentiques fait apparaître une différence de sens que l'application des articles 31 et 32 ne permet pas d'éliminer, on adoptera le sens qui, compte tenu de l'objet et du but du traité, concilie le mieux ces textes».

La Cour passera donc maintenant à l'examen de l'objet et du but du Statut, ainsi que du contexte de l'article 41 du Statut.

102. L'objet et le but du Statut sont de permettre à la Cour de remplir les fonctions qui lui sont dévolues par cet instrument, et en particulier de s'acquitter de sa mission fondamentale, qui est le règlement judiciaire des différends internationaux au moyen de décisions obligatoires conformément à l'article 59 du Statut. L'article 41, analysé dans le contexte du Sta-

being hampered in the exercise of its functions because the respective rights of the parties to a dispute before the Court are not preserved. It follows from the object and purpose of the Statute, as well as from the terms of Article 41 when read in their context, that the power to indicate provisional measures entails that such measures should be binding, inasmuch as the power in question is based on the necessity, when the circumstances call for it, to safeguard, and to avoid prejudice to, the rights of the parties as determined by the final judgment of the Court. The contention that provisional measures indicated under Article 41 might not be binding would be contrary to the object and purpose of that Article.

103. A related reason which points to the binding character of orders made under Article 41 and to which the Court attaches importance is the existence of a principle which has already been recognized by the Permanent Court of International Justice when it spoke of

> "the principle universally accepted by international tribunals and likewise laid down in many conventions . . . to the effect that the parties to a case must abstain from any measure capable of exercising a prejudicial effect in regard to the execution of the decision to be given, and, in general, not allow any step of any kind to be taken which might aggravate or extend the dispute" (*Electricity Company of Sofia and Bulgaria, Order of 5 December 1939, P.C.I.J, Series A/B, No. 79*, p. 199).

Furthermore measures designed to avoid aggravating or extending disputes have frequently been indicated by the Court. They were indicated with the purpose of being implemented (see *Nuclear Tests (Australia* v. *France), Interim Protection, Order of 22 June 1973, I.C.J. Reports 1973*, p. 106; *Nuclear Tests (New Zealand* v. *France), Interim Protection, Order of 22 June 1973, I.C.J. Reports 1973*, p. 142; *Frontier Dispute, Provisional Measures, Order of 10 January 1986, I.C.J. Reports 1986*, p. 9, para. 18, and p. 11, para. 32, point 1 A; *Application of the Convention on the Prevention and Punishment of the Crime of Genocide, Provisional Measures, Order of 8 April 1993, I.C.J. Reports 1993*, p. 23, para. 48, and p. 24, para. 52 B; *Application of the Convention on the Prevention and Punishment of the Crime of Genocide, Provisional Measures, Order of 13 September 1993, I.C.J. Reports 1993*, p. 349, para. 57, and p. 350, para. 61 (3); *Land and Maritime Boundary between Cameroon and Nigeria, Provisional Measures, Order of 15 March 1996, I.C.J. Reports 1996 (I)*, pp. 22-23, para. 41, and p. 24, para. 49 (1)).

104. Given the conclusions reached by the Court above in interpreting the text of Article 41 of the Statute in the light of its object and purpose, it does not consider it necessary to resort to the preparatory work in order to determine the meaning of that Article. The Court would nevertheless point out that the preparatory work of the Statute

tut, a pour but d'éviter que la Cour soit empêchée d'exercer ses fonctions du fait de l'atteinte portée aux droits respectifs des parties à un différend soumis à la Cour. Il ressort de l'objet et du but du Statut, ainsi que des termes de l'article 41 lus dans leur contexte, que le pouvoir d'indiquer des mesures conservatoires emporte le caractère obligatoire desdites mesures, dans la mesure où le pouvoir en question est fondé sur la nécessité, lorsque les circonstances l'exigent, de sauvegarder les droits des parties, tels que déterminés par la Cour dans son arrêt définitif, et d'éviter qu'il y soit porté préjudice. Prétendre que des mesures conservatoires indiquées en vertu de l'article 41 ne seraient pas obligatoires serait contraire à l'objet et au but de cette disposition.

103. Un motif connexe qui va dans le sens du caractère obligatoire des ordonnances rendues au titre de l'article 41, et auquel la Cour attache de l'importance, est l'existence d'un principe que la Cour permanente de Justice internationale a déjà reconnu lorsqu'elle a évoqué le

> «principe universellement admis devant les juridictions internationales et consacré d'ailleurs dans maintes conventions ... d'après lequel les parties en cause doivent s'abstenir de toute mesure susceptible d'avoir une répercussion préjudiciable à l'exécution de la décision à intervenir et, en général, ne laisser procéder à aucun acte, de quelque nature qu'il soit, susceptible d'aggraver ou d'étendre le différend» (*Compagnie d'électricité de Sofia et de Bulgarie, ordonnance du 5 décembre 1939, C.P.J.I. série A/B n° 79*, p. 199).

Aussi bien des mesures tendant à éviter l'aggravation ou l'extension des différends ont-elles fréquemment été indiquées par la Cour. Ces mesures étaient destinées à être exécutées (voir *Essais nucléaires (Australie c. France), mesures conservatoires, ordonnance du 22 juin 1973, C.I.J. Recueil 1973*, p. 106; *Essais nucléaires (Nouvelle-Zélande c. France), mesures conservatoires, ordonnance du 22 juin 1973, C.I.J. Recueil 1973*, p. 142; *Différend frontalier, mesures conservatoires, ordonnance du 10 janvier 1986, C.I.J. Recueil 1986*, p. 9, par. 18, et p. 11, par. 32, point 1 A; *Application de la convention pour la prévention et la répression du crime de génocide, mesures conservatoires, ordonnance du 8 avril 1993, C.I.J. Recueil 1993*, p. 23, par. 48, et p. 24, par. 52 B; *Application de la convention pour la prévention et la répression du crime de génocide, mesures conservatoires, ordonnance du 13 septembre 1993, C.I.J. Recueil 1993*, p. 349, par. 57, et p. 350, par. 61, alinéa 3; *Frontière terrestre et maritime entre le Cameroun et le Nigéria, mesures conservatoires, ordonnance du 15 mars 1996, C.I.J. Recueil 1996 (I)*, p. 22-23, par. 41, et p. 24, par. 49, alinéa 1).

104. Compte tenu des conclusions auxquelles la Cour est parvenue ci-dessus en interprétant le texte de l'article 41 du Statut à la lumière de son objet et de son but, elle n'estime pas nécessaire de faire appel aux travaux préparatoires pour déterminer le sens de cet article. La Cour fera néanmoins observer que les travaux préparatoires relatifs au Statut ne

does not preclude the conclusion that orders under Article 41 have binding force.

105. The initial preliminary draft of the Statute of the Permanent Court of International Justice, as prepared by the Committee of Jurists established by the Council of the League of Nations, made no mention of provisional measures. A provision to this effect was inserted only at a later stage in the draft prepared by the Committee, following a proposal from the Brazilian jurist Raul Fernandes.

Basing himself on the Bryan Treaty of 13 October 1914 between the United States and Sweden, Raul Fernandes had submitted the following text:

> "Dans le cas où la cause du différend consiste en actes déterminés déjà effectués ou sur le point de l'être, la Cour pourra ordonner, dans le plus bref délai, à titre provisoire, des mesures conservatoires adéquates, en attendant le jugement définitif." (Comité consultatif de juristes, *Procès-verbaux des séances du comité*, 16 juin-24 juillet 1920 (avec annexes), La Haye, 1920, p. 609.)

In its English translation this text read as follows:

> "In case the cause of the dispute should consist of certain acts already committed or about to be committed, the Court may, provisionally and with the least possible delay, order adequate protective measures to be taken, pending the final judgment of the Court." (Advisory Committee of Jurists, *Procès-verbaux of the Proceedings of the Committee*, 16 June-24 July 1920 (with Annexes), The Hague, 1920, p. 609.)

The Drafting Committee prepared a new version of this text, to which two main amendments were made: on the one hand, the words "la Cour pourra ordonner" ("the Court may . . . order") were replaced by "la Cour a le pouvoir d'indiquer" ("the Court shall have the power to suggest"), while, on the other, a second paragraph was added providing for notice to be given to the parties and to the Council of the "measures suggested" by the Court. The draft Article 2*bis* as submitted by the Drafting Committee thus read as follows:

> "Dans le cas où la cause du différend consiste en un acte effectué ou sur le point de l'être, la Cour a le pouvoir d'indiquer, si elle estime que les circonstances l'exigent, quelles mesures conservatoires du droit de chacun doivent être prises à titre provisoire.
>
> En attendant son arrêt, cette suggestion de la Cour est immédiatement transmise aux parties et au Conseil." (Comité consultatif de juristes, *Procès-verbaux des séances du comité*, 16 juin-24 juillet 1920 (avec annexes), La Haye, 1920, p. 567-568.)

The English version read:

> "If the dispute arises out of an act which has already taken place or which is imminent, the Court shall have the power to suggest, if it

s'opposent pas à la conclusion que les ordonnances rendues en vertu de l'article 41 ont force obligatoire.

105. La première version de l'avant-projet de Statut de la Cour permanente de Justice internationale, tel que préparé par le comité de juristes constitué par le Conseil de la Société des Nations, ne traitait pas des mesures conservatoires. Une disposition à cet égard ne fut incorporée que plus tard dans le projet élaboré par le comité, à la suite d'une proposition du juriste brésilien Raul Fernandes.

S'inspirant du traité Bryan conclu le 13 octobre 1914 entre les Etats-Unis et la Suède, Raul Fernandes avait soumis le texte suivant:

> «Dans le cas où la cause du différend consiste en actes déterminés déjà effectués ou sur le point de l'être, la Cour pourra ordonner, dans le plus bref délai, à titre provisoire, des mesures conservatoires adéquates, en attendant le jugement définitif.» (Comité consultatif de juristes, *Procès-verbaux des séances du comité*, 16 juin-24 juillet 1920 (avec annexes), La Haye, 1920, p. 609.)

Dans sa traduction anglaise, ce texte se lisait comme suit:

> «In case the cause of the dispute should consist of certain acts already committed or about to be committed, the Court may, provisionally and with the least possible delay, order adequate protective measures to be taken, pending the final judgment of the Court.» (Advisory Committee of Jurists, *Procès-verbaux of the Proceedings of the Committee*, 16 June-24 July 1920 (with Annexes), The Hague, 1920, p. 609.)

Le comité de rédaction établit une nouvelle version de ce texte auquel deux modifications principales furent apportées: d'une part, l'expression «la Cour pourra ordonner» («the Court may ... order») fut remplacée par «la Cour a le pouvoir d'indiquer» («the Court shall have the power to suggest») et, d'autre part, un second alinéa fut ajouté, prévoyant la transmission aux parties et au Conseil de la «suggestion de la Cour». Le projet d'article 2*bis* du comité de rédaction était en conséquence libellé comme suit:

> «Dans le cas où la cause du différend consiste en un acte effectué ou sur le point de l'être, la Cour a le pouvoir d'indiquer, si elle estime que les circonstances l'exigent, quelles mesures conservatoires du droit de chacun doivent être prises à titre provisoire.
>
> En attendant son arrêt, cette suggestion de la Cour est immédiatement transmise aux parties et au Conseil.» (Comité consultatif de juristes, *Procès-verbaux des séances du comité*, 16 juin-24 juillet 1920 (avec annexes), La Haye, 1920, p. 567-568.)

Sa version anglaise se lisait ainsi:

> «If the dispute arises out of an act which has already taken place or which is imminent, the Court shall have the power to suggest, if it

> considers that circumstances so require, the provisional measures that should be taken to preserve the respective rights of either party.
>
> Pending the final decision, notice of the measures suggested shall forthwith be given to the parties and the Council." (Advisory Committee of Jurists, *Procès-verbaux of the Proceedings of the Committee*, 16 June-24 July 1920 (with Annexes), The Hague, 1920, pp. 567-568.)

The Committee of Jurists eventually adopted a draft Article 39, which amended the former Article 2*bis* only in its French version: in the second paragraph, the words "cette suggestion" were replaced in French by the words "l'indication".

106. When the draft Article 39 was examined by the Sub-Committee of the Third Committee of the first Assembly of the League of Nations, a number of amendments were considered. Raul Fernandes suggested again to use the word "ordonner" in the French version. The Sub-Committee decided to stay with the word "indiquer", the Chairman of the Sub-Committee observing that the Court lacked the means to execute its decisions. The language of the first paragraph of the English version was then made to conform to the French text: thus the word "suggest" was replaced by "indicate", and "should" by "ought to". However, in the second paragraph of the English version, the phrase "measures suggested" remained unchanged.

The provision thus amended in French and in English by the Sub-Committee was adopted as Article 41 of the Statute of the Permanent Court of International Justice. It passed as such into the Statute of the present Court without any discussion in 1945.

107. The preparatory work of Article 41 shows that the preference given in the French text to "indiquer" over "ordonner" was motivated by the consideration that the Court did not have the means to assure the execution of its decisions. However, the lack of means of execution and the lack of binding force are two different matters. Hence, the fact that the Court does not itself have the means to ensure the execution of orders made pursuant to Article 41 is not an argument against the binding nature of such orders.

108. The Court finally needs to consider whether Article 94 of the United Nations Charter precludes attributing binding effect to orders indicating provisional measures. That Article reads as follows:

> "1. Each Member of the United Nations undertakes to comply with the decision of the International Court of Justice in any case to which it is a party.
>
> 2. If any party to a case fails to perform the obligations incumbent upon it under a judgment rendered by the Court, the other party may have recourse to the Security Council, which may, if it

considers that circumstances so require, the provisional measures that should be taken to preserve the respective rights of either party.

Pending the final decision, notice of the measures suggested shall forthwith be given to the parties and the Council.» (Advisory Committee of Jurists, *Procès-verbaux of the Proceedings of the Committee*, 16 June-24 July 1920 (with Annexes), The Hague, 1920, pp. 567-568.)

Le comité de juristes adopta finalement un projet d'article 39, qui ne modifiait l'ancien projet d'article 2*bis* que dans sa version française: au second alinéa, les termes «cette suggestion» furent remplacés par les mots «l'indication».

106. Lorsque la Sous-Commission de la Troisième Commission de la première Assemblée de la Société des Nations examina le projet d'article 39, plusieurs amendements furent considérés. Raul Fernandes suggéra à nouveau d'employer le verbe «ordonner» dans la version française. La Sous-Commission décida de maintenir le verbe «indiquer», le président de la Sous-Commission relevant que la Cour n'avait pas les moyens d'assurer l'exécution de ses décisions. La terminologie utilisée au premier alinéa de la version anglaise fut alignée sur le texte français: ainsi, le mot «suggest» fut remplacé par le terme «indicate», et «should» par «ought to». Toutefois, dans le second alinéa de la version anglaise, l'expression «measures suggested» ne fut pas modifiée.

La disposition ainsi amendée en français et en anglais par la Sous-Commission fut adoptée comme article 41 du Statut de la Cour permanente de Justice internationale. Elle passa comme telle dans le Statut de la présente Cour sans faire l'objet d'aucune discussion en 1945.

107. Les travaux préparatoires de l'article 41 font ainsi apparaître que la préférence donnée dans le texte français au verbe «indiquer» au lieu d'«ordonner» a été motivée par la considération que la Cour n'avait pas les moyens d'assurer l'exécution de ses décisions. Mais l'absence de voies d'exécution et le défaut de caractère obligatoire d'une disposition sont deux questions différentes. Dès lors, le fait que la Cour ne dispose pas de moyens pour assurer elle-même l'exécution des ordonnances prises en vertu de l'article 41 ne constitue pas un argument contre le caractère obligatoire de ces ordonnances.

108. La Cour doit enfin examiner si l'article 94 de la Charte des Nations Unies s'oppose à ce qu'effet obligatoire soit reconnu aux ordonnances indiquant des mesures conservatoires. Cet article se lit comme suit:

«1. Chaque Membre des Nations Unies s'engage à se conformer à la décision de la Cour internationale de Justice dans tout litige auquel il est partie.

2. Si une partie à un litige ne satisfait pas aux obligations qui lui incombent en vertu d'un arrêt rendu par la Cour, l'autre partie peut recourir au Conseil de sécurité et celui-ci, s'il le juge nécessaire, peut

> deems necessary, make recommendations or decide upon measures to be taken to give effect to the judgment."

The question arises as to the meaning to be attributed to the words "the decision of the International Court of Justice" in paragraph 1 of this Article. This wording could be understood as referring not merely to the Court's judgments but to any decision rendered by it, thus including orders indicating provisional measures. It could also be interpreted to mean only judgments rendered by the Court as provided in paragraph 2 of Article 94. In this regard, the fact that in Articles 56 to 60 of the Court's Statute both the word "decision" and the word "judgment" are used does little to clarify the matter.

Under the first interpretation of paragraph 1 of Article 94, the text of the paragraph would confirm the binding nature of provisional measures; whereas the second interpretation would in no way preclude their being accorded binding force under Article 41 of the Statute. The Court accordingly concludes that Article 94 of the Charter does not prevent orders made under Article 41 from having a binding character.

109. In short, it is clear that none of the sources of interpretation referred to in the relevant Articles of the Vienna Convention on the Law of Treaties, including the preparatory work, contradict the conclusions drawn from the terms of Article 41 read in their context and in the light of the object and purpose of the Statute. Thus, the Court has reached the conclusion that orders on provisional measures under Article 41 have binding effect.

*

110. The Court will now consider the Order of 3 March 1999. This Order was not a mere exhortation. It had been adopted pursuant to Article 41 of the Statute. This Order was consequently binding in character and created a legal obligation for the United States.

*

111. As regards the question whether the United States has complied with the obligation incumbent upon it as a result of the Order of 3 March 1999, the Court observes that the Order indicated two provisional measures, the first of which states that

> "[t]he United States of America should take all measures at its disposal to ensure that Walter LaGrand is not executed pending the final decision in these proceedings, and should inform the Court of all the measures which it has taken in implementation of this Order".

The second measure required the Government of the United States to

> faire des recommandations ou décider des mesures à prendre pour faire exécuter l'arrêt.»

La question se pose de savoir quel sens doit être attribué aux mots «la décision de la Cour internationale de Justice» au paragraphe 1 de cet article. Ce libellé pourrait s'entendre comme visant non seulement les arrêts de la Cour, mais toute décision rendue par elle, et s'appliquant ainsi aux ordonnances en indication de mesures conservatoires. Ces mots pourraient aussi être interprétés comme désignant seulement les arrêts rendus par la Cour tels que visés au paragraphe 2 de l'article 94. A cet égard, l'utilisation faite aux articles 56 à 60 du Statut de la Cour des mots «décision» et «arrêt» n'ajoute guère de clarté au débat.

Dans la première interprétation du paragraphe 1 de l'article 94, celui-ci confirmerait le caractère obligatoire des mesures conservatoires; dans la seconde, il ne s'opposerait nullement à ce que ce caractère obligatoire leur soit reconnu au titre de l'article 41 du Statut. La Cour en conclut que l'article 94 de la Charte ne fait en tout état de cause pas obstacle au caractère obligatoire des ordonnances rendues au titre de l'article 41.

109. En définitive, aucune des sources d'interprétation mentionnées dans les articles pertinents de la convention de Vienne sur le droit des traités, y compris les travaux préparatoires, ne contredit les conclusions tirées des termes de l'article 41 lus dans son contexte à la lumière de l'objet et du but du Statut. Ainsi, la Cour parvient à la conclusion que les ordonnances indiquant des mesures conservatoires au titre de l'article 41 ont un caractère obligatoire.

*

110. La Cour passera maintenant à l'examen de l'ordonnance du 3 mars 1999. Celle-ci ne constituait pas une simple exhortation. Elle avait été adoptée en vertu de l'article 41 du Statut. Ladite ordonnance avait par suite un caractère obligatoire et mettait une obligation juridique à la charge des Etats-Unis.

*

111. S'agissant de la question de savoir si les Etats-Unis se sont acquittés de l'obligation découlant pour eux de l'ordonnance du 3 mars 1999, la Cour observe qu'elle a indiqué, dans cette ordonnance, deux mesures conservatoires, dont la première énonce ce qui suit:

> «[l]es Etats-Unis d'Amérique doivent prendre toutes les mesures dont ils disposent pour que M. Walter LaGrand ne soit pas exécuté tant que la décision définitive en la présente instance n'aura pas été rendue, et doivent porter à la connaissance de la Cour toutes les mesures qui auront été prises en application de la présente ordonnance».

Par la seconde mesure indiquée, la Cour demandait aux Etats-Unis de "transmit this Order to the Governor of the State of Arizona". The information required on the measures taken in implementation of this Order was given to the Court by a letter of 8 March 1999 from the Legal Counsellor of the United States Embassy at The Hague. According to this letter, on 3 March 1999 the State Department had transmitted to the Governor of Arizona a copy of the Court's Order. "In view of the extremely late hour of the receipt of the Court's Order", the letter of 8 March went on to say, "no further steps were feasible".

The United States authorities have thus limited themselves to the mere transmission of the text of the Order to the Governor of Arizona. This certainly met the requirement of the second of the two measures indicated. As to the first measure, the Court notes that it did not create an obligation of result, but that the United States was asked to "take all measures at its disposal to ensure that Walter LaGrand is not executed pending the final decision in these proceedings". The Court agrees that due to the extremely late presentation of the request for provisional measures, there was certainly very little time for the United States authorities to act.

112. The Court observes, nevertheless, that the mere transmission of its Order to the Governor of Arizona without any comment, particularly without even so much as a plea for a temporary stay and an explanation that there is no general agreement on the position of the United States that orders of the International Court of Justice on provisional measures are non-binding, was certainly less than could have been done even in the short time available. The same is true of the United States Solicitor General's categorical statement in his brief letter to the United States Supreme Court that "an order of the International Court of Justice indicating provisional measures is not binding and does not furnish a basis for judicial relief" (see paragraph 33 above). This statement went substantially further than the amicus brief referred to in a mere footnote in his letter, which was filed on behalf of the United States in earlier proceedings before the United States Supreme Court in the case of Angel Francisco Breard (see *Breard* v. *Greene*, United States Supreme Court, 14 April 1998, *International Legal Materials*, Vol. 37 (1998), p. 824; Memorial of Germany, Ann. 34). In that amicus brief, the same Solicitor General had declared less than a year earlier that "there is substantial disagreement among jurists as to whether an ICJ order indicating provisional measures is binding . . . The better reasoned position is that such an order is not binding."

113. It is also noteworthy that the Governor of Arizona, to whom the

«transmettre la présente ordonnance au gouverneur de l'Etat de l'Arizona». Les renseignements demandés quant aux mesures prises en application de l'ordonnance ont été fournis à la Cour par une lettre du 8 mars 1999 du conseiller juridique de l'ambassade des Etats-Unis aux Pays-Bas. Aux termes de cette lettre, le département d'Etat a transmis, le 3 mars 1999, copie de l'ordonnance de la Cour au gouverneur de l'Arizona. «Vu l'heure extrêmement tardive à laquelle l'ordonnance de la Cour a été reçue», est-il expliqué dans la lettre du 8 mars, «aucune autre démarche n'a pu être entreprise».

Les autorités des Etats-Unis se sont ainsi limitées à transmettre le texte de l'ordonnance au gouverneur de l'Arizona. C'était là certainement satisfaire aux conditions posées dans la seconde des deux mesures indiquées. Quant à la première mesure, la Cour relève qu'elle ne créait pas une obligation de résultat, mais qu'il était demandé aux Etats-Unis de «prendre toutes les mesures dont ils disposent pour que M. Walter LaGrand ne soit pas exécuté tant que la décision définitive en la présente instance n'aura[it] pas été rendue». La Cour reconnaît que, en raison de la présentation extrêmement tardive de la demande en indication de mesures conservatoires, il est certain que les autorités des Etats-Unis ont disposé de très peu de temps pour agir.

112. La Cour relève néanmoins que la simple transmission de son ordonnance au gouverneur de l'Arizona, sans l'accompagner d'aucun commentaire, sans même demander en particulier de surseoir temporairement à l'exécution et sans expliquer qu'il n'existait pas de consensus sur la position des Etats-Unis selon laquelle les ordonnances de la Cour internationale de Justice indiquant des mesures conservatoires n'ont pas force obligatoire, était assurément très en deçà de ce que l'on aurait pu attendre des autorités des Etats-Unis, dans les délais — si brefs eussent-ils été — dont elles disposaient. Il en va de même de la déclaration catégorique faite par le *Solicitor General*, dans la brève lettre qu'il a adressée à la Cour suprême des Etats-Unis, selon laquelle «une ordonnance de la Cour internationale de Justice en indication de mesures conservatoires ne revêt pas un caractère obligatoire et ne peut fonder un recours susceptible d'être exercé en justice» (voir paragraphe 33 ci-dessus). Cette déclaration allait considérablement plus loin que celle figurant dans le mémoire soumis par les Etats-Unis à titre d'*amicus curiae* dans le cadre d'un recours antérieur devant la Cour suprême des Etats-Unis en l'affaire relative à Angel Francisco Breard (voir *Breard c. Greene*, Cour suprême des Etats-Unis, 14 avril 1998, *International Legal Materials*, vol. 37, 1998, p. 824; mémoire de l'Allemagne, annexe 34), auquel elle se borne à faire référence dans une simple note au bas de sa lettre. Dans ce mémoire, le même *Solicitor General* avait en effet déclaré moins d'un an auparavant que «quant à l'effet obligatoire qu'aurait une ordonnance en indication de mesures conservatoires rendue par la Cour internationale de Justice, les juristes sont profondément divisés sur cette question... La thèse la meilleure est qu'une telle ordonnance n'a pas un caractère obligatoire.»

113. Il y a par ailleurs lieu de relever que le gouverneur de l'Arizona

Court's Order had been transmitted, decided not to give effect to it, even though the Arizona Clemency Board had recommended a stay of execution for Walter LaGrand.

114. Finally, the United States Supreme Court rejected a separate application by Germany for a stay of execution, "[g]iven the tardiness of the pleas and the jurisdictional barriers they implicate". Yet it would have been open to the Supreme Court, as one of its members urged, to grant a preliminary stay, which would have given it "time to consider, after briefing from all interested parties, the jurisdictional and international legal issues involved . . ." (*Federal Republic of Germany et al.* v. *United States et al.*, United States Supreme Court, 3 March 1999).

115. The review of the above steps taken by the authorities of the United States with regard to the Order of the International Court of Justice of 3 March 1999 indicates that the various competent United States authorities failed to take all the steps they could have taken to give effect to the Court's Order. The Order did not require the United States to exercise powers it did not have; but it did impose the obligation to "take all measures at its disposal to ensure that Walter LaGrand is not executed pending the final decision in these proceedings . . .". The Court finds that the United States did not discharge this obligation.

Under these circumstances the Court concludes that the United States has not complied with the Order of 3 March 1999.

116. The Court observes finally that in the third submission Germany requests the Court to adjudge and declare only that the United States violated its international legal obligation to comply with the Order of 3 March 1999; it contains no other request regarding that violation. Moreover, the Court points out that the United States was under great time pressure in this case, due to the circumstances in which Germany had instituted the proceedings. The Court notes moreover that at the time when the United States authorities took their decision the question of the binding character of orders indicating provisional measures had been extensively discussed in the literature, but had not been settled by its jurisprudence. The Court would have taken these factors into consideration had Germany's submission included a claim for indemnification.

* *

117. Finally, the Court will consider Germany's fourth submission, in which it asks the Court to adjudge and declare

> "that the United States shall provide Germany an assurance that it will not repeat its unlawful acts and that, in any future cases of detention of or criminal proceedings against German nationals, the United States will ensure in law and practice the effective exercise of

auquel l'ordonnance de la Cour avait été transmise a décidé de ne pas donner suite à cette ordonnance, alors que la commission des grâces de l'Arizona lui avait recommandé de surseoir à l'exécution de Walter LaGrand.

114. Enfin, la Cour suprême des Etats-Unis a rejeté la demande de l'Allemagne tendant également au sursis à l'exécution, «[e]u égard à la tardiveté de la procédure engagée et aux obstacles d'ordre juridictionnel que cela soulève». Elle eût cependant pu, comme l'un de ses membres le lui avait demandé, ordonner un sursis temporaire qui lui aurait donné «le temps d'étudier, après avoir entendu toutes les parties concernées, les questions juridictionnelles et les questions de droit international en jeu...» (*République fédérale d'Allemagne et autres c. Etats-Unis et autre*, Cour suprême des Etats-Unis, 3 mars 1999).

115. L'examen des mesures prises par les autorités des Etats-Unis et rappelées ci-dessus révèle que les diverses autorités compétentes des Etats-Unis n'ont pas pris toutes les mesures qu'elles auraient pu prendre pour donner effet à l'ordonnance que la Cour internationale de Justice a rendue le 3 mars 1999. Celle-ci n'exigeait pas des Etats-Unis qu'ils exercent des pouvoirs qu'ils n'avaient pas; mais elle leur imposait effectivement l'obligation de «prendre toutes les mesures dont ils disposent pour que M. Walter LaGrand ne soit pas exécuté tant que la décision définitive en la présente instance [n'aurait] pas été rendue...». La Cour estime que les Etats-Unis ne se sont pas acquittés de cette obligation.

Dans ces conditions, la Cour conclut que les Etats-Unis n'ont pas respecté l'ordonnance du 3 mars 1999.

116. La Cour relève finalement que dans sa troisième conclusion l'Allemagne demande seulement à la Cour de dire et juger que les Etats-Unis ont violé leur obligation juridique internationale de se conformer à l'ordonnance du 3 mars 1999; ladite conclusion ne contient pas d'autre demande au sujet de cette violation. De plus, la Cour souligne que les Etats-Unis étaient confrontés en l'espèce à de fortes contraintes de temps, résultant des conditions dans lesquelles l'Allemagne avait introduit l'instance. Elle relève également qu'à l'époque où les autorités des Etats-Unis ont pris leur décision la question du caractère obligatoire des ordonnances en indication de mesures conservatoires avait été abondamment discutée dans la doctrine, mais n'avait pas été tranchée par la jurisprudence. La Cour aurait pris ces facteurs en considération si la conclusion de l'Allemagne avait comporté une demande à fin d'indemnité.

* *

117. La Cour examinera enfin la quatrième conclusion de l'Allemagne, par laquelle cette dernière demande à la Cour de dire et juger que:

> «les Etats-Unis devront donner à l'Allemagne l'assurance qu'ils ne répéteront pas de tels actes illicites et que, dans tous les cas futurs de détention de ressortissants allemands ou d'actions pénales à l'encontre de tels ressortissants, les Etats-Unis veilleront à assurer en droit

> the rights under Article 36 of the Vienna Convention on Consular Relations. In particular in cases involving the death penalty, this requires the United States to provide effective review of and remedies for criminal convictions impaired by a violation of the rights under Article 36."

118. Germany states that:

> "[c]oncerning the requested assurances and guarantees of non-repetition of the United States, they are appropriate because of the existence of a real risk of repetition and the seriousness of the injury suffered by Germany. Further, the choice of means by which full conformity of the future conduct of the United States with Article 36 of the Vienna Convention is to be ensured may be left to the United States."

Germany explains that:

> "the effective exercise of the right to consular notification embodied in [Article 36,] paragraph 2, requires that, where it cannot be excluded that the judgment was impaired by the violation of the right to consular notification, appellate proceedings allow for a reversal of the judgment and for either a retrial or a re-sentencing".

Finally, Germany points out that its fourth submission has been so worded "as to . . . leave the choice of means by which to implement the remedy [it seeks] to the United States".

119. In reply, the United States argues as follows:

> "Germany's fourth submission is clearly of a wholly different nature than its first three submissions. Each of the first three submissions seeks a judgment and declaration by the Court that a violation of a stated international legal obligation has occurred. Such judgments are at the core of the Court's function, as an aspect of reparation.
>
> . . . .
>
> In contrast, however, to the character of the relief sought in the first three submissions, the requirement of assurances of non-repetition sought in the fourth submission has no precedent in the jurisprudence of this Court and would exceed the Court's jurisdiction and authority in this case. It is exceptional even as a non-legal undertaking in State practice, and it would be entirely inappropriate for the Court to require such assurances with respect to the duty to inform undertaken in the Consular Convention in the circumstances of this case."

et en pratique l'exercice effectif des droits visés à l'article 36 de la convention de Vienne sur les relations consulaires. En particulier dans les cas où un accusé est passible de la peine de mort, cela entraîne pour les Etats-Unis l'obligation de prévoir le réexamen effectif des condamnations pénales entachées d'une violation des droits énoncés à l'article 36 de la convention, ainsi que les moyens pour y porter remède.»

118. L'Allemagne expose que:

«[s]'agissant des assurances et garanties de non-répétition à fournir par les Etats-Unis, cette mesure est appropriée en raison de l'existence d'un véritable risque de répétition et de la gravité du préjudice subi par l'Allemagne. En outre, les Etats-Unis peuvent se voir accorder le soin de choisir les moyens permettant d'assurer la pleine conformité de leur comportement futur à l'égard de l'article 36 de la convention de Vienne.»

Elle précise que:

«l'exercice effectif du droit à la notification consulaire énoncée au paragraphe 2 [de l'article 36] exige que, dans les cas où il n'est pas exclu que le jugement prononcé soit vicié par la violation du droit à la notification consulaire, des procédures de recours permettent de revenir sur la décision et soit de revoir le verdict de culpabilité, soit de prononcer une autre peine».

Enfin, l'Allemagne souligne que sa quatrième conclusion a été libellée «de façon à laisser aux Etats-Unis le choix des moyens propres à mettre en œuvre les mesures [qui leur sont demandées]».

119. En réponse, les Etats-Unis exposent ce qui suit:

«La quatrième conclusion de l'Allemagne est à l'évidence d'une nature complètement différente de celle des trois premières. Dans chacune des trois premières conclusions, l'Allemagne demande à la Cour un prononcé déclarant qu'il y a eu violation d'une obligation juridique internationale déterminée. Pareils prononcés sont au cœur même de la fonction de la Cour, représentant un aspect de la réparation.

. . . .

Contrairement, toutefois, à la forme de réparation demandée dans les trois premières conclusions, la demande d'assurances de non-répétition formulée dans la quatrième est sans précédent dans la jurisprudence de la Cour et outrepasserait sa compétence et son pouvoir en la présente affaire. Il est exceptionnel dans la pratique des Etats, même à titre d'engagement non juridique, et il serait parfaitement incongru pour la Cour d'exiger de telles assurances à propos de l'obligation d'informer énoncée dans la convention sur les relations consulaires, vu les autres circonstances de l'affaire.»

It points out that "US authorities are working energetically to strengthen the regime of consular notification at the state and local level throughout the United States, in order to reduce the chances of cases such as this recurring" and adds that:

> "the German request for an assurance as to the duty to inform foreign nationals without delay of their right to consular notification . . . seeks to have the Court require the United States to assure that it will never again fail to inform a German foreign national of his or her right to consular notification",

and that "the Court is aware that the United States is not in a position to provide such an assurance". The United States further contends that it "has already provided appropriate assurances to Germany on this point".

Finally, the United States recalls that:

> "[w]ith respect to the alleged breach of Article 36, paragraph 2, . . . Germany seeks an assurance that, 'in any future cases of detention of or criminal proceedings against German nationals, the United States will ensure in law and practice the effective exercise of the rights under Article 36' ".

According to the United States,

> "[such an assurance] is again absolute in character . . . [and] seeks to create obligations on the United States that exceed those that are contained in the Vienna Convention. For example, the requirement of consular notification under Article 36, paragraph 1 *(b)*, of the Convention applies when a foreign national is arrested, committed to prison or to custody pending trial or detained in any other manner. It does not apply, as the submission would have it, to any future criminal proceedings. That is a new obligation, and it does not arise out of the Vienna Convention."

The United States further observes that:

> "[e]ven if this Court were to agree that, as a result of the application of procedural default with respect to the claims of the LaGrands, the United States committed a second internationally wrongful act, it should limit that judgment to the application of that law in the particular case of the LaGrands. It should resist the invitation to require an absolute assurance as to the application of US domestic law in all such future cases. The imposition of such an additional obligation on the United States would . . . be unprecedented in international jurisprudence and would exceed the Court's authority and jurisdiction."

120. The Court observes that in its fourth submission Germany seeks

Ils font valoir que «les autorités américaines s'emploient résolument à renforcer l'application des règles en matière de notification consulaire au niveau des Etats et au niveau local sur tout [leur] territoire ... afin de réduire les risques de voir se reproduire une situation comme celle» advenue en l'espèce et ajoutent que:

> «la demande d'assurance présentée par l'Allemagne en ce qui concerne l'obligation d'informer sans retard les ressortissants étrangers de leur droit à notification consulaire ... tend à ce que la Cour ordonne aux Etats-Unis d'assurer qu'ils ne manqueront plus jamais d'informer un ressortissant étranger allemand de son droit à la notification consulaire»,

et que: «la Cour sait bien qu'[ils] ne sont pas en mesure d'offrir une telle assurance». Ils soutiennent par ailleurs avoir «déjà fourni des assurances appropriées à l'Allemagne sur ce point».

Enfin, les Etats-Unis rappellent que:

> «[e]n ce qui concerne la violation alléguée du paragraphe 2 de l'article 36 ..., [l']Allemagne cherche à obtenir l'assurance que, «dans tous les cas futurs de détention de ressortissants allemands ou d'actions pénales à l'encontre de tels ressortissants, les Etats-Unis veilleront à assurer en droit et en pratique l'exercice effectif des droits visés à l'article 36».

Selon eux,

> «[une telle mesure] est là encore d'un caractère absolu ... [et] tend à créer pour [eux] des obligations excédant celles qui sont prévues dans la convention de Vienne. Ainsi, la notification consulaire exigée par l'alinéa *b)* du paragraphe 1 de l'article 36 de la convention s'applique aux cas où un ressortissant étranger est arrêté, incarcéré ou mis en état de détention préventive ou autre. Elle ne s'applique pas, comme le voudrait la conclusion de l'Allemagne, à toute future action pénale. C'est là une nouvelle obligation, qui ne découle pas de la convention de Vienne.»

Les Etats-Unis font de surcroît observer que:

> «[q]uand bien même la Cour estimerait qu'en opposant la règle de la carence procédurale aux recours des LaGrand les Etats-Unis ont commis un deuxième acte internationalement illicite, elle devrait limiter ce prononcé à l'application qui a été faite de cette règle dans le cas particulier des LaGrand. Elle doit résister à l'invitation qui lui est faite de prescrire une assurance absolue couvrant l'application future par les Etats-Unis de leur droit interne dans toutes les affaires de ce genre. Imposer une telle obligation additionnelle aux Etats-Unis serait ... sans précédent dans la jurisprudence internationale et outrepasserait le pouvoir et la compétence de la Cour.»

120. La Cour relève que, dans sa quatrième conclusion, l'Allemagne

several assurances. First it seeks a straightforward assurance that the United States will not repeat its unlawful acts. This request does not specify the means by which non-repetition is to be assured.

Additionally, Germany seeks from the United States that

> "in any future cases of detention of or criminal proceedings against German nationals, the United States will ensure in law and practice the effective exercise of the rights under Article 36 of the Vienna Convention on Consular Relations".

This request goes further, for, by referring to the law of the United States, it appears to require specific measures as a means of preventing recurrence.

Germany finally requests that

> "[i]n particular in cases involving the death penalty, this requires the United States to provide effective review of and remedies for criminal convictions impaired by a violation of the rights under Article 36".

This request goes even further, since it is directed entirely towards securing specific measures in cases involving the death penalty.

121. Turning first to the general demand for an assurance of non-repetition, the Court observes that it has been informed by the United States of the "substantial measures [which it is taking] aimed at preventing any recurrence" of the breach of Article 36, paragraph 1 *(b)*. Throughout these proceedings, oral as well as written, the United States has insisted that it "keenly appreciates the importance of the Vienna Convention's consular notification obligation for foreign citizens in the United States as well as for United States citizens travelling and living abroad"; that "effective compliance with the consular notification requirements of Article 36 of the Vienna Convention requires constant effort and attention"; and that

> "the Department of State is working intensively to improve understanding of and compliance with consular notification and access requirements throughout the United States, so as to guard against future violations of these requirements".

The United States points out that

> "[t]his effort has included the January 1998 publication of a booklet entitled 'Consular Notification and Access: Instructions for Federal, State and Local Law Enforcement and Other Officials Regarding

veut obtenir plusieurs assurances. En premier lieu, elle veut obtenir des Etats-Unis une assurance pure et simple qu'ils ne répéteront pas leurs actes illicites. Cette demande ne précise pas les moyens à mettre en œuvre pour assurer la non-répétition de tels actes.

En outre, l'Allemagne cherche à obtenir des Etats-Unis que

> «pour toutes les affaires futures impliquant la détention de ressortissants allemands ou des actions pénales à leur encontre, le droit et la pratique internes des Etats-Unis ne feront pas obstacle à l'exercice effectif des droits prévus à l'article 36 de la convention de Vienne sur les relations consulaires».

Cette demande va plus loin, dans la mesure où, en se référant au droit des Etats-Unis, elle paraît appeler l'adoption de mesures spécifiques visant à empêcher que de tels actes illicites se reproduisent.

L'Allemagne demande enfin que

> «dans les cas où un accusé est passible de la peine de mort, cela entraîne pour les Etats-Unis l'obligation de prévoir le réexamen effectif des condamnations pénales entachées d'une violation des droits énoncés à l'article 36 de la convention, ainsi que les moyens pour y porter remède».

Cette demande va encore plus loin, car elle tend exclusivement à ce que des mesures spécifiques soient prises dans les cas où un accusé est passible de la peine de mort.

121. Concernant tout d'abord la demande, de caractère général, visant l'obtention d'une assurance de non-répétition, la Cour relève que les Etats-Unis l'ont informée des «mesures importantes [qu'ils prennent] visant à empêcher que [cette violation de l'alinéa *b)* du paragraphe 1 de l'article 36] se reproduise». Tout au long de la procédure, tant orale qu'écrite, dans cette affaire, les Etats-Unis ont insisté sur le fait qu'ils étaient «profondément conscients de l'importance de l'obligation de notification consulaire prévue par la convention de Vienne pour les citoyens étrangers se trouvant aux Etats-Unis ainsi que pour les citoyens américains voyageant et demeurant à l'étranger», «qu'il faut, pour assurer le plein et entier respect des conditions qu'impose l'article 36 de la convention de Vienne en matière de notification consulaire, déployer des efforts constants et faire preuve d'une vigilance continuelle» et que

> «le département d'Etat ne ménage aucun effort pour mieux faire connaître et mieux faire respecter sur tout le territoire des Etats-Unis les prescriptions applicables en matière de notification consulaire et de communication entre consulats et ressortissants étrangers afin de prévenir toute nouvelle violation de celles-ci».

Les Etats-Unis soulignent que

> «parmi ces efforts, on relève notamment la publication en janvier 1998 d'une brochure intitulée «Communications entre les consulats et les ressortissants étrangers et informations à fournir aux uns

> Foreign Nationals in the United States and the Rights of Consular Officials to Assist Them', and development of a small reference card designed to be carried by individual arresting officers".

According to the United States, it is estimated that until now over 60,000 copies of the brochure as well as over 400,000 copies of the pocket card have been distributed to federal, state and local law enforcement and judicial officials throughout the United States. The United States is also conducting training programmes reaching out to all levels of government. In the Department of State a permanent office to focus on United States and foreign compliance with consular notification and access requirements has been created.

122. Germany has stated that it "does not consider the so-called 'assurances' offered by the Respondent as adequate". It says

> "[v]iolations of Article 36 followed by death sentences and executions cannot be remedied by apologies or the distribution of leaflets. An effective remedy requires certain changes in US law and practice".

In order to illustrate its point, Germany has presented to the Court a "[l]ist of German nationals detained after January 1, 1998, who claim not to have been informed of their consular rights". The United States has criticized this list as misleading and inaccurate.

123. The Court notes that the United States has acknowledged that, in the case of the LaGrand brothers, it did not comply with its obligations to give consular notification. The United States has presented an apology to Germany for this breach. The Court considers however that an apology is not sufficient in this case, as it would not be in other cases where foreign nationals have not been advised without delay of their rights under Article 36, paragraph 1, of the Vienna Convention and have been subjected to prolonged detention or sentenced to severe penalties.

In this respect, the Court has taken note of the fact that the United States repeated in all phases of these proceedings that it is carrying out a vast and detailed programme in order to ensure compliance by its competent authorities at the federal as well as at the state and local levels with its obligation under Article 36 of the Vienna Convention.

124. The United States has provided the Court with information, which it considers important, on its programme. If a State, in proceedings before this Court, repeatedly refers to substantial activities which it

> et aux autres: directives à l'intention des fonctionnaires fédéraux, fonctionnaires des Etats, fonctionnaires locaux et autres fonctionnaires chargés de l'application des lois concernant les ressortissants étrangers aux Etats-Unis et le droit des fonctionnaires consulaires de leur prêter assistance» et la mise au point d'une petite carte dont seront porteurs les agents autorisés à procéder à des arrestations».

D'après les Etats-Unis, on estime à l'heure actuelle à soixante mille exemplaires le nombre de brochures diffusées et à plus de quatre cent mille le nombre de petites cartes remises aux agents de la force publique et aux autorités judiciaires au niveau fédéral, au niveau des Etats et au niveau local dans l'ensemble du pays. Les Etats-Unis ont lancé en outre des programmes de formation s'adressant aux fonctionnaires à tous les échelons de l'administration. Un bureau permanent chargé de veiller au respect par les Etats-Unis et les pays étrangers de leurs obligations en matière de notification et de communication consulaires a été créé au sein du département d'Etat.

122. L'Allemagne a déclaré qu'elle ne considérait pas «les prétendues «assurances» proposées par le défendeur comme adéquates». Elle ajoute que

> «lorsque des violations de l'article 36 sont suivies par des condamnations à mort et des exécutions, il n'est pas possible, pour toute mesure de réparation, de formuler des excuses ou de distribuer des brochures. Pour que la mesure soit efficace, il faut apporter certains changements au droit et à la pratique des Etats-Unis.»

Pour illustrer son propos, l'Allemagne a présenté à la Cour «une liste de ressortissants allemands mis en détention aux Etats-Unis après le 1er janvier 1998 qui affirment ne pas avoir été informés de leurs droits consulaires». Les Etats-Unis ont critiqué cette liste comme fournissant des informations trompeuses et inexactes.

123. La Cour relève que les Etats-Unis ont reconnu, dans le cas des frères LaGrand, qu'ils avaient manqué à leurs obligations en matière de notification consulaire. Les Etats-Unis ont présenté des excuses à l'Allemagne pour ce manquement. La Cour considère cependant que des excuses ne suffisent pas en l'espèce, comme d'ailleurs chaque fois que des étrangers n'ont pas été avisés sans retard de leurs droits en vertu du paragraphe 1 de l'article 36 de la convention de Vienne et qu'ils ont fait l'objet d'une détention prolongée ou été condamnés à des peines sévères.

A cet égard, la Cour a pris note du fait que, à tous les stades de la procédure, les Etats-Unis ont rappelé qu'ils mettaient en œuvre un programme vaste et détaillé pour assurer le respect par les autorités compétentes, tant au niveau fédéral qu'au niveau des Etats et au niveau local, de leurs obligations résultant de l'article 36 de la convention de Vienne.

124. Les Etats-Unis ont communiqué à la Cour des informations qu'ils jugent importantes sur leur programme. Or si, dans le cadre d'une instance, un Etat fait référence de manière répétée devant la Cour aux

is carrying out in order to achieve compliance with certain obligations under a treaty, then this expresses a commitment to follow through with the efforts in this regard. The programme in question certainly cannot provide an assurance that there will never again be a failure by the United States to observe the obligation of notification under Article 36 of the Vienna Convention. But no State could give such a guarantee and Germany does not seek it. The Court considers that the commitment expressed by the United States to ensure implementation of the specific measures adopted in performance of its obligations under Article 36, paragraph 1 *(b)*, must be regarded as meeting Germany's request for a general assurance of non-repetition.

125. The Court will now examine the other assurances sought by Germany in its fourth submission. The Court observes in this regard that it can determine the existence of a violation of an international obligation. If necessary, it can also hold that a domestic law has been the cause of this violation. In the present case the Court has made its findings of violations of the obligations under Article 36 of the Vienna Convention when it dealt with the first and the second submission of Germany. But it has not found that a United States law, whether substantive or procedural in character, is inherently inconsistent with the obligations undertaken by the United States in the Vienna Convention. In the present case the violation of Article 36, paragraph 2, was caused by the circumstances in which the procedural default rule was applied, and not by the rule as such.

In the present proceedings the United States has apologized to Germany for the breach of Article 36, paragraph 1, and Germany has not requested material reparation for this injury to itself and to the LaGrand brothers. It does, however, seek assurances:

> "that, in any future cases of detention or of criminal proceedings against German nationals, the United States will ensure in law and practice the effective exercise of the rights under Article 36 of the Vienna Convention on Consular Relations",

and that

> "[i]n particular in cases involving the death penalty, this requires the United States to provide effective review of and remedies for criminal convictions impaired by the violation of the rights under Article 36".

The Court considers in this respect that if the United States, notwithstanding its commitment referred to in paragraph 124 above, should fail in its obligation of consular notification to the detriment of German nationals, an apology would not suffice in cases where the individuals concerned have been subjected to prolonged detention or convicted and activités substantielles auxquelles il se livre aux fins de mettre en œuvre certaines obligations découlant d'un traité, cela traduit un engagement de sa part de poursuivre les efforts entrepris à cet effet. Certes, le programme en cause ne peut fournir l'assurance qu'il n'y aura plus jamais de manquement des autorités des Etats-Unis à l'obligation de notification prévue à l'article 36 de la convention de Vienne. Mais aucun Etat ne pourrait fournir une telle garantie, et l'Allemagne ne cherche pas à l'obtenir. La Cour estime que l'engagement pris par les Etats-Unis d'assurer la mise en œuvre des mesures spécifiques adoptées en exécution de leurs obligations au titre de l'alinéa *b)* du paragraphe 1 de l'article 36 doit être considéré comme satisfaisant à la demande de l'Allemagne visant à obtenir une assurance générale de non-répétition.

125. La Cour passera maintenant à l'examen des autres assurances demandées par l'Allemagne dans sa quatrième conclusion. A cet égard, la Cour constate qu'elle peut établir la violation d'une obligation internationale. Si nécessaire, elle peut aussi constater qu'une loi interne a été la cause de cette violation. La Cour, en la présente instance, a conclu, lorsqu'elle a traité de la première et de la deuxième conclusion de l'Allemagne, à la violation des obligations existant au titre de l'article 36 de la convention de Vienne. Mais elle n'a pas trouvé de loi américaine, de fond ou de procédure, qui, par nature, soit incompatible avec les obligations que la convention de Vienne impose aux Etats-Unis. En la présente instance, la violation du paragraphe 2 de l'article 36 a découlé des circonstances dans lesquelles a été appliquée la règle de la carence procédurale, et non de la règle elle-même.

Les Etats-Unis ont en l'espèce présenté leurs excuses à l'Allemagne pour la violation du paragraphe 1 de l'article 36 et l'Allemagne n'a pas sollicité réparation matérielle du préjudice subi tant par elle que par les frères LaGrand. Elle n'en cherche pas moins à obtenir l'assurance que:

> «dans tous les cas futurs de détention de ressortissants allemands ou d'actions pénales à l'encontre de tels ressortissants, les Etats-Unis veille[nt] à assurer, en droit et en pratique, l'exercice effectif des droits visés à l'article 36 de la convention de Vienne sur les relations consulaires»

et que

> «[e]n particulier, dans les cas où un accusé est passible de la peine de mort, cela entraîne pour les Etats-Unis l'obligation de prévoir le réexamen effectif des condamnations pénales entachées d'une violation des droits énoncés à l'article 36 de la convention, ainsi que les moyens pour y porter remède».

La Cour estime à cet égard que, si les Etats-Unis, en dépit de l'engagement visé au paragraphe 124 ci-dessus, manquaient à leur obligation de notification consulaire au détriment de ressortissants allemands, des excuses ne suffiraient pas dans les cas où les intéressés auraient fait l'objet d'une détention prolongée ou été condamnés à des peines sévères.

sentenced to severe penalties. In the case of such a conviction and sentence, it would be incumbent upon the United States to allow the review and reconsideration of the conviction and sentence by taking account of the violation of the rights set forth in the Convention. This obligation can be carried out in various ways. The choice of means must be left to the United States.

126. Given the foregoing ruling by the Court regarding the obligation of the United States under certain circumstances to review and reconsider convictions and sentences, the Court need not examine Germany's further argument which seeks to found a like obligation on the contention that the right of a detained person to be informed without delay pursuant to Article 36, paragraph 1, of the Vienna Convention is not only an individual right but has today assumed the character of a human right.

127. In reply to the fourth submission of Germany, the Court will therefore limit itself to taking note of the commitment undertaken by the United States to ensure implementation of the specific measures adopted in performance of its obligations under Article 36, paragraph 1 *(b)*, of the Vienna Convention, as well as the aforementioned duty of the United States to address violations of that Convention should they still occur in spite of its efforts to achieve compliance.

* * *

128. For these reasons,

The Court,

(1) By fourteen votes to one,

Finds that it has jurisdiction, on the basis of Article I of the Optional Protocol concerning the Compulsory Settlement of Disputes to the Vienna Convention on Consular Relations of 24 April 1963, to entertain the Application filed by the Federal Republic of Germany on 2 March 1999;

in favour: *President* Guillaume; *Vice-President* Shi; *Judges* Oda, Bedjaoui, Ranjeva, Herczegh, Fleischhauer, Koroma, Vereshchetin, Higgins, Kooijmans, Rezek, Al-Khasawneh, Buergenthal:

against: *Judge* Parra-Aranguren;

(2) *(a)* By thirteen votes to two,

Finds that the first submission of the Federal Republic of Germany is admissible;

in favour: *President* Guillaume; *Vice-President* Shi; *Judges* Bedjaoui, Ranjeva, Herczegh, Fleischhauer, Koroma, Vereshchetin, Higgins, Kooijmans, Rezek, Al-Khasawneh, Buergenthal;

against: *Judges* Oda, Parra-Aranguren;

Dans le cas d'une telle condamnation, les Etats-Unis devraient permettre le réexamen et la revision du verdict de culpabilité et de la peine en tenant compte de la violation des droits prévus par la convention. Cette obligation peut être mise en œuvre de diverses façons. Le choix des moyens doit revenir aux Etats-Unis.

126. Etant donné la conclusion à laquelle elle est ainsi parvenue concernant l'obligation pour les Etats-Unis, dans certaines circonstances, de réexaminer et de reviser le verdict de culpabilité et la peine, point n'est besoin pour la Cour d'examiner l'argumentation supplémentaire de l'Allemagne tendant à fonder une telle obligation sur le fait que le droit d'une personne détenue d'être informée sans retard aux termes du paragraphe 1 de l'article 36 de la convention de Vienne ne serait pas seulement un droit individuel, mais aurait aujourd'hui acquis le caractère d'un droit de l'homme.

127. En réponse à la quatrième conclusion de l'Allemagne, la Cour se bornera donc à prendre acte de l'engagement pris par les Etats-Unis d'assurer la mise en œuvre des mesures spécifiques adoptées en exécution de leurs obligations au titre de l'alinéa *b)* du paragraphe 1 de l'article 36 de la convention de Vienne, ainsi que de l'obligation susvisée qu'ont les Etats-Unis de prendre les mesures qui s'imposent en cas de violation de cette convention, si de telles violations se produisaient en dépit des efforts déployés pour en assurer le respect.

* * *

128. Par ces motifs,

LA COUR,

1) Par quatorze voix contre une,

Dit qu'elle a compétence, sur la base de l'article premier du protocole de signature facultative concernant le règlement obligatoire des différends à la convention de Vienne sur les relations consulaires du 24 avril 1963, pour connaître de la requête déposée par la République fédérale d'Allemagne le 2 mars 1999;

POUR : M. Guillaume, *président*; M. Shi, *vice-président*; MM. Oda, Bedjaoui, Ranjeva, Herczegh, Fleischhauer, Koroma, Vereshchetin, Mme Higgins, MM. Kooijmans, Rezek, Al-Khasawneh, Buergenthal;

CONTRE : M. Parra-Aranguren;

2) *a)* Par treize voix contre deux,

Dit que la première conclusion de la République fédérale d'Allemagne est recevable;

POUR : M. Guillaume, *président*; M. Shi, *vice-président*; MM. Bedjaoui, Ranjeva, Herczegh, Fleischhauer, Koroma, Vereshchetin, Mme Higgins, MM. Kooijmans, Rezek, Al-Khasawneh, Buergenthal;

CONTRE : MM. Oda, Parra-Aranguren;

(b) By fourteen votes to one,

Finds that the second submission of the Federal Republic of Germany is admissible;

IN FAVOUR: *President* Guillaume; *Vice-President* Shi; *Judges* Bedjaoui, Ranjeva, Herczegh, Fleischhauer, Koroma, Vereshchetin, Higgins, Parra-Aranguren, Kooijmans, Rezek, Al-Khasawneh, Buergenthal;

AGAINST: *Judge* Oda;

(c) By twelve votes to three,

Finds that the third submission of the Federal Republic of Germany is admissible;

IN FAVOUR: *President* Guillaume; *Vice-President* Shi; *Judges* Bedjaoui, Ranjeva, Herczegh, Fleischhauer, Koroma, Vereshchetin, Higgins, Kooijmans, Rezek, Al-Khasawneh;

AGAINST: *Judges* Oda, Parra-Aranguren, Buergenthal;

(d) By fourteen votes to one,

Finds that the fourth submission of the Federal Republic of Germany is admissible;

IN FAVOUR: *President* Guillaume; *Vice-President* Shi; *Judges* Bedjaoui, Ranjeva, Herczegh, Fleischhauer, Koroma, Vereshchetin, Higgins, Parra-Aranguren, Kooijmans, Rezek, Al-Khasawneh, Buergenthal;

AGAINST: *Judge* Oda;

(3) By fourteen votes to one,

Finds that, by not informing Karl and Walter LaGrand without delay following their arrest of their rights under Article 36, paragraph 1 *(b)*, of the Convention, and by thereby depriving the Federal Republic of Germany of the possibility, in a timely fashion, to render the assistance provided for by the Convention to the individuals concerned, the United States of America breached its obligations to the Federal Republic of Germany and to the LaGrand brothers under Article 36, paragraph 1;

IN FAVOUR: *President* Guillaume; *Vice-President* Shi; *Judges* Bedjaoui, Ranjeva, Herczegh, Fleischhauer, Koroma, Vereshchetin, Higgins, Parra-Aranguren, Kooijmans, Rezek, Al-Khasawneh, Buergenthal;

AGAINST: *Judge* Oda;

(4) By fourteen votes to one,

Finds that, by not permitting the review and reconsideration, in the light of the rights set forth in the Convention, of the convictions and sentences of the LaGrand brothers after the violations referred to in paragraph (3) above had been established, the United States of America breached its obligation to the Federal Republic of Ger-

b) Par quatorze voix contre une,

Dit que la deuxième conclusion de la République fédérale d'Allemagne est recevable;

POUR: M. Guillaume, *président*; M. Shi, *vice-président*; MM. Bedjaoui, Ranjeva, Herczegh, Fleischhauer, Koroma, Vereshchetin, Mme Higgins, MM. Parra-Aranguren, Kooijmans, Rezek, Al-Khasawneh, Buergenthal;

CONTRE: M. Oda;

c) Par douze voix contre trois,

Dit que la troisième conclusion de la République fédérale d'Allemagne est recevable;

POUR: M. Guillaume, *président*; M. Shi, *vice-président*; MM. Bedjaoui, Ranjeva, Herczegh, Fleischhauer, Koroma, Vereshchetin, Mme Higgins, MM. Kooijmans, Rezek, Al-Khasawneh;

CONTRE: MM. Oda, Parra-Aranguren, Buergenthal;

d) Par quatorze voix contre une,

Dit que la quatrième conclusion de la République fédérale d'Allemagne est recevable;

POUR: M. Guillaume, *président*; M. Shi, *vice-président*; MM. Bedjaoui, Ranjeva, Herczegh, Fleischhauer, Koroma, Vereshchetin, Mme Higgins, MM. Parra-Aranguren, Kooijmans, Rezek, Al-Khasawneh, Buergenthal;

CONTRE: M. Oda;

3) Par quatorze voix contre une,

Dit que, en n'informant pas sans retard Karl et Walter LaGrand, après leur arrestation, des droits qui étaient les leurs en vertu de l'alinéa *b)* du paragraphe 1 de l'article 36 de la convention et en privant de ce fait la République fédérale d'Allemagne de la possibilité de fournir aux intéressés, en temps opportun, l'assistance prévue par la convention, les Etats-Unis d'Amérique ont violé les obligations dont ils étaient tenus envers la République fédérale d'Allemagne et envers les frères LaGrand en vertu du paragraphe 1 de l'article 36;

POUR: M. Guillaume, *président*; M. Shi, *vice-président*; MM. Bedjaoui, Ranjeva, Herczegh, Fleischhauer, Koroma, Vereshchetin, Mme Higgins, MM. Parra-Aranguren, Kooijmans, Rezek, Al-Khasawneh, Buergenthal;

CONTRE: M. Oda;

4) Par quatorze voix contre une,

Dit que, en ne permettant pas, à la lumière des droits reconnus par la convention, le réexamen et la revision des verdicts de culpabilité des frères LaGrand et de leurs peines, une fois constatées les violations rappelées au paragraphe 3) ci-dessus, les Etats-Unis d'Amérique ont violé l'obligation dont ils étaient tenus envers la République fédérale d'Allemany and to the LaGrand brothers under Article 36, paragraph 2, of the Convention;

IN FAVOUR: *President* Guillaume; *Vice-President* Shi; *Judges* Bedjaoui, Ranjeva, Herczegh, Fleischhauer, Koroma, Vereshchetin, Higgins, Parra-Aranguren, Kooijmans, Rezek, Al-Khasawneh, Buergenthal;

AGAINST: *Judge* Oda;

(5) By thirteen votes to two,

Finds that, by failing to take all measures at its disposal to ensure that Walter LaGrand was not executed pending the final decision of the International Court of Justice in the case, the United States of America breached the obligation incumbent upon it under the Order indicating provisional measures issued by the Court on 3 March 1999;

IN FAVOUR: *President* Guillaume; *Vice-President* Shi; *Judges* Bedjaoui, Ranjeva, Herczegh, Fleischhauer, Koroma, Vereshchetin, Higgins, Kooijmans, Rezek, Al-Khasawneh, Buergenthal;

AGAINST: *Judges* Oda, Parra-Aranguren;

(6) Unanimously,

Takes note of the commitment undertaken by the United States of America to ensure implementation of the specific measures adopted in performance of its obligations under Article 36, paragraph 1 *(b)*, of the Convention; and *finds* that this commitment must be regarded as meeting the Federal Republic of Germany's request for a general assurance of non-repetition;

(7) By fourteen votes to one,

Finds that should nationals of the Federal Republic of Germany nonetheless be sentenced to severe penalties, without their rights under Article 36, paragraph 1 *(b)*, of the Convention having been respected, the United States of America, by means of its own choosing, shall allow the review and reconsideration of the conviction and sentence by taking account of the violation of the rights set forth in that Convention.

IN FAVOUR: *President* Guillaume; *Vice-President* Shi; *Judges* Bedjaoui, Ranjeva, Herczegh, Fleischhauer, Koroma, Vereshchetin, Higgins, Parra-Aranguren, Kooijmans, Rezek, Al-Khasawneh, Buergenthal;

AGAINST: *Judge* Oda.

Done in English and in French, the English text being authoritative, at the Peace Palace, The Hague, this twenty-seventh day of June, two thousand and one, in three copies, one of which will be placed in the archives magne et envers les frères LaGrand en vertu du paragraphe 2 de l'article 36 de la convention;

POUR: M. Guillaume, *président*; M. Shi, *vice-président*; MM. Bedjaoui, Ranjeva, Herczegh, Fleischhauer, Koroma, Vereshchetin, Mme Higgins, MM. Parra-Aranguren, Kooijmans, Rezek, Al-Khasawneh, Buergenthal;

CONTRE: M. Oda;

5) Par treize voix contre deux,

Dit que, en ne prenant pas toutes les mesures dont ils disposaient pour que Walter LaGrand ne soit pas exécuté tant que la Cour internationale de Justice n'aurait pas rendu sa décision définitive en l'affaire, les Etats-Unis d'Amérique ont violé l'obligation dont ils étaient tenus en vertu de l'ordonnance en indication de mesures conservatoires rendue par la Cour le 3 mars 1999;

POUR: M. Guillaume, président; M. Shi, *vice-président*; MM. Bedjaoui, Ranjeva, Herczegh, Fleischhauer, Koroma, Vereshchetin, Mme Higgins, MM. Kooijmans, Rezek, Al-Khasawneh, Buergenthal;

CONTRE: MM. Oda, Parra-Aranguren;

6) A l'unanimité,

Prend acte de l'engagement pris par les Etats-Unis d'Amérique d'assurer la mise en œuvre des mesures spécifiques adoptées en exécution de leurs obligations au titre de l'alinéa *b)* du paragraphe 1 de l'article 36 de la convention; et *dit* que cet engagement doit être considéré comme satisfaisant à la demande de la République fédérale d'Allemagne visant à obtenir une assurance générale de non-répétition;

7) Par quatorze voix contre une,

Dit que, si des ressortissants allemands devaient néanmoins être condamnés à une peine sévère sans que les droits qu'ils tiennent de l'alinéa *b)* du paragraphe 1 de l'article 36 de la convention aient été respectés, les Etats-Unis d'Amérique devront, en mettant en œuvre les moyens de leur choix, permettre le réexamen et la revision du verdict de culpabilité et de la peine en tenant compte de la violation des droits prévus par la convention.

POUR: M. Guillaume, *président*; M. Shi, *vice-président*; MM. Bedjaoui, Ranjeva, Herczegh, Fleischhauer, Koroma, Vereshchetin, Mme Higgins, MM. Parra-Aranguren, Kooijmans, Rezek, Al-Khasawneh, Buergenthal;

CONTRE: M. Oda.

Fait en anglais et en français, le texte anglais faisant foi, au Palais de la Paix, à La Haye, le vingt-sept juin deux mille un, en trois exemplaires, dont l'un restera déposé aux archives de la Cour et les autres seront of the Court and the others transmitted to the Government of the Federal Republic of Germany and the Government of the United States of America, respectively.

(Signed) Gilbert GUILLAUME,
President.

(Signed) Philippe COUVREUR,
Registrar.

President GUILLAUME makes the following declaration:

Subparagraph (7) of the operative part of the Court's Judgment envisages a situation where, despite the commitment by the United States noted by the Court in subparagraph (6), a severe penalty is imposed upon a German national without his or her rights under Article 36, paragraph 1 *(b)*, of the Vienna Convention on Consular Relations having been respected. The Court states that, in such a case, "the United States, by means of its own choosing, shall allow the review and reconsideration of the conviction and sentence by taking account of the violation of the rights set forth in that Convention".

This subparagraph represents a response to certain submissions by Germany and hence rules only on the obligations of the United States in cases of severe penalties imposed upon German nationals.

Thus, subparagraph (7) does not address the position of nationals of other countries or that of individuals sentenced to penalties that are not of a severe nature. However, in order to avoid any ambiguity, it should be made clear that there can be no question of applying an *a contrario* interpretation to this paragraph.

(Signed) Gilbert GUILLAUME.

Vice-President SHI appends a separate opinion to the Judgment of the Court; Judge ODA appends a dissenting opinion to the Judgment of the Court; Judges KOROMA and PARRA-ARANGUREN append separate opinions to the Judgment of the Court; Judge BUERGENTHAL appends a dissenting opinion to the Judgment of the Court.

(Initialled) G.G.

(Initialled) Ph.C.

transmis respectivement au Gouvernement de la République fédérale d'Allemagne et au Gouvernement des Etats-Unis d'Amérique.

Le président,
(Signé) Gilbert GUILLAUME.

Le greffier,
(Signé) Philippe COUVREUR.

M. GUILLAUME, président, fait la déclaration suivante:

L'alinéa 7) du dispositif de l'arrêt de la Cour envisage le cas où, malgré l'engagement des Etats-Unis dont la Cour a pris acte à l'alinéa 6), des ressortissants allemands seraient condamnés à une peine sévère sans que les droits qu'ils tiennent de l'alinéa *b)* du paragraphe 1 de l'article 36 de la convention de Vienne sur les relations consulaires aient été respectés. La Cour dit qu'en pareille hypothèse «les Etats-Unis devront, en mettant en œuvre les moyens de leur choix, permettre le réexamen et la revision du verdict de culpabilité et de la peine en tenant compte de la violation des droits prévus par la convention».

Cet alinéa du dispositif répond à certaines conclusions de l'Allemagne et statue de ce fait exclusivement sur les obligations des Etats-Unis dans le cas où des ressortissants allemands seraient condamnés à des peines sévères.

L'alinéa 7) ne se prononce donc pas sur la situation des ressortissants d'autres pays ou sur celle de personnes condamnées à des peines n'ayant pas un caractère sévère. En vue cependant d'éviter toute ambiguïté, il convient de préciser qu'il ne saurait faire l'objet d'une interprétation *a contrario*.

(Signé) Gilbert GUILLAUME.

M. SHI, vice-président, joint à l'arrêt l'exposé de son opinion individuelle; M. ODA, juge, joint à l'arrêt l'exposé de son opinion dissidente; MM. KOROMA et PARRA-ARANGUREN, juges, joignent à l'arrêt les exposés de leur opinion individuelle; M. BUERGENTHAL, juge, joint à l'arrêt l'exposé de son opinion dissidente.

(Paraphé) G.G.
(Paraphé) Ph.C.

COUR INTERNATIONALE DE JUSTICE

RECUEIL DES ARRÊTS,
AVIS CONSULTATIFS ET ORDONNANCES

CONSÉQUENCES JURIDIQUES DE L'ÉDIFICATION D'UN MUR DANS LE TERRITOIRE PALESTINIEN OCCUPÉ

AVIS CONSULTATIF DU 9 JUILLET 2004

2004

INTERNATIONAL COURT OF JUSTICE

REPORTS OF JUDGMENTS,
ADVISORY OPINIONS AND ORDERS

LEGAL CONSEQUENCES OF THE CONSTRUCTION OF A WALL IN THE OCCUPIED PALESTINIAN TERRITORY

ADVISORY OPINION OF 9 JULY 2004

COUR INTERNATIONALE DE JUSTICE

ANNÉE 2004

9 juillet 2004

CONSÉQUENCES JURIDIQUES DE L'ÉDIFICATION D'UN MUR DANS LE TERRITOIRE PALESTINIEN OCCUPÉ

Compétence de la Cour pour donner l'avis consultatif demandé.

Paragraphe 1 de l'article 65 du Statut — Paragraphe 1 de l'article 96 de la Charte — Pouvoir de l'Assemblée générale de solliciter des avis consultatifs — Activités de l'Assemblée.

Evénements ayant conduit à l'adoption de la résolution ES-10/14 de l'Assemblée générale portant demande de l'avis consultatif.

Allégation selon laquelle l'Assemblée générale aurait outrepassé la compétence que lui confère la Charte — Paragraphe 1 de l'article 12 et article 24 de la Charte — Pratique de l'Organisation des Nations Unies concernant l'interprétation du paragraphe 1 de l'article 12 de la Charte — Assemblée générale n'ayant pas outrepassé sa compétence.

Demande d'avis adoptée par la dixième session extraordinaire d'urgence de l'Assemblée générale — Session convoquée sur la base de la résolution 377 A (V) («L'union pour le maintien de la paix») — Conditions prévues par cette résolution — Régularité de la procédure suivie.

Manque de clarté allégué du libellé de la question — Nature prétendument abstraite de la question — Aspects politiques de la question — Mobiles qui auraient inspiré la requête et implications que pourrait avoir l'avis — Caractère «juridique» de la question non affecté.

Cour compétente pour donner l'avis consultatif demandé.

* *

Pouvoir discrétionnaire de la Cour de décider s'il échet de donner un avis.

Paragraphe 1 de l'article 65 du Statut — Pertinence du défaut de consentement d'un Etat intéressé — Question ne pouvant être considérée seulement comme une question bilatérale entre Israël et la Palestine, mais intéressant directement l'Organisation des Nations Unies — Effets possibles de l'avis sur un règlement politique négocié du conflit israélo-palestinien — Question ne constituant qu'un aspect du conflit israélo-palestinien — Suffisance des renseigne-

INTERNATIONAL COURT OF JUSTICE

YEAR 2004

9 July 2004

LEGAL CONSEQUENCES OF THE CONSTRUCTION OF A WALL IN THE OCCUPIED PALESTINIAN TERRITORY

Jurisdiction of the Court to give the advisory opinion requested.

Article 65, paragraph 1, of the Statute — Article 96, paragraph 1, of the Charter — Power of General Assembly to request advisory opinions — Activities of Assembly.

Events leading to the adoption of General Assembly resolution ES-10/14 requesting the advisory opinion.

Contention that General Assembly acted ultra vires *under the Charter — Article 12, paragraph 1, and Article 24 of the Charter — United Nations practice concerning the interpretation of Article 12, paragraph 1, of Charter — General Assembly did not exceed its competence.*

Request for opinion adopted by the Tenth Emergency Special Session of the General Assembly — Session convened pursuant to resolution 377 A (V) ("Uniting for Peace") — Conditions set by that resolution — Regularity of procedure followed.

Alleged lack of clarity of the terms of the question — Purportedly abstract nature of the question — Political aspects of the question — Motives said to have inspired the request and opinion's possible implications — "Legal" nature of question unaffected.

Court having jurisdiction to give advisory opinion requested.

* *

Discretionary power of Court to decide whether it should give an opinion.

Article 65, paragraph 1, of Statute — Relevance of lack of consent of a State concerned — Question cannot be regarded only as a bilateral matter between Israel and Palestine but is directly of concern to the United Nations — Possible effects of opinion on a political, negotiated solution to the Israeli-Palestinian conflict — Question representing only one aspect of Israeli-Palestinian conflict — Sufficiency of information and evidence available to Court — Useful purpose ments et éléments de preuve à la disposition de la Cour — Utilité de l'avis — Nullus commodum capere potest de sua injuria propria — *Avis donné à l'Assemblée générale et non à un Etat ou une entité déterminés.*

Absence de «raisons décisives» pour que la Cour use de son pouvoir discrétionnaire de ne pas donner l'avis consultatif.

* *

«Conséquences juridiques» de l'édification d'un mur dans le territoire palestinien occupé, y compris à l'intérieur et sur le pourtour de Jérusalem-Est — Portée de la question posée — Demande d'avis limitée aux conséquences juridiques de la construction des parties du mur situées dans le territoire palestinien occupé — Emploi du terme «mur».

Contexte historique.

Description du mur.

* *

Droit applicable.

Charte des Nations Unies — Résolution 2625 (XXV) de l'Assemblée générale — Illicéité de toute acquisition de territoire résultant de la menace ou de l'emploi de la force — Droit des peuples à disposer d'eux-mêmes.

Droit international humanitaire — Règlement annexé à la quatrième convention de La Haye de 1907 — Quatrième convention de Genève de 1949 — Applicabilité de la quatrième convention de Genève dans le territoire palestinien occupé — Droits de l'homme — Pacte international relatif aux droits civils et politiques — Pacte international relatif aux droits économiques, sociaux et culturels — Convention relative aux droits de l'enfant — Rapport entre droit international humanitaire et droits de l'homme — Applicabilité des instruments relatifs aux droits de l'homme hors du territoire national — Applicabilité de ces instruments dans le territoire palestinien occupé.

* *

Colonies de peuplement installées par Israël en méconnaissance du droit international dans le territoire palestinien occupé — Construction du mur et régime qui lui est associé créant sur le terrain un «fait accompli» susceptible de devenir permanent — Risque d'une situation équivalant à une annexion de facto — *Construction du mur dressant un obstacle grave à l'exercice par le peuple palestinien de son droit à l'autodétermination et violant de ce fait l'obligation incombant à Israël de respecter ce droit.*

Dispositions applicables du droit international humanitaire et des conventions relatives aux droits de l'homme pertinentes en l'espèce — Destruction et réquisition de propriétés — Restrictions à la liberté de circulation des habitants du territoire palestinien occupé — Entraves à l'exercice par les intéressés des droits au travail, à la santé, à l'éducation et à un niveau de vie suffisant — Changements démographiques dans le territoire palestinien occupé — Dispositions du droit international humanitaire permettant de tenir compte des impératifs militaires — Clauses de limitation des droits garantis et clauses de dérogation dans les conventions relatives aux droits de l'homme — Construction du mur et régime qui lui est associé ne pouvant être justifiés par des impératifs militaires ou des nécessités de sécurité nationale ou d'ordre public — Violation par Israël of opinion — Nullus commodum capere potest de sua injuria propria — *Opinion to be given to the General Assembly, not to a specific State or entity.*

No "compelling reason" for Court to use its discretionary power not to give an advisory opinion.

* *

"Legal consequences" of the construction of a wall in the Occupied Palestinian Territory, including in and around East Jerusalem — Scope of question posed — Request for opinion limited to the legal consequences of the construction of those parts of the wall situated in Occupied Palestinian Territory — Use of the term "wall".

Historical background.

Description of the wall.

* *

Applicable law.

United Nations Charter — General Assembly resolution 2625 (XXV) — Illegality of any territorial acquisition resulting from the threat or use of force — Right of peoples to self-determination.

International humanitarian law — Regulations annexed to the Fourth Hague Convention of 1907 — Fourth Geneva Convention of 1949 — Applicability of Fourth Geneva Convention in the Occupied Palestinian Territory — Human rights law — International Covenant on Civil and Political Rights — International Covenant on Economic, Social and Cultural Rights — Convention on the Rights of the Child — Relationship between international humanitarian law and human rights law — Applicability of human rights instruments outside national territory — Applicability of those instruments in the Occupied Palestinian Territory.

* *

Settlements established by Israel in breach of international law in the Occupied Palestinian Territory — Construction of the wall and its associated régime create a "fait accompli" on the ground that could well become permanent — Risk of situation tantamount to de facto *annexation — Construction of the wall severely impedes the exercise by the Palestinian people of its right to self-determination and is therefore a breach of Israel's obligation to respect that right.*

Applicable provisions of international humanitarian law and human rights instruments relevant to the present case — Destruction and requisition of properties — Restrictions on freedom of movement of inhabitants of the Occupied Palestinian Territory — Impediments to the exercise by those concerned of the right to work, to health, to education and to an adequate standard of living — Demographic changes in the Occupied Palestinian Territory — Provisions of international humanitarian law enabling account to be taken of military exigencies — Clauses in human rights instruments qualifying rights guaranteed or providing for derogation — Construction of the wall and its associated régime cannot be justified by military exigencies or by the requirements of national security or public order — Breach by Israel of various of its obligations under de diverses obligations lui incombant en vertu des dispositions applicables du droit international humanitaire et des conventions relatives aux droits de l'homme.

Légitime défense — Article 51 de la Charte — Violences contre Israël non imputables à un Etat étranger — Menace invoquée pour justifier la construction du mur trouvant son origine à l'intérieur d'un territoire sur lequel Israël exerce son contrôle — Article 51 sans pertinence au cas particulier.

Etat de nécessité — Droit international coutumier — Conditions — Construction du mur ne constituant pas le seul moyen de protéger les intérêts d'Israël contre le péril invoqué.

Construction du mur et régime qui lui est associé étant contraires au droit international.

* *

Conséquences juridiques de la violation des obligations incombant à Israël.

Responsabilité internationale d'Israël — Israël tenu de respecter les obligations internationales auxquelles il a contrevenu par la construction du mur — Israël tenu de mettre un terme à la violation de ses obligations internationales — Obligation de cesser immédiatement les travaux d'édification du mur, de démanteler immédiatement celui-ci et d'abroger immédiatement ou de priver immédiatement d'effet les actes législatifs et réglementaires adoptés en vue de son édification, sous réserve des actes pertinents dans le contexte du respect par Israël de son obligation de réparer les dommages causés — Israël tenu de réparer tous les dommages causés à toutes les personnes physiques ou morales affectées par la construction du mur.

Conséquences juridiques pour les Etats autres qu'Israël — Caractère erga omnes *de certaines obligations violées par Israël — Obligation de tous les Etats de ne pas reconnaître la situation illicite découlant de la construction du mur et de ne pas prêter aide ou assistance au maintien de la situation créée par cette construction — Obligation de tous les Etats de veiller, dans le respect de la Charte et du droit international, à ce qu'il soit mis fin aux entraves, résultant de la construction du mur, à l'exercice par le peuple palestinien de son droit à l'autodétermination — Obligation de tous les Etats parties à la quatrième convention de Genève, dans le respect de la Charte et du droit international, de faire respecter par Israël le droit international humanitaire incorporé dans la convention — Nécessité pour l'Organisation des Nations Unies, et spécialement l'Assemblée générale et le Conseil de sécurité, d'examiner, en tenant dûment compte de l'avis consultatif, quelles nouvelles mesures doivent être prises afin de mettre un terme à la situation illicite découlant de la construction du mur et du régime qui lui est associé.*

* *

Construction du mur devant être replacée dans un contexte plus général — Obligation incombant à Israël et à la Palestine de respecter de manière scrupuleuse le droit international humanitaire — Mise en œuvre de bonne foi de toutes les résolutions pertinentes du Conseil de sécurité, en particulier les résolutions 242 (1967) et 338 (1973) — « Feuille de route » — Nécessité d'encourager les efforts en vue d'aboutir le plus tôt possible, sur la base du droit international, à une solution négociée des problèmes pendants et à la constitution d'un Etat palestinien, et d'assurer à chacun dans la région paix et sécurité.

the applicable provisions of international humanitarian law and human rights instruments.

Self-defence — Article 51 of the Charter — Attacks against Israel not imputable to a foreign State — Threat invoked to justify the construction of the wall originating within a territory over which Israel exercises control — Article 51 not relevant in the present case.

State of necessity — Customary international law — Conditions — Construction of the wall not the only means to safeguard Israel's interests against the peril invoked.

Construction of the wall and its associated régime are contrary to international law.

* *

Legal consequences of the violation by Israel of its obligations.

Israel's international responsibility — Israel obliged to comply with the international obligations it has breached by the construction of the wall — Israel obliged to put an end to the violation of its international obligations — Obligation to cease forthwith the works of construction of the wall, to dismantle it forthwith and to repeal or render ineffective forthwith the legislative and regulatory acts relating to its construction, save where relevant for compliance by Israel with its obligation to make reparation for the damage caused — Israel obliged to make reparation for the damage caused to all natural or legal persons affected by construction of the wall.

Legal consequences for States other than Israel — Erga omnes *character of certain obligations violated by Israel — Obligation for all States not to recognize the illegal situation resulting from construction of the wall and not to render aid or assistance in maintaining the situation created by such construction — Obligation for all States, while respecting the Charter and international law, to see to it that any impediment, resulting from the construction of the wall, to the exercise by the Palestinian people of its right to self-determination is brought to an end — Obligation for all States parties to the Fourth Geneva Convention, while respecting the Charter and international law, to ensure compliance by Israel with international humanitarian law as embodied in that Convention — Need for the United Nations, and especially the General Assembly and the Security Council, to consider what further action is required to bring to an end the illegal situation resulting from the construction of the wall and its associated régime, taking due account of the Advisory Opinion.*

* *

Construction of the wall must be placed in a more general context — Obligation of Israel and Palestine scrupulously to observe international humanitarian law — Implementation in good faith of all relevant Security Council resolutions, in particular resolutions 242 (1967) and 338 (1973) — "Roadmap" — Need for efforts to be encouraged with a view to achieving as soon as possible, on the basis of international law, a negotiated solution to the outstanding problems and the establishment of a Palestinian State, with peace and security for all in the region.

AVIS CONSULTATIF

Présents: M. SHI, *président*; M. RANJEVA, *vice-président*; MM. GUILLAUME, KOROMA, VERESHCHETIN, Mme HIGGINS, MM. PARRA-ARANGUREN, KOOIJMANS, REZEK, AL-KHASAWNEH, BUERGENTHAL, ELARABY, OWADA, SIMMA, TOMKA, *juges*; M. COUVREUR, *greffier*.

Sur les conséquences juridiques de l'édification d'un mur dans le territoire palestinien occupé,

LA COUR,

ainsi composée,

donne l'avis consultatif suivant:

1. La question sur laquelle un avis consultatif est demandé à la Cour est énoncée dans la résolution ES-10/14 que l'Assemblée générale des Nations Unies (ci-après dénommée l'«Assemblée générale») a adoptée le 8 décembre 2003 lors de sa dixième session extraordinaire d'urgence. Par une lettre datée du 8 décembre 2003 et reçue au Greffe par télécopie le 10 décembre 2003, dont l'original est parvenu au Greffe ultérieurement, le Secrétaire général de l'Organisation des Nations Unies a officiellement communiqué à la Cour la décision prise par l'Assemblée générale de lui soumettre cette question pour avis consultatif. Des copies certifiées conformes des versions française et anglaise de la résolution ES-10/14 étaient jointes à cette lettre. La résolution se lit comme suit:

«*L'Assemblée générale*,

Réaffirmant sa résolution ES-10/13 du 21 octobre 2003,

Guidée par les principes énoncés dans la Charte des Nations Unies,

Tenant compte du principe, reconnu en droit international, de l'inadmissibilité de l'acquisition de territoire par la force,

Consciente que le développement entre les nations de relations amicales fondées sur le respect du principe de l'égalité de droits des peuples et de leur droit à disposer d'eux-mêmes fait partie des buts et des principes énoncés dans la Charte des Nations Unies,

Rappelant ses résolutions pertinentes, notamment la résolution 181 (II) du 29 novembre 1947, qui portait partition de la Palestine sous mandat en deux Etats, l'un arabe, l'autre juif,

Rappelant également les résolutions de sa dixième session extraordinaire d'urgence,

Rappelant en outre les résolutions pertinentes du Conseil de sécurité, notamment les résolutions 242 (1967) du 22 novembre 1967, 338 (1973) du 22 octobre 1973, 267 (1969) du 3 juillet 1969, 298 (1971) du 25 septembre 1971, 446 (1979) du 22 mars 1979, 452 (1979) du 20 juillet 1979, 465 (1980) du 1er mars 1980, 476 (1980) du 30 juin 1980, 478 (1980) du 20 août 1980, 904 (1994) du 18 mars 1994, 1073 (1996) du 28 septembre 1996, 1397 (2002) du 12 mars 2002 et 1515 (2003) du 19 novembre 2003,

ADVISORY OPINION

Present: *President* SHI; *Vice-President* RANJEVA; *Judges* GUILLAUME, KOROMA, VERESHCHETIN, HIGGINS, PARRA-ARANGUREN, KOOIJMANS, REZEK, AL-KHASAWNEH, BUERGENTHAL, ELARABY, OWADA, SIMMA, TOMKA; *Registrar* COUVREUR.

On the legal consequences of the construction of a wall in the Occupied Palestinian Territory,

THE COURT,

composed as above,

gives the following Advisory Opinion:

1. The question on which the advisory opinion of the Court has been requested is set forth in resolution ES-10/14 adopted by the General Assembly of the United Nations (hereinafter the "General Assembly") on 8 December 2003 at its Tenth Emergency Special Session. By a letter dated 8 December 2003 and received in the Registry by facsimile on 10 December 2003, the original of which reached the Registry subsequently, the Secretary-General of the United Nations officially communicated to the Court the decision taken by the General Assembly to submit the question for an advisory opinion. Certified true copies of the English and French versions of resolution ES-10/14 were enclosed with the letter. The resolution reads as follows:

"*The General Assembly*,

Reaffirming its resolution ES-10/13 of 21 October 2003,

Guided by the principles of the Charter of the United Nations,

Aware of the established principle of international law on the inadmissibility of the acquisition of territory by force,

Aware also that developing friendly relations among nations based on respect for the principle of equal rights and self-determination of peoples is among the purposes and principles of the Charter of the United Nations,

Recalling relevant General Assembly resolutions, including resolution 181 (II) of 29 November 1947, which partitioned mandated Palestine into two States, one Arab and one Jewish,

Recalling also the resolutions of the tenth emergency special session of the General Assembly,

Recalling further relevant Security Council resolutions, including resolutions 242 (1967) of 22 November 1967, 338 (1973) of 22 October 1973, 267 (1969) of 3 July 1969, 298 (1971) of 25 September 1971, 446 (1979) of 22 March 1979, 452 (1979) of 20 July 1979, 465 (1980) of 1 March 1980, 476 (1980) of 30 June 1980, 478 (1980) of 20 August 1980, 904 (1994) of 18 March 1994, 1073 (1996) of 28 September 1996, 1397 (2002) of 12 March 2002 and 1515 (2003) of 19 November 2003,

Réaffirmant l'applicabilité au territoire palestinien occupé, y compris Jérusalem-Est, de la quatrième convention de Genève[1] et du protocole additionnel I aux conventions de Genève[2],

Rappelant le règlement annexé à la convention de La Haye concernant les lois et coutumes de la guerre sur terre de 1907[3],

Se félicitant de la tenue à Genève, le 15 juillet 1999, de la conférence des Hautes Parties contractantes à la quatrième convention de Genève sur les mesures à prendre pour assurer l'application de la convention dans le territoire palestinien occupé, y compris Jérusalem,

Se déclarant favorable à la déclaration adoptée par la conférence des Hautes Parties contractantes réunie de nouveau à Genève le 5 décembre 2001,

Rappelant en particulier les résolutions pertinentes des Nations Unies dans lesquelles il est affirmé que les colonies de peuplement israéliennes dans le territoire palestinien occupé, y compris Jérusalem-Est, sont illégales et constituent un obstacle à la paix et au développement économique et social, ainsi que les résolutions exigeant la cessation complète des activités d'implantation de colonies de peuplement,

Rappelant les résolutions pertinentes des Nations Unies dans lesquelles il est affirmé que les mesures prises par Israël, puissance occupante, pour modifier le statut et la composition démographique de Jérusalem-Est occupée n'ont aucun fondement juridique et sont nulles et non avenues,

Notant les accords auxquels sont parvenus le Gouvernement israélien et l'Organisation de libération de la Palestine dans le contexte du processus de paix au Moyen-Orient,

Gravement préoccupée par le fait qu'Israël, puissance occupante, a commencé et continue à construire un mur dans le territoire palestinien occupé, y compris à l'intérieur et sur le pourtour de Jérusalem-Est, dont le tracé s'écarte de la ligne d'armistice de 1949 (Ligne verte) et qui a entraîné la confiscation et la destruction de terres et de ressources palestiniennes, le bouleversement de la vie de milliers de civils jouissant d'une protection et l'annexion de fait de vastes parties du territoire, et soulignant que la communauté internationale tout entière est opposée à la construction de ce mur,

Gravement préoccupée également par les effets encore plus dévastateurs qu'auraient les parties du mur dont la construction est prévue sur la population civile palestinienne et sur les perspectives de règlement du conflit israélo-palestinien et l'établissement de la paix dans la région,

Prenant note avec satisfaction du rapport du rapporteur spécial de la Commission des droits de l'homme, en date du 8 septembre 2003, sur la situation des droits de l'homme dans les territoires palestiniens occupés par Israël depuis 1967[4], en particulier la partie du rapport relative au mur,

---

[1] Nations Unies, *Recueil des traités*, vol. 75, n° 973.

[2] *Ibid.*, vol. 1125, n° 17512.

[3] Voir Dotation Carnegie pour la paix internationale, *Les conventions et déclarations de La Haye de 1899 et 1907*, New York, Oxford University Press, 1918.

[4] E/CN.4/2004/6.

Reaffirming the applicability of the Fourth Geneva Convention[1] as well as Additional Protocol I to the Geneva Conventions[2] to the Occupied Palestinian Territory, including East Jerusalem,

Recalling the Regulations annexed to the Hague Convention Respecting the Laws and Customs of War on Land of 1907[3],

Welcoming the convening of the Conference of High Contracting Parties to the Fourth Geneva Convention on measures to enforce the Convention in the Occupied Palestinian Territory, including Jerusalem, at Geneva on 15 July 1999,

Expressing its support for the declaration adopted by the reconvened Conference of High Contracting Parties at Geneva on 5 December 2001,

Recalling in particular relevant United Nations resolutions affirming that Israeli settlements in the Occupied Palestinian Territory, including East Jerusalem, are illegal and an obstacle to peace and to economic and social development as well as those demanding the complete cessation of settlement activities,

Recalling relevant United Nations resolutions affirming that actions taken by Israel, the occupying Power, to change the status and demographic composition of Occupied East Jerusalem have no legal validity and are null and void,

Noting the agreements reached between the Government of Israel and the Palestine Liberation Organization in the context of the Middle East peace process,

Gravely concerned at the commencement and continuation of construction by Israel, the occupying Power, of a wall in the Occupied Palestinian Territory, including in and around East Jerusalem, which is in departure from the Armistice Line of 1949 (Green Line) and which has involved the confiscation and destruction of Palestinian land and resources, the disruption of the lives of thousands of protected civilians and the de facto annexation of large areas of territory, and underlining the unanimous opposition by the international community to the construction of that wall,

Gravely concerned also at the even more devastating impact of the projected parts of the wall on the Palestinian civilian population and on the prospects for solving the Palestinian-Israeli conflict and establishing peace in the region,

Welcoming the report of 8 September 2003 of the Special Rapporteur of the Commission on Human Rights on the situation of human rights in the Palestinian territories occupied by Israel since 1967[4], in particular the section regarding the wall,

---

[1] United Nations, *Treaty Series*, Vol. 75, No. 973.

[2] *Ibid.*, Vol. 1125, No. 17512.

[3] See Carnegie Endowment for International Peace, *The Hague Conventions and Declarations of 1899 and 1907* (New York, Oxford University Press, 1915).

[4] E/CN.4/2004/6.

Affirmant qu'il est nécessaire de mettre fin au conflit sur la base d'une solution permettant aux deux Etats, Israël et la Palestine, de vivre côte à côte dans la paix et la sécurité et dans le respect de la ligne d'armistice de 1949, conformément aux résolutions pertinentes du Conseil de sécurité et de l'Assemblée générale,

Ayant reçu avec satisfaction le rapport du Secrétaire général établi en application de la résolution ES-10/13[5],

Ayant à l'esprit que les difficultés sur le terrain ne font que s'aggraver avec le temps, Israël, puissance occupante, continuant à refuser de respecter le droit international pour ce qui est de l'édification du mur susmentionné, avec toutes les répercussions et conséquences néfastes qu'elle entraîne,

Décide, en vertu de l'article 96 de la Charte des Nations Unies, de demander à la Cour internationale de Justice, conformément aux dispositions de l'article 65 du Statut de la Cour, de rendre d'urgence un avis consultatif sur la question suivante:

> Quelles sont en droit les conséquences de l'édification du mur qu'Israël, puissance occupante, est en train de construire dans le territoire palestinien occupé, y compris à l'intérieur et sur le pourtour de Jérusalem-Est, selon ce qui est exposé dans le rapport du Secrétaire général, compte tenu des règles et des principes du droit international, notamment la quatrième convention de Genève de 1949 et les résolutions consacrées à la question par le Conseil de sécurité et l'Assemblée générale?

[5] A/ES-10/248.»

Etaient également joints à la lettre les textes français et anglais certifiés conformes du rapport du Secrétaire général daté du 24 novembre 2003 et établi en application de la résolution ES-10/13 de l'Assemblée générale (A/ES-10/248), auquel la résolution ES-10/14 fait référence.

2. Par des lettres en date du 10 décembre 2003, le greffier a notifié la requête pour avis consultatif à tous les Etats admis à ester devant la Cour, conformément au paragraphe 1 de l'article 66 du Statut.

3. Par une lettre en date du 11 décembre 2003, le Gouvernement d'Israël a informé la Cour de sa position à l'égard tant de la requête pour avis consultatif que de la procédure à suivre.

4. Par une ordonnance en date du 19 décembre 2003, la Cour a décidé que l'Organisation des Nations Unies et ses Etats Membres étaient susceptibles de fournir des renseignements sur l'ensemble des aspects soulevés par la question soumise à la Cour pour avis consultatif, conformément au paragraphe 2 de l'article 66 du Statut, et a fixé au 30 janvier 2004 la date d'expiration du délai dans lequel des exposés écrits pourraient lui être présentés sur cette question conformément au paragraphe 4 de l'article 66 du Statut. Par la même ordonnance, la Cour a décidé par ailleurs que, au vu de la résolution ES-10/14 et du rapport du Secrétaire général transmis avec la requête, et compte tenu du fait que l'Assemblée générale avait accordé à la Palestine un statut spécial d'observateur et que celle-ci était coauteur du projet de résolution demandant l'avis consultatif, la Palestine pourrait également soumettre un exposé écrit sur la question posée, dans le délai sus-indiqué.

5. Par ladite ordonnance, la Cour a en outre décidé, conformément au para-

Affirming the necessity of ending the conflict on the basis of the two-State solution of Israel and Palestine living side by side in peace and security based on the Armistice Line of 1949, in accordance with relevant Security Council and General Assembly resolutions,

Having received with appreciation the report of the Secretary-General, submitted in accordance with resolution ES-10/13[5],

Bearing in mind that the passage of time further compounds the difficulties on the ground, as Israel, the occupying Power, continues to refuse to comply with international law vis-à-vis its construction of the above-mentioned wall, with all its detrimental implications and consequences,

Decides, in accordance with Article 96 of the Charter of the United Nations, to request the International Court of Justice, pursuant to Article 65 of the Statute of the Court, to urgently render an advisory opinion on the following question:

> What are the legal consequences arising from the construction of the wall being built by Israel, the occupying Power, in the Occupied Palestinian Territory, including in and around East Jerusalem, as described in the report of the Secretary-General, considering the rules and principles of international law, including the Fourth Geneva Convention of 1949, and relevant Security Council and General Assembly resolutions?

[5] A/ES-10/248."

Also enclosed with the letter were the certified English and French texts of the report of the Secretary-General dated 24 November 2003, prepared pursuant to General Assembly resolution ES-10/13 (A/ES-10/248), to which resolution ES-10/14 makes reference.

2. By letters dated 10 December 2003, the Registrar notified the request for an advisory opinion to all States entitled to appear before the Court, in accordance with Article 66, paragraph 1, of the Statute.

3. By a letter dated 11 December 2003, the Government of Israel informed the Court of its position on the request for an advisory opinion and on the procedure to be followed.

4. By an Order of 19 December 2003, the Court decided that the United Nations and its Member States were likely, in accordance with Article 66, paragraph 2, of the Statute, to be able to furnish information on all aspects raised by the question submitted to the Court for an advisory opinion and fixed 30 January 2004 as the time-limit within which written statements might be submitted to it on the question in accordance with Article 66, paragraph 4, of the Statute. By the same Order, the Court further decided that, in the light of resolution ES-10/14 and the report of the Secretary-General transmitted with the request, and taking into account the fact that the General Assembly had granted Palestine a special status of observer and that the latter was co-sponsor of the draft resolution requesting the advisory opinion, Palestine might also submit a written statement on the question within the above time-limit.

5. By the aforesaid Order, the Court also decided, in accordance with

graphe 4 de l'article 105 du Règlement, de tenir des audiences publiques au cours desquelles des exposés et observations pourraient être présentés devant elle par l'Organisation des Nations Unies et ses Etats Membres, qu'ils aient ou non déposé des exposés écrits, et a fixé au 23 février 2004 la date d'ouverture desdites audiences. Toujours par la même ordonnance, la Cour a décidé que, pour les motifs exposés ci-dessus (voir paragraphe 4), la Palestine pourrait également participer à la procédure orale. Elle a enfin prié l'Organisation des Nations Unies et ses Etats Membres, ainsi que la Palestine, de faire connaître au Greffe, le 13 février 2004 au plus tard, s'ils entendaient prendre part aux audiences susmentionnées. Par des lettres du 19 décembre 2004, le greffier les a informés des décisions de la Cour et leur a fait tenir copie de l'ordonnance.

6. Statuant sur des demandes présentées ultérieurement par la Ligue des Etats arabes et l'Organisation de la Conférence islamique, la Cour a décidé, conformément à l'article 66 de son Statut, que ces deux organisations internationales étaient susceptibles de fournir des renseignements sur la question dont la Cour est saisie, et qu'en conséquence elles pourraient présenter à cette fin des exposés écrits dans le délai fixé par la Cour dans son ordonnance du 19 décembre 2003 et participer à la procédure orale.

7. Conformément au paragraphe 2 de l'article 65 du Statut, le Secrétaire général de l'Organisation des Nations Unies a communiqué à la Cour un dossier contenant des documents pouvant servir à élucider la question.

8. Par une ordonnance motivée en date du 30 janvier 2004 concernant sa composition en l'espèce, la Cour a décidé que les éléments portés à son attention par le Gouvernement d'Israël dans une lettre du 31 décembre 2003, ainsi que dans une lettre confidentielle du 15 janvier 2004 adressée au président en vertu du paragraphe 2 de l'article 34 du Règlement, n'étaient pas de nature à empêcher le juge Elaraby de siéger en l'espèce.

9. Dans le délai fixé par la Cour à cette fin, des exposés écrits ont été déposés, selon l'ordre de réception, par: la Guinée, l'Arabie saoudite, la Ligue des Etats arabes, l'Egypte, le Cameroun, la Fédération de Russie, l'Australie, la Palestine, l'Organisation des Nations Unies, la Jordanie, le Koweït, le Liban, le Canada, la Syrie, la Suisse, Israël, le Yémen, les Etats-Unis d'Amérique, le Maroc, l'Indonésie, l'Organisation de la Conférence islamique, la France, l'Italie, le Soudan, l'Afrique du Sud, l'Allemagne, le Japon, la Norvège, le Royaume-Uni, le Pakistan, la République tchèque, la Grèce, l'Irlande en son nom propre, l'Irlande au nom de l'Union européenne, Chypre, le Brésil, la Namibie, Malte, la Malaisie, les Pays-Bas, Cuba, la Suède, l'Espagne, la Belgique, Palau, les Etats fédérés de Micronésie, les Iles Marshall, le Sénégal et la République populaire démocratique de Corée. Dès réception de ces exposés, le greffier en a transmis le texte à l'Organisation des Nations Unies et ses Etats Membres, à la Palestine, à la Ligue des Etats arabes, ainsi qu'à l'Organisation de la Conférence islamique.

10. Diverses correspondances ont été adressées par le Greffe à ces derniers, concernant notamment les dispositions prises pour l'organisation de la procédure orale. Par des communications du 20 février 2004, le Greffe a fait tenir le calendrier détaillé des audiences à ceux d'entre eux qui avaient manifesté, dans le délai fixé par la Cour à cet effet, leur intention de prendre part à ladite procédure.

11. Conformément à l'article 106 du Règlement, la Cour a décidé de rendre accessible au public le texte des exposés écrits à la date d'ouverture de la procédure orale.

Article 105, paragraph 4, of the Rules of Court, to hold public hearings during which oral statements and comments might be presented to it by the United Nations and its Member States, regardless of whether or not they had submitted written statements, and fixed 23 February 2004 as the date for the opening of the said hearings. By the same Order, the Court decided that, for the reasons set out above (see paragraph 4), Palestine might also take part in the hearings. Lastly, it invited the United Nations and its Member States, as well as Palestine, to inform the Registry, by 13 February 2004 at the latest, if they were intending to take part in the above-mentioned hearings. By letters of 19 December 2004, the Registrar informed them of the Court's decisions and transmitted to them a copy of the Order.

6. Ruling on requests submitted subsequently by the League of Arab States and the Organization of the Islamic Conference, the Court decided, in accordance with Article 66 of its Statute, that those two international organizations were likely to be able to furnish information on the question submitted to the Court, and that consequently they might for that purpose submit written statements within the time-limit fixed by the Court in its Order of 19 December 2003 and take part in the hearings.

7. Pursuant to Article 65, paragraph 2, of the Statute, the Secretary-General of the United Nations communicated to the Court a dossier of documents likely to throw light upon the question.

8. By a reasoned Order of 30 January 2004 regarding its composition in the case, the Court decided that the matters brought to its attention by the Government of Israel in a letter of 31 December 2003, and in a confidential letter of 15 January 2004 addressed to the President pursuant to Article 34, paragraph 2, of the Rules of Court, were not such as to preclude Judge Elaraby from sitting in the case.

9. Within the time-limit fixed by the Court for that purpose, written statements were filed by, in order of their receipt: Guinea, Saudi Arabia, League of Arab States, Egypt, Cameroon, Russian Federation, Australia, Palestine, United Nations, Jordan, Kuwait, Lebanon, Canada, Syria, Switzerland, Israel, Yemen, United States of America, Morocco, Indonesia, Organization of the Islamic Conference, France, Italy, Sudan, South Africa, Germany, Japan, Norway, United Kingdom, Pakistan, Czech Republic, Greece, Ireland on its own behalf, Ireland on behalf of the European Union, Cyprus, Brazil, Namibia, Malta, Malaysia, Netherlands, Cuba, Sweden, Spain, Belgium, Palau, Federated States of Micronesia, Marshall Islands, Senegal, Democratic People's Republic of Korea. Upon receipt of those statements, the Registrar transmitted copies thereof to the United Nations and its Member States, to Palestine, to the League of Arab States and to the Organization of the Islamic Conference.

10. Various communications were addressed to these latter by the Registry, concerning in particular the measures taken for the organization of the oral proceedings. By communications of 20 February 2004, the Registry transmitted a detailed timetable of the hearings to those of the latter who, within the time-limit fixed for that purpose by the Court, had expressed their intention of taking part in the aforementioned proceedings.

11. Pursuant to Article 106 of the Rules of Court, the Court decided to make the written statements accessible to the public, with effect from the opening of the oral proceedings.

12. Au cours d'audiences tenues du 23 au 25 février 2004, la Cour a entendu en leurs exposés oraux et dans l'ordre suivant:

pour la Palestine:

S. Exc. M. Nasser Al-Kidwa, ambassadeur, observateur permanent de la Palestine auprès de l'Organisation des Nations Unies,

Mme Stephanie Koury, membre du groupe d'appui aux négociations, conseil,

M. James Crawford, S.C., professeur de droit international à l'Université de Cambridge (chaire Whewell), membre de l'Institut de droit international, conseil et avocat,

M. Georges Abi-Saab, professeur de droit international à l'Institut universitaire de hautes études internationales de Genève, membre de l'Institut de droit international, conseil et avocat,

M. Vaughan Lowe, professeur de droit international à l'Université d'Oxford (chaire Chichele), conseil et avocat,

M. Jean Salmon, professeur émérite de droit international à l'Université libre de Bruxelles, membre de l'Institut de droit international, conseil et avocat;

pour la République sud-africaine:

S. Exc. M. Aziz Pahad, vice-ministre des affaires étrangères, chef de délégation,

M. M. R. W. Madlanga, S.C., juge;

pour la République algérienne démocratique et populaire:

M. Ahmed Laraba, professeur de droit international;

pour le Royaume d'Arabie saoudite:

S. Exc. M. Fawzi A. Shobokshi, ambassadeur et représentant permanent du Royaume d'Arabie saoudite auprès de l'Organisation des Nations Unies à New York, chef de délégation;

pour la République populaire du Bangladesh:

S. Exc. M. Liaquat Ali Choudhury, ambassadeur de la République populaire du Bangladesh auprès du Royaume des Pays-Bas;

pour Belize:

M. Jean-Marc Sorel, professeur à l'Université de Paris I (Panthéon-Sorbonne);

pour la République de Cuba:

S. Exc. M. Abelardo Moreno Fernández, vice-ministre des affaires étrangères;

pour la République d'Indonésie:

S. Exc. M. Mohammad Jusuf, ambassadeur de la République d'Indonésie auprès du Royaume des Pays-Bas, chef de délégation;

pour le Royaume hachémite de Jordanie:

S. A. R. Zeid Ra'ad Zeid Al-Hussein, ambassadeur, représentant permanent du Royaume hachémite de Jordanie auprès de l'Organisation des Nations Unies, chef de délégation,

sir Arthur Watts, K.C.M.G., Q.C., conseiller juri-

12. In the course of hearings held from 23 to 25 February 2004, the Court heard oral statements, in the following order, by:

for Palestine:	H.E. Mr. Nasser Al-Kidwa, Ambassador, Permanent Observer of Palestine to the United Nations, Ms Stephanie Koury, Member, Negotiations Support Unit, Counsel, Mr. James Crawford, S.C., Whewell Professor of International Law, University of Cambridge, Member of the Institute of International Law, Counsel and Advocate, Mr. Georges Abi-Saab, Professor of International Law, Graduate Institute of International Studies, Geneva, Member of the Institute of International Law, Counsel and Advocate, Mr. Vaughan Lowe, Chichele Professor of International Law, University of Oxford, Counsel and Advocate, Mr. Jean Salmon, Professor Emeritus of International Law, Université libre de Bruxelles, Member of the Institute of International Law, Counsel and Advocate;
for the Republic of South Africa:	H.E. Mr. Aziz Pahad, Deputy Minister for Foreign Affairs, Head of Delegation, Judge M. R. W. Madlanga, S.C.;
for the People's Democratic Republic of Algeria:	Mr. Ahmed Laraba, Professor of International Law;
for the Kingdom of Saudi Arabia:	H.E. Mr. Fawzi A. Shobokshi, Ambassador and Permanent Representative of the Kingdom of Saudi Arabia to the United Nations in New York, Head of Delegation;
for the People's Republic of Bangladesh:	H.E. Mr. Liaquat Ali Choudhury, Ambassador of the People's Republic of Bangladesh to the Kingdom of the Netherlands;
for Belize:	Mr. Jean-Marc Sorel, Professor at the University of Paris I (Panthéon-Sorbonne);
for the Republic of Cuba:	H.E. Mr. Abelardo Moreno Fernández, Deputy Minister for Foreign Affairs;
for the Republic of Indonesia:	H.E. Mr. Mohammad Jusuf, Ambassador of the Republic of Indonesia to the Kingdom of the Netherlands, Head of Delegation;
for the Hashemite Kingdom of Jordan:	H.R.H. Ambassador Zeid Ra'ad Zeid Al-Hussein, Permanent Representative of the Hashemite Kingdom of Jordan to the United Nations, New York, Head of Delegation, Sir Arthur Watts, K.C.M.G., Q.C., Senior Legal

	dique principal du Gouvernement du Royaume hachémite de Jordanie;
pour la République de Madagascar:	S. Exc. M. Alfred Rambeloson, représentant permanent de Madagascar auprès de l'Office des Nations Unies et des institutions spécialisées à Genève, chef de délégation;
pour la Malaisie:	S. Exc. Datuk Seri Syed Hamid Albar, ministre des affaires étrangères, chef de délégation;
pour la République du Sénégal:	S. Exc. M. Saliou Cissé, ambassadeur de la République du Sénégal auprès du Royaume des Pays-Bas, chef de délégation;
pour la République du Soudan:	S. Exc. M. Abuelgasim A. Idris, ambassadeur de la République du Soudan auprès du Royaume des Pays-Bas;
pour la Ligue des Etats arabes:	M. Michael Bothe, professeur de droit, chef de l'équipe juridique;
pour l'Organisation de la Conférence islamique:	S. Exc. M. Abdelouahed Belkeziz, Secrétaire général de l'Organisation de la Conférence islamique, Mme Monique Chemillier-Gendreau, professeur de droit public à l'Université Paris VII-Denis Diderot, conseil.

* * *

13. Lorsqu'elle est saisie d'une demande d'avis consultatif, la Cour doit commencer par déterminer si elle a compétence pour donner l'avis demandé et, dans l'affirmative, s'il existe une quelconque raison pour elle de refuser d'exercer une telle compétence (voir *Licéité de la menace ou de l'emploi d'armes nucléaires, avis consultatif, C.I.J. Recueil 1996 (I)*, p. 232, par. 10).

* *

14. La Cour se penchera donc en premier lieu sur la question de savoir si elle a compétence pour donner l'avis consultatif demandé par l'Assemblée générale le 8 décembre 2003. La compétence de la Cour en la matière est fondée sur le paragraphe 1 de l'article 65 de son Statut, aux termes duquel la Cour «peut donner un avis consultatif sur toute question juridique, à la demande de tout organe ou institution qui aura été autorisé par la Charte des Nations Unies ou conformément à ses dispositions à demander cet avis». La Cour a déjà eu l'occasion d'indiquer que:

> «pour qu[elle] ait compétence, il faut que l'avis consultatif soit demandé par un organe dûment habilité à cet effet conformément à la Charte, qu'il porte sur une question juridique et que, sauf dans le cas de l'Assemblée générale et du Conseil de sécurité, cette question se pose dans le cadre de l'activité de cet organe» (*Demande de réformation du jugement n° 273 du Tribunal administratif des Nations Unies, avis consultatif, C.I.J. Recueil 1982*, p. 333-334, par. 21).

Adviser to the Government of the Hashemite Kingdom of Jordan;

for the Republic of Madagascar:	H.E. Mr. Alfred Rambeloson, Permanent Representative of Madagascar to the Office of the United Nations at Geneva and to the Specialized Agencies, Head of Delegation;
for Malaysia:	H.E. Datuk Seri Syed Hamid Albar, Foreign Minister of Malaysia, Head of Delegation;
for the Republic of Senegal:	H.E. Mr. Saliou Cissé, Ambassador of the Republic of Senegal to the Kingdom of the Netherlands, Head of Delegation;
for the Republic of the Sudan:	H.E. Mr. Abuelgasim A. Idris, Ambassador of the Republic of the Sudan to the Kingdom of the Netherlands;
for the League of Arab States:	Mr. Michael Bothe, Professor of Law, Head of the Legal Team;
for the Organization of the Islamic Conference:	H.E. Mr. Abdelouahed Belkeziz, Secretary General of the Organization of the Islamic Conference, Ms Monique Chemillier-Gendreau, Professor of Public Law, University of Paris VII-Denis Diderot, as Counsel.

* * *

13. When seised of a request for an advisory opinion, the Court must first consider whether it has jurisdiction to give the opinion requested and whether, should the answer be in the affirmative, there is any reason why it should decline to exercise any such jurisdiction (see *Legality of the Threat or Use of Nuclear Weapons, Advisory Opinion, I.C.J. Reports 1996 (I)*, p. 232, para. 10).

* *

14. The Court will thus first address the question whether it possesses jurisdiction to give the advisory opinion requested by the General Assembly on 8 December 2003. The competence of the Court in this regard is based on Article 65, paragraph 1, of its Statute, according to which the Court "may give an advisory opinion on any legal question at the request of whatever body may be authorized by or in accordance with the Charter of the United Nations to make such a request". The Court has already had occasion to indicate that:

> "It is . . . a precondition of the Court's competence that the advisory opinion be requested by an organ duly authorized to seek it under the Charter, that it be requested on a legal question, and that, except in the case of the General Assembly or the Security Council, that question should be one arising within the scope of the activities of the requesting organ." (*Application for Review of Judgement No. 273 of the United Nations Administrative Tribunal, Advisory Opinion, I.C.J. Reports 1982,* pp. 333-334, para. 21.)

15. C'est à la Cour qu'il appartient de s'assurer que la demande d'avis consultatif émane d'un organe ou d'une institution ayant compétence pour ce faire. Dans la présente espèce, la Cour relève que l'Assemblée générale, qui demande l'avis consultatif, est autorisée à le faire en vertu du paragraphe 1 de l'article 96 de la Charte, qui dispose que «[l]'Assemblée générale ou le Conseil de sécurité peut demander à la Cour internationale de Justice un avis consultatif sur toute question juridique».

16. Bien que la disposition précitée prévoie que l'Assemblée générale peut demander un avis consultatif «sur toute question juridique», la Cour a parfois, dans le passé, donné certaines indications quant à la relation entre la question faisant l'objet d'une demande d'avis consultatif et les activités de l'Assemblée générale (*Interprétation des traités de paix conclus avec la Bulgarie, la Hongrie et la Roumanie, C.I.J. Recueil 1950*, p. 70; *Licéité de la menace ou de l'emploi d'armes nucléaires, C.I.J. Recueil 1996 (I)*, p. 232 et 233, par. 11 et 12).

17. La Cour fera de même en l'espèce. Elle relèvera à cet égard que l'article 10 de la Charte a conféré à l'Assemblée générale une compétence à l'égard de «toutes questions ou affaires» entrant dans le cadre de la Charte, et que le paragraphe 2 de l'article 11 lui a spécifiquement donné compétence à l'égard de «toutes questions se rattachant au maintien de la paix et de la sécurité internationales dont elle aura été saisie par l'une quelconque des Nations Unies...» et pour faire des recommandations sous certaines conditions posées dans ces deux articles. Comme il sera expliqué plus loin, la question de la construction du mur dans le territoire palestinien occupé a été soumise à l'Assemblée générale par un certain nombre d'Etats Membres dans le cadre de sa dixième session extraordinaire d'urgence, convoquée pour examiner ce que l'Assemblée, dans sa résolution ES-10/2 du 25 avril 1997, avait considéré comme constituant une menace à la paix et à la sécurité internationales.

*

18. Avant de se pencher plus avant sur les questions de compétence qui ont été soulevées dans la présente affaire, la Cour estime nécessaire de décrire les événements qui ont conduit à l'adoption de la résolution ES-10/14, par laquelle l'Assemblée générale a demandé un avis consultatif sur les conséquences juridiques de la construction du mur dans le territoire palestinien occupé.

19. La dixième session extraordinaire d'urgence de l'Assemblée générale, au cours de laquelle a été adoptée cette résolution, fut convoquée pour la première fois après que, les 7 et 21 mars 1997, le Conseil de sécurité, du fait du vote négatif de l'un de ses membres permanents, eut rejeté deux projets de résolution relatifs à certaines colonies israéliennes dans le territoire palestinien occupé (voir, respectivement, S/1997/199 et S/PV.3747, S/1997/241 et S/PV.3756). Par une lettre du 31 mars 1997, le président du Groupe arabe demanda alors «que l'Assemblée générale soit convoquée en session extraordinaire d'urgence, conformément à la réso-

15. It is for the Court to satisfy itself that the request for an advisory opinion comes from an organ or agency having competence to make it. In the present instance, the Court notes that the General Assembly, which seeks the advisory opinion, is authorized to do so by Article 96, paragraph 1, of the Charter, which provides: "The General Assembly or the Security Council may request the International Court of Justice to give an advisory opinion on any legal question."

16. Although the above-mentioned provision states that the General Assembly may seek an advisory opinion "on any legal question", the Court has sometimes in the past given certain indications as to the relationship between the question the subject of a request for an advisory opinion and the activities of the General Assembly (*Interpretation of Peace Treaties with Bulgaria, Hungary and Romania, I.C.J. Reports 1950*, p. 70; *Legality of the Threat or Use of Nuclear Weapons, I.C.J. Reports 1996 (I)*, pp. 232 and 233, paras. 11 and 12).

17. The Court will so proceed in the present case. The Court would observe that Article 10 of the Charter has conferred upon the General Assembly a competence relating to "any questions or any matters" within the scope of the Charter, and that Article 11, paragraph 2, has specifically provided it with competence on "questions relating to the maintenance of international peace and security brought before it by any Member of the United Nations . . ." and to make recommendations under certain conditions fixed by those Articles. As will be explained below, the question of the construction of the wall in the Occupied Palestinian Territory was brought before the General Assembly by a number of Member States in the context of the Tenth Emergency Special Session of the Assembly, convened to deal with what the Assembly, in its resolution ES-10/2 of 25 April 1997, considered to constitute a threat to international peace and security.

*

18. Before further examining the problems of jurisdiction that have been raised in the present proceedings, the Court considers it necessary to describe the events that led to the adoption of resolution ES-10/14, by which the General Assembly requested an advisory opinion on the legal consequences of the construction of the wall in the Occupied Palestinian Territory.

19. The Tenth Emergency Special Session of the General Assembly, at which that resolution was adopted, was first convened following the rejection by the Security Council, on 7 March and 21 March 1997, as a result of negative votes by a permanent member, of two draft resolutions concerning certain Israeli settlements in the Occupied Palestinian Territory (see, respectively, S/1997/199 and S/PV.3747, and S/1997/241 and S/PV.3756). By a letter of 31 March 1997, the Chairman of the Arab Group then requested "that an emergency special session of the General Assembly be convened pursuant to resolution 377 A (V) entitled 'Uniting

lution 377 A (V) intitulée «L'union pour le maintien de la paix»», en vue de débattre des «mesures illégales prises par les autorités israéliennes à Jérusalem-Est occupée ainsi que dans le reste du territoire palestinien occupé» (lettre du 31 mars 1997, adressée au Secrétaire général par le représentant permanent du Qatar auprès de l'Organisation des Nations Unies, A/ES-10/1, 22 avril 1997, annexe). Cette demande ayant recueilli l'agrément de la majorité des Membres de l'Organisation des Nations Unies, la première séance de la dixième session extraordinaire d'urgence de l'Assemblée générale eut lieu le 24 avril 1997 (voir A/ES-10/1, 22 avril 1997). Dans sa résolution ES-10/2 adoptée le jour suivant, l'Assemblée générale se déclarait convaincue que

> «les violations répétées du droit international par Israël, puissance occupante, et la non-application par ce pays des résolutions pertinentes du Conseil de sécurité et de l'Assemblée générale et des accords auxquels sont parvenues les parties, portent atteinte au processus de paix au Moyen-Orient et constituent une menace à la paix et à la sécurité internationales»,

et condamnait les «mesures illégales prises par Israël» à Jérusalem-Est occupée et dans le reste du territoire palestinien occupé, en particulier la construction de colonies dans ce territoire. La dixième session extraordinaire d'urgence fut ensuite temporairement ajournée, et a été depuis lors convoquée à nouveau onze fois (les 15 juillet 1997, 13 novembre 1997, 17 mars 1998, 5 février 1999, 18 octobre 2000, 20 décembre 2001, 7 mai 2002, 5 août 2002, 19 septembre 2003, 20 octobre 2003 et 8 décembre 2003).

20. Par une lettre du 9 octobre 2003, le président du Groupe arabe, agissant au nom des Etats membres de la Ligue des Etats arabes, demanda que le Conseil de sécurité se réunisse sans délai pour examiner les «graves violations du droit international, y compris le droit international humanitaire, qu'Israël continue de commettre et [prendre] les mesures qui s'imposent en la matière» (lettre du 9 octobre 2003, adressée au président du Conseil de sécurité par le représentant permanent de la République arabe syrienne auprès de l'Organisation des Nations Unies, S/2003/973, 9 octobre 2003). Cette lettre était accompagnée d'un projet de résolution soumis à l'examen du Conseil, projet qui condamnait comme illicite la construction par Israël d'un mur dans le territoire palestinien occupé selon un tracé s'écartant de la ligne d'armistice de 1949. Le Conseil de sécurité tint ses 4841e et 4842e séances le 14 octobre 2003 pour examiner le point intitulé «La situation au Moyen-Orient, y compris la question de Palestine». Un autre projet de résolution lui avait été soumis le même jour par la Guinée, la Malaisie, le Pakistan et la République arabe syrienne, condamnant également la construction du mur. Ce dernier projet de résolution, mis aux voix au terme d'un débat ouvert, fut rejeté en raison du vote négatif de l'un des membres permanents du Conseil (S/PV.4841 et S/PV.4842).

Le 15 octobre 2003, le président du Groupe arabe, agissant au nom des for Peace' " with a view to discussing "Illegal Israeli actions in occupied East Jerusalem and the rest of the Occupied Palestinian Territory" (letter dated 31 March 1997 from the Permanent Representative of Qatar to the United Nations addressed to the Secretary-General, A/ES-10/1, 22 April 1997, Annex). The majority of Members of the United Nations having concurred in this request, the first meeting of the Tenth Emergency Special Session of the General Assembly took place on 24 April 1997 (see A/ES-10/1, 22 April 1997). Resolution ES-10/2 was adopted the following day; the General Assembly thereby expressed its conviction that:

> "the repeated violation by Israel, the occupying Power, of international law and its failure to comply with relevant Security Council and General Assembly resolutions and the agreements reached between the parties undermine the Middle East peace process and constitute a threat to international peace and security",

and condemned the "illegal Israeli actions" in occupied East Jerusalem and the rest of the Occupied Palestinian Territory, in particular the construction of settlements in that territory. The Tenth Emergency Special Session was then adjourned temporarily and has since been reconvened 11 times (on 15 July 1997, 13 November 1997, 17 March 1998, 5 February 1999, 18 October 2000, 20 December 2001, 7 May 2002, 5 August 2002, 19 September 2003, 20 October 2003 and 8 December 2003).

20. By a letter dated 9 October 2003, the Chairman of the Arab Group, on behalf of the States Members of the League of Arab States, requested an immediate meeting of the Security Council to consider the "grave and ongoing Israeli violations of international law, including international humanitarian law, and to take the necessary measures in this regard" (letter of 9 October 2003 from the Permanent Representative of the Syrian Arab Republic to the United Nations to the President of the Security Council, S/2003/973, 9 October 2003). This letter was accompanied by a draft resolution for consideration by the Council, which condemned as illegal the construction by Israel of a wall in the Occupied Palestinian Territory departing from the Armistice Line of 1949. The Security Council held its 4841st and 4842nd meetings on 14 October 2003 to consider the item entitled "The situation in the Middle East, including the Palestine question". It then had before it another draft resolution proposed on the same day by Guinea, Malaysia, Pakistan and the Syrian Arab Republic, which also condemned the construction of the wall. This latter draft resolution was put to a vote after an open debate and was not adopted owing to the negative vote of a permanent member of the Council (S/PV.4841 and S/PV.4842).

On 15 October 2003, the Chairman of the Arab Group, on behalf of

Etats membres de la Ligue des Etats arabes, demanda la reprise de la dixième session extraordinaire d'urgence de l'Assemblée générale en vue d'examiner le point intitulé «Mesures illégales prises par Israël à Jérusalem-Est occupée et dans le reste du territoire palestinien occupé» (A/ES-10/242); cette demande fut soutenue par le Mouvement des pays non alignés (A/ES-10/243) et par le groupe de l'Organisation de la Conférence islamique à l'Organisation des Nations Unies (A/ES-10/244). La dixième session extraordinaire d'urgence reprit ses travaux le 20 octobre 2003.

21. Le 27 octobre 2003, l'Assemblée générale adoptait la résolution ES-10/13, par laquelle elle exigeait que

> «Israël arrête la construction du mur dans le territoire palestinien occupé, y compris Jérusalem-Est et ses alentours, et revienne sur ce projet, qui s'écarte de la ligne d'armistice de 1949 et qui est contraire aux dispositions pertinentes du droit international» (par. 1).

Au paragraphe 3, elle priait le Secrétaire général

> «de rendre compte périodiquement de la façon dont la ... résolution [serait] respectée, son premier rapport sur l'application du paragraphe 1 [de ladite résolution] devant être présenté dans un délai d'un mois...».

La clôture de la dixième session extraordinaire d'urgence fut temporairement prononcée, et le rapport du Secrétaire général établi en application de la résolution ES-10/13 de l'Assemblée générale (ci-après dénommé le «rapport du Secrétaire général») fut publié le 24 novembre 2003 (A/ES-10/248).

22. Entre-temps, le 19 novembre 2003, le Conseil de sécurité avait adopté la résolution 1515 (2003), par laquelle il «*[a]pprouv[ait]* la feuille de route axée sur les résultats en vue d'un règlement permanent du conflit israélo-palestinien prévoyant deux Etats, établie par le Quatuor». Le Quatuor est composé des représentants des Etats-Unis d'Amérique, de l'Union européenne, de la Fédération de Russie et de l'Organisation des Nations Unies. La résolution

> «*[d]emand[ait]* aux parties de s'acquitter des obligations ... leur incomb[a]nt en vertu de la feuille de route, en coopération avec le Quatuor, et de concrétiser la vision de deux Etats vivant côte à côte dans la paix et la sécurité».

Ni ladite «feuille de route» ni la résolution 1515 (2003) ne contenaient de disposition concernant explicitement la construction du mur, question qui ne fut pas alors examinée par le Conseil de sécurité.

23. Dix-neuf jours plus tard, le 8 décembre 2003, la dixième session extraordinaire d'urgence de l'Assemblée générale reprenait ses travaux, à la suite d'une nouvelle demande présentée par le président du Groupe des Etats arabes, au nom des Etats membres de la Ligue des Etats arabes, et conformément à la résolution ES-10/13 (lettre du 1er décembre 2003, adressée au président de l'Assemblée générale par le chargé d'affaires par

the States Members of the League of Arab States, requested the resumption of the Tenth Emergency Special Session of the General Assembly to consider the item of "Illegal Israeli actions in Occupied East Jerusalem and the rest of the Occupied Palestinian Territory" (A/ES-10/242); this request was supported by the Non-Aligned Movement (A/ES-10/243) and the Organization of the Islamic Conference Group at the United Nations (A/ES-10/244). The Tenth Emergency Special Session resumed its work on 20 October 2003.

21. On 27 October 2003, the General Assembly adopted resolution ES-10/13, by which it demanded that

> "Israel stop and reverse the construction of the wall in the Occupied Palestinian Territory, including in and around East Jerusalem, which is in departure of the Armistice Line of 1949 and is in contradiction to relevant provisions of international law" (para. 1).

In paragraph 3, the Assembly requested the Secretary-General

> "to report on compliance with the . . . resolution periodically, with the first report on compliance with paragraph 1 [of that resolution] to be submitted within one month . . .".

The Tenth Emergency Special Session was temporarily adjourned and, on 24 November 2003, the report of the Secretary-General prepared pursuant to General Assembly resolution ES-10/13 (hereinafter the "report of the Secretary-General") was issued (A/ES-10/248).

22. Meanwhile, on 19 November 2003, the Security Council adopted resolution 1515 (2003), by which it "*Endorse[d]* the Quartet Performance-based Roadmap to a Permanent Two-State Solution to the Israeli-Palestinian Conflict". The Quartet consists of representatives of the United States of America, the European Union, the Russian Federation and the United Nations. That resolution

> "*Call[ed] on* the parties to fulfil their obligations under the Roadmap in cooperation with the Quartet and to achieve the vision of two States living side by side in peace and security."

Neither the "Roadmap" nor resolution 1515 (2003) contained any specific provision concerning the construction of the wall, which was not discussed by the Security Council in this context.

23. Nineteen days later, on 8 December 2003, the Tenth Emergency Special Session of the General Assembly again resumed its work, following a new request by the Chairman of the Arab Group, on behalf of the States Members of the League of Arab States, and pursuant to resolution ES-10/13 (letter dated 1 December 2003 to the President of the General Assembly from the Chargé d'affaires a.i. of the Permanent Mission

intérim de la mission permanente du Koweït auprès de l'Organisation des Nations Unies, doc. A/ES-10/249, 2 décembre 2003). C'est au cours de la séance convoquée ce jour-là qu'a été adoptée la résolution ES-10/14 portant demande du présent avis consultatif.

*

24. Ayant ainsi rappelé la chronologie des événements qui ont conduit à l'adoption de la résolution ES-10/14, la Cour abordera maintenant les questions de compétence soulevées en la présente espèce. Tout d'abord, Israël a prétendu que, compte tenu du rôle actif joué par le Conseil de sécurité à l'égard de la situation au Moyen-Orient, y compris la question palestinienne, l'Assemblée générale, en demandant un avis consultatif sur les conséquences juridiques de l'édification du mur dans le territoire palestinien occupé, avait outrepassé la compétence que lui confère la Charte.

25. La Cour a déjà indiqué que l'objet de la requête portant demande du présent avis consultatif relevait de la compétence de l'Assemblée générale en vertu de la Charte (voir paragraphes 15 à 17 ci-dessus). Le paragraphe 1 de l'article 12 de la Charte dispose toutefois que:

> «Tant que le Conseil de sécurité remplit, à l'égard d'un différend ou d'une situation quelconque, les fonctions qui lui sont attribuées par la présente Charte, l'Assemblée générale ne doit faire aucune recommandation sur ce différend ou cette situation, à moins que le Conseil de sécurité ne le lui demande.»

Une requête pour avis consultatif ne constitue pas en soi une «recommandation» de l'Assemblée générale «sur [un] différend ou [une] situation». Il a cependant été soutenu en l'espèce que l'adoption de la résolution ES-10/14 par l'Assemblée générale avait outrepassé la compétence de celle-ci, en tant qu'elle n'était pas conforme à l'article 12. Aussi la Cour juge-t-elle opportun d'examiner le sens qu'il convient de donner à cet article, compte tenu des textes pertinents et de la pratique des Nations Unies.

26. En vertu de l'article 24 de la Charte, le Conseil de sécurité a «la responsabilité principale du maintien de la paix et de la sécurité internationales». Ainsi a-t-il à cet égard la faculté d'imposer aux Etats «l'obligation explicite de se conformer aux ordres qu'il peut émettre au titre du chapitre VII» et, à cette fin, de «prescrire des mesures d'exécution par une action coercitive» (*Certaines dépenses des Nations Unies (article 17, paragraphe 2 de la Charte), avis consultatif, C.I.J. Recueil 1962*, p. 163). La Cour relèvera toutefois que l'article 24 fait mention d'une compétence principale, mais pas nécessairement exclusive. L'Assemblée générale a par exemple le pouvoir, en vertu de l'article 14 de la Charte, de «recommander les mesures propres à assurer l'ajustement pacifique» de diverses situations (*ibid.*).

> «[L]a seule restriction que l'article 14 impose à l'Assemblée géné-

of Kuwait to the United Nations, A/ES-10/249, 2 December 2003). It was during the meeting convened on that day that resolution ES-10/14 requesting the present advisory opinion was adopted.

*

24. Having thus recalled the sequence of events that led to the adoption of resolution ES-10/14, the Court will now turn to the questions of jurisdiction that have been raised in the present proceedings. First, Israel has alleged that, given the active engagement of the Security Council with the situation in the Middle East, including the Palestinian question, the General Assembly acted *ultra vires* under the Charter when it requested an advisory opinion on the legal consequences of the construction of the wall in the Occupied Palestinian Territory.

25. The Court has already indicated that the subject of the present request for an advisory opinion falls within the competence of the General Assembly under the Charter (see paragraphs 15-17 above). However, Article 12, paragraph 1, of the Charter provides that:

> "While the Security Council is exercising in respect of any dispute or situation the functions assigned to it in the present Charter, the General Assembly shall not make any recommendation with regard to that dispute or situation unless the Security Council so requests."

A request for an advisory opinion is not in itself a "recommendation" by the General Assembly "with regard to [a] dispute or situation". It has however been argued in this case that the adoption by the General Assembly of resolution ES-10/14 was *ultra vires* as not in accordance with Article 12. The Court thus considers that it is appropriate for it to examine the significance of that Article, having regard to the relevant texts and the practice of the United Nations.

26. Under Article 24 of the Charter the Security Council has "primary responsibility for the maintenance of international peace and security". In that regard it can impose on States "an explicit obligation of compliance if for example it issues an order or command . . . under Chapter VII" and can, to that end, "require enforcement by coercive action" (*Certain Expenses of the United Nations (Article 17, paragraph 2, of the Charter), Advisory Opinion, I.C.J. Reports 1962*, p. 163). However, the Court would emphasize that Article 24 refers to a primary, but not necessarily exclusive, competence. The General Assembly does have the power, *inter alia*, under Article 14 of the Charter, to "recommend measures for the peaceful adjustment" of various situations (*ibid.*).

> "[T]he only limitation which Article 14 imposes on the General

rale est celle qui figure à l'article 12, c'est-à-dire que l'Assemblée ne peut recommander de mesures tant que le Conseil de sécurité traite de la même question, à moins que [celui-ci] ne le lui demande.» (*C.I.J. Recueil 1962*, p. 163.)

27. S'agissant de la pratique de l'Organisation des Nations Unies, l'Assemblée générale et le Conseil de sécurité interprétèrent et appliquèrent l'un et l'autre, dans un premier temps, l'article 12 comme faisant obstacle à ce que l'Assemblée puisse formuler des recommandations sur une question relative au maintien de la paix et de la sécurité internationales restant inscrite à l'ordre du jour du Conseil. Ainsi l'Assemblée refusa-t-elle, durant sa quatrième session, de recommander certaines mesures concernant la question indonésienne, au motif, entre autres, que le Conseil demeurait saisi de la question (*Documents officiels de la quatrième session de l'Assemblée générale, Commission politique spéciale, comptes rendus analytiques des séances, 27 septembre-7 décembre 1949*, 56e séance, 3 décembre 1949, p. 361, par. 118). Le Conseil lui-même raya à plusieurs reprises certains points de son ordre du jour afin de permettre à l'Assemblée de délibérer sur ceux-ci (par exemple, en ce qui concerne la question espagnole (*Procès-verbaux officiels du Conseil de sécurité, première année: seconde série, n° 21*, 79e séance, 4 novembre 1946, p. 498), certains incidents à la frontière grecque (*Procès-verbaux officiels du Conseil de sécurité, deuxième année, n° 89*, 202e séance, 15 septembre 1947, p. 2404-2405) et l'île de Taïwan (Formose) (*Procès-verbaux officiels du Conseil de sécurité, cinquième année, n° 48*, 506e séance, 29 septembre 1950, p. 5)). Dans le cas de la République de Corée, le Conseil décida le 31 janvier 1951 de retirer le point pertinent de la liste des questions dont il était saisi afin de permettre à l'Assemblée de délibérer à cet égard (*Procès-verbaux officiels du Conseil de sécurité, sixième année*, S/PV.531, 531e séance, 31 janvier 1951, p. 11-12, par. 57).

Cette interprétation de l'article 12 devait cependant évoluer par la suite. Ainsi l'Assemblée générale estima-t-elle pouvoir adopter des recommandations sur la question du Congo en 1961 (résolutions 1955 (XV) et 1600 (XVI)) et sur celle des colonies portugaises en 1963 (résolution 1913 (XVIII)), alors que ces questions étaient toujours inscrites à l'ordre du jour du Conseil, sans que celui-ci eût adopté de résolutions récentes à leur égard. En réponse à une question posée par le Pérou lors de la vingt-troisième session de l'Assemblée générale, le conseiller juridique de l'Organisation des Nations Unies confirma que l'Assemblée avait interprété les mots «remplit ... les fonctions» employés à l'article 12 de la Charte comme signifiant «remplit ... les fonctions en ce moment» (Assemblée générale, vingt-troisième session, Troisième Commission, 1637[e] séance, A/C.3/SR.1637, par. 9). De fait, la Cour relève l'existence d'une tendance croissante à voir l'Assemblée générale et le Conseil de sécurité examiner parallèlement une même question relative au maintien de la paix et de la sécurité internationales (voir, par exemple, les cas de Chypre, de l'Afrique du Sud, de l'Angola, de la Rhodésie du Sud et, plus récemment, de la

Assembly is the restriction found in Article 12, namely, that the Assembly should not recommend measures while the Security Council is dealing with the same matter unless the Council requests it to do so." *(I.C.J. Reports 1962*, p. 163.)

27. As regards the practice of the United Nations, both the General Assembly and the Security Council initially interpreted and applied Article 12 to the effect that the Assembly could not make a recommendation on a question concerning the maintenance of international peace and security while the matter remained on the Council's agenda. Thus the Assembly during its fourth session refused to recommend certain measures on the question of Indonesia, on the ground, *inter alia*, that the Council remained seised of the matter (*Official Records of the General Assembly, Fourth Session,* Ad Hoc *Political Committee, Summary Records of Meetings, 27 September-7 December 1949*, 56th Meeting, 3 December 1949, p. 339, para. 118). As for the Council, on a number of occasions it deleted items from its agenda in order to enable the Assembly to deliberate on them (for example, in respect of the Spanish question (*Official Records of the Security Council, First Year: Second Series, No. 21*, 79th Meeting, 4 November 1946, p. 498), in connection with incidents on the Greek border (*Official Records of the Security Council, Second Year, No. 89*, 202nd Meeting, 15 September 1947, pp. 2404-2405) and in regard to the Island of Taiwan (Formosa) (*Official Records of the Security Council, Fifth Year, No. 48*, 506th Meeting, 29 September 1950, p. 5)). In the case of the Republic of Korea, the Council decided on 31 January 1951 to remove the relevant item from the list of matters of which it was seised in order to enable the Assembly to deliberate on the matter (*Official Records of the Security Council, Sixth Year*, S/PV.531, 531st Meeting, 31 January 1951, pp. 11-12, para. 57).

However, this interpretation of Article 12 has evolved subsequently. Thus the General Assembly deemed itself entitled in 1961 to adopt recommendations in the matter of the Congo (resolutions 1955 (XV) and 1600 (XVI)) and in 1963 in respect of the Portuguese colonies (resolution 1913 (XVIII)) while those cases still appeared on the Council's agenda, without the Council having adopted any recent resolution concerning them. In response to a question posed by Peru during the twenty-third session of the General Assembly, the Legal Counsel of the United Nations confirmed that the Assembly interpreted the words "is exercising the functions" in Article 12 of the Charter as meaning "is exercising the functions at this moment" (General Assembly, Twenty-third Session, Third Committee, 1637th meeting, A/C.3/SR.1637, para. 9). Indeed, the Court notes that there has been an increasing tendency over time for the General Assembly and the Security Council to deal in parallel with the same matter concerning the maintenance of international peace and security (see, for example, the matters involving Cyprus, South Africa, Angola, Southern Rhodesia and more recently Bosnia and Herzegovina and

Bosnie-Herzégovine et de la Somalie). Il est souvent arrivé que, alors que le Conseil de sécurité tendait à privilégier les aspects de ces questions touchant à la paix et à la sécurité internationales, l'Assemblée générale les envisage sous un angle plus large et en examine également les aspects humanitaires, sociaux et économiques.

28. La Cour estime que la pratique acceptée de l'Assemblée générale, telle qu'elle a évolué, est compatible avec le paragraphe 1 de l'article 12 de la Charte.

La Cour est en conséquence d'avis que l'Assemblée générale, en adoptant la résolution ES-10/14 portant demande d'un avis consultatif de la Cour, n'a pas enfreint les dispositions du paragraphe 1 de l'article 12 de la Charte. Elle conclut que, en présentant la demande d'avis consultatif, l'Assemblée générale n'a pas outrepassé sa compétence.

29. Il a cependant été soutenu devant la Cour que la présente demande d'avis consultatif ne satisfaisait pas aux conditions essentielles énoncées dans la résolution 377 A (V), au titre de laquelle la dixième session extraordinaire d'urgence a été convoquée et a poursuivi ses travaux. A ce propos, il a tout d'abord été affirmé que «[l]e Conseil de sécurité n'a jamais été saisi d'un projet de résolution visant à ce qu'il demande lui-même un avis consultatif à la Cour sur les questions aujourd'hui en cause»; le Conseil n'ayant jamais été saisi de cette question précise, l'Assemblée générale ne pouvait, selon cet argument, invoquer un quelconque défaut d'action du Conseil pour soumettre une telle demande. Il a ensuite été prétendu que, en adoptant sa résolution 1515 (2003) approuvant la «feuille de route» avant que l'Assemblée générale prenne sa résolution ES-10/14, le Conseil de sécurité avait continué d'exercer sa responsabilité en matière de maintien de la paix et de la sécurité internationales et que, partant, l'Assemblée générale n'était pas en droit d'agir à sa place. La régularité de la procédure suivie par la dixième session extraordinaire d'urgence, en particulier le «caractère continu» de cette session, ainsi que le fait qu'elle ait été convoquée pour débattre de la demande d'avis consultatif au moment où l'Assemblée générale siégeait en session ordinaire ont également été contestés.

30. La Cour rappellera que, aux termes de la résolution 377 A (V):

> «dans tout cas où paraît exister une menace contre la paix, une rupture de la paix ou un acte d'agression et où, du fait que l'unanimité n'a pas pu se réaliser parmi ses membres permanents, le Conseil de sécurité manque à s'acquitter de sa responsabilité principale dans le maintien de la paix et de la sécurité internationales, l'Assemblée générale examinera immédiatement la question afin de faire aux Membres les recommandations appropriées sur les mesures collectives à prendre...».

Pour que la procédure prévue par cette résolution puisse être enclenchée, deux conditions doivent être remplies, à savoir, d'une part, que le Conseil ait manqué à s'acquitter de sa responsabilité principale en matière de maintien de la paix et de la sécurité internationales du fait du vote négatif

Somalia). It is often the case that, while the Security Council has tended to focus on the aspects of such matters related to international peace and security, the General Assembly has taken a broader view, considering also their humanitarian, social and economic aspects.

28. The Court considers that the accepted practice of the General Assembly, as it has evolved, is consistent with Article 12, paragraph 1, of the Charter.

The Court is accordingly of the view that the General Assembly, in adopting resolution ES-10/14, seeking an advisory opinion from the Court, did not contravene the provisions of Article 12, paragraph 1, of the Charter. The Court concludes that by submitting that request the General Assembly did not exceed its competence.

29. It has however been contended before the Court that the present request for an advisory opinion did not fulfil the essential conditions set by resolution 377 A (V), under which the Tenth Emergency Special Session was convened and has continued to act. In this regard, it has been said, first, that "The Security Council was never seised of a draft resolution proposing that the Council itself should request an advisory opinion from the Court on the matters now in contention", and, that specific issue having thus never been brought before the Council, the General Assembly could not rely on any inaction by the Council to make such a request. Secondly, it has been claimed that, in adopting resolution 1515 (2003), which endorsed the "Roadmap", before the adoption by the General Assembly of resolution ES-10/14, the Security Council continued to exercise its responsibility for the maintenance of international peace and security and that, as a result, the General Assembly was not entitled to act in its place. The validity of the procedure followed by the Tenth Emergency Special Session, especially the Session's "rolling character" and the fact that its meeting was convened to deliberate on the request for the advisory opinion at the same time as the General Assembly was meeting in regular session, has also been questioned.

30. The Court would recall that resolution 377 A (V) states that:

> "if the Security Council, because of lack of unanimity of the permanent members, fails to exercise its primary responsibility for the maintenance of international peace and security in any case where there appears to be a threat to the peace, breach of the peace, or act of aggression, the General Assembly shall consider the matter immediately with a view to making appropriate recommendations to Members for collective measures . . .".

The procedure provided for by that resolution is premised on two conditions, namely that the Council has failed to exercise its primary responsibility for the maintenance of international peace and security as a result of a negative vote of one or more permanent members, and that the situade l'un ou de plusieurs de ses membres permanents et que, d'autre part, la situation soit de celles dans lesquelles paraît exister une menace contre la paix, une rupture de la paix ou un acte d'agression. La Cour doit en conséquence déterminer si ces conditions étaient effectivement remplies lors de la convocation de la dixième session extraordinaire d'urgence de l'Assemblée générale, en particulier lorsque celle-ci a décidé de demander un avis consultatif à la Cour.

31. Au vu de la série d'événements décrits aux paragraphes 18 à 23 ci-dessus, la Cour constate que, lorsque la dixième session extraordinaire d'urgence fut convoquée en 1997, le Conseil s'était effectivement trouvé, en raison du vote négatif d'un membre permanent, dans l'incapacité de prendre une décision concernant l'implantation de certaines colonies de peuplement dans le territoire palestinien occupé et que, comme l'indique la résolution ES-10/2 (voir paragraphe 19 ci-dessus), il existait une menace à la paix et à la sécurité internationales.

La Cour constate en outre que la dixième session extraordinaire d'urgence, convoquée à nouveau le 20 octobre 2003, le fut sur la même base qu'en 1997 (voir les déclarations des représentants de la Palestine et d'Israël, A/ES-10/PV.21, p. 2 et 5), après le rejet par le Conseil de sécurité, le 14 octobre 2003, d'un projet de résolution portant sur la construction par Israël du mur dans le territoire palestinien occupé, du fait une nouvelle fois du vote négatif d'un membre permanent. La Cour considère que le Conseil de sécurité a là encore manqué à agir au sens de la résolution 377 A (V). Il ne semble pas à la Cour que la situation à cet égard ait évolué entre le 20 octobre 2003 et le 8 décembre 2003, le Conseil de sécurité n'ayant ni débattu de la construction du mur, ni adopté une quelconque résolution sur ce point. La Cour estime donc que, à la date du 8 décembre 2003, le Conseil n'était pas revenu sur le vote négatif du 14 octobre 2003. Il s'ensuit que, au cours de cette période, la dixième session extraordinaire d'urgence a été dûment convoquée à nouveau et pouvait régulièrement, en vertu de la résolution 377 A (V), être saisie de la question dont la Cour doit aujourd'hui connaître.

32. La Cour relèvera aussi qu'au cours de cette session extraordinaire d'urgence l'Assemblée générale pouvait adopter toute résolution ayant trait à la question pour laquelle avait été convoquée la session, et entrant par ailleurs dans les compétences de l'Assemblée, y compris une résolution demandant un avis à la Cour. Qu'il n'ait pas été proposé au Conseil de sécurité de solliciter un tel avis est sans pertinence à cet égard.

33. Abordant maintenant les autres irrégularités procédurales dont serait entachée la dixième session extraordinaire d'urgence, la Cour ne considère pas que le fait que cette session ait présenté un caractère «continu» — ayant été convoquée en avril 1997 et convoquée à nouveau onze fois depuis lors — ait quelque pertinence que ce soit en ce qui concerne la validité de la demande de l'Assemblée générale. La Cour fait observer à cet égard que la septième session extraordinaire d'urgence de l'Assemblée générale, convoquée le 22 juillet 1980, fut, par la suite, convoquée à nouveau à quatre reprises (les 20 avril, 25 juin, 16 août et

tion is one in which there appears to be a threat to the peace, breach of the peace, or act of aggression. The Court must accordingly ascertain whether these conditions were fulfilled as regards the convening of the Tenth Emergency Special Session of the General Assembly, in particular at the time when the Assembly decided to request an advisory opinion from the Court.

31. In the light of the sequence of events described in paragraphs 18 to 23 above, the Court observes that, at the time when the Tenth Emergency Special Session was convened in 1997, the Council had been unable to take a decision on the case of certain Israeli settlements in the Occupied Palestinian Territory, due to negative votes of a permanent member; and that, as indicated in resolution ES-10/2 (see paragraph 19 above), there existed a threat to international peace and security.

The Court further notes that, on 20 October 2003, the Tenth Emergency Special Session of the General Assembly was reconvened on the same basis as in 1997 (see the statements by the representatives of Palestine and Israel, A/ES-10/PV.21, pp. 2 and 5), after the rejection by the Security Council, on 14 October 2003, again as a result of the negative vote of a permanent member, of a draft resolution concerning the construction by Israel of the wall in the Occupied Palestinian Territory. The Court considers that the Security Council again failed to act as contemplated in resolution 377 A (V). It does not appear to the Court that the situation in this regard changed between 20 October 2003 and 8 December 2003, since the Council neither discussed the construction of the wall nor adopted any resolution in that connection. Thus, the Court is of the view that, up to 8 December 2003, the Council had not reconsidered the negative vote of 14 October 2003. It follows that, during that period, the Tenth Emergency Special Session was duly reconvened and could properly be seised, under resolution 377 A (V), of the matter now before the Court.

32. The Court would also emphasize that, in the course of this Emergency Special Session, the General Assembly could adopt any resolution falling within the subject-matter for which the Session had been convened, and otherwise within its powers, including a resolution seeking the Court's opinion. It is irrelevant in that regard that no proposal had been made to the Security Council to request such an opinion.

33. Turning now to alleged further procedural irregularities of the Tenth Emergency Special Session, the Court does not consider that the "rolling" character of that Session, namely the fact of its having been convened in April 1997 and reconvened 11 times since then, has any relevance with regard to the validity of the request by the General Assembly. The Court observes in that regard that the Seventh Emergency Special Session of the General Assembly, having been convened on 22 July 1980, was subsequently reconvened four times (on 20 April 1982, 25 June 1982, 16 August 1982 and 24 September 1982), and that the validity of

24 septembre 1982), sans que la validité des résolutions ou des décisions adoptées par elle dans ce contexte ait jamais été contestée. La validité des résolutions précédemment adoptées dans le cadre de la dixième session extraordinaire d'urgence n'a pas davantage été contestée.

34. La Cour note aussi l'argument avancé par Israël selon lequel la nouvelle convocation de la dixième session extraordinaire d'urgence était inappropriée, une session ordinaire de l'Assemblée générale étant alors en cours. Elle observe que, même si, à l'origine, il a pu ne pas sembler approprié que l'Assemblée générale tienne simultanément une session extraordinaire d'urgence et une session ordinaire, aucune règle constitutionnelle de l'Organisation n'a été identifiée, dont la méconnaissance aurait rendu nulle la résolution portant adoption de la demande d'avis consultatif en l'espèce.

35. Enfin, la Cour relèvera que la dixième session extraordinaire d'urgence a été convoquée conformément à l'alinéa *b)* de l'article 9 du règlement intérieur de l'Assemblée générale, et que les séances pertinentes ont été convoquées selon les règles en vigueur. Ainsi que la Cour l'a dit dans son avis consultatif du 21 juin 1971 sur les *Conséquences juridiques pour les Etats de la présence continue de l'Afrique du Sud en Namibie (Sud-Ouest africain) nonobstant la résolution 276 (1970) du Conseil de sécurité*, une

> «résolution émanant d'un organe des Nations Unies régulièrement constitué, prise conformément à son règlement et déclarée adoptée par son président, doit être présumée valable» (*C.I.J. Recueil 1971*, p. 22, par. 20).

La Cour ne voit aucune raison d'écarter cette présomption en l'espèce.

*

36. La Cour abordera à présent une autre question soulevée à l'égard de sa compétence en l'espèce, à savoir que la demande d'avis consultatif émanant de l'Assemblée générale ne porterait pas sur une «question juridique» au sens du paragraphe 1 de l'article 96 de la Charte et du paragraphe 1 de l'article 65 du Statut de la Cour. Il a été soutenu à cet égard que, pour constituer une question juridique au sens des deux dispositions susmentionnées, une question doit être raisonnablement précise, faute de quoi elle ne saurait se prêter à une réponse de la Cour. S'agissant de la demande formulée dans la présente procédure consultative, il a été fait valoir qu'il n'était pas possible d'appréhender avec une certitude raisonnable le sens juridique de la question posée à la Cour, et ce pour deux raisons.

En premier lieu, il a été prétendu que la question concernant les «conséquences» «en droit» de la construction du mur n'admettait que deux interprétations possibles, et que chacune de ces interprétations resolutions or decisions of the Assembly adopted under such circumstances was never disputed. Nor has the validity of any previous resolutions adopted during the Tenth Emergency Special Session been challenged.

34. The Court also notes the contention by Israel that it was improper to reconvene the Tenth Emergency Special Session at a time when the regular session of the General Assembly was in progress. The Court considers that, while it may not have been originally contemplated that it would be appropriate for the General Assembly to hold simultaneous emergency and regular sessions, no rule of the Organization has been identified which would be thereby violated, so as to render invalid the resolution adopting the present request for an advisory opinion.

35. Finally, the Tenth Emergency Special Session appears to have been convened in accordance with Rule 9 *(b)* of the Rules of Procedure of the General Assembly, and the relevant meetings have been convened in pursuance of the applicable rules. As the Court stated in its Advisory Opinion of 21 June 1971 concerning the *Legal Consequences for States of the Continued Presence of South Africa in Namibia (South West Africa) notwithstanding Security Council Resolution 276 (1970)*, a

> "resolution of a properly constituted organ of the United Nations which is passed in accordance with that organ's rules of procedure, and is declared by its President to have been so passed, must be presumed to have been validly adopted" (*I.C.J. Reports 1971*, p. 22, para. 20).

In view of the foregoing, the Court cannot see any reason why that presumption is to be rebutted in the present case.

*

36. The Court now turns to a further issue related to jurisdiction in the present proceedings, namely the contention that the request for an advisory opinion by the General Assembly is not on a "legal question" within the meaning of Article 96, paragraph 1, of the Charter and Article 65, paragraph 1, of the Statute of the Court. It has been contended in this regard that, for a question to constitute a "legal question" for the purposes of these two provisions, it must be reasonably specific, since otherwise it would not be amenable to a response by the Court. With regard to the request made in the present advisory proceedings, it has been argued that it is not possible to determine with reasonable certainty the legal meaning of the question asked of the Court for two reasons.

First, it has been argued that the question regarding the "legal consequences" of the construction of the wall only allows for two possible interpretations, each of which would lead to a course of action that is conduirait la Cour à adopter une ligne de conduite qu'elle ne saurait retenir. La question posée pourrait tout d'abord être interprétée comme une invitation faite à la Cour de constater l'illicéité de la construction du mur, puis de donner son avis sur les conséquences juridiques de cette illicéité. Dans ce cas, a-t-il été soutenu, la Cour devrait refuser de répondre à la question posée pour plusieurs raisons, certaines d'entre elles concernant la compétence, et d'autres plutôt l'opportunité. S'agissant de la compétence, il a été dit que, si l'Assemblée générale avait voulu obtenir l'avis de la Cour sur la question particulièrement complexe et délicate de la licéité de la construction du mur, elle aurait demandé expressément un avis à cet effet (voir *Echange des populations grecques et turques, avis consultatif, 1925, C.P.J.I. série B n° 10*, p. 17). Il a été affirmé qu'une seconde interprétation possible de la demande consisterait pour la Cour à présumer illicite la construction du mur, pour ensuite se prononcer sur les conséquences juridiques de cette illicéité présumée. Dans cette hypothèse aussi, la Cour devrait refuser de répondre à la question posée, puisque la demande serait alors fondée sur un postulat contestable et qu'il serait en tout état de cause impossible de se prononcer sur les conséquences juridiques de cette illicéité sans avoir précisé la nature de cette dernière.

Il a été prétendu en second lieu que, en raison de son manque de clarté et de son caractère abstrait, la question posée à la Cour ne serait pas de nature «juridique». En particulier, il a été soutenu à cet égard que la question ne précise pas si les conséquences juridiques que la Cour est priée d'examiner concernent «l'Assemblée générale ou quelque autre organe des Nations Unies», les «Etats Membres de l'Organisation des Nations Unies», «Israël», la «Palestine» ou «certaines des entités précitées, ou quelque autre entité».

37. En ce qui concerne le manque de clarté allégué des termes employés dans la requête de l'Assemblée générale et son incidence sur la «nature juridique» de la question soumise à la Cour, celle-ci observera tout d'abord que cette question vise les conséquences juridiques d'une situation de fait donnée, compte tenu des règles et des principes du droit international, notamment de la convention de Genève relative à la protection des personnes civiles en temps de guerre, du 12 août 1949 (ci-après dénommée la «quatrième convention de Genève»), et des résolutions consacrées à la question par le Conseil de sécurité et l'Assemblée générale. La question posée par l'Assemblée générale a donc, pour reprendre les termes employés par la Cour dans son avis consultatif sur le *Sahara occidental*, «été libell[ée] en termes juridiques et soulèv[e] des problèmes de droit international»; elle est, par sa nature même, susceptible de recevoir une réponse fondée en droit; elle ne serait guère susceptible d'ailleurs de recevoir une autre réponse. La Cour est d'avis que cette question a bien un caractère juridique (voir *Sahara occidental, avis consultatif, C.I.J. Recueil 1975*, p. 18, par. 15).

38. La Cour fera observer qu'un manque de clarté dans le libellé d'une question ne saurait priver la Cour de sa compétence. Tout au plus, du fait

precluded for the Court. The question asked could first be interpreted as a request for the Court to find that the construction of the wall is illegal, and then to give its opinion on the legal consequences of that illegality. In this case, it has been contended, the Court should decline to respond to the question asked for a variety of reasons, some of which pertain to jurisdiction and others rather to the issue of propriety. As regards jurisdiction, it is said that, if the General Assembly had wished to obtain the view of the Court on the highly complex and sensitive question of the legality of the construction of the wall, it should have expressly sought an opinion to that effect (cf. *Exchange of Greek and Turkish Populations, Advisory Opinion, 1925, P.C.I.J., Series B, No. 10*, p. 17). A second possible interpretation of the request, it is said, is that the Court should assume that the construction of the wall is illegal, and then give its opinion on the legal consequences of that assumed illegality. It has been contended that the Court should also decline to respond to the question on this hypothesis, since the request would then be based on a questionable assumption and since, in any event, it would be impossible to rule on the legal consequences of illegality without specifying the nature of that illegality.

Secondly, it has been contended that the question asked of the Court is not of a "legal" character because of its imprecision and abstract nature. In particular, it has been argued in this regard that the question fails to specify whether the Court is being asked to address legal consequences for "the General Assembly or some other organ of the United Nations", "Member States of the United Nations", "Israel", "Palestine" or "some combination of the above, or some different entity".

37. As regards the alleged lack of clarity of the terms of the General Assembly's request and its effect on the "legal nature" of the question referred to the Court, the Court observes that this question is directed to the legal consequences arising from a given factual situation considering the rules and principles of international law, including the Geneva Convention relative to the Protection of Civilian Persons in Time of War of 12 August 1949 (hereinafter the "Fourth Geneva Convention") and relevant Security Council and General Assembly resolutions. The question submitted by the General Assembly has thus, to use the Court's phrase in its Advisory Opinion on *Western Sahara*, "been framed in terms of law and raise[s] problems of international law"; it is by its very nature susceptible of a reply based on law; indeed it is scarcely susceptible of a reply otherwise than on the basis of law. In the view of the Court, it is indeed a question of a legal character (see *Western Sahara, Advisory Opinion, I.C.J. Reports 1975*, p. 18, para. 15).

38. The Court would point out that lack of clarity in the drafting of a question does not deprive the Court of jurisdiction. Rather, such uncer-

de ces incertitudes, la Cour devra-t-elle préciser l'interprétation à donner à la question, ce qu'elle a souvent fait.

La Cour permanente et la Cour actuelle ont toutes deux fait observer dans plusieurs affaires que le libellé d'une requête pour avis consultatif n'explicitait pas suffisamment la question sur laquelle l'avis de la Cour était demandé (*Interprétation de l'accord gréco-turc du 1er décembre 1926 (protocole final, article IV), avis consultatif, 1928, C.P.J.I. série B nº 16 (I)*, p. 14-16) ou ne correspondait pas à la «véritable question juridique» qui se posait (*Interprétation de l'accord du 25 mars 1951 entre l'OMS et l'Egypte, avis consultatif, C.I.J. Recueil 1980*, p. 87-89, par. 34-36). Elle a constaté dans une affaire que «la question soumise à la Cour, considérée en elle-même, apparai[ssai]t à la fois mal posée et vague» (*Demande de réformation du jugement nº 273 du Tribunal administratif des Nations Unies, avis consultatif, C.I.J. Recueil 1982*, p. 348, par. 46).

De ce fait, la Cour a souvent été amenée à élargir, interpréter, voire reformuler les questions qui lui étaient posées (voir les trois avis cités plus haut; voir également *Jaworzina, avis consultatif, 1923, C.P.J.I. série B nº 8*; *Admissibilité de l'audition de pétitionnaires par le Comité du Sud-Ouest africain, avis consultatif, C.I.J. Recueil 1956*, p. 25; *Certaines dépenses des Nations Unies (article 17, paragraphe 2, de la Charte), avis consultatif, C.I.J. Recueil 1962*, p. 157-162).

Dans la présente espèce, la Cour n'aura à faire que ce qu'elle a souvent fait par le passé, c'est-à-dire «déterminer les principes et règles existants, les interpréter et les appliquer..., apportant ainsi à la question posée une réponse fondée en droit» (*Licéité de la menace ou de l'emploi d'armes nucléaires, avis consultatif, C.I.J. Recueil 1996 (I)*, p. 234, par. 13).

39. En l'espèce, si l'Assemblée générale prie la Cour de dire «[q]uelles sont en droit les conséquences» de la construction du mur, l'emploi de ces termes implique nécessairement de déterminer si cette construction viole ou non certaines règles et certains principes de droit international. Il est donc clair que la Cour est tout d'abord invitée à déterminer si ces règles et principes ont été violés et le demeurent du fait de la construction du mur selon le tracé projeté.

40. La Cour ne considère pas que la nature prétendument abstraite de la question qui lui est posée soulève un problème de compétence. Même lorsque, dans l'affaire de la *Licéité de la menace ou de l'emploi d'armes nucléaires*, cet aspect fut soulevé sous l'angle de l'opportunité judiciaire plutôt que sous celui de la compétence, la Cour déclara que l'allégation selon laquelle elle ne pourrait connaître d'une question posée en termes abstraits n'était qu'«une pure affirmation dénuée de toute justification», et qu'elle pouvait «donner un avis consultatif sur toute question juridique, abstraite ou non» (*C.I.J. Recueil 1996 (I)*, p. 236, par. 15, citant les affaires suivantes: *Conditions de l'admission d'un Etat comme Membre des Nations Unies (article 4 de la Charte), avis consultatif, 1948, C.I.J. Recueil 1947-1948*, p. 61; *Effet de jugements du Tribunal administratif des Nations Unies accordant indemnité, avis consultatif, C.I.J. Recueil*

tainty will require clarification in interpretation, and such necessary clarifications of interpretation have frequently been given by the Court.

In the past, both the Permanent Court and the present Court have observed in some cases that the wording of a request for an advisory opinion did not accurately state the question on which the Court's opinion was being sought (*Interpretation of the Greco-Turkish Agreement of 1 December 1926 (Final Protocol, Article IV), Advisory Opinion, 1928, P.C.I.J., Series B, No. 16 (I)*, pp. 14-16), or did not correspond to the "true legal question" under consideration (*Interpretation of the Agreement of 25 March 1951 between the WHO and Egypt, Advisory Opinion, I.C.J. Reports 1980*, pp. 87-89, paras. 34-36). The Court noted in one case that "the question put to the Court is, on the face of it, at once infelicitously expressed and vague" (*Application for Review of Judgement No. 273 of the United Nations Administrative Tribunal, Advisory Opinion, I.C.J. Reports 1982*, p. 348, para. 46).

Consequently, the Court has often been required to broaden, interpret and even reformulate the questions put (see the three Opinions cited above; see also *Jaworzina, Advisory Opinion, 1923, P.C.I.J., Series B, No. 8*; *Admissibility of Hearings of Petitioners by the Committee on South West Africa, Advisory Opinion, I.C.J. Reports 1956*, p. 25; *Certain Expenses of the United Nations (Article 17, paragraph 2, of the Charter), Advisory Opinion, I.C.J. Reports 1962*, pp. 157-162).

In the present instance, the Court will only have to do what it has often done in the past, namely "identify the existing principles and rules, interpret them and apply them . . ., thus offering a reply to the question posed based on law" (*Legality of the Threat or Use of Nuclear Weapons, I.C.J. Reports 1996 (I)*, p. 234, para. 13).

39. In the present instance, if the General Assembly requests the Court to state the "legal consequences" arising from the construction of the wall, the use of these terms necessarily encompasses an assessment of whether that construction is or is not in breach of certain rules and principles of international law. Thus, the Court is first called upon to determine whether such rules and principles have been and are still being breached by the construction of the wall along the planned route.

40. The Court does not consider that what is contended to be the abstract nature of the question posed to it raises an issue of jurisdiction. Even when the matter was raised as an issue of propriety rather than one of jurisdiction, in the case concerning the *Legality of the Threat or Use of Nuclear Weapons*, the Court took the position that to contend that it should not deal with a question couched in abstract terms is "a mere affirmation devoid of any justification" and that "the Court may give an advisory opinion on any legal question, abstract or otherwise" (*I.C.J. Reports 1996 (I)*, p. 236, para. 15, referring to *Conditions of Admission of a State to Membership in the United Nations (Article 4 of the Charter), Advisory Opinion, 1948, I.C.J. Reports 1947-1948*, p. 61; *Effect of Awards of Compensation Made by the United Nations Administrative Tribunal, Advisory Opinion, I.C.J. Reports 1954*, p. 51; and *Legal Con-*

1954, p. 51; et *Conséquences juridiques pour les Etats de la présence continue de l'Afrique du Sud en Namibie (Sud-Ouest africain) nonobstant la résolution 276 (1970) du Conseil de sécurité, avis consultatif, C.I.J. Recueil 1971*, p. 27, par. 40). En tout état de cause, la Cour considère que la question qui lui a été posée quant aux conséquences juridiques de la construction du mur n'est pas de nature abstraite et que c'est en outre à elle qu'il appartiendrait de déterminer à l'égard de qui ces conséquences devraient être précisées.

41. La Cour ne saurait par ailleurs accepter le point de vue, également avancé au cours de la procédure, selon lequel elle n'aurait pas compétence en raison du caractère «politique» de la question posée. Ainsi qu'il ressort à cet égard de sa jurisprudence constante, la Cour estime que le fait qu'une question juridique présente également des aspects politiques,

> «comme c'est, par la nature des choses, le cas de bon nombre de questions qui viennent à se poser dans la vie internationale, ne suffit pas à la priver de son caractère de «question juridique» et à «enlever à la Cour une compétence qui lui est expressément conférée par son Statut» (*Demande de réformation du jugement n° 158 du Tribunal administratif des Nations Unies, avis consultatif, C.I.J. Recueil 1973*, p. 172, par. 14). Quels que soient les aspects politiques de la question posée, la Cour ne saurait refuser un caractère juridique à une question qui l'invite à s'acquitter d'une tâche essentiellement judiciaire, à savoir l'appréciation de la licéité de la conduite éventuelle d'Etats au regard des obligations que le droit international leur impose (voir *Conditions de l'admission d'un Etat comme Membre des Nations Unies (article 4 de la Charte), avis consultatif, 1948, C.I.J. Recueil 1947-1948*, p. 61-62; *Compétence de l'Assemblée générale pour l'admission d'un Etat aux Nations Unies, avis consultatif, C.I.J. Recueil 1950*, p. 6-7; *Certaines dépenses des Nations Unies (article 17, paragraphe 2, de la Charte), avis consultatif, C.I.J. Recueil 1962*, p. 155).» (*Licéité de la menace ou de l'emploi d'armes nucléaires, avis consultatif, C.I.J. Recueil 1996 (I)*, p. 234, par. 13.)

Dans son avis concernant l'*Interprétation de l'accord du 25 mars 1951 entre l'OMS et l'Egypte*, la Cour a même souligné que

> «lorsque des considérations politiques jouent un rôle marquant il peut être particulièrement nécessaire à une organisation internationale d'obtenir un avis consultatif de la Cour sur les principes juridiques applicables à la matière en discussion...» (*C.I.J. Recueil 1980*, p. 87, par. 33).

La Cour a en outre affirmé, dans son avis sur la *Licéité de la menace ou de l'emploi d'armes nucléaires*, que

> «la nature politique des mobiles qui auraient inspiré la requête et les implications politiques que pourrait avoir l'avis donné sont sans pertinence au regard de l'établissement de sa compétence pour donner un tel avis» (*C.I.J. Recueil 1996 (I)*, p. 234, par. 13).

sequences for States of the Continued Presence of South Africa in Namibia (South West Africa) notwithstanding Security Council Resolution 276 (1970), Advisory Opinion, I.C.J. Reports 1971, p. 27, para. 40). In any event, the Court considers that the question posed to it in relation to the legal consequences of the construction of the wall is not an abstract one, and moreover that it would be for the Court to determine for whom any such consequences arise.

41. Furthermore, the Court cannot accept the view, which has also been advanced in the present proceedings, that it has no jurisdiction because of the "political" character of the question posed. As is clear from its long-standing jurisprudence on this point, the Court considers that the fact that a legal question also has political aspects,

> "as, in the nature of things, is the case with so many questions which arise in international life, does not suffice to deprive it of its character as a 'legal question' and to 'deprive the Court of a competence expressly conferred on it by its Statute' (*Application for Review of Judgement No. 158 of the United Nations Administrative Tribunal, Advisory Opinion, I.C.J. Reports 1973*, p. 172, para. 14). Whatever its political aspects, the Court cannot refuse to admit the legal character of a question which invites it to discharge an essentially judicial task, namely, an assessment of the legality of the possible conduct of States with regard to the obligations imposed upon them by international law (cf. *Conditions of Admission of a State to Membership in the United Nations (Article 4 of the Charter), Advisory Opinion, 1948, I.C.J. Reports 1947-1948*, pp. 61-62; *Competence of the General Assembly for the Admission of a State to the United Nations, Advisory Opinion, I.C.J. Reports 1950*, pp. 6-7; *Certain Expenses of the United Nations (Article 17, paragraph 2, of the Charter), Advisory Opinion, I.C.J. Reports 1962*, p. 155)." (*Legality of the Threat or Use of Nuclear Weapons, Advisory Opinion, I.C.J. Reports 1996 (I)*, p. 234, para. 13.)

In its Opinion concerning the *Interpretation of the Agreement of 25 March 1951 between the WHO and Egypt*, the Court indeed emphasized that,

> "in situations in which political considerations are prominent it may be particularly necessary for an international organization to obtain an advisory opinion from the Court as to the legal principles applicable with respect to the matter under debate . . ." (*I.C.J. Reports 1980*, p. 87, para. 33).

Moreover, the Court has affirmed in its Opinion on the *Legality of the Threat or Use of Nuclear Weapons* that

> "the political nature of the motives which may be said to have inspired the request and the political implications that the opinion given might have are of no relevance in the establishment of its jurisdiction to give such an opinion" (*I.C.J. Reports 1996 (I)*, p. 234, para. 13).

La Cour estime qu'il n'existe en l'espèce aucun élément susceptible de l'amener à conclure différemment.

*

42. La Cour en conséquence a compétence pour donner l'avis consultatif demandé par la résolution ES-10/14 de l'Assemblée générale.

* *

43. Il a cependant été soutenu au cours de la procédure que la Cour devrait refuser d'exercer sa compétence en raison de la présence, dans la requête de l'Assemblée générale, d'un certain nombre d'éléments qui rendraient l'exercice par la Cour de sa compétence malvenu et étranger à sa fonction judiciaire.

44. La Cour a maintes fois eu par le passé l'occasion de rappeler que le paragraphe 1 de l'article 65 de son Statut, selon lequel «[l]a Cour *peut* donner un avis consultatif...» (les italiques sont de la Cour), devait être interprété comme reconnaissant à la Cour le pouvoir discrétionnaire de refuser de donner un avis consultatif même lorsque les conditions pour qu'elle soit compétente sont remplies (*Licéité de la menace ou de l'emploi d'armes nucléaires, avis consultatif, C.I.J. Recueil 1996 (I)*, p. 234-235, par. 14). La Cour n'en garde pas moins présent à l'esprit que sa réponse à une demande d'avis consultatif «constitue [sa] participation ... à l'action de l'Organisation et [que], en principe, elle ne devrait pas être refusée» (*Interprétation des traités de paix conclus avec la Bulgarie, la Hongrie et la Roumanie, première phase, avis consultatif, C.I.J. Recueil 1950*, p. 71; voir également, par exemple, *Différend relatif à l'immunité de juridiction d'un rapporteur spécial de la Commission des droits de l'homme, avis consultatif, C.I.J. Recueil 1999 (I)*, p. 78-79, par. 29). Compte tenu de ses responsabilités en tant qu'«organe judiciaire principal des Nations Unies» (article 92 de la Charte), la Cour ne devrait pas en principe refuser de donner un avis consultatif. Conformément à la jurisprudence constante de la Cour, il faudrait des «raisons décisives» pour l'amener à opposer un tel refus (*Certaines dépenses des Nations Unies (article 17, paragraphe 2, de la Charte), avis consultatif, C.I.J. Recueil 1962*, p. 155; voir également, par exemple, *Différend relatif à l'immunité de juridiction d'un rapporteur spécial de la Commission des droits de l'homme, avis consultatif, C.I.J. Recueil 1999 (I)*, p. 78-79, par. 29).

La Cour actuelle n'a jamais, dans l'exercice de ce pouvoir discrétionnaire, refusé de répondre à une demande d'avis consultatif. La décision de ne pas donner l'avis consultatif que sollicitait l'Organisation mondiale de la Santé sur la *Licéité de l'utilisation des armes nucléaires par un Etat dans un conflit armé* a été fondée sur le défaut de compétence de la Cour, et non sur des considérations touchant à l'opportunité judiciaire (voir *C.I.J. Recueil 1996 (I)*, p. 235, par. 14). La devancière de la Cour, la Cour permanente de Justice internationale, estima une seule fois ne pas

The Court is of the view that there is no element in the present proceedings which could lead it to conclude otherwise.

*

42. The Court accordingly has jurisdiction to give the advisory opinion requested by resolution ES-10/14 of the General Assembly.

* *

43. It has been contended in the present proceedings, however, that the Court should decline to exercise its jurisdiction because of the presence of specific aspects of the General Assembly's request that would render the exercise of the Court's jurisdiction improper and inconsistent with the Court's judicial function.

44. The Court has recalled many times in the past that Article 65, paragraph 1, of its Statute, which provides that "The Court *may* give an advisory opinion . . ." (emphasis added), should be interpreted to mean that the Court has a discretionary power to decline to give an advisory opinion even if the conditions of jurisdiction are met (*Legality of the Threat or Use of Nuclear Weapons, Advisory Opinion, I.C.J. Reports 1996 (I)*, pp. 234-235, para. 14). The Court however is mindful of the fact that its answer to a request for an advisory opinion "represents its participation in the activities of the Organization, and, in principle, should not be refused" (*Interpretation of Peace Treaties with Bulgaria, Hungary and Romania, First Phase, Advisory Opinion, I.C.J. Reports 1950*, p. 71; see also, for example, *Difference Relating to Immunity from Legal Process of a Special Rapporteur of the Commission on Human Rights, Advisory Opinion, I.C.J. Reports 1999 (I)*, pp. 78-79, para. 29.) Given its responsibilities as the "principal judicial organ of the United Nations" (Article 92 of the Charter), the Court should in principle not decline to give an advisory opinion. In accordance with its consistent jurisprudence, only "compelling reasons" should lead the Court to refuse its opinion (*Certain Expenses of the United Nations (Article 17, paragraph 2, of the Charter), Advisory Opinion, I.C.J. Reports 1962*, p. 155; see also, for example, *Difference Relating to Immunity from Legal Process of a Special Rapporteur of the Commission on Human Rights, Advisory Opinion, I.C.J. Reports 1999 (I)*, pp. 78-79, para. 29.)

The present Court has never, in the exercise of this discretionary power, declined to respond to a request for an advisory opinion. Its decision not to give the advisory opinion on the *Legality of the Use by a State of Nuclear Weapons in Armed Conflict* requested by the World Health Organization was based on the Court's lack of jurisdiction, and not on considerations of judicial propriety (see *I.C.J. Reports 1996 (I)*, p. 235, para. 14). Only on one occasion did the Court's predecessor, the Permanent Court of International Justice, take the view that it should devoir répondre à la question qui lui avait été posée (*Statut de la Carélie orientale, avis consultatif, 1923, C.P.J.I. série B n° 5*), mais cela en raison des

> «circonstances toutes particulières de l'espèce, à savoir, notamment, [du fait] que cette question concernait directement un différend déjà né auquel était partie un Etat qui n'avait pas adhéré au Statut de la Cour permanente, n'était pas membre de la Société des Nations, s'opposait à la procédure et refusait d'y prendre part de quelque manière que ce [fût]» (*Licéité de la menace ou de l'emploi d'armes nucléaires, avis consultatif, C.I.J. Recueil 1996 (I)*, p. 235-236, par. 14).

45. Ces considérations ne dispensent pas la Cour de l'obligation de s'assurer, chaque fois qu'elle est saisie d'une demande d'avis, de l'opportunité d'exercer sa fonction judiciaire, sur la base du critère des «raisons décisives» tel que rappelé ci-dessus. La Cour examinera donc en détail, et à la lumière de sa jurisprudence, chacun des arguments qui lui a été présenté à cet égard.

*

46. Selon le premier de ces arguments, la Cour ne devrait pas exercer sa compétence en l'espèce, au motif que la demande concernerait un différend entre Israël et la Palestine à l'égard duquel Israël n'a pas accepté la juridiction de la Cour. Ainsi, l'objet de la question posée par l'Assemblée générale ferait «partie intégrante du différend israélo-palestinien plus large qui concerne des questions liées au terrorisme, à la sécurité, aux frontières, aux colonies de peuplement, à Jérusalem et à d'autres questions connexes». Israël a insisté sur le fait qu'il n'avait jamais consenti à voir ce différend plus large tranché par la Cour ou dans le cadre de tout autre mode de règlement obligatoire; il affirme au contraire que les parties ont convenu à plusieurs reprises que ces questions devaient être réglées par la voie de la négociation, le recours à l'arbitrage étant envisageable en cas d'accord. Il est donc soutenu que la Cour devrait refuser de donner l'avis qui lui est demandé, en s'appuyant notamment sur le précédent constitué par la décision de la Cour permanente de Justice internationale relative au *Statut de la Carélie orientale*.

47. La Cour relève que l'absence de consentement à la juridiction contentieuse de la Cour de la part des Etats intéressés est sans effet sur la compétence qu'a celle-ci de donner un avis consultatif. Dans un avis consultatif de 1950, la Cour a expliqué que:

> «Le consentement des Etats parties à un différend est le fondement de la juridiction de la Cour en matière contentieuse. Il en est autrement en matière d'avis, alors même que la demande d'avis a trait à une question juridique actuellement pendante entre Etats. La réponse de la Cour n'a qu'un caractère consultatif: comme telle, elle ne saurait avoir d'effet obligatoire. Il en résulte qu'aucun Etat,

not reply to a question put to it (*Status of Eastern Carelia, Advisory Opinion, 1923, P.C.I.J., Series B, No. 5*), but this was due to

> "the very particular circumstances of the case, among which were that the question directly concerned an already existing dispute, one of the States parties to which was neither a party to the Statute of the Permanent Court nor a Member of the League of Nations, objected to the proceedings, and refused to take part in any way" (*Legality of the Threat or Use of Nuclear Weapons, I.C.J. Reports 1996 (I)*, pp. 235-236, para. 14).

45. These considerations do not release the Court from the duty to satisfy itself, each time it is seised of a request for an opinion, as to the propriety of the exercise of its judicial function, by reference to the criterion of "compelling reasons" as cited above. The Court will accordingly examine in detail and in the light of its jurisprudence each of the arguments presented to it in this regard.

*

46. The first such argument is to the effect that the Court should not exercise its jurisdiction in the present case because the request concerns a contentious matter between Israel and Palestine, in respect of which Israel has not consented to the exercise of that jurisdiction. According to this view, the subject-matter of the question posed by the General Assembly "is an integral part of the wider Israeli-Palestinian dispute concerning questions of terrorism, security, borders, settlements, Jerusalem and other related matters". Israel has emphasized that it has never consented to the settlement of this wider dispute by the Court or by any other means of compulsory adjudication; on the contrary, it contends that the parties repeatedly agreed that these issues are to be settled by negotiation, with the possibility of an agreement that recourse could be had to arbitration. It is accordingly contended that the Court should decline to give the present Opinion, on the basis *inter alia* of the precedent of the decision of the Permanent Court of International Justice on the *Status of Eastern Carelia*.

47. The Court observes that the lack of consent to the Court's contentious jurisdiction by interested States has no bearing on the Court's jurisdiction to give an advisory opinion. In an Advisory Opinion of 1950, the Court explained that:

> "The consent of States, parties to a dispute, is the basis of the Court's jurisdiction in contentious cases. The situation is different in regard to advisory proceedings even where the Request for an Opinion relates to a legal question actually pending between States. The Court's reply is only of an advisory character: as such, it has no binding force. It follows that no State, whether a Member of the

> Membre ou non membre des Nations Unies, n'a qualité pour empêcher que soit donné suite à une demande d'avis dont les Nations Unies, pour s'éclairer dans leur action propre, auraient reconnu l'opportunité. L'avis est donné par la Cour non aux Etats, mais à l'organe habilité pour le lui demander; la réponse constitue une participation de la Cour, elle-même «organe des Nations Unies», à l'action de l'Organisation et, en principe, elle ne devrait pas être refusée.» (*Interprétation des traités de paix conclus avec la Bulgarie, la Hongrie et la Roumanie, première phase, C.I.J. Recueil 1950*, p. 71; voir également *Sahara occidental, C.I.J. Recueil 1975*, p. 24, par. 31.)

Il en résulte que, dans cette affaire, la Cour n'a pas refusé de répondre à la demande d'avis consultatif au motif que, dans les circonstances en question, elle n'aurait pas eu compétence pour ce faire. Elle a toutefois examiné l'opposition marquée par certains Etats intéressés à la requête émanant de l'Assemblée générale sous l'angle de l'opportunité judiciaire. Commentant sa décision de 1950, la Cour a expliqué dans son avis consultatif sur le *Sahara occidental* qu'elle avait «ainsi reconnu que le défaut de consentement pourrait l'amener à ne pas émettre d'avis si, dans les circonstances d'une espèce donnée, des considérations tenant à son caractère judiciaire imposaient un refus de répondre». Et la Cour de poursuivre:

> «le défaut de consentement d'un Etat intéressé peut, dans certaines circonstances, rendre le prononcé d'un avis consultatif incompatible avec le caractère judiciaire de la Cour. Tel serait le cas si les faits montraient qu'accepter de répondre aurait pour effet de tourner le principe selon lequel un Etat n'est pas tenu de soumettre un différend au règlement judiciaire s'il n'est pas consentant.» (*Sahara occidental, C.I.J. Recueil 1975*, p. 25, par. 32-33.)

Appliquant le principe ainsi libellé à la demande relative au *Sahara occidental*, la Cour constata qu'existait certes une controverse juridique, mais une controverse qui avait surgi lors des débats de l'Assemblée générale et au sujet de problèmes traités par celle-ci. Cette controverse n'était pas née indépendamment, dans le cadre de relations bilatérales (*ibid.*, p. 25, par. 34).

48. S'agissant de la requête pour avis consultatif dont elle est saisie, la Cour prend acte du fait qu'Israël et la Palestine ont exprimé des vues radicalement opposées sur les conséquences juridiques de l'édification du mur par Israël, sur lesquelles la Cour a été priée de se prononcer. Toutefois, ainsi que la Cour l'a elle-même noté, «[p]resque toutes les procédures consultatives ont été marquées par des divergences de vues» (*Conséquences juridiques pour les Etats de la présence continue de l'Afrique du Sud en Namibie (Sud-Ouest africain) nonobstant la résolution 276 (1970) du Conseil de sécurité, avis consultatif, C.I.J. Recueil 1971*, p. 24, par. 34).

49. En outre, la Cour n'estime pas que la question qui fait l'objet de la

> United Nations or not, can prevent the giving of an Advisory Opinion which the United Nations considers to be desirable in order to obtain enlightenment as to the course of action it should take. The Court's Opinion is given not to the States, but to the organ which is entitled to request it; the reply of the Court, itself an 'organ of the United Nations', represents its participation in the activities of the Organization, and, in principle, should not be refused." (*Interpretation of Peace Treaties with Bulgaria, Hungary and Romania, First Phase, Advisory Opinion, I.C.J. Reports 1950*, p. 71; see also *Western Sahara, I.C.J. Reports 1975*, p. 24, para. 31.)

It followed from this that, in those proceedings, the Court did not refuse to respond to the request for an advisory opinion on the ground that, in the particular circumstances, it lacked jurisdiction. The Court did however examine the opposition of certain interested States to the request by the General Assembly in the context of issues of judicial propriety. Commenting on its 1950 decision, the Court explained in its Advisory Opinion on *Western Sahara* that it had "Thus . . . recognized that lack of consent might constitute a ground for declining to give the opinion requested if, in the circumstances of a given case, considerations of judicial propriety should oblige the Court to refuse an opinion." The Court continued:

> "In certain circumstances . . . the lack of consent of an interested State may render the giving of an advisory opinion incompatible with the Court's judicial character. An instance of this would be when the circumstances disclose that to give a reply would have the effect of circumventing the principle that a State is not obliged to allow its disputes to be submitted to judicial settlement without its consent." (*Western Sahara, I.C.J. Reports 1975*, p. 25, paras. 32-33.)

In applying that principle to the request concerning *Western Sahara*, the Court found that a legal controversy did indeed exist, but one which had arisen during the proceedings of the General Assembly and in relation to matters with which the Assembly was dealing. It had not arisen independently in bilateral relations (*ibid.*, p. 25, para. 34).

48. As regards the request for an advisory opinion now before it, the Court acknowledges that Israel and Palestine have expressed radically divergent views on the legal consequences of Israel's construction of the wall, on which the Court has been asked to pronounce. However, as the Court has itself noted, "Differences of views . . . on legal issues have existed in practically every advisory proceeding" (*Legal Consequences for States of the Continued Presence of South Africa in Namibia (South West Africa) notwithstanding Security Council Resolution 276 (1970), Advisory Opinion, I.C.J. Reports 1971*, p. 24, para. 34).

49. Furthermore, the Court does not consider that the subject-matter

requête de l'Assemblée générale puisse être considérée seulement comme une question bilatérale entre Israël et la Palestine. Compte tenu des pouvoirs et responsabilités de l'Organisation des Nations Unies à l'égard des questions se rattachant au maintien de la paix et de la sécurité internationales, la Cour est d'avis que la construction du mur doit être regardée comme intéressant directement l'Organisation des Nations Unies. La responsabilité de l'Organisation à cet égard trouve également son origine dans le mandat et dans la résolution relative au plan de partage de la Palestine (voir paragraphes 70 et 71 ci-après). Cette responsabilité a été décrite par l'Assemblée générale comme «une responsabilité permanente à assumer en ce qui concerne la question de Palestine jusqu'à ce qu'elle soit réglée sous tous ses aspects de manière satisfaisante et dans le respect de la légitimité internationale» (résolution 57/107 de l'Assemblée générale, en date du 3 décembre 2002). Dans le cadre institutionnel de l'Organisation, cette responsabilité s'est concrétisée par l'adoption de nombreuses résolutions du Conseil de sécurité et de l'Assemblée générale, ainsi que par la création de plusieurs organes subsidiaires spécifiquement établis pour œuvrer à la réalisation des droits inaliénables du peuple palestinien.

50. L'objet de la requête dont la Cour est saisie est d'obtenir de celle-ci un avis que l'Assemblée générale estime utile pour exercer comme il convient ses fonctions. L'avis est demandé à l'égard d'une question qui intéresse tout particulièrement les Nations Unies, et qui s'inscrit dans un cadre bien plus large que celui d'un différend bilatéral. Dans ces conditions, la Cour estime que rendre un avis n'aurait pas pour effet de tourner le principe du consentement au règlement judiciaire et qu'elle ne saurait dès lors, dans l'exercice de son pouvoir discrétionnaire, refuser de donner un avis pour ce motif.

*

51. La Cour passera maintenant à un autre argument avancé au cours de la présente procédure pour étayer la thèse selon laquelle elle devrait refuser d'exercer sa compétence. Certains participants ont soutenu qu'un avis consultatif de la Cour sur la licéité du mur et les conséquences juridiques de son édification pourrait faire obstacle à un règlement politique négocié du conflit israélo-palestinien. En particulier, selon cette thèse, une telle opinion pourrait porter atteinte à la «feuille de route» (voir paragraphe 22 ci-dessus), qui prescrit à Israël et à la Palestine le respect d'un certain nombre d'obligations au cours des différentes phases qui y sont prévues. Il a été affirmé que l'avis demandé pourrait compliquer les négociations envisagées dans la «feuille de route» et que la Cour devrait en conséquence exercer son pouvoir discrétionnaire et refuser de répondre à la question qui lui a été posée.

La Cour a déjà été appelée à examiner des arguments analogues plusieurs fois par le passé. Ainsi, dans son avis consultatif sur la *Licéité de la menace ou de l'emploi d'armes nucléaires*, la Cour a-t-elle déclaré:

of the General Assembly's request can be regarded as only a bilateral matter between Israel and Palestine. Given the powers and responsibilities of the United Nations in questions relating to international peace and security, it is the Court's view that the construction of the wall must be deemed to be directly of concern to the United Nations. The responsibility of the United Nations in this matter also has its origin in the Mandate and the Partition Resolution concerning Palestine (see paragraphs 70 and 71 below). This responsibility has been described by the General Assembly as "a permanent responsibility towards the question of Palestine until the question is resolved in all its aspects in a satisfactory manner in accordance with international legitimacy" (General Assembly resolution 57/107 of 3 December 2002). Within the institutional framework of the Organization, this responsibility has been manifested by the adoption of many Security Council and General Assembly resolutions, and by the creation of several subsidiary bodies specifically established to assist in the realization of the inalienable rights of the Palestinian people.

50. The object of the request before the Court is to obtain from the Court an opinion which the General Assembly deems of assistance to it for the proper exercise of its functions. The opinion is requested on a question which is of particularly acute concern to the United Nations, and one which is located in a much broader frame of reference than a bilateral dispute. In the circumstances, the Court does not consider that to give an opinion would have the effect of circumventing the principle of consent to judicial settlement, and the Court accordingly cannot, in the exercise of its discretion, decline to give an opinion on that ground.

*

51. The Court now turns to another argument raised in the present proceedings in support of the view that it should decline to exercise its jurisdiction. Some participants have argued that an advisory opinion from the Court on the legality of the wall and the legal consequences of its construction could impede a political, negotiated solution to the Israeli-Palestinian conflict. More particularly, it has been contended that such an opinion could undermine the scheme of the "Roadmap" (see paragraph 22 above), which requires Israel and Palestine to comply with certain obligations in various phases referred to therein. The requested opinion, it has been alleged, could complicate the negotiations envisaged in the "Roadmap", and the Court should therefore exercise its discretion and decline to reply to the question put.

This is a submission of a kind which the Court has already had to consider several times in the past. For instance, in its Advisory Opinion on the *Legality of the Threat or Use of Nuclear Weapons*, the Court stated:

« Il a ... été soutenu qu'une réponse de la Cour en l'espèce pourrait être préjudiciable aux négociations sur le désarmement et serait, en conséquence, contraire à l'intérêt de l'Organisation des Nations Unies. La Cour sait que, quelles que soient les conclusions auxquelles elle pourrait parvenir dans l'avis qu'elle donnerait, ces conclusions seraient pertinentes au regard du débat qui se poursuit à l'Assemblée générale, et apporteraient dans les négociations sur la question un élément supplémentaire. Mais, au-delà de cette constatation, l'effet qu'aurait cet avis est une question d'appréciation. Des opinions contraires ont été exposées devant la Cour et il n'est pas de critère évident qui permettrait à celle-ci de donner la préférence à une position plutôt qu'à une autre. » (*C.I.J. Recueil 1996 (I)*, p. 237, par. 17; voir également *Sahara occidental, C.I.J. Recueil 1975*, p. 37, par. 73.)

52. Un participant à la présente procédure a dit que la Cour, si elle devait répondre à la requête, devrait en tout cas garder présents à l'esprit

« deux aspects essentiels du processus de paix: le principe fondamental selon lequel les questions relatives au statut définitif doivent être résolues par la négociation; et le fait que le processus de paix ne pourra aboutir que si, pendant la période intérimaire, les parties s'acquittent de leurs responsabilités en matière de sécurité ».

53. La Cour n'ignore pas que la « feuille de route », entérinée par le Conseil de sécurité dans sa résolution 1515 (2003) (voir paragraphe 22 ci-dessus), constitue un cadre de négociation visant au règlement du conflit israélo-palestinien. L'influence que l'avis de la Cour pourrait avoir sur ces négociations n'apparaît cependant pas de façon évidente: les participants à la présente procédure ont exprimé à cet égard des vues divergentes. La Cour ne saurait considérer ce facteur comme une raison décisive de refuser d'exercer sa compétence.

54. Certains participants ont par ailleurs affirmé devant la Cour que la question de la construction du mur n'était qu'un aspect du conflit israélo-palestinien, à l'examen duquel la présente procédure ne saurait servir de cadre approprié. Toutefois, la Cour estime que cela ne saurait justifier qu'elle refuse de répondre à la question posée. La Cour est certes consciente que la question du mur fait partie d'un ensemble, et elle prendrait soigneusement en considération cette circonstance dans tout avis qu'elle pourrait rendre. En même temps, la question que l'Assemblée générale a choisi de lui soumettre pour avis est limitée aux conséquences juridiques de la construction du mur, et la Cour ne tiendrait compte d'autres éléments que dans la mesure où ceux-ci seraient nécessaires aux fins de l'examen de cette question.

*

55. Plusieurs participants à la procédure ont encore soutenu que la

> "It has . . . been submitted that a reply from the Court in this case might adversely affect disarmament negotiations and would, therefore, be contrary to the interest of the United Nations. The Court is aware that, no matter what might be its conclusions in any opinion it might give, they would have relevance for the continuing debate on the matter in the General Assembly and would present an additional element in the negotiations on the matter. Beyond that, the effect of the opinion is a matter of appreciation. The Court has heard contrary positions advanced and there are no evident criteria by which it can prefer one assessment to another." (*I.C.J. Reports 1996 (I)*, p. 237, para. 17; see also *Western Sahara, I.C.J. Reports 1975*, p. 37, para. 73.)

52. One participant in the present proceedings has indicated that the Court, if it were to give a response to the request, should in any event do so keeping in mind

> "two key aspects of the peace process: the fundamental principle that permanent status issues must be resolved through negotiations; and the need during the interim period for the parties to fulfil their security responsibilities so that the peace process can succeed".

53. The Court is conscious that the "Roadmap", which was endorsed by the Security Council in resolution 1515 (2003) (see paragraph 22 above), constitutes a negotiating framework for the resolution of the Israeli-Palestinian conflict. It is not clear, however, what influence the Court's opinion might have on those negotiations: participants in the present proceedings have expressed differing views in this regard. The Court cannot regard this factor as a compelling reason to decline to exercise its jurisdiction.

54. It was also put to the Court by certain participants that the question of the construction of the wall was only one aspect of the Israeli-Palestinian conflict, which could not be properly addressed in the present proceedings. The Court does not however consider this a reason for it to decline to reply to the question asked. The Court is indeed aware that the question of the wall is part of a greater whole, and it would take this circumstance carefully into account in any opinion it might give. At the same time, the question that the General Assembly has chosen to ask of the Court is confined to the legal consequences of the construction of the wall, and the Court would only examine other issues to the extent that they might be necessary to its consideration of the question put to it.

*

55. Several participants in the proceedings have raised the further

Cour devrait refuser d'exercer sa compétence parce qu'elle ne dispose pas des faits et des éléments de preuve nécessaires pour lui permettre de formuler des conclusions. Israël a en particulier fait valoir, en se référant à l'avis consultatif relatif à l'*Interprétation des traités de paix conclus avec la Bulgarie, la Hongrie et la Roumanie*, que la Cour ne saurait donner un avis sur des questions soulevant des points de fait qui ne peuvent être éclaircis que contradictoirement. Selon Israël, si la Cour décidait de donner l'avis demandé, elle en serait réduite à des conjectures sur des faits essentiels et à des hypothèses sur des arguments de droit. Israël a précisé que la Cour ne pourrait se prononcer sur les conséquences juridiques de l'édification du mur sans examiner, d'une part, la nature et la portée des menaces pour la sécurité auxquelles le mur entend répondre, ainsi que l'efficacité de cette réponse, et, d'autre part, l'effet de la construction du mur pour les Palestiniens. Cette tâche, qui serait déjà difficile dans une affaire contentieuse, serait encore plus complexe dans une procédure consultative, d'autant qu'Israël serait seul à posséder une grande partie des renseignements nécessaires et qu'il a indiqué avoir choisi de ne pas traiter du fond. Israël a conclu que la Cour, face à des questions de fait impossibles à éclaircir dans la présente procédure, devrait user de son pouvoir discrétionnaire et refuser de donner suite à la demande d'avis consultatif.

56. La Cour fera observer que la question de savoir si les éléments de preuve dont elle dispose sont suffisants pour donner un avis consultatif doit être tranchée dans chaque cas particulier. Dans son avis relatif à l'*Interprétation des traités de paix conclus avec la Bulgarie, la Hongrie et la Roumanie* (*C.I.J. Recueil 1950*, p. 72), et de nouveau dans son avis relatif au *Sahara occidental*, la Cour a bien indiqué que ce qui était décisif dans ces circonstances était de savoir

> «si la Cour dispose de renseignements et d'éléments de preuve suffisants pour être à même de porter un jugement sur toute question de fait contestée et qu'il lui faudrait établir pour se prononcer d'une manière conforme à son caractère judiciaire» (*Sahara occidental, C.I.J. Recueil 1975*, p. 28-29, par. 46).

Ainsi, par exemple, dans la procédure concernant le *Statut de la Carélie orientale*, la Cour permanente de Justice internationale a décidé de refuser de donner un avis, entre autres, parce que la question posée «soulevait des points de fait qui ne pouvaient être éclaircis que contradictoirement» (*Interprétation des traités de paix conclus avec la Bulgarie, la Hongrie et la Roumanie, C.I.J. Recueil 1950*, p. 72; voir *Statut de la Carélie orientale, C.P.J.I série B n° 5*, p. 28). En revanche, dans l'avis sur le *Sahara occidental*, la Cour a noté qu'elle avait reçu une très abondante documentation permettant d'établir les faits pertinents (*C.I.J. Recueil 1975*, p. 29, par. 47).

57. En l'espèce, la Cour a à sa disposition le rapport du Secrétaire général, ainsi qu'un dossier volumineux soumis par celui-ci à la Cour, qui contient des informations détaillées non seulement quant au tracé du mur

argument that the Court should decline to exercise its jurisdiction because it does not have at its disposal the requisite facts and evidence to enable it to reach its conclusions. In particular, Israel has contended, referring to the Advisory Opinion on the *Interpretation of Peace Treaties with Bulgaria, Hungary and Romania*, that the Court could not give an opinion on issues which raise questions of fact that cannot be elucidated without hearing all parties to the conflict. According to Israel, if the Court decided to give the requested opinion, it would be forced to speculate about essential facts and make assumptions about arguments of law. More specifically, Israel has argued that the Court could not rule on the legal consequences of the construction of the wall without enquiring, first, into the nature and scope of the security threat to which the wall is intended to respond and the effectiveness of that response, and, second, into the impact of the construction for the Palestinians. This task, which would already be difficult in a contentious case, would be further complicated in an advisory proceeding, particularly since Israel alone possesses much of the necessary information and has stated that it chooses not to address the merits. Israel has concluded that the Court, confronted with factual issues impossible to clarify in the present proceedings, should use its discretion and decline to comply with the request for an advisory opinion.

56. The Court observes that the question whether the evidence available to it is sufficient to give an advisory opinion must be decided in each particular instance. In its Opinion concerning the *Interpretation of Peace Treaties with Bulgaria, Hungary and Romania* (*I.C.J. Reports 1950*, p. 72) and again in its Opinion on the *Western Sahara*, the Court made it clear that what is decisive in these circumstances is

> "whether the Court has before it sufficient information and evidence to enable it to arrive at a judicial conclusion upon any disputed questions of fact the determination of which is necessary for it to give an opinion in conditions compatible with its judicial character" (*Western Sahara, I.C.J. Reports 1975*, pp. 28-29, para. 46).

Thus, for instance, in the proceedings concerning the *Status of Eastern Carelia*, the Permanent Court of International Justice decided to decline to give an Opinion *inter alia* because the question put "raised a question of fact which could not be elucidated without hearing both parties" (*Interpretation of Peace Treaties with Bulgaria, Hungary and Romania, I.C.J. Reports 1950*, p. 72; see *Status of Eastern Carelia, P.C.I.J., Series B, No. 5*, p. 28). On the other hand, in the *Western Sahara* Opinion, the Court observed that it had been provided with very extensive documentary evidence of the relevant facts (*I.C.J. Reports 1975*, p. 29, para. 47).

57. In the present instance, the Court has at its disposal the report of the Secretary-General, as well as a voluminous dossier submitted by him to the Court, comprising not only detailed information on the route of

mais aussi quant aux conséquences humanitaires et socio-économiques de celui-ci sur la population palestinienne. Le dossier inclut de nombreux rapports fondés sur des visites effectuées sur le terrain par des rapporteurs spéciaux et des organes compétents des Nations Unies. Le Secrétaire général a par ailleurs soumis à la Cour un exposé écrit complétant les informations fournies dans son rapport, aux fins de mettre celui-ci à jour. Nombre d'autres participants ont en outre présenté à la Cour des exposés écrits qui renferment des informations pertinentes pour une réponse à la question posée par l'Assemblée générale. La Cour relève en particulier que l'exposé écrit d'Israël, bien que se limitant aux questions de compétence et d'opportunité judiciaire, comporte des observations concernant d'autres sujets, y compris les préoccupations d'Israël en matière de sécurité, et est accompagné d'annexes correspondantes; de nombreux autres documents émanant du Gouvernement israélien et concernant ces mêmes sujets sont dans le domaine public.

58. La Cour estime qu'elle dispose de renseignements et d'éléments de preuve suffisants pour lui permettre de donner l'avis consultatif demandé par l'Assemblée générale. La circonstance que d'autres pourraient évaluer et interpréter ces faits de manière subjective ou politique ne saurait au demeurant constituer un motif pour qu'une cour de justice s'abstienne d'assumer sa tâche judiciaire. Il n'y a donc pas, en l'espèce, insuffisance d'éléments d'information qui constituerait une raison décisive pour la Cour de refuser de donner l'avis sollicité.

*

59. Dans leurs exposés écrits, certains participants ont également avancé l'argument selon lequel la Cour devrait refuser de donner l'avis consultatif demandé sur les conséquences juridiques de l'édification du mur, parce que pareil avis consultatif ne serait d'aucune utilité. Ils ont soutenu que les avis consultatifs de la Cour seraient à considérer comme un moyen devant permettre à un organe ou à une institution, qui a besoin pour ses activités futures qu'un point de droit soit élucidé, d'obtenir ladite élucidation. Dans le cas d'espèce, est-il encore soutenu, l'Assemblée générale n'aurait pas besoin d'un tel avis de la Cour, parce qu'elle a déjà déclaré la construction du mur illégale, qu'elle a déjà déterminé les conséquences juridiques de cette construction en exigeant qu'Israël l'arrête et revienne sur le projet, et parce que, en outre, l'Assemblée générale n'a jamais fait clairement connaître ce qu'elle entendait faire de l'avis demandé.

60. Comme il ressort de la jurisprudence de la Cour, les avis consultatifs servent à fournir aux organes qui les sollicitent les éléments de caractère juridique qui leur sont nécessaires dans le cadre de leurs activités. Dans son avis sur les *Réserves à la convention pour la prévention et la répression du crime de génocide*, la Cour a observé: «L'objet de la présente demande d'avis est d'éclairer les Nations Unies dans leur action propre.» (*C.I.J. Recueil 1951*, p. 19.) De la même manière, dans son avis sur les *Conséquences juridiques pour les Etats de la présence continue de l'Afrique du Sud*

the wall but also on its humanitarian and socio-economic impact on the Palestinian population. The dossier includes several reports based on on-site visits by special rapporteurs and competent organs of the United Nations. The Secretary-General has further submitted to the Court a written statement updating his report, which supplemented the information contained therein. Moreover, numerous other participants have submitted to the Court written statements which contain information relevant to a response to the question put by the General Assembly. The Court notes in particular that Israel's Written Statement, although limited to issues of jurisdiction and judicial propriety, contained observations on other matters, including Israel's concerns in terms of security, and was accompanied by corresponding annexes; many other documents issued by the Israeli Government on those matters are in the public domain.

58. The Court finds that it has before it sufficient information and evidence to enable it to give the advisory opinion requested by the General Assembly. Moreover, the circumstance that others may evaluate and interpret these facts in a subjective or political manner can be no argument for a court of law to abdicate its judicial task. There is therefore in the present case no lack of information such as to constitute a compelling reason for the Court to decline to give the requested opinion.

*

59. In their written statements, some participants have also put forward the argument that the Court should decline to give the requested opinion on the legal consequences of the construction of the wall because such opinion would lack any useful purpose. They have argued that the advisory opinions of the Court are to be seen as a means to enable an organ or agency in need of legal clarification for its future action to obtain that clarification. In the present instance, the argument continues, the General Assembly would not need an opinion of the Court because it has already declared the construction of the wall to be illegal and has already determined the legal consequences by demanding that Israel stop and reverse its construction, and further, because the General Assembly has never made it clear how it intended to use the opinion.

60. As is clear from the Court's jurisprudence, advisory opinions have the purpose of furnishing to the requesting organs the elements of law necessary for them in their action. In its Opinion concerning *Reservations to the Convention on the Prevention and Punishment of the Crime of Genocide*, the Court observed: "The object of this request for an Opinion is to guide the United Nations in respect of its own action." (*I.C.J. Reports 1951*, p. 19.) Likewise, in its Opinion on the *Legal Consequences for States of the Continued Presence of South Africa in Namibia (South*

en Namibie (Sud-Ouest africain) nonobstant la résolution 276 (1970) du Conseil de sécurité, la Cour a rappelé qu'«[i]l s'agi[ssait] d'une requête présentée par un organe des Nations Unies, à propos de ses propres décisions, en vue d'obtenir de la Cour un avis juridique sur les conséquences et les incidences de ces décisions» (*C.I.J. Recueil 1971*, p. 24, par. 32). En une autre occasion, la Cour a déclaré que l'avis consultatif qui lui était demandé «fournira[it] à l'Assemblée générale des éléments de caractère juridique qui lui ser[aient] utiles quand elle traitera[it] à nouveau de la décolonisation du Sahara occidental» (*Sahara occidental, C.I.J. Recueil 1975*, p. 37, par. 72).

61. Quant à l'argument selon lequel l'Assemblée générale n'a pas fait connaître clairement quel usage elle entendait faire d'un avis consultatif sur le mur, la Cour rappellera ce qu'elle a déclaré dans son avis consultatif sur la *Licéité de la menace ou de l'emploi d'armes nucléaires*, une déclaration qui est également pertinente en la présente espèce:

> «Certains Etats ont observé que l'Assemblée générale n'a pas expliqué à la Cour à quelles fins précises elle sollicitait l'avis consultatif. Toutefois, il n'appartient pas à la Cour de prétendre décider si l'Assemblée a ou non besoin d'un avis consultatif pour s'acquitter de ses fonctions. L'Assemblée générale est habilitée à décider elle-même de l'utilité d'un avis au regard de ses besoins propres.» (*C.I.J. Recueil 1996 (I)*, p. 237, par. 16.)

62. Il s'ensuit que la Cour ne saurait refuser de répondre à la question posée au motif que son avis ne serait d'aucune utilité. La Cour ne peut substituer sa propre appréciation de l'utilité de l'avis demandé à celle de l'organe qui le sollicite, en l'occurrence l'Assemblée générale. En outre, et en tout état de cause, la Cour estime que l'Assemblée générale n'a pas encore procédé à la détermination de toutes les conséquences possibles de sa propre résolution. La tâche de la Cour consisterait à déterminer l'ensemble des conséquences juridiques de l'édification du mur, alors que l'Assemblée générale — et le Conseil de sécurité — pourrait ensuite tirer des conclusions de ces déterminations de la Cour.

*

63. Enfin, la Cour examinera un autre argument avancé en ce qui concerne l'opportunité de donner un avis consultatif en l'espèce. Israël a soutenu que la Palestine, compte tenu de la responsabilité qui est la sienne dans les actes de violence auxquels le mur vise à parer, commis contre Israël et sa population, ne saurait demander à la Cour de remédier à une situation résultant de ses propres actes illicites. A ce propos, Israël a invoqué la maxime *nullus commodum capere potest de sua injuria propria*, qu'il considère comme aussi pertinente dans une procédure consultative que dans une affaire contentieuse. Dès lors, conclut Israël, la bonne foi et le principe des «mains propres» constituent une raison décisive qui devrait conduire la Cour à refuser d'accéder à la demande de l'Assemblée générale.

West Africa) notwithstanding Security Council Resolution 276 (1970), the Court noted: "The request is put forward by a United Nations organ with reference to its own decisions and it seeks legal advice from the Court on the consequences and implications of these decisions." (*I.C.J. Reports 1971*, p. 24, para. 32.) The Court found on another occasion that the advisory opinion it was to give would "furnish the General Assembly with elements of a legal character relevant to its further treatment of the decolonization of Western Sahara" (*Western Sahara, I.C.J. Reports 1975*, p. 37, para. 72).

61. With regard to the argument that the General Assembly has not made it clear what use it would make of an advisory opinion on the wall, the Court would recall, as equally relevant in the present proceedings, what it stated in its Opinion on the *Legality of the Threat or Use of Nuclear Weapons*:

> "Certain States have observed that the General Assembly has not explained to the Court for what precise purposes it seeks the advisory opinion. Nevertheless, it is not for the Court itself to purport to decide whether or not an advisory opinion is needed by the Assembly for the performance of its functions. The General Assembly has the right to decide for itself on the usefulness of an opinion in the light of its own needs." (*I.C.J. Reports 1996 (I)*, p. 237, para. 16.)

62. It follows that the Court cannot decline to answer the question posed based on the ground that its opinion would lack any useful purpose. The Court cannot substitute its assessment of the usefulness of the opinion requested for that of the organ that seeks such opinion, namely the General Assembly. Furthermore, and in any event, the Court considers that the General Assembly has not yet determined all the possible consequences of its own resolution. The Court's task would be to determine in a comprehensive manner the legal consequences of the construction of the wall, while the General Assembly — and the Security Council — may then draw conclusions from the Court's findings.

*

63. Lastly, the Court will turn to another argument advanced with regard to the propriety of its giving an advisory opinion in the present proceedings. Israel has contended that Palestine, given its responsibility for acts of violence against Israel and its population which the wall is aimed at addressing, cannot seek from the Court a remedy for a situation resulting from its own wrongdoing. In this context, Israel has invoked the maxim *nullus commodum capere potest de sua injuria propria*, which it considers to be as relevant in advisory proceedings as it is in contentious cases. Therefore, Israel concludes, good faith and the principle of "clean hands" provide a compelling reason that should lead the Court to refuse the General Assembly's request.

64. De l'avis de la Cour, cet argument est dénué de pertinence. Comme cela a déjà été souligné précédemment, c'est l'Assemblée générale qui a sollicité un avis consultatif, et un tel avis serait donné à l'Assemblée générale et non à un Etat ou une entité déterminés.

* *

65. A la lumière de ce qui précède, la Cour conclut non seulement qu'elle a compétence pour donner un avis sur la question qui lui a été posée par l'Assemblée générale (voir paragraphe 42 ci-dessus), mais encore qu'il n'existe aucune raison décisive pour qu'elle use de son pouvoir discrétionnaire de ne pas donner cet avis.

* * *

66. La Cour abordera maintenant l'examen de la question qui lui a été adressée par l'Assemblée générale par résolution ES-10/14. Il est rappelé que cette question est la suivante:

> «Quelles sont en droit les conséquences de l'édification du mur qu'Israël, puissance occupante, est en train de construire dans le territoire palestinien occupé, y compris à l'intérieur et sur le pourtour de Jérusalem-Est, selon ce qui est exposé dans le rapport du Secrétaire général, compte tenu des règles et des principes du droit international, notamment la quatrième convention de Genève de 1949 et les résolutions consacrées à la question par le Conseil de sécurité et l'Assemblée générale?»

67. Comme la Cour l'expliquera au paragraphe 82 ci-après, le «mur» en question est un ouvrage complexe, de sorte que ce terme ne peut être entendu dans son sens physique strict. Toutefois, les autres termes utilisés par Israël («clôture») ou par le Secrétaire général («barrière»), pris dans leur acception physique, ne sont pas plus exacts. De ce fait, dans le présent avis, la Cour a choisi d'user de la terminologie employée par l'Assemblée générale.

La Cour relèvera par ailleurs que la requête de l'Assemblée générale a trait aux conséquences juridiques de l'édification du mur «dans le territoire palestinien occupé, y compris à l'intérieur et sur le pourtour de Jérusalem-Est». Comme la Cour l'expliquera également plus loin (voir paragraphes 79 à 84 ci-après), certaines parties de l'ouvrage sont en cours de construction, ou leur construction est prévue, sur le territoire même d'Israël; la Cour ne considère pas qu'elle a à examiner les conséquences juridiques de la construction de telles parties du mur.

68. La question posée par l'Assemblée générale porte sur les conséquences juridiques de l'édification du mur dans le territoire palestinien occupé. Toutefois, en vue de préciser ces conséquences à l'intention de l'Assemblée générale, la Cour doit au préalable déterminer si l'édification de ce mur est ou non contraire au droit international (voir paragraphe 39

64. The Court does not consider this argument to be pertinent. As was emphasized earlier, it was the General Assembly which requested the advisory opinion, and the opinion is to be given to the General Assembly, and not to a specific State or entity.

* *

65. In the light of the foregoing, the Court concludes not only that it has jurisdiction to give an opinion on the question put to it by the General Assembly (see paragraph 42 above), but also that there is no compelling reason for it to use its discretionary power not to give that opinion.

* * *

66. The Court will now address the question put to it by the General Assembly in resolution ES-10/14. The Court recalls that the question is as follows:

> "What are the legal consequences arising from the construction of the wall being built by Israel, the occupying Power, in the Occupied Palestinian Territory, including in and around East Jerusalem, as described in the report of the Secretary-General, considering the rules and principles of international law, including the Fourth Geneva Convention of 1949, and relevant Security Council and General Assembly resolutions?"

67. As explained in paragraph 82 below, the "wall" in question is a complex construction, so that that term cannot be understood in a limited physical sense. However, the other terms used, either by Israel ("fence") or by the Secretary-General ("barrier"), are no more accurate if understood in the physical sense. In this Opinion, the Court has therefore chosen to use the terminology employed by the General Assembly.

The Court notes furthermore that the request of the General Assembly concerns the legal consequences of the wall being built "in the Occupied Palestinian Territory, including in and around East Jerusalem". As also explained below (see paragraphs 79-84 below), some parts of the complex are being built, or are planned to be built, on the territory of Israel itself; the Court does not consider that it is called upon to examine the legal consequences arising from the construction of those parts of the wall.

68. The question put by the General Assembly concerns the legal consequences of the construction of the wall in the Occupied Palestinian Territory. However, in order to indicate those consequences to the General Assembly the Court must first determine whether or not the construction of that wall breaches international law (see paragraph 39 above). It will

ci-dessus). Elle procédera donc à cette détermination avant de traiter des conséquences de la construction.

69. Pour ce faire, la Cour effectuera tout d'abord une brève analyse du statut du territoire en cause, puis décrira les ouvrages construits ou en cours de construction sur ce territoire. Elle indiquera ensuite quel est le droit applicable, avant de rechercher si celui-ci a été méconnu.

* *

70. La Palestine avait fait partie de l'Empire ottoman. A l'issue de la première guerre mondiale, un mandat «A» pour la Palestine fut confié à la Grande-Bretagne par la Société des Nations en application du paragraphe 4 de l'article 22 du Pacte, qui disposait que

> «[c]ertaines communautés, qui appartenaient autrefois à l'Empire ottoman, ont atteint un degré de développement tel que leur existence comme nations indépendantes peut être reconnue provisoirement, à la condition que les conseils et l'aide d'un mandataire guident leur administration jusqu'au moment où elles seront capables de se conduire seules».

La Cour rappellera ce qu'elle avait relevé dans son avis consultatif sur le *Statut international du Sud-Ouest africain*, alors qu'elle s'exprimait de manière générale sur les mandats, à savoir que «[l]e Mandat a été créé, dans l'intérêt des habitants du Territoire et de l'humanité en général, comme une institution internationale à laquelle était assigné un but international: une mission sacrée de civilisation» (*C.I.J. Recueil 1950*, p. 132). Elle avait également constaté à cet égard que «deux principes furent considérés comme étant d'importance primordiale: celui de la non-annexion et celui qui proclamait que le bien-être et le développement de ces peuples [qui n'étaient pas encore capables de se gouverner eux-mêmes] formaient «une mission sacrée de civilisation»» (*ibid.*, p. 131).

Les limites territoriales du mandat pour la Palestine furent fixées par divers instruments, notamment, en ce qui concerne sa frontière orientale, par un mémorandum britannique du 16 septembre 1922 et un traité anglo-transjordanien du 20 février 1928.

71. En 1947, le Royaume-Uni fit connaître son intention de procéder à l'évacuation complète du territoire sous mandat pour le 1er août 1948, date qui fut par la suite avancée au 15 mai 1948. Dans l'intervalle, l'Assemblée générale des Nations Unies avait adopté le 29 novembre 1947 une résolution 181 (II) sur le gouvernement futur de la Palestine, résolution qui «*[r]ecommande* au Royaume-Uni ... ainsi qu'à tous les autres Membres de l'Organisation des Nations Unies, l'adoption et la mise à exécution ... du plan de partage» du territoire, prévu dans la résolution, entre deux Etats indépendants, l'un arabe, l'autre juif, ainsi que la mise sur pied d'un régime international particulier pour la ville de Jérusalem. La population arabe de Palestine et les Etats arabes rejetèrent ce

therefore make this determination before dealing with the consequences of the construction.

69. To do so, the Court will first make a brief analysis of the status of the territory concerned, and will then describe the works already constructed or in course of construction in that territory. It will then indicate the applicable law before seeking to establish whether that law has been breached.

* *

70. Palestine was part of the Ottoman Empire. At the end of the First World War, a class "A" Mandate for Palestine was entrusted to Great Britain by the League of Nations, pursuant to paragraph 4 of Article 22 of the Covenant, which provided that:

> "Certain communities, formerly belonging to the Turkish Empire have reached a stage of development where their existence as independent nations can be provisionally recognized subject to the rendering of administrative advice and assistance by a Mandatory until such time as they are able to stand alone."

The Court recalls that in its Advisory Opinion on the *International Status of South West Africa*, speaking of mandates in general, it observed that "The Mandate was created, in the interest of the inhabitants of the territory, and of humanity in general, as an international institution with an international object — a sacred trust of civilization." (*I.C.J. Reports 1950*, p. 132.) The Court also held in this regard that "two principles were considered to be of paramount importance: the principle of non-annexation and the principle that the well-being and development of . . . peoples [not yet able to govern themselves] form[ed] 'a sacred trust of civilization' " (*ibid.*, p. 131).

The territorial boundaries of the Mandate for Palestine were laid down by various instruments, in particular on the eastern border by a British memorandum of 16 September 1922 and an Anglo-Transjordanian Treaty of 20 February 1928.

71. In 1947 the United Kingdom announced its intention to complete evacuation of the mandated territory by 1 August 1948, subsequently advancing that date to 15 May 1948. In the meantime, the General Assembly had on 29 November 1947 adopted resolution 181 (II) on the future government of Palestine, which "*Recommends* to the United Kingdom . . . and to all other Members of the United Nations the adoption and implementation . . . of the Plan of Partition" of the territory, as set forth in the resolution, between two independent States, one Arab, the other Jewish, as well as the creation of a special international régime for the City of Jerusalem. The Arab population of Palestine and the Arab States rejected this plan, contending that it was unbalanced; on 14 May

plan qu'ils estimaient déséquilibré; Israël proclama son indépendance le 14 mai 1948 en vertu de la résolution de l'Assemblée générale; un conflit armé éclata alors entre Israël et plusieurs Etats arabes et le plan de partage ne fut pas appliqué.

72. Par résolution 62 (1948) du 16 novembre 1948, le Conseil de sécurité décida qu'«il sera[it] conclu un armistice dans tous les secteurs de la Palestine» et invita les parties directement impliquées dans le conflit à rechercher un accord à cette fin. Conformément à cette décision, des conventions générales d'armistice furent conclues en 1949 entre Israël et les Etats voisins grâce à la médiation des Nations Unies. Une telle convention fut en particulier signée à Rhodes le 3 avril 1949 entre Israël et la Jordanie. Les articles V et VI de cette convention fixaient la ligne de démarcation de l'armistice entre les forces israéliennes et les forces arabes (ligne souvent appelée par la suite «Ligne verte» du fait de la couleur retenue pour la tracer sur les cartes, et qui sera ainsi dénommée ci-après). Il était précisé au paragraphe 2 de l'article III qu'«[a]ucun élément des forces militaires ou paramilitaires ... de l'une ou l'autre partie ... ne franchira[it], pour quelque motif que ce soit, la ligne de démarcation...». Il était convenu au paragraphe 8 de l'article VI que ces dispositions ne seraient pas «interprétées comme préjugeant en aucune façon un règlement ... définitif entre les parties». En outre, il était précisé que «[l]a ligne de démarcation de l'armistice définie aux articles V et VI de la ... convention [était] acceptée par les parties sans préjudice de règlements territoriaux ultérieurs, du tracé des frontières ou des revendications de chacune des parties à ce sujet». La ligne de démarcation était susceptible de subir des ajustements par accord entre les parties.

73. Lors du conflit armé de 1967, les forces armées israéliennes occupèrent l'ensemble des territoires qui avaient constitué la Palestine sous mandat britannique (y compris les territoires désignés sous le nom de Cisjordanie situés à l'est de la Ligne verte).

74. Le 22 novembre 1967, le Conseil de sécurité adopta à l'unanimité la résolution 242 (1967) qui soulignait l'inadmissibilité de l'acquisition de territoire par la guerre et appelait au «[r]etrait des forces armées israéliennes des territoires occupés lors du récent conflit», et à la «cessation de toutes assertions de belligérance ou de tous états de belligérance».

75. A partir de 1967, Israël a pris dans ces territoires diverses mesures tendant à modifier le statut de la ville de Jérusalem. Le Conseil de sécurité, après avoir rappelé à plusieurs reprises que «le principe que l'acquisition d'un territoire par la conquête militaire est inadmissible», a condamné ces mesures et a confirmé, par résolution 298 du 25 septembre 1971 (1971), de la façon la plus explicite que:

> «toutes les dispositions législatives et administratives prises par Israël en vue de modifier le statut de la ville de Jérusalem, y compris l'expropriation de terres et de biens immeubles, le transfert de populations et la législation visant à incorporer la partie occupée, sont totalement nulles et non avenues et ne peuvent modifier le statut de la ville».

1948, Israel proclaimed its independence on the strength of the General Assembly resolution; armed conflict then broke out between Israel and a number of Arab States and the Plan of Partition was not implemented.

72. By resolution 62 (1948) of 16 November 1948, the Security Council decided that "an armistice shall be established in all sectors of Palestine" and called upon the parties directly involved in the conflict to seek agreement to this end. In conformity with this decision, general armistice agreements were concluded in 1949 between Israel and the neighbouring States through mediation by the United Nations. In particular, one such agreement was signed in Rhodes on 3 April 1949 between Israel and Jordan. Articles V and VI of that Agreement fixed the armistice demarcation line between Israeli and Arab forces (often later called the "Green Line" owing to the colour used for it on maps; hereinafter the "Green Line"). Article III, paragraph 2, provided that "No element of the . . . military or para-military forces of either Party . . . shall advance beyond or pass over for any purpose whatsoever the Armistice Demarcation Lines . . ." It was agreed in Article VI, paragraph 8, that these provisions would not be "interpreted as prejudicing, in any sense, an ultimate political settlement between the Parties". It was also stated that "the Armistice Demarcation Lines defined in articles V and VI of [the] Agreement [were] agreed upon by the Parties without prejudice to future territorial settlements or boundary lines or to claims of either Party relating thereto". The Demarcation Line was subject to such rectification as might be agreed upon by the parties.

73. In the 1967 armed conflict, Israeli forces occupied all the territories which had constituted Palestine under British Mandate (including those known as the West Bank, lying to the east of the Green Line).

74. On 22 November 1967, the Security Council unanimously adopted resolution 242 (1967), which emphasized the inadmissibility of acquisition of territory by war and called for the "Withdrawal of Israel armed forces from territories occupied in the recent conflict", and "Termination of all claims or states of belligerency".

75. From 1967 onwards, Israel took a number of measures in these territories aimed at changing the status of the City of Jerusalem. The Security Council, after recalling on a number of occasions "the principle that acquisition of territory by military conquest is inadmissible", condemned those measures and, by resolution 298 (1971) of 25 September 1971, confirmed in the clearest possible terms that:

> "all legislative and administrative actions taken by Israel to change the status of the City of Jerusalem, including expropriation of land and properties, transfer of populations and legislation aimed at the incorporation of the occupied section, are totally invalid and cannot change that status".

Puis, à la suite de l'adoption par Israël le 30 juillet 1980 de la loi fondamentale faisant de Jérusalem la capitale «entière et réunifiée» d'Israël, le Conseil de sécurité, par résolution 478 (1980) du 20 août 1980, a précisé que l'adoption de cette loi constituait une violation du droit international et que «toutes les mesures et dispositions législatives et administratives prises par Israël, la puissance occupante, qui ont modifié ou visent à modifier le caractère et le statut de la Ville sainte de Jérusalem ... étaient nulles et non avenues». Il a en outre décidé «de ne pas reconnaître la «loi fondamentale» et les autres actions d'Israël qui, du fait de cette loi, cherchent à modifier le caractère et le statut de Jérusalem».

76. Par la suite, un traité de paix est intervenu le 26 octobre 1994 entre Israël et la Jordanie. Ce traité fixe la frontière entre les deux Etats «par référence à la frontière sous le mandat ... telle qu'elle est décrite en annexe I *a)* ..., sans préjudice aucun au statut de tout territoire placé sous le contrôle du gouvernement militaire israélien en 1967» (article 3, paragraphes 1 et 2). Quant à l'annexe I, elle fournit les cartes correspondantes et ajoute que, en ce qui concerne «le territoire passé sous le contrôle du gouvernement militaire israélien en 1967», la ligne ainsi tracée «est la frontière administrative» avec la Jordanie.

77. Enfin, plusieurs accords sont intervenus depuis 1993 entre Israël et l'Organisation de libération de la Palestine mettant diverses obligations à la charge de chacune des parties. En vertu de ces accords, Israël devait notamment transférer à des autorités palestiniennes certains pouvoirs et responsabilités exercés dans le territoire palestinien occupé par ses autorités militaires et son administration civile. De tels transferts ont eu lieu, mais, du fait d'événements ultérieurs, ils demeurent partiels et limités.

78. La Cour observera que, selon le droit international coutumier tel que reflété (voir paragraphe 89 ci-après) à l'article 42 du règlement concernant les lois et coutumes de la guerre sur terre annexé à la quatrième convention de La Haye du 18 octobre 1907 (ci-après dénommé le «règlement de La Haye de 1907»), un territoire est considéré comme occupé lorsqu'il se trouve placé de fait sous l'autorité de l'armée ennemie, et l'occupation ne s'étend qu'aux territoires où cette autorité est établie et en mesure de s'exercer.

Les territoires situés entre la Ligne verte (voir paragraphe 72 ci-dessus) et l'ancienne frontière orientale de la Palestine sous mandat ont été occupés par Israël en 1967 au cours du conflit armé ayant opposé Israël à la Jordanie. Selon le droit international coutumier, il s'agissait donc de territoires occupés dans lesquels Israël avait la qualité de puissance occupante. Les événements survenus depuis lors dans ces territoires tels que rapportés aux paragraphes 75 à 77 ci-dessus n'ont rien changé à cette situation. L'ensemble de ces territoires (y compris Jérusalem-Est) demeurent des territoires occupés et Israël y a conservé la qualité de puissance occupante.

*

Later, following the adoption by Israel on 30 July 1980 of the Basic Law making Jerusalem the "complete and united" capital of Israel, the Security Council, by resolution 478 (1980) of 20 August 1980, stated that the enactment of that Law constituted a violation of international law and that "all legislative and administrative measures and actions taken by Israel, the occupying Power, which have altered or purport to alter the character and status of the Holy City of Jerusalem . . . are null and void". It further decided "not to recognize the 'basic law' and such other actions by Israel that, as a result of this law, seek to alter the character and status of Jerusalem".

76. Subsequently, a peace treaty was signed on 26 October 1994 between Israel and Jordan. That treaty fixed the boundary between the two States "with reference to the boundary definition under the Mandate as is shown in Annex I *(a)* . . . without prejudice to the status of any territories that came under Israeli military government control in 1967" (Article 3, paragraphs 1 and 2). Annex I provided the corresponding maps and added that, with regard to the "territory that came under Israeli military government control in 1967", the line indicated "is the administrative boundary" with Jordan.

77. Lastly, a number of agreements have been signed since 1993 between Israel and the Palestine Liberation Organization imposing various obligations on each party. Those agreements *inter alia* required Israel to transfer to Palestinian authorities certain powers and responsibilities exercised in the Occupied Palestinian Territory by its military authorities and civil administration. Such transfers have taken place, but, as a result of subsequent events, they remained partial and limited.

78. The Court would observe that, under customary international law as reflected (see paragraph 89 below) in Article 42 of the Regulations Respecting the Laws and Customs of War on Land annexed to the Fourth Hague Convention of 18 October 1907 (hereinafter "the Hague Regulations of 1907"), territory is considered occupied when it is actually placed under the authority of the hostile army, and the occupation extends only to the territory where such authority has been established and can be exercised.

The territories situated between the Green Line (see paragraph 72 above) and the former eastern boundary of Palestine under the Mandate were occupied by Israel in 1967 during the armed conflict between Israel and Jordan. Under customary international law, these were therefore occupied territories in which Israel had the status of occupying Power. Subsequent events in these territories, as described in paragraphs 75 to 77 above, have done nothing to alter this situation. All these territories (including East Jerusalem) remain occupied territories and Israel has continued to have the status of occupying Power.

*

79. C'est pour l'essentiel dans ces territoires qu'Israël a construit ou projette de construire les ouvrages décrits dans le rapport du Secrétaire général. La Cour décrira maintenant ces ouvrages en s'appuyant sur ce rapport. Pour ce qui est des développements postérieurs à la diffusion dudit rapport, la Cour se référera aux informations complémentaires contenues dans l'exposé écrit de l'Organisation des Nations Unies, par lequel le Secrétaire général a entendu mettre à jour son rapport (dénommé ci-après l'«exposé écrit du Secrétaire général»).

80. Aux termes du rapport du Secrétaire général, «[d]epuis 1996, le Gouvernement israélien examine des plans qui visent à enrayer les infiltrations en Israël à partir du centre et du nord de la Cisjordanie...» (paragraphe 4). D'après le même rapport, un plan de ce type a été approuvé pour la première fois par le conseil des ministres israélien en juillet 2001. Puis le conseil a, le 14 avril 2002, adopté une décision prévoyant la construction d'ouvrages formant, selon Israël, une «clôture de sécurité» sur 80 kilomètres dans trois secteurs de la Cisjordanie.

Allant au-delà, le conseil des ministres israélien a, le 23 juin 2002, approuvé la première phase de construction d'une «clôture continue» en Cisjordanie (y compris Jérusalem-Est). Le 14 août 2002, il a adopté le tracé de ladite «clôture» pour les travaux de la phase A, en vue de la construction d'un ouvrage de 123 kilomètres de long dans le nord de la Cisjordanie à partir du poste de contrôle de Salem (au nord de Djénine) jusqu'à la colonie de peuplement d'Elkana. La phase B des travaux a été approuvée en décembre 2002. Il s'agit d'un tronçon d'environ 40 kilomètres à l'est du poste de contrôle de Salem, en direction de Beth Shean, le long de la partie nord de la Ligne verte jusqu'à la vallée du Jourdain. En outre, le 1er octobre 2003, le conseil des ministres israélien a adopté un tracé complet qui, selon le rapport du Secrétaire général, «formera une ligne continue qui s'étendra sur une distance de 720 kilomètres le long de la Cisjordanie». Une carte indiquant les tronçons achevés et les tronçons planifiés a été affichée sur le site de la toile Internet du ministère israélien de la défense le 23 octobre 2003. Selon les indications fournies sur cette carte, un tronçon continu (phase C) et englobant plusieurs colonies importantes reliera l'extrémité nord-ouest de la «clôture de sécurité» édifiée autour de Jérusalem à la pointe sud des travaux de la phase A à Elkana. Selon la même carte, la «clôture de sécurité» s'étendra sur 115 kilomètres de la colonie de Har Gilo près de Jérusalem à la colonie du Carmel au sud-est d'Hébron (phase D). D'après les documents du ministère de la défense, les travaux dans ce secteur doivent en principe s'achever en 2005. Il est enfin fait état au dossier de projets de construction par Israël d'une «clôture de sécurité» qui longerait la vallée du Jourdain le long de la chaîne montagneuse située à l'ouest de cette vallée.

81. Selon l'exposé écrit du Secrétaire général, la première partie de ces travaux (phase A), qui s'étend finalement sur 150 kilomètres, a été déclarée achevée le 31 juillet 2003. 56 000 Palestiniens environ auraient ainsi été placés dans des enclaves. Au cours de cette phase ont été édifiés deux tronçons d'un total de 19,5 kilomètres sur le pourtour de Jérusalem. La

79. It is essentially in these territories that Israel has constructed or plans to construct the works described in the report of the Secretary-General. The Court will now describe those works, basing itself on that report. For developments subsequent to the publication of that report, the Court will refer to complementary information contained in the Written Statement of the United Nations, which was intended by the Secretary-General to supplement his report (hereinafter "Written Statement of the Secretary-General").

80. The report of the Secretary-General states that "The Government of Israel has since 1996 considered plans to halt infiltration into Israel from the central and northern West Bank . . ." (para. 4). According to that report, a plan of this type was approved for the first time by the Israeli Cabinet in July 2001. Then, on 14 April 2002, the Cabinet adopted a decision for the construction of works, forming what Israel describes as a "security fence", 80 kilometres in length, in three areas of the West Bank.

The project was taken a stage further when, on 23 June 2002, the Israeli Cabinet approved the first phase of the construction of a "continuous fence" in the West Bank (including East Jerusalem). On 14 August 2002, it adopted the line of that "fence" for the work in Phase A, with a view to the construction of a complex 123 kilometres long in the northern West Bank, running from the Salem checkpoint (north of Jenin) to the settlement at Elkana. Phase B of the work was approved in December 2002. It entailed a stretch of some 40 kilometres running east from the Salem checkpoint towards Beth Shean along the northern part of the Green Line as far as the Jordan Valley. Furthermore, on 1 October 2003, the Israeli Cabinet approved a full route, which, according to the report of the Secretary-General, "will form one continuous line stretching 720 kilometres along the West Bank". A map showing completed and planned sections was posted on the Israeli Ministry of Defence website on 23 October 2003. According to the particulars provided on that map, a continuous section (Phase C) encompassing a number of large settlements will link the north-western end of the "security fence" built around Jerusalem with the southern point of Phase A construction at Elkana. According to the same map, the "security fence" will run for 115 kilometres from the Har Gilo settlement near Jerusalem to the Carmel settlement south-east of Hebron (Phase D). According to Ministry of Defence documents, work in this sector is due for completion in 2005. Lastly, there are references in the case file to Israel's planned construction of a "security fence" following the Jordan Valley along the mountain range to the west.

81. According to the Written Statement of the Secretary-General, the first part of these works (Phase A), which ultimately extends for a distance of 150 kilometres, was declared completed on 31 July 2003. It is reported that approximately 56,000 Palestinians would be encompassed in enclaves. During this phase, two sections totalling 19.5 kilometres

construction d'une nouvelle section a par ailleurs été entamée en novembre 2003 le long de la Ligne verte à l'ouest de l'enclave de Nazlat Issa-Baqa al-Sharqiya, laquelle était presque achevée en janvier 2004 lors du dépôt de l'exposé écrit du Secrétaire général.

Suivant l'exposé écrit du Secrétaire général, les travaux entrepris au titre de la phase B étaient toujours en cours en janvier 2004. Une première section de ce tronçon, qui suit de près la Ligne verte jusqu'au village d'Al-Mutilla, était ainsi en voie d'achèvement en janvier 2004. A cet endroit, deux sections partent dans des directions différentes. Les travaux de construction de la première section, qui s'étend plein est jusqu'à la frontière avec la Jordanie, ont débuté en janvier 2004. La construction de la seconde section, qui devrait s'étendre de la Ligne verte au village de Taysir, a été à peine entamée. L'Organisation des Nations Unies a néanmoins été informée que cette seconde section pourrait ne pas être construite.

L'exposé écrit du Secrétaire général précise en outre que la phase C des travaux, selon un tracé partant du point d'aboutissement de celui de la phase A, près de la colonie d'Elkana, jusqu'au village de Nu'man, au sud-est de Jérusalem, a débuté en décembre 2003. Ce tronçon est divisé en trois parties et en autant de phases de travaux. Pour la phase C1, les travaux engagés, entre les villages de Rantis et de Budrus notamment, ont abouti à l'édification d'un tronçon de 4 kilomètres environ, sur un total de 40 kilomètres prévus. Le tronçon de la phase C2 devrait entourer «le saillant d'Ariel» en pénétrant de 22 kilomètres à l'intérieur de la Cisjordanie et inclure ainsi 52 000 colons israéliens. La phase C3 devrait donner lieu à l'édification de deux «barrières avancées»: l'une d'elles suit une direction nord-sud globalement parallèle au tronçon de la phase C1 actuellement en cours de construction entre Rantis et Budrus; l'autre suit une direction est-ouest le long d'une crête qui ferait partie de l'itinéraire de la Route 45, une autoroute en construction. Si la construction de ces deux tronçons était achevée, elle entraînerait la formation de deux enclaves peuplées de 72 000 Palestiniens dans 24 localités.

De nouveaux travaux ont aussi débuté à la fin du mois de novembre 2003 le long de la partie sud-est de la limite de la municipalité de Jérusalem, selon un tracé qui, d'après l'exposé écrit du Secrétaire général, coupe la localité suburbaine d'El-Ezariya de Jérusalem et divise la localité voisine d'Abou Dis en deux.

Au 25 janvier 2004, selon l'exposé écrit du Secrétaire général, les travaux avaient été achevés sur environ 190 kilomètres, couvrant la phase A et la majeure partie de la phase B; de nouveaux travaux de construction concernant la phase C avaient été entrepris dans certaines parties du centre de la Cisjordanie et à Jérusalem; et la phase D, prévue pour le sud de la Cisjordanie, n'avait pas encore débuté.

Selon le Gouvernement israélien, les tracés et le calendrier susmentionnés sont susceptibles de modifications. C'est ainsi qu'en février 2004 un tronçon de 8 kilomètres proche de la ville de Baqa al-Sharqiya a été were built around Jerusalem. In November 2003 construction of a new section was begun along the Green Line to the west of the Nazlat Issa-Baqa al-Sharqiya enclave, which in January 2004 was close to completion at the time when the Secretary-General submitted his Written Statement.

According to the Written Statement of the Secretary-General, the works carried out under Phase B were still in progress in January 2004. Thus an initial section of this stretch, which runs near or on the Green Line to the village of al-Mutilla, was almost complete in January 2004. Two additional sections diverge at this point. Construction started in early January 2004 on one section that runs due east as far as the Jordanian border. Construction of the second section, which is planned to run from the Green Line to the village of Taysir, has barely begun. The United Nations has, however, been informed that this second section might not be built.

The Written Statement of the Secretary-General further states that Phase C of the work, which runs from the terminus of Phase A, near the Elkana settlement, to the village of Nu'man, south-east of Jerusalem, began in December 2003. This section is divided into three stages. In Stage C1, between *inter alia* the villages of Rantis and Budrus, approximately 4 kilometres out of a planned total of 40 kilometres have been constructed. Stage C2, which will surround the so-called "Ariel Salient" by cutting 22 kilometres into the West Bank, will incorporate 52,000 Israeli settlers. Stage C3 is to involve the construction of two "depth barriers"; one of these is to run north-south, roughly parallel with the section of Stage C1 currently under construction between Rantis and Budrus, whilst the other runs east-west along a ridge said to be part of the route of Highway 45, a motorway under construction. If construction of the two barriers were completed, two enclaves would be formed, encompassing 72,000 Palestinians in 24 communities.

Further construction also started in late November 2003 along the south-eastern part of the municipal boundary of Jerusalem, following a route that, according to the Written Statement of the Secretary-General, cuts off the suburban village of El-Ezariya from Jerusalem and splits the neighbouring Abu Dis in two.

As at 25 January 2004, according to the Written Statement of the Secretary-General, some 190 kilometres of construction had been completed, covering Phase A and the greater part of Phase B. Further construction in Phase C had begun in certain areas of the central West Bank and in Jerusalem. Phase D, planned for the southern part of the West Bank, had not yet begun.

The Israeli Government has explained that the routes and timetable as described above are subject to modification. In February 2004, for example, an 8-kilometre section near the town of Baqa al-Sharqiya was détruit, et que la longueur du mur semble avoir été quelque peu réduite.

82. Les travaux réalisés ou décidés, tels que décrits dans le rapport et l'exposé écrit du Secrétaire général, ont conduit ou conduiront à la construction d'un dispositif comprenant en sa majeure partie:

1) une clôture équipée de détecteurs électroniques;
2) un fossé (pouvant atteindre 4 mètres de profondeur);
3) une route de patrouille asphaltée à deux voies;
4) une route de dépistage (bande de sable lisse permettant de détecter des empreintes de pieds) parallèle à la clôture;
5) six boudins de barbelés empilés qui marquent le périmètre des installations.

L'ouvrage a une largeur de 50 à 70 mètres, mais peut atteindre 100 mètres à certains endroits. Des barrières dites «avancées» peuvent s'ajouter à ce dispositif.

Par ailleurs, sur les quelque 180 kilomètres de l'ouvrage construits ou en cours de construction au moment où le Secrétaire général a déposé son rapport, des murs en béton couvraient une distance de 8,5 kilomètres environ. Ils sont généralement situés là où des agglomérations palestiniennes sont proches de ou contiguës à Israël (par exemple près de Qalqiliya et de Tulkarem ou dans certaines parties de Jérusalem).

83. Selon le rapport du Secrétaire général, le mur construit ou en cours de construction ne s'éloigne guère, en son extrémité nord, de la Ligne verte. Il n'en est pas moins situé dans les territoires occupés sur la majeure partie de son parcours. A certains endroits, les ouvrages s'écartent de la Ligne verte de plus de 7,5 kilomètres pour incorporer des colonies de peuplement, en encerclant des agglomérations palestiniennes. A l'ouest de Tulkarem, ils semblent suivre un tracé situé du côté israélien de la Ligne verte sur une distance de 1 à 2 kilomètres. En d'autres endroits, le tracé projeté impliquerait en revanche un écart allant jusqu'à 22 kilomètres vers l'est. Dans le cas de Jérusalem, les ouvrages existants et le tracé prévu se trouvent très au-delà de la Ligne verte, et même, dans certains cas, au-delà de la limite orientale de la municipalité de Jérusalem telle que fixée par Israël.

84. D'après ce même tracé, approximativement 975 kilomètres carrés (soit 16,6% de la superficie de la Cisjordanie) seraient, selon le rapport du Secrétaire général, situés entre la Ligne verte et le mur. Environ 237 000 Palestiniens vivraient dans cette zone. Si le mur était intégralement construit comme prévu, 160 000 autres Palestiniens vivraient dans des agglomérations presque totalement encerclées, qualifiées d'enclaves dans le rapport. Selon le tracé projeté, près de 320 000 colons israéliens (dont 178 000 environ à Jérusalem-Est) vivraient dans la zone comprise entre la Ligne verte et le mur.

85. Il convient enfin de relever que la construction du mur s'est accompagnée de la mise sur pied d'un régime administratif nouveau. Les forces de défense israéliennes ont en effet édicté en octobre 2003 des ordon-

demolished, and the planned length of the wall appears to have been slightly reduced.

82. According to the description in the report and the Written Statement of the Secretary-General, the works planned or completed have resulted or will result in a complex consisting essentially of:

(1) a fence with electronic sensors;
(2) a ditch (up to 4 metres deep);
(3) a two-lane asphalt patrol road;
(4) a trace road (a strip of sand smoothed to detect footprints) running parallel to the fence;
(5) a stack of six coils of barbed wire marking the perimeter of the complex.

The complex has a width of 50 to 70 metres, increasing to as much as 100 metres in some places. "Depth barriers" may be added to these works.

The approximately 180 kilometres of the complex completed or under construction as of the time when the Secretary-General submitted his report included some 8.5 kilometres of concrete wall. These are generally found where Palestinian population centres are close to or abut Israel (such as near Qalqiliya and Tulkarm or in parts of Jerusalem).

83. According to the report of the Secretary-General, in its northernmost part, the wall as completed or under construction barely deviates from the Green Line. It nevertheless lies within occupied territories for most of its course. The works deviate more than 7.5 kilometres from the Green Line in certain places to encompass settlements, while encircling Palestinian population areas. A stretch of 1 to 2 kilometres west of Tulkarm appears to run on the Israeli side of the Green Line. Elsewhere, on the other hand, the planned route would deviate eastward by up to 22 kilometres. In the case of Jerusalem, the existing works and the planned route lie well beyond the Green Line and even in some cases beyond the eastern municipal boundary of Jerusalem as fixed by Israel.

84. On the basis of that route, approximately 975 square kilometres (or 16.6 per cent of the West Bank) would, according to the report of the Secretary-General, lie between the Green Line and the wall. This area is stated to be home to 237,000 Palestinians. If the full wall were completed as planned, another 160,000 Palestinians would live in almost completely encircled communities, described as enclaves in the report. As a result of the planned route, nearly 320,000 Israeli settlers (of whom 178,000 in East Jerusalem) would be living in the area between the Green Line and the wall.

85. Lastly, it should be noted that the construction of the wall has been accompanied by the creation of a new administrative régime. Thus in October 2003 the Israeli Defence Forces issued Orders establishing the

nances établissant comme «zone fermée» la partie de la Cisjordanie qui se trouve entre la Ligne verte et le mur. Les résidents de cette zone ne peuvent désormais y demeurer et les non-résidents, y accéder, que s'ils sont porteurs d'un permis ou d'une carte d'identité délivrés par les autorités israéliennes. Selon le rapport du Secrétaire général, la plupart des résidents ont reçu des permis pour une durée limitée. Les citoyens israéliens, les résidents permanents en Israël et les personnes admises à immigrer en Israël en vertu de la loi du retour peuvent demeurer dans la zone fermée, s'y déplacer librement et en sortir sans avoir besoin de permis. L'entrée et la sortie de la zone fermée ne peuvent être opérées que par des portes d'accès qui sont ouvertes peu fréquemment et pour de courtes durées.

* *

86. La Cour déterminera maintenant les règles et principes de droit international qui sont pertinents pour l'appréciation de la licéité des mesures prises par Israël. Ces règles et principes figurent dans la Charte des Nations Unies et certains autres traités, dans le droit international coutumier et dans les résolutions pertinentes adoptées en vertu de la Charte par l'Assemblée générale et le Conseil de sécurité. Des doutes ont toutefois été exprimés par Israël en ce qui concerne l'applicabilité dans le territoire palestinien occupé de certaines règles de droit international humanitaire et des conventions relatives aux droits de l'homme. La Cour examinera maintenant ces diverses questions.

87. La Cour rappellera tout d'abord que, selon le paragraphe 4 de l'article 2 de la Charte des Nations Unies:

> «Les Membres de l'Organisation s'abstiennent, dans leurs relations internationales, de recourir à la menace ou à l'emploi de la force, soit contre l'intégrité territoriale ou l'indépendance politique de tout Etat, soit de toute autre manière incompatible avec les buts des Nations Unies.»

L'Assemblée générale a, le 24 octobre 1970, adopté la résolution 2625 (XXV) intitulée «Déclaration relative aux principes du droit international touchant les relations amicales et la coopération entre Etats» (ci-après dénommée la «résolution 2625 (XXV)»), dans laquelle elle a souligné que «[n]ulle acquisition territoriale obtenue par la menace ou l'emploi de la force ne sera reconnue comme légale». Comme la Cour l'a dit dans l'affaire des *Activités militaires et paramilitaires au Nicaragua et contre celui-ci (Nicaragua c. Etats-Unis d'Amérique)*, les principes énoncés dans la Charte au sujet de l'usage de la force reflètent le droit international coutumier (voir *C.I.J. Recueil 1986*, p. 98-101, par. 187-190); cela vaut également pour ce qui en est le corollaire, l'illicéité de toute acquisition de territoire résultant de la menace ou de l'emploi de la force.

88. La Cour relèvera également que le principe du droit des peuples à disposer d'eux-mêmes a été consacré dans la Charte des Nations Unies et réaffirmé par la résolution 2625 (XXV) de l'Assemblée générale déjà

part of the West Bank lying between the Green Line and the wall as a "Closed Area". Residents of this area may no longer remain in it, nor may non-residents enter it, unless holding a permit or identity card issued by the Israeli authorities. According to the report of the Secretary-General, most residents have received permits for a limited period. Israeli citizens, Israeli permanent residents and those eligible to immigrate to Israel in accordance with the Law of Return may remain in, or move freely to, from and within the Closed Area without a permit. Access to and exit from the Closed Area can only be made through access gates, which are opened infrequently and for short periods.

* *

86. The Court will now determine the rules and principles of international law which are relevant in assessing the legality of the measures taken by Israel. Such rules and principles can be found in the United Nations Charter and certain other treaties, in customary international law and in the relevant resolutions adopted pursuant to the Charter by the General Assembly and the Security Council. However, doubts have been expressed by Israel as to the applicability in the Occupied Palestinian Territory of certain rules of international humanitarian law and human rights instruments. The Court will now consider these various questions.

87. The Court first recalls that, pursuant to Article 2, paragraph 4, of the United Nations Charter:

> "All Members shall refrain in their international relations from the threat or use of force against the territorial integrity or political independence of any State, or in any other manner inconsistent with the Purposes of the United Nations."

On 24 October 1970, the General Assembly adopted resolution 2625 (XXV), entitled "Declaration on Principles of International Law concerning Friendly Relations and Co-operation among States" (hereinafter "resolution 2625 (XXV)"), in which it emphasized that "No territorial acquisition resulting from the threat or use of force shall be recognized as legal." As the Court stated in its Judgment in the case concerning *Military and Paramilitary Activities in and against Nicaragua (Nicaragua* v. *United States of America)*, the principles as to the use of force incorporated in the Charter reflect customary international law (see *I.C.J. Reports 1986*, pp. 98-101, paras. 187-190); the same is true of its corollary entailing the illegality of territorial acquisition resulting from the threat or use of force.

88. The Court also notes that the principle of self-determination of peoples has been enshrined in the United Nations Charter and reaffirmed by the General Assembly in resolution 2625 (XXV) cited above, pursuant

mentionnée, selon laquelle «[t]out Etat a le devoir de s'abstenir de recourir à toute mesure de coercition qui priverait de leur droit à l'autodétermination ... les peuples mentionnés [dans ladite résolution]». L'article 1er commun au pacte international relatif aux droits économiques, sociaux et culturels et au pacte international relatif aux droits civils et politiques réaffirme le droit de tous les peuples à disposer d'eux-mêmes et fait obligation aux Etats parties de faciliter la réalisation de ce droit et de le respecter, conformément aux dispositions de la Charte des Nations Unies.

La Cour rappellera qu'en 1971 elle a souligné que l'évolution actuelle du «droit international à l'égard des territoires non autonomes, tel qu'il est consacré par la Charte des Nations Unies, a fait de l'autodétermination un principe applicable à tous ces territoires». La Cour a ajouté que «[d]u fait de cette évolution il n'y a[vait] guère de doute que la «mission sacrée»» visée au paragraphe 1 de l'article 22 du Pacte de la Société des Nations «avait pour objectif ultime l'autodétermination ... des peuples en cause» (*Conséquences juridiques pour les Etats de la présence continue de l'Afrique du Sud en Namibie (Sud-Ouest africain) nonobstant la résolution 276 (1970) du Conseil de sécurité, avis consultatif, C.I.J. Recueil 1971*, p. 31, par. 52-53). La Cour s'est référée à ce principe à plusieurs reprises dans sa jurisprudence (*ibid.*; voir aussi *Sahara occidental, avis consultatif, C.I.J. Recueil 1975*, p. 68, par. 162). La Cour a même précisé qu'aujourd'hui le droit des peuples à disposer d'eux-mêmes est un droit opposable *erga omnes* (voir *Timor oriental (Portugal c. Australie), arrêt, C.I.J. Recueil 1995*, p. 102, par. 29).

89. Pour ce qui concerne le droit international humanitaire, la Cour relèvera en premier lieu qu'Israël n'est pas partie à la quatrième convention de La Haye de 1907 à laquelle le règlement est annexé. La Cour observera qu'aux termes de la convention ce règlement avait pour objet de «reviser les lois et coutumes générales de la guerre» telles qu'elles existaient à l'époque. Depuis lors cependant, le Tribunal militaire international de Nuremberg a jugé que les «règles définies dans la convention étaient reconnues par toutes les nations civilisées et étaient considérées comme une formulation des lois et coutumes de guerre» (jugement du Tribunal militaire international de Nuremberg du 30 septembre et 1er octobre 1946, p. 65). La Cour elle-même a abouti à la même conclusion en examinant les droits et devoirs des belligérants dans la conduite des opérations militaires (*Licéité de la menace ou de l'emploi d'armes nucléaires, avis consultatif, C.I.J. Recueil 1996 (I)*, p. 256, par. 75). La Cour estime que les dispositions du règlement de La Haye de 1907 ont acquis un caractère coutumier, comme d'ailleurs tous les participants à la procédure devant la Cour le reconnaissent.

La Cour observera en outre que, conformément à l'article 154 de la quatrième convention de Genève, le règlement de La Haye a été complété en ses sections II et III par les dispositions de ladite convention. La section III dudit règlement, qui concerne «l'autorité militaire sur le territoire de l'Etat ennemi», est particulièrement pertinente en l'espèce.

to which "Every State has the duty to refrain from any forcible action which deprives peoples referred to [in that resolution] . . . of their right to self-determination." Article 1 common to the International Covenant on Economic, Social and Cultural Rights and the International Covenant on Civil and Political Rights reaffirms the right of all peoples to self-determination, and lays upon the States parties the obligation to promote the realization of that right and to respect it, in conformity with the provisions of the United Nations Charter.

The Court would recall that in 1971 it emphasized that current developments in "international law in regard to non-self-governing territories, as enshrined in the Charter of the United Nations, made the principle of self-determination applicable to all [such territories]". The Court went on to state that "These developments leave little doubt that the ultimate objective of the sacred trust" referred to in Article 22, paragraph 1, of the Covenant of the League of Nations "was the self-determination . . . of the peoples concerned" (*Legal Consequences for States of the Continued Presence of South Africa in Namibia (South West Africa) notwithstanding Security Council Resolution 276 (1970), Advisory Opinion, I.C.J. Reports 1971*, p. 31, paras. 52-53). The Court has referred to this principle on a number of occasions in its jurisprudence (*ibid.*; see also *Western Sahara, Advisory Opinion, I.C.J. Reports 1975*, p. 68, para. 162). The Court indeed made it clear that the right of peoples to self-determination is today a right *erga omnes* (see *East Timor (Portugal* v. *Australia), Judgment, I.C.J. Reports 1995*, p. 102, para. 29).

89. As regards international humanitarian law, the Court would first note that Israel is not a party to the Fourth Hague Convention of 1907, to which the Hague Regulations are annexed. The Court observes that, in the words of the Convention, those Regulations were prepared "to revise the general laws and customs of war" existing at that time. Since then, however, the International Military Tribunal of Nuremberg has found that the "rules laid down in the Convention were recognised by all civilised nations, and were regarded as being declaratory of the laws and customs of war" (Judgment of the International Military Tribunal of Nuremberg, 30 September and 1 October 1946, p. 65). The Court itself reached the same conclusion when examining the rights and duties of belligerents in their conduct of military operations (*Legality of the Threat or Use of Nuclear Weapons, Advisory Opinion, I.C.J. Reports 1996 (I)*, p. 256, para. 75). The Court considers that the provisions of the Hague Regulations have become part of customary law, as is in fact recognized by all the participants in the proceedings before the Court.

The Court also observes that, pursuant to Article 154 of the Fourth Geneva Convention, that Convention is supplementary to Sections II and III of the Hague Regulations. Section III of those Regulations, which concerns "Military authority over the territory of the hostile State", is particularly pertinent in the present case.

90. S'agissant en second lieu de la quatrième convention de Genève, des points de vue divergents ont été exprimés par les participants à la procédure devant la Cour. Contrairement à la grande majorité des autres participants, Israël conteste en effet l'applicabilité *de jure* de la convention au territoire palestinien occupé. Au paragraphe 3 de l'annexe I au rapport du Secrétaire général intitulée «Résumé de la position juridique du Gouvernement israélien», il est en particulier précisé qu'Israël ne considère pas que la quatrième convention de Genève «soit applicable au territoire palestinien occupé», dans la mesure où «le territoire n'était pas reconnu comme souverain avant son annexion par la Jordanie et l'Egypte et où, en conséquence, il ne s'agit pas d'un territoire d'une Haute Partie contractante au regard de la convention».

91. La Cour rappellera que la quatrième convention de Genève a été ratifiée par Israël le 6 juillet 1951 et qu'Israël est partie à cette convention. La Jordanie y est aussi partie depuis le 29 mai 1951. Aucun des deux Etats n'a formulé de réserve pertinente au cas particulier.

La Palestine s'est par ailleurs engagée unilatéralement, par déclaration du 7 juin 1982, à appliquer la quatrième convention de Genève. La Suisse, en qualité d'Etat dépositaire, a estimé valable cet engagement unilatéral. En revanche, elle a conclu qu'elle «n'[était] pas — en tant que dépositaire — en mesure de trancher le point de savoir si» «la demande [en date du 14 juin 1989] de l'Organisation de libération de la Palestine, au nom de l'«Etat de Palestine», d'adhérer» notamment à la quatrième convention «[devait] être considérée comme un instrument d'adhésion».

92. En outre, en vue de déterminer le champ d'application de la quatrième convention de Genève, il convient de rappeler que selon l'article 2 commun aux quatre conventions du 12 août 1949:

> «En dehors des dispositions qui doivent entrer en vigueur dès le temps de paix, la présente convention s'appliquera en cas de guerre déclarée ou de tout autre conflit armé surgissant entre deux ou plusieurs des Hautes Parties contractantes même si l'état de guerre n'est pas reconnu par l'une d'elles.
>
> La convention s'appliquera également dans tous les cas d'occupation de tout ou partie du territoire d'une Haute Partie contractante, même si cette occupation ne rencontre aucune résistance militaire.
>
> Si l'une des puissances en conflit n'est pas partie à la présente convention, les puissances parties à celle-ci resteront néanmoins liées par elle dans leurs rapports réciproques. Elles seront liées en outre par la convention envers ladite puissance, si celle-ci en accepte et en applique les dispositions.»

93. Après l'occupation de la Cisjordanie en 1967, les autorités israéliennes ont promulgué l'ordonnance n° 3 qui stipule en son article 35 que

> «Le tribunal militaire ... doit appliquer les dispositions de la convention de Genève du 12 août 1949 relative à la protection des

90. Secondly, with regard to the Fourth Geneva Convention, differing views have been expressed by the participants in these proceedings. Israel, contrary to the great majority of the other participants, disputes the applicability *de jure* of the Convention to the Occupied Palestinian Territory. In particular, in paragraph 3 of Annex I to the report of the Secretary-General, entitled "Summary Legal Position of the Government of Israel", it is stated that Israel does not agree that the Fourth Geneva Convention "is applicable to the occupied Palestinian Territory", citing "the lack of recognition of the territory as sovereign prior to its annexation by Jordan and Egypt" and inferring that it is "not a territory of a High Contracting Party as required by the Convention".

91. The Court would recall that the Fourth Geneva Convention was ratified by Israel on 6 July 1951 and that Israel is a party to that Convention. Jordan has also been a party thereto since 29 May 1951. Neither of the two States has made any reservation that would be pertinent to the present proceedings.

Furthermore, Palestine gave a unilateral undertaking, by declaration of 7 June 1982, to apply the Fourth Geneva Convention. Switzerland, as depositary State, considered that unilateral undertaking valid. It concluded, however, that it "[was] not — as a depositary — in a position to decide whether" "the request [dated 14 June 1989] from the Palestine Liberation Movement in the name of the 'State of Palestine' to accede" *inter alia* to the Fourth Geneva Convention "can be considered as an instrument of accession".

92. Moreover, for the purpose of determining the scope of application of the Fourth Geneva Convention, it should be recalled that under common Article 2 of the four Conventions of 12 August 1949:

> "In addition to the provisions which shall be implemented in peacetime, the present Convention shall apply to all cases of declared war or of any other armed conflict which may arise between two or more of the High Contracting Parties, even if the state of war is not recognized by one of them.
>
> The Convention shall also apply to all cases of partial or total occupation of the territory of a High Contracting Party, even if the said occupation meets with no armed resistance.
>
> Although one of the Powers in conflict may not be a party to the present Convention, the Powers who are parties thereto shall remain bound by it in their mutual relations. They shall furthermore be bound by the Convention in relation to the said Power, if the latter accepts and applies the provisions thereof."

93. After the occupation of the West Bank in 1967, the Israeli authorities issued an order No. 3 stating in its Article 35 that:

> "the Military Court . . . must apply the provisions of the Geneva Convention dated 12 August 1949 relative to the Protection of

> personnes civiles en temps de guerre en ce qui concerne les procédures judiciaires. En cas d'incompatibilité entre la présente ordonnance et ladite convention, cette dernière prévaudra.» *[Traduction du Greffe.]*

Par la suite, les autorités israéliennes ont déclaré à plusieurs reprises qu'en fait elles appliquaient de manière générale les dispositions humanitaires de la quatrième convention de Genève dans les territoires occupés. Toutefois, selon la thèse israélienne telle que rappelée brièvement au paragraphe 90 ci-dessus, cette convention ne serait pas applicable *de jure* dans ces territoires car, conformément au deuxième alinéa de son article 2, elle s'appliquerait seulement en cas d'occupation de territoires relevant de la souveraineté d'un Etat contractant partie à un conflit armé. Israël expose que la Jordanie était certes partie à la quatrième convention de Genève en 1967 et qu'un conflit armé a alors éclaté entre Israël et la Jordanie, mais il ajoute que les territoires occupés par Israël à la suite de ce conflit ne relevaient pas auparavant de la souveraineté jordanienne. Il en déduit que ladite convention n'est pas applicable *de jure* dans ces territoires. En revanche, selon la grande majorité des autres participants à la procédure, la quatrième convention de Genève y serait applicable, en vertu du premier alinéa de l'article 2, et ce quels qu'aient pu être les droits de la Jordanie sur ces territoires avant 1967.

94. La Cour rappellera que, selon le droit international coutumier tel qu'exprimé à l'article 31 de la convention de Vienne sur le droit des traités du 23 mai 1969, un traité doit être interprété de bonne foi suivant le sens ordinaire à attribuer à ses termes dans leur contexte et à la lumière de son objet et de son but. Selon l'article 32:

> «Il peut être fait appel à des moyens complémentaires d'interprétation, et notamment aux travaux préparatoires et aux circonstances dans lesquelles le traité a été conclu, en vue soit de confirmer le sens résultant de l'application de l'article 31, soit de déterminer le sens lorsque l'interprétation donnée conformément à l'article 31 ... [l]aisse le sens ambigu ou obscur; ou ... [c]onduit à un résultat qui est manifestement absurde ou déraisonnable.» (Voir *Plates-formes pétrolières (République islamique d'Iran c. Etats-Unis d'Amérique), exception préliminaire, arrêt, C.I.J. Recueil 1996 (II)*, p. 812, par. 23; voir dans le même sens *Ile de Kasikili/Sedudu (Botswana/Namibie), arrêt, C.I.J. Recueil 1999 (II)*, p. 1059, par. 18, et *Souveraineté sur Pulau Ligitan et Pulau Sipadan (Indonésie/Malaisie), arrêt, C.I.J. Recueil 2002*, p. 645, par. 37.)

95. La Cour relèvera que, selon le premier alinéa de l'article 2 de la quatrième convention de Genève, celle-ci est applicable dès lors que deux conditions sont remplies: existence d'un conflit armé (que l'état de guerre ait ou non été reconnu); survenance de ce conflit entre deux parties contractantes. Si ces deux conditions sont réunies, la convention s'ap-

> Civilian Persons in Time of War with respect to judicial procedures. In case of conflict between this Order and the said Convention, the Convention shall prevail."

Subsequently, the Israeli authorities have indicated on a number of occasions that in fact they generally apply the humanitarian provisions of the Fourth Geneva Convention within the occupied territories. However, according to Israel's position as briefly recalled in paragraph 90 above, that Convention is not applicable *de jure* within those territories because, under Article 2, paragraph 2, it applies only in the case of occupation of territories falling under the sovereignty of a High Contracting Party involved in an armed conflict. Israel explains that Jordan was admittedly a party to the Fourth Geneva Convention in 1967, and that an armed conflict broke out at that time between Israel and Jordan, but it goes on to observe that the territories occupied by Israel subsequent to that conflict had not previously fallen under Jordanian sovereignty. It infers from this that that Convention is not applicable *de jure* in those territories. According however to the great majority of other participants in the proceedings, the Fourth Geneva Convention is applicable to those territories pursuant to Article 2, paragraph 1, whether or not Jordan had any rights in respect thereof prior to 1967.

94. The Court would recall that, according to customary international law as expressed in Article 31 of the Vienna Convention on the Law of Treaties of 23 May 1969, a treaty must be interpreted in good faith in accordance with the ordinary meaning to be given to its terms in their context and in the light of its object and purpose. Article 32 provides that:

> "Recourse may be had to supplementary means of interpretation, including the preparatory work of the treaty and the circumstances of its conclusion, in order to confirm the meaning resulting from the application of article 31, or to determine the meaning when the interpretation according to article 31 . . . leaves the meaning ambiguous or obscure; or . . . leads to a result which is manifestly obscure or unreasonable." (See *Oil Platforms (Islamic Republic of Iran* v. *United States of America), Preliminary Objection, Judgment, I.C.J. Reports 1996 (II)*, p. 812, para. 23; see, similarly, *Kasikili/Sedudu Island (Botswana/Namibia), Judgment, I.C.J. Reports 1999 (II)*, p. 1059, para. 18, and *Sovereignty over Pulau Ligitan and Pulau Sipadan (Indonesia/Malaysia), Judgment, I.C.J. Reports 2002*, p. 645, para. 37.)

95. The Court notes that, according to the first paragraph of Article 2 of the Fourth Geneva Convention, that Convention is applicable when two conditions are fulfilled: that there exists an armed conflict (whether or not a state of war has been recognized); and that the conflict has arisen between two contracting parties. If those two conditions are satis-

plique en particulier dans tout territoire occupé au cours d'un tel conflit par l'une des parties contractantes.

Le deuxième alinéa de l'article 2 n'a pas pour objet de restreindre le champ d'application de la convention ainsi fixé par l'alinéa premier, en excluant de ce champ d'application les territoires qui ne relèveraient pas de la souveraineté de l'une des parties contractantes. Il tend seulement à préciser que, même si l'occupation opérée au cours du conflit a eu lieu sans rencontrer de résistance militaire, la convention demeure applicable.

Cette interprétation reflète l'intention des auteurs de la quatrième convention de Genève de protéger les personnes civiles se trouvant d'une manière ou d'une autre au pouvoir de la puissance occupante. Alors que les rédacteurs du règlement de La Haye de 1907 s'étaient préoccupés tout autant de préserver les droits de l'Etat dont le territoire est occupé que de protéger les populations vivant sur ce territoire, les auteurs de la quatrième convention de Genève ont cherché à assurer la protection des personnes civiles en temps de guerre indépendamment du statut des territoires occupés, comme en témoigne l'article 47 de la convention.

Ladite interprétation est confirmée par les travaux préparatoires de la convention. La conférence d'experts gouvernementaux convoquée par le Comité international de la Croix-Rouge (ci-après dénommé le «CICR») au lendemain de la seconde guerre mondiale en vue de la préparation des futures conventions de Genève recommanda que ces conventions soient applicables dans tout conflit armé, «qu'il soit reconnu ou non comme état de guerre par les parties», et «dans les cas d'occupation de territoire auxquels il serait procédé sans qu'il existe un état de guerre» (*Rapport sur les travaux de la conférence d'experts gouvernementaux pour l'étude des conventions protégeant les victimes de la guerre*, Genève, 14-26 avril 1947, p. 8). Ainsi les rédacteurs du deuxième alinéa de l'article 2 n'avaient-ils nullement l'intention, en insérant cet alinéa dans la convention, d'en restreindre le champ d'application. Ils entendaient seulement couvrir le cas d'occupation sans combats, comme par exemple celle de la Bohême et de la Moravie par l'Allemagne en 1939.

96. La Cour relèvera par ailleurs que les Etats parties à la quatrième convention de Genève ont retenu cette interprétation lors de la conférence qu'ils ont tenue le 15 juillet 1999. En effet, ils ont alors adopté une déclaration aux termes de laquelle ils «ont réaffirmé que la quatrième convention de Genève était applicable au territoire palestinien occupé, y compris Jérusalem-Est». Puis, le 5 décembre 2001, les Hautes Parties contractantes, eu égard notamment à l'article 1er de la quatrième convention de Genève de 1949, ont réaffirmé une nouvelle fois «l'applicabilité de la convention au territoire palestinien occupé, y compris Jérusalem-Est». Elles ont en outre rappelé à leurs obligations respectives les Parties contractantes participantes à la conférence, les parties au conflit et l'Etat d'Israël en tant que puissance occupante.

97. De plus, la Cour observera que le CICR, dont la situation particulière en ce qui concerne l'exécution de la quatrième convention de Genève doit être «en tout temps reconnue et respectée» par les parties

fied, the Convention applies, in particular, in any territory occupied in the course of the conflict by one of the contracting parties.

The object of the second paragraph of Article 2 is not to restrict the scope of application of the Convention, as defined by the first paragraph, by excluding therefrom territories not falling under the sovereignty of one of the contracting parties. It is directed simply to making it clear that, even if occupation effected during the conflict met no armed resistance, the Convention is still applicable.

This interpretation reflects the intention of the drafters of the Fourth Geneva Convention to protect civilians who find themselves, in whatever way, in the hands of the occupying Power. Whilst the drafters of the Hague Regulations of 1907 were as much concerned with protecting the rights of a State whose territory is occupied, as with protecting the inhabitants of that territory, the drafters of the Fourth Geneva Convention sought to guarantee the protection of civilians in time of war, regardless of the status of the occupied territories, as is shown by Article 47 of the Convention.

That interpretation is confirmed by the Convention's *travaux préparatoires*. The Conference of Government Experts convened by the International Committee of the Red Cross (hereinafter, "ICRC") in the aftermath of the Second World War for the purpose of preparing the new Geneva Conventions recommended that these conventions be applicable to any armed conflict "whether [it] is or is not recognized as a state of war by the parties" and "in cases of occupation of territories in the absence of any state of war" (*Report on the Work of the Conference of Government Experts for the Study of the Conventions for the Protection of War Victims, Geneva, 14-26 April 1947*, p. 8). The drafters of the second paragraph of Article 2 thus had no intention, when they inserted that paragraph into the Convention, of restricting the latter's scope of application. They were merely seeking to provide for cases of occupation without combat, such as the occupation of Bohemia and Moravia by Germany in 1939.

96. The Court would moreover note that the States parties to the Fourth Geneva Convention approved that interpretation at their Conference on 15 July 1999. They issued a statement in which they "reaffirmed the applicability of the Fourth Geneva Convention to the Occupied Palestinian Territory, including East Jerusalem". Subsequently, on 5 December 2001, the High Contracting Parties, referring in particular to Article 1 of the Fourth Geneva Convention of 1949, once again reaffirmed the "applicability of the Fourth Geneva Convention to the Occupied Palestinian Territory, including East Jerusalem". They further reminded the Contracting Parties participating in the Conference, the parties to the conflict, and the State of Israel as occupying Power, of their respective obligations.

97. Moreover, the Court would observe that the ICRC, whose special position with respect to execution of the Fourth Geneva Convention must be "recognized and respected at all times" by the parties pursuant

conformément à l'article 142 de la convention, a, lui aussi, pris parti sur l'interprétation à donner à la convention. Par déclaration du 5 décembre 2001, il a en effet rappelé que «le CICR a toujours affirmé l'applicabilité *de jure* de la IVe convention de Genève aux territoires occupés depuis 1967 par l'Etat d'Israël, y compris Jérusalem-Est».

98. La Cour notera que l'Assemblée générale a pris position dans le même sens dans de multiples résolutions. C'est ainsi que, les 10 décembre 2001 et 9 décembre 2003, elle a, par résolutions 56/60 et 58/97, réaffirmé

> «que la convention de Genève relative à la protection des personnes civiles en temps de guerre, du 12 août 1949, est applicable au territoire palestinien occupé, y compris Jérusalem-Est, et aux autres territoires occupés par Israël depuis 1967».

99. Le Conseil de sécurité, quant à lui, avait dès le 14 juin 1967 considéré, par résolution 237 (1967), que «les parties impliquées dans le conflit doivent se conformer à toutes les obligations de la convention de Genève relative au traitement des prisonniers de guerre». Puis, le 15 septembre 1969, le Conseil avait, par résolution 271 (1969), demandé «à Israël d'observer scrupuleusement les dispositions des conventions de Genève et du droit international régissant l'occupation militaire».

Dix ans plus tard, le Conseil de sécurité s'est penché sur «la politique et les pratiques israéliennes consistant à établir des colonies de peuplement dans les territoires palestiniens et autres territoires arabes occupés depuis 1967». Par résolution 446 (1979) du 22 mars 1979, il a estimé que celles-ci n'ont «aucune validité en droit» et affirmé «*une fois encore* que la convention de Genève relative à la protection des personnes civiles ..., du 12 août 1949, est applicable aux territoires arabes occupés par Israël depuis 1967, y compris Jérusalem». Il a demandé «*une fois encore* à Israël, en tant que puissance occupante, de respecter scrupuleusement» cette convention.

Le 20 décembre 1990, le Conseil de sécurité, par résolution 681 (1990), a engagé «le Gouvernement israélien à reconnaître l'applicabilité *de jure* de la convention ... à tous les territoires occupés par Israël depuis 1967 et à se conformer scrupuleusement aux dispositions de la convention». Il a demandé en outre «aux Hautes Parties contractantes à ladite convention de veiller à ce qu'Israël, puissance occupante, s'acquitte des obligations qu'il a contractées aux termes de l'article 1 de la convention».

Enfin, par résolutions 799 (1992) du 18 décembre 1992 et 904 (1994) du 18 mars 1994, le Conseil a réaffirmé sa position en ce qui concerne l'applicabilité de la quatrième convention de Genève dans les territoires occupés.

100. La Cour relèvera enfin que la Cour suprême d'Israël, dans un arrêt du 30 mai 2004, a aussi jugé que

> «les opérations militaires des forces de défense israéliennes à Rafah,

to Article 142 of the Convention, has also expressed its opinion on the interpretation to be given to the Convention. In a declaration of 5 December 2001, it recalled that "the ICRC has always affirmed the *de jure* applicability of the Fourth Geneva Convention to the territories occupied since 1967 by the State of Israel, including East Jerusalem".

98. The Court notes that the General Assembly has, in many of its resolutions, taken a position to the same effect. Thus on 10 December 2001 and 9 December 2003, in resolutions 56/60 and 58/97, it reaffirmed

> "that the Geneva Convention relative to the Protection of Civilian Persons in Time of War, of 12 August 1949, is applicable to the Occupied Palestinian Territory, including East Jerusalem, and other Arab territories occupied by Israel since 1967".

99. The Security Council, for its part, had already on 14 June 1967 taken the view in resolution 237 (1967) that "all the obligations of the Geneva Convention relative to the Treatment of Prisoners of War . . . should be complied with by the parties involved in the conflict". Subsequently, on 15 September 1969, the Security Council, in resolution 271 (1969), called upon "Israel scrupulously to observe the provisions of the Geneva Conventions and international law governing military occupation".

Ten years later, the Security Council examined "the policy and practices of Israel in establishing settlements in the Palestinian and other Arab territories occupied since 1967". In resolution 446 (1979) of 22 March 1979, the Security Council considered that those settlements had "no legal validity" and affirmed "*once more* that the Geneva Convention relative to the Protection of Civilian Persons in Time of War, of 12 August 1949, is applicable to the Arab territories occupied by Israel since 1967, including Jerusalem". It called "*once more upon* Israel, as the occupying Power, to abide scrupulously" by that Convention.

On 20 December 1990, the Security Council, in resolution 681 (1990), urged "the Government of Israel to accept the *de jure* applicability of the Fourth Geneva Convention . . . to all the territories occupied by Israel since 1967 and to abide scrupulously by the provisions of the Convention". It further called upon "the high contracting parties to the said Fourth Geneva Convention to ensure respect by Israel, the occupying Power, for its obligations under the Convention in accordance with article 1 thereof".

Lastly, in resolutions 799 (1992) of 18 December 1992 and 904 (1994) of 18 March 1994, the Security Council reaffirmed its position concerning the applicability of the Fourth Geneva Convention in the occupied territories.

100. The Court would note finally that the Supreme Court of Israel, in a judgment dated 30 May 2004, also found that:

> "The military operations of the [Israeli Defence Forces] in Rafah,

dans la mesure où elles affectent des civils, sont régies par la quatrième convention de La Haye concernant les lois et coutumes de la guerre sur terre de 1907 ... et par la convention de Genève relative à la protection des personnes civiles en temps de guerre de 1949».

101. Au vu de ce qui précède, la Cour estime que la quatrième convention de Genève est applicable dans tout territoire occupé en cas de conflit armé surgissant entre deux ou plusieurs parties contractantes. Israël et la Jordanie étaient parties à cette convention lorsque éclata le conflit armé de 1967. Dès lors ladite convention est applicable dans les territoires palestiniens qui étaient avant le conflit à l'est de la Ligne verte, et qui ont à l'occasion de ce conflit été occupés par Israël, sans qu'il y ait lieu de rechercher quel était auparavant le statut exact de ces territoires.

*

102. Les participants à la procédure devant la Cour sont également divisés en ce qui concerne l'applicabilité dans le territoire palestinien occupé des conventions internationales concernant les droits de l'homme auxquelles Israël est partie. A l'annexe I au rapport du Secrétaire général, il est précisé:

> «4. Israël conteste que le pacte international relatif aux droits civils et politiques et le pacte international relatif aux droits économiques, sociaux et culturels, qu'il a signés l'un et l'autre, soient applicables au territoire palestinien occupé. Il affirme que le droit humanitaire est le type de protection qui convient dans un conflit tel que celui qui existe en Cisjordanie et dans la bande de Gaza, tandis que les instruments relatifs aux droits de l'homme ont pour objet d'assurer la protection des citoyens vis-à-vis de leur propre gouvernement en temps de paix.»

Ceux des autres participants à la procédure devant la Cour qui traitent de cette question soutiennent en revanche que les deux pactes sont applicables dans le territoire palestinien occupé.

103. Israël a ratifié le 3 octobre 1991 le pacte international relatif aux droits économiques, sociaux et culturels du 19 décembre 1966, le pacte international relatif aux droits civils et politiques du même jour, ainsi que la convention des Nations Unies relative aux droits de l'enfant du 20 novembre 1989. Il est partie à ces trois instruments.

104. En vue de déterminer si ces derniers sont applicables dans le territoire palestinien occupé, la Cour s'interrogera d'une part sur les rapports entre droit international humanitaire et droits de l'homme et d'autre part sur l'applicabilité des instruments relatifs aux droits de l'homme hors des territoires nationaux.

105. La Cour, dans son avis consultatif du 8 juillet 1996 sur la *Licéité de la menace ou de l'emploi d'armes nucléaires*, a été amenée à aborder la première question en ce qui concerne le pacte international relatif aux

to the extent they affect civilians, are governed by Hague Convention IV Respecting the Laws and Customs of War on Land 1907 . . . and the Geneva Convention relative to the Protection of Civilian Persons in Time of War 1949."

101. In view of the foregoing, the Court considers that the Fourth Geneva Convention is applicable in any occupied territory in the event of an armed conflict arising between two or more High Contracting Parties. Israel and Jordan were parties to that Convention when the 1967 armed conflict broke out. The Court accordingly finds that that Convention is applicable in the Palestinian territories which before the conflict lay to the east of the Green Line and which, during that conflict, were occupied by Israel, there being no need for any enquiry into the precise prior status of those territories.

*

102. The participants in the proceedings before the Court also disagree whether the international human rights conventions to which Israel is party apply within the Occupied Palestinian Territory. Annex I to the report of the Secretary-General states:

> "4. Israel denies that the International Covenant on Civil and Political Rights and the International Covenant on Economic, Social and Cultural Rights, both of which it has signed, are applicable to the occupied Palestinian territory. It asserts that humanitarian law is the protection granted in a conflict situation such as the one in the West Bank and Gaza Strip, whereas human rights treaties were intended for the protection of citizens from their own Government in times of peace."

Of the other participants in the proceedings, those who addressed this issue contend that, on the contrary, both Covenants are applicable within the Occupied Palestinian Territory.

103. On 3 October 1991 Israel ratified both the International Covenant on Economic, Social and Cultural Rights of 19 December 1966 and the International Covenant on Civil and Political Rights of the same date, as well as the United Nations Convention on the Rights of the Child of 20 November 1989. It is a party to these three instruments.

104. In order to determine whether these texts are applicable in the Occupied Palestinian Territory, the Court will first address the issue of the relationship between international humanitarian law and human rights law and then that of the applicability of human rights instruments outside national territory.

105. In its Advisory Opinion of 8 July 1996 on the *Legality of the Threat or Use of Nuclear Weapons*, the Court had occasion to address the first of these issues in relation to the International Covenant on Civil

droits civils et politiques. Certains Etats avaient, à l'occasion de cette demande d'avis, soutenu que «le pacte vise la protection des droits de l'homme en temps de paix, alors que les questions relatives à la privation illicite de la vie au cours d'hostilités sont régies par le droit international applicable dans les conflits armés» (*C.I.J. Recueil 1996 (I)*, p. 239, par. 24).

La Cour a écarté cette thèse en observant que

> «la protection offerte par le pacte international relatif aux droits civils et politiques ne cesse pas en temps de guerre, si ce n'est par l'effet de l'article 4 du pacte, qui prévoit qu'il peut être dérogé, en cas de danger public, à certaines des obligations qu'impose cet instrument. Le respect du droit à la vie ne constitue cependant pas une prescription à laquelle il peut être dérogé. En principe, le droit de ne pas être arbitrairement privé de la vie vaut aussi pendant des hostilités. C'est toutefois, en pareil cas, à la *lex specialis* applicable, à savoir le droit applicable dans les conflits armés, conçu pour régir la conduite des hostilités, qu'il appartient de déterminer ce qui constitue une privation arbitraire de la vie.» (*Ibid.*, p. 240, par. 25.)

106. De manière plus générale, la Cour estime que la protection offerte par les conventions régissant les droits de l'homme ne cesse pas en cas de conflit armé, si ce n'est par l'effet de clauses dérogatoires du type de celle figurant à l'article 4 du pacte international relatif aux droits civils et politiques. Dans les rapports entre droit international humanitaire et droits de l'homme, trois situations peuvent dès lors se présenter: certains droits peuvent relever exclusivement du droit international humanitaire; d'autres peuvent relever exclusivement des droits de l'homme; d'autres enfin peuvent relever à la fois de ces deux branches du droit international. Pour répondre à la question qui lui est posée, la Cour aura en l'espèce à prendre en considération les deux branches du droit international précitées, à savoir les droits de l'homme et, en tant que *lex specialis*, le droit international humanitaire.

107. Reste à déterminer si les deux pactes internationaux et la convention relative aux droits de l'enfant sont applicables sur le seul territoire des Etats parties, ou s'ils sont également applicables hors de ce territoire et, si oui, dans quelles circonstances.

108. Le champ d'application du pacte international relatif aux droits civils et politiques est fixé par le paragraphe 1 de l'article 2 de cet instrument selon lequel:

> «Les Etats parties au présent pacte s'engagent à respecter et à garantir à tous les individus se trouvant sur leur territoire et relevant de leur compétence les droits reconnus dans le présent pacte, sans distinction aucune, notamment de race, de couleur, de sexe, de lanue, de religion, d'opinion politique ou de toute autre opinion, d'origine nationale ou sociale, de fortune, de naissance ou de toute autre situation.»

and Political Rights. In those proceedings certain States had argued that "the Covenant was directed to the protection of human rights in peacetime, but that questions relating to unlawful loss of life in hostilities were governed by the law applicable in armed conflict" (*I.C.J. Reports 1996 (I)*, p. 239, para. 24).

The Court rejected this argument, stating that:

> "the protection of the International Covenant of Civil and Political Rights does not cease in times of war, except by operation of Article 4 of the Covenant whereby certain provisions may be derogated from in a time of national emergency. Respect for the right to life is not, however, such a provision. In principle, the right not arbitrarily to be deprived of one's life applies also in hostilities. The test of what is an arbitrary deprivation of life, however, then falls to be determined by the applicable *lex specialis*, namely, the law applicable in armed conflict which is designed to regulate the conduct of hostilities." (*Ibid.*, p. 240, para. 25.)

106. More generally, the Court considers that the protection offered by human rights conventions does not cease in case of armed conflict, save through the effect of provisions for derogation of the kind to be found in Article 4 of the International Covenant on Civil and Political Rights. As regards the relationship between international humanitarian law and human rights law, there are thus three possible situations: some rights may be exclusively matters of international humanitarian law; others may be exclusively matters of human rights law; yet others may be matters of both these branches of international law. In order to answer the question put to it, the Court will have to take into consideration both these branches of international law, namely human rights law and, as *lex specialis*, international humanitarian law.

107. It remains to be determined whether the two international Covenants and the Convention on the Rights of the Child are applicable only on the territories of the States parties thereto or whether they are also applicable outside those territories and, if so, in what circumstances.

108. The scope of application of the International Covenant on Civil and Political Rights is defined by Article 2, paragraph 1, thereof, which provides:

> "Each State Party to the present Covenant undertakes to respect and to ensure to all individuals within its territory and subject to its jurisdiction the rights recognized in the present Covenant, without distinction of any kind, such as race, colour, sex, language, religion, political or other opinion, national or social origin, property, birth or other status."

Cette disposition peut être interprétée comme couvrant seulement les individus se trouvant sur le territoire d'un Etat dans la mesure où ils relèvent en outre de la compétence de cet Etat. Elle peut aussi être comprise comme couvrant à la fois les individus se trouvant sur le territoire d'un Etat et ceux se trouvant hors de ce territoire, mais relevant de la compétence de cet Etat. La Cour recherchera donc quel sens il convient de donner à ce texte.

109. La Cour observera que, si la compétence des Etats est avant tout territoriale, elle peut parfois s'exercer hors du territoire national. Compte tenu de l'objet et du but du pacte international relatif aux droits civils et politiques, il apparaîtrait naturel que, même dans cette dernière hypothèse, les Etats parties au pacte soient tenus d'en respecter les dispositions.

La pratique constante du Comité des droits de l'homme est en ce sens. Il a estimé en effet que le pacte est applicable dans le cas où un Etat exerce sa compétence en territoire étranger. Il s'est prononcé sur la licéité de l'action de l'Uruguay dans le cas d'arrestation opérée par des agents uruguayens au Brésil ou en Argentine (affaire 52/79, *López Burgos c. Uruguay*; affaire 56/79, *Lilian Celiberti de Casariego c. Uruguay*). Le Comité a procédé de même dans le cas de la confiscation d'un passeport par un consulat de l'Uruguay en Allemagne (affaire 106/81, *Montero c. Uruguay*).

Les travaux préparatoires du pacte confirment l'interprétation donnée par le Comité de l'article 2 de cet instrument. Il en résulte en effet que, en adoptant la rédaction qu'ils ont retenue, les auteurs du pacte n'ont pas entendu faire échapper les Etats aux obligations qui sont les leurs lorsqu'ils exercent leur compétence hors du territoire national. Ils ont seulement voulu éviter que des personnes résidant à l'étranger puissent se prévaloir envers leur Etat d'origine de droits ne relevant pas de la compétence de ce dernier, mais de celle de l'Etat de résidence (voir la discussion de l'avant-projet à la Commission des droits de l'homme, E/CN.4/SR.194, par. 46; et Nations Unies, *Documents officiels de l'Assemblée générale, dixième session, annexes*, A/2929, part. 2, chap. V, par. 4 (1955)).

110. La Cour note à cet égard la position adoptée par Israël, en ce qui concerne l'applicabilité du pacte, dans ses communications au Comité des droits de l'homme, ainsi que les vues du Comité.

En 1998, Israël déclarait avoir eu, au moment de la rédaction de son rapport au Comité, à examiner la question de savoir «si les personnes résidant dans les territoires occupés relevaient effectivement de la compétence d'Israël» aux fins de l'application du pacte (CCPR/C/SR.1675, par. 21 *[traduction du Greffe]*). Cet Etat estima que «le pacte et les instruments de même nature ne s'appliqu[aient] pas directement à la situation [qui prévalait alors] dans les territoires occupés» (*ibid.*, par. 27).

Dans les observations finales qu'il formula après avoir examiné le rapport, le Comité se déclara préoccupé par l'attitude d'Israël, relevant «la durée de la présence [de celui-ci] dans [les] territoires [occupés], [son] atti-

This provision can be interpreted as covering only individuals who are both present within a State's territory and subject to that State's jurisdiction. It can also be construed as covering both individuals present within a State's territory and those outside that territory but subject to that State's jurisdiction. The Court will thus seek to determine the meaning to be given to this text.

109. The Court would observe that, while the jurisdiction of States is primarily territorial, it may sometimes be exercised outside the national territory. Considering the object and purpose of the International Covenant on Civil and Political Rights, it would seem natural that, even when such is the case, States parties to the Covenant should be bound to comply with its provisions.

The constant practice of the Human Rights Committee is consistent with this. Thus, the Committee has found the Covenant applicable where the State exercises its jurisdiction on foreign territory. It has ruled on the legality of acts by Uruguay in cases of arrests carried out by Uruguayan agents in Brazil or Argentina (case No. 52/79, *López Burgos* v. *Uruguay*; case No. 56/79, *Lilian Celiberti de Casariego* v. *Uruguay*). It decided to the same effect in the case of the confiscation of a passport by a Uruguayan consulate in Germany (case No. 106/81, *Montero* v. *Uruguay*).

The *travaux préparatoires* of the Covenant confirm the Committee's interpretation of Article 2 of that instrument. These show that, in adopting the wording chosen, the drafters of the Covenant did not intend to allow States to escape from their obligations when they exercise jurisdiction outside their national territory. They only intended to prevent persons residing abroad from asserting, vis-à-vis their State of origin, rights that do not fall within the competence of that State, but of that of the State of residence (see the discussion of the preliminary draft in the Commission on Human Rights, E/CN.4/SR.194, para. 46; and United Nations, *Official Records of the General Assembly, Tenth Session, Annexes*, A/2929, Part II, Chap. V, para. 4 (1955)).

110. The Court takes note in this connection of the position taken by Israel, in relation to the applicability of the Covenant, in its communications to the Human Rights Committee, and of the view of the Committee.

In 1998, Israel stated that, when preparing its report to the Committee, it had had to face the question "whether individuals resident in the occupied territories were indeed subject to Israel's jurisdiction" for purposes of the application of the Covenant (CCPR/C/SR.1675, para. 21). Israel took the position that "the Covenant and similar instruments did not apply directly to the current situation in the occupied territories" (*ibid.*, para. 27).

The Committee, in its concluding observations after examination of the report, expressed concern at Israel's attitude and pointed "to the long-standing presence of Israel in [the occupied] territories, Israel's tude ambiguë ... quant à leur statut futur, ainsi que la juridiction de fait qu'y exer[çaien]t les forces de sécurité israéliennes» (CCPR/C/79/Add.93, par. 10). En 2003, face à la position inchangée d'Israël, qui considérait que «le pacte ne s'appliqu[ait] pas au-delà de son propre territoire, notamment en Cisjordanie et à Gaza ...», le Comité arriva à la conclusion suivante:

> «dans les circonstances actuelles, les dispositions du pacte s'appliquent au profit de la population des territoires occupés, en ce qui concerne tous les actes accomplis par les autorités ou les agents de l'Etat partie dans ces territoires, qui compromettent la jouissance des droits consacrés dans le pacte et relèvent de la responsabilité de l'Etat d'Israël conformément aux principes du droit international public» (CCPR/CO/78/ISR, par. 11).

111. En définitive, la Cour estime que le pacte international relatif aux droits civils et politiques est applicable aux actes d'un Etat agissant dans l'exercice de sa compétence en dehors de son propre territoire.

112. Le pacte international relatif aux droits économiques, sociaux et culturels ne comporte aucune disposition quant à son champ d'application. Cette situation peut trouver son explication dans le fait que les droits garantis par ce pacte ont pour l'essentiel une portée territoriale. Mais on ne saurait exclure qu'il s'applique à la fois aux territoires placés sous la souveraineté d'un Etat partie et à ceux sur lesquels un tel Etat exerce une juridiction territoriale. Ainsi l'article 14 du pacte prévoit-il des mesures transitoires pour tout Etat qui, «au moment où il devient partie, n'a pas encore pu assurer dans sa métropole ou dans les territoires placés sous sa juridiction le caractère obligatoire et la gratuité de l'enseignement primaire».

Il n'est pas inutile de rappeler sur ce point la position prise par Israël dans ses rapports au Comité des droits économiques, sociaux et culturels. Dans son rapport initial au Comité en date du 4 décembre 1998, Israël a fourni «des statistiques d'où il ressort que les colons israéliens établis dans les territoires occupés jouissent des droits inscrits dans le pacte». Le Comité a constaté que, selon Israël, «la population palestinienne des mêmes zones de juridiction se trouve exclue aussi bien du rapport que de la protection du pacte» (E/C.12/1/Add.27, par. 8). Le Comité s'en est ému et Israël a fait valoir dans un nouveau rapport en date du 19 octobre 2001 qu'il «a toujours soutenu que le pacte ne s'appliquait pas aux zones qui ne sont pas soumises à sa souveraineté territoriale et à sa juridiction» (formule inspirée de celle employée par le pacte international relatif aux droits civils et politiques). Cette position, a poursuivi Israël, est «fondée sur la distinction nette qu'établit le droit international entre le droit relatif aux droits de l'homme et le droit humanitaire». Il ajoutait: «le mandat du Comité ne peut pas porter sur ce qui se passe en Cisjordanie et dans la bande de Gaza, car les événements s'inscrivent dans le cadre d'un conflit armé et ne relèvent pas du domaine des droits de l'homme» (E/1990/6/Add.32, par. 5). Au vu de ces observations, le Comité a réafambiguous attitude towards their future status, as well as the exercise of effective jurisdiction by Israeli security forces therein" (CCPR/C/79/Add.93, para. 10). In 2003 in face of Israel's consistent position, to the effect that "the Covenant does not apply beyond its own territory, notably in the West Bank and Gaza . . .", the Committee reached the following conclusion:

> "in the current circumstances, the provisions of the Covenant apply to the benefit of the population of the Occupied Territories, for all conduct by the State party's authorities or agents in those territories that affect the enjoyment of rights enshrined in the Covenant and fall within the ambit of State responsibility of Israel under the principles of public international law" (CCPR/CO/78/ISR, para. 11).

111. In conclusion, the Court considers that the International Covenant on Civil and Political Rights is applicable in respect of acts done by a State in the exercise of its jurisdiction outside its own territory.

112. The International Covenant on Economic, Social and Cultural Rights contains no provision on its scope of application. This may be explicable by the fact that this Covenant guarantees rights which are essentially territorial. However, it is not to be excluded that it applies both to territories over which a State party has sovereignty and to those over which that State exercises territorial jurisdiction. Thus Article 14 makes provision for transitional measures in the case of any State which "at the time of becoming a Party, has not been able to secure in its metropolitan territory or other territories under its jurisdiction compulsory primary education, free of charge".

It is not without relevance to recall in this regard the position taken by Israel in its reports to the Committee on Economic, Social and Cultural Rights. In its initial report to the Committee of 4 December 1998, Israel provided "statistics indicating the enjoyment of the rights enshrined in the Covenant by Israeli settlers in the occupied Territories". The Committee noted that, according to Israel, "the Palestinian population within the same jurisdictional areas were excluded from both the report and the protection of the Covenant" (E/C.12/1/Add.27, para. 8). The Committee expressed its concern in this regard, to which Israel replied in a further report of 19 October 2001 that it has "consistently maintained that the Covenant does not apply to areas that are not subject to its sovereign territory and jurisdiction" (a formula inspired by the language of the International Covenant on Civil and Political Rights). This position, continued Israel, is "based on the well-established distinction between human rights and humanitarian law under international law". It added: "the Committee's mandate cannot relate to events in the West Bank and the Gaza Strip, inasmuch as they are part and parcel of the context of armed conflict as distinct from a relationship of human rights" (E/1990/6/Add.32, para. 5). In view of these observations, the Committee reiterated firmé sa préoccupation au sujet de la position d'Israël et s'est à nouveau déclaré «d'avis que les obligations de l'Etat partie en vertu du pacte s'appliquent à l'ensemble des territoires et des populations qui sont effectivement sous son contrôle» (E/C.12/1/Add.90, par. 15 et 31).

Pour les motifs développés au paragraphe 106 ci-dessus, la Cour ne saurait souscrire à la thèse d'Israël. Elle observe aussi que les territoires occupés par Israël sont soumis depuis plus de trente-sept ans à la juridiction territoriale d'Israël en tant que puissance occupante. Dans l'exercice des compétences dont il dispose à ce titre, Israël est tenu par les dispositions du pacte international relatif aux droits économiques, sociaux et culturels. En outre, il est tenu de ne pas faire obstacle à l'exercice de tels droits dans les domaines où compétence a été transférée à des autorités palestiniennes.

113. Quant à la convention relative aux droits de l'enfant du 20 novembre 1989, elle comporte un article 2 en vertu duquel «[l]es Etats parties s'engagent à respecter les droits qui sont énoncés dans la ... convention et à les garantir à tout enfant relevant de leur juridiction...». Elle est donc applicable dans le territoire palestinien occupé.

* *

114. Ayant déterminé les règles et les principes de droit international qui sont applicables pour répondre à la question posée par l'Assemblée générale, et s'étant prononcée en particulier sur l'applicabilité dans le territoire palestinien occupé du droit international humanitaire et des droits de l'homme, la Cour recherchera maintenant si la construction du mur a porté atteinte à ces règles et principes.

*

115. A cet égard, il est exposé à l'annexe II au rapport du Secrétaire général intitulée «Résumé de la position juridique de l'Organisation de libération de la Palestine» que «[l]a construction du mur est une tentative d'annexion du territoire qui constitue une transgression du droit international» et que «[l]'annexion *de facto* de terres constitue une atteinte à la souveraineté territoriale et en conséquence au droit des Palestiniens à l'autodétermination». Ce point de vue a été repris dans certains des exposés écrits présentés à la Cour ainsi qu'à l'audience. Il a notamment été prétendu que:

> «[l]e mur ampute l'assise territoriale sur laquelle le peuple palestinien est fondé à exercer son droit à l'autodétermination et contrevient au principe interdisant l'acquisition de territoire par le recours à la force».

A ce propos, il a en particulier été souligné que «le tracé du mur est conçu pour modifier la composition démographique du territoire palestinien occupé, y compris Jérusalem-Est, par le renforcement des colonies its concern about Israel's position and reaffirmed "its view that the State party's obligations under the Covenant apply to all territories and populations under its effective control" (E/C.12/1/Add.90, paras. 15 and 31).

For the reasons explained in paragraph 106 above, the Court cannot accept Israel's view. It would also observe that the territories occupied by Israel have for over 37 years been subject to its territorial jurisdiction as the occupying Power. In the exercise of the powers available to it on this basis, Israel is bound by the provisions of the International Covenant on Economic, Social and Cultural Rights. Furthermore, it is under an obligation not to raise any obstacle to the exercise of such rights in those fields where competence has been transferred to Palestinian authorities.

113. As regards the Convention on the Rights of the Child of 20 November 1989, that instrument contains an Article 2 according to which "States Parties shall respect and ensure the rights set forth in the . . . Convention to each child within their jurisdiction . . .". That Convention is therefore applicable within the Occupied Palestinian Territory.

* *

114. Having determined the rules and principles of international law relevant to reply to the question posed by the General Assembly, and having ruled in particular on the applicability within the Occupied Palestinian Territory of international humanitarian law and human rights law, the Court will now seek to ascertain whether the construction of the wall has violated those rules and principles.

*

115. In this regard, Annex II to the report of the Secretary-General, entitled "Summary Legal Position of the Palestine Liberation Organization", states that "The construction of the Barrier is an attempt to annex the territory contrary to international law" and that "The de facto annexation of land interferes with the territorial sovereignty and consequently with the right of the Palestinians to self-determination." This view was echoed in certain of the written statements submitted to the Court and in the views expressed at the hearings. *Inter alia*, it was contended that:

> "The wall severs the territorial sphere over which the Palestinian people are entitled to exercise their right of self-determination and constitutes a violation of the legal principle prohibiting the acquisition of territory by the use of force."

In this connection, it was in particular emphasized that "[t]he route of the wall is designed to change the demographic composition of the Occupied Palestinian Territory, including East Jerusalem, by reinforcing the Israeli de peuplement israéliennes» installées illégalement en territoire palestinien occupé. Le mur viserait en outre à «réduire et morceler le territoire sur lequel le peuple palestinien est fondé à exercer son droit à l'autodétermination».

116. Israël expose pour sa part que le mur a pour seul objet de permettre de lutter efficacement contre le terrorisme en provenance de Cisjordanie. En outre, Israël a déclaré à plusieurs reprises que l'édification de la barrière a un caractère temporaire (voir rapport du Secrétaire général, par. 29). Il l'a fait notamment par la bouche de son représentant permanent auprès des Nations Unies lors de la réunion du Conseil de sécurité du 14 octobre 2003, en soulignant que «[la clôture] n'annexe aucun territoire à l'Etat d'Israël» et qu'Israël est «disposé en encourant des dépenses considérables à réaménager ou à démanteler la clôture, si cela est exigé dans le cadre d'un règlement politique» (S/PV.4841, p. 10). Le représentant permanent d'Israël a réitéré cette position devant l'Assemblée générale les 20 octobre et 8 décembre 2003. A cette dernière occasion, il a ajouté:

> «La clôture [de sécurité] ne sera plus nécessaire dès qu'il sera mis un terme à la terreur. Cette clôture ne constitue pas une frontière et n'a aucune portée politique. Elle ne modifie en rien le statut juridique du territoire.» (A/ES-10/PV.23, p. 7.)

117. La Cour rappellera que tant l'Assemblée générale que le Conseil de sécurité se sont référés, à propos de la Palestine, à la règle coutumière de «l'inadmissibilité de l'acquisition de territoire par la guerre» (voir paragraphes 74 et 87 ci-dessus). C'est ainsi que, par résolution 242 (1967) du 22 novembre 1967, le Conseil a affirmé, après avoir rappelé cette règle, que

> «l'accomplissement des principes de la Charte exige l'instauration d'une paix juste et durable au Moyen-Orient qui devrait comprendre l'application des deux principes suivants:
>
> i) Retrait des forces armées israéliennes des territoires occupés lors du récent conflit;
> ii) Cessation de toutes assertions de belligérance ou de tous états de belligérance et respect et reconnaissance de la souveraineté, de l'intégrité territoriale et de l'indépendance politique de chaque Etat de la région et de leur droit de vivre en paix à l'intérieur de frontières sûres et reconnues à l'abri de menaces ou d'acte de force».

C'est sur la même base que le Conseil a condamné à plusieurs reprises les mesures prises par Israël en vue de modifier le statut de Jérusalem (voir paragraphe 75 ci-dessus).

118. S'agissant du principe du droit des peuples à disposer d'eux-mêmes, la Cour observera que l'existence d'un «peuple palestinien» ne

settlements" illegally established on the Occupied Palestinian Territory. It was further contended that the wall aimed at "reducing and parcelling out the territorial sphere over which the Palestinian people are entitled to exercise their right of self-determination".

116. For its part, Israel has argued that the wall's sole purpose is to enable it effectively to combat terrorist attacks launched from the West Bank. Furthermore, Israel has repeatedly stated that the Barrier is a temporary measure (see report of the Secretary-General, para. 29). It did so *inter alia* through its Permanent Representative to the United Nations at the Security Council meeting of 14 October 2003, emphasizing that "[the fence] does not annex territories to the State of Israel", and that Israel is "ready and able, at tremendous cost, to adjust or dismantle a fence if so required as part of a political settlement" (S/PV.4841, p. 10). Israel's Permanent Representative restated this view before the General Assembly on 20 October and 8 December 2003. On this latter occasion, he added:

> "As soon as the terror ends, the fence will no longer be necessary. The fence is not a border and has no political significance. It does not change the legal status of the territory in any way." (A/ES-10/PV.23, p. 6.)

117. The Court would recall that both the General Assembly and the Security Council have referred, with regard to Palestine, to the customary rule of "the inadmissibility of the acquisition of territory by war" (see paragraphs 74 and 87 above). Thus in resolution 242 (1967) of 22 November 1967, the Security Council, after recalling this rule, affirmed that:

> "the fulfilment of Charter principles requires the establishment of a just and lasting peace in the Middle East which should include the application of both the following principles:
>
> (i) Withdrawal of Israel armed forces from territories occupied in the recent conflict;
> (ii) Termination of all claims or states of belligerency and respect for and acknowledgement of the sovereignty, territorial integrity and political independence of every State in the area and their right to live in peace within secure and recognized boundaries free from threats or acts of force".

It is on this same basis that the Council has several times condemned the measures taken by Israel to change the status of Jerusalem (see paragraph 75 above).

118. As regards the principle of the right of peoples to self-determination, the Court observes that the existence of a "Palestinian people" is no

saurait plus faire débat. En outre, cette existence a été reconnue par Israël dans l'échange de lettres intervenu le 9 septembre 1993 entre M. Yasser Arafat, président de l'Organisation de libération de la Palestine (OLP), et M. Yitzhak Rabin, premier ministre d'Israël. Dans cette correspondance, le président de l'OLP reconnaissait «le droit d'Israël à vivre en paix et dans la sécurité» et prenait divers autres engagements. En réponse, le premier ministre israélien lui faisait connaître que, à la lumière des engagements ainsi pris, «le Gouvernement d'Israël a décidé de reconnaître l'OLP comme le représentant du peuple palestinien». L'accord intérimaire israélo-palestinien sur la Cisjordanie et la bande de Gaza du 28 septembre 1995 mentionne à son tour à plusieurs reprises le peuple palestinien et ses «droits légitimes» (Préambule, par. 4, 7, 8; art. II, par. 2; art. III, par. 1 et 3; art. XXII, par. 2). De l'avis de la Cour, parmi ces droits figure le droit à l'autodétermination, comme l'Assemblée générale l'a d'ailleurs reconnu à plusieurs occasions (voir par exemple la résolution 58/163 du 22 décembre 2003).

119. La Cour relèvera que le tracé du mur tel qu'il a été fixé par le Gouvernement israélien incorpore dans la «zone fermée» (voir paragraphe 85 ci-dessus) environ 80% des colons installés dans le territoire palestinien occupé. Par ailleurs, l'examen de la carte mentionnée au paragraphe 80 ci-dessus montre que ce tracé sinueux a été fixé de manière à inclure dans la zone la plus grande partie des colonies de peuplement installées par Israël dans le territoire palestinien occupé (y compris Jérusalem-Est).

120. En ce qui concerne ces colonies, la Cour notera que, selon le sixième alinéa de l'article 49 de la quatrième convention de Genève: «La puissance occupante ne pourra procéder à la déportation ou au transfert d'une partie de sa propre population civile dans le territoire occupé par elle.» Cette disposition prohibe non seulement les déportations ou transferts forcés de population tels qu'intervenus au cours de la seconde guerre mondiale, mais encore toutes les mesures que peut prendre une puissance occupante en vue d'organiser et de favoriser des transferts d'une partie de sa propre population dans le territoire occupé.

A cet égard, les informations fournies à la Cour montrent qu'à partir de 1977 Israël a mené une politique et développé des pratiques consistant à établir des colonies de peuplement dans le territoire palestinien occupé, contrairement aux prescriptions ainsi rappelées du sixième alinéa de l'article 49.

Aussi bien le Conseil de sécurité a-t-il considéré que cette politique et ces pratiques «n'ont aucune validité en droit». Il a en outre demandé «à Israël en tant que puissance occupante de respecter scrupuleusement» la quatrième convention de Genève, et

> «de rapporter les mesures qui ont déjà été prises et de s'abstenir de toute mesure qui modifierait le statut juridique et le caractère géographique des territoires arabes occupés depuis 1967, y compris Jérusalem, et influerait sensiblement sur leur composition démogra-

longer in issue. Such existence has moreover been recognized by Israel in the exchange of letters of 9 September 1993 between Mr. Yasser Arafat, President of the Palestine Liberation Organization (PLO) and Mr. Yitzhak Rabin, Israeli Prime Minister. In that correspondence, the President of the PLO recognized "the right of the State of Israel to exist in peace and security" and made various other commitments. In reply, the Israeli Prime Minister informed him that, in the light of those commitments, "the Government of Israel has decided to recognize the PLO as the representative of the Palestinian people". The Israeli-Palestinian Interim Agreement on the West Bank and the Gaza Strip of 28 September 1995 also refers a number of times to the Palestinian people and its "legitimate rights" (Preamble, paras. 4, 7, 8; Article II, para. 2; Article III, paras. 1 and 3; Article XXII, para. 2). The Court considers that those rights include the right to self-determination, as the General Assembly has moreover recognized on a number of occasions (see, for example, resolution 58/163 of 22 December 2003).

119. The Court notes that the route of the wall as fixed by the Israeli Government includes within the "Closed Area" (see paragraph 85 above) some 80 per cent of the settlers living in the Occupied Palestinian Territory. Moreover, it is apparent from an examination of the map mentioned in paragraph 80 above that the wall's sinuous route has been traced in such a way as to include within that area the great majority of the Israeli settlements in the occupied Palestinian Territory (including East Jerusalem).

120. As regards these settlements, the Court notes that Article 49, paragraph 6, of the Fourth Geneva Convention provides: "The Occupying Power shall not deport or transfer parts of its own civilian population into the territory it occupies." That provision prohibits not only deportations or forced transfers of population such as those carried out during the Second World War, but also any measures taken by an occupying Power in order to organize or encourage transfers of parts of its own population into the occupied territory.

In this respect, the information provided to the Court shows that, since 1977, Israel has conducted a policy and developed practices involving the establishment of settlements in the Occupied Palestinian Territory, contrary to the terms of Article 49, paragraph 6, just cited.

The Security Council has thus taken the view that such policy and practices "have no legal validity". It has also called upon "Israel, as the occupying Power, to abide scrupulously" by the Fourth Geneva Convention and:

> "to rescind its previous measures and to desist from taking any action which would result in changing the legal status and geographical nature and materially affecting the demographic composition of the Arab territories occupied since 1967, including Jerusalem

phique, et en particulier de ne pas transférer des éléments de sa propre population civile dans les territoires arabes occupés» (résolution 446 (1979) du 22 mars 1979).

Le Conseil a réaffirmé cette position par résolutions 452 (1979) du 20 juillet 1979 et 465 (1980) du 1er mars 1980. Il a même dans ce dernier cas qualifié «la politique et les pratiques d'Israël consistant à installer des éléments de sa population et de nouveaux immigrants dans [l]es territoires [occupés]» de «violation flagrante» de la quatrième convention de Genève.

La Cour conclut que les colonies de peuplement installées par Israël dans le territoire palestinien occupé (y compris Jérusalem-Est) l'ont été en méconnaissance du droit international.

121. Tout en notant l'assurance donnée par Israël que la construction du mur n'équivaut pas à une annexion et que le mur est de nature temporaire (voir paragraphe 116 ci-dessus), la Cour ne saurait pour autant rester indifférente à certaines craintes exprimées devant elle d'après lesquelles le tracé du mur préjugerait la frontière future entre Israël et la Palestine, et à la crainte qu'Israël pourrait intégrer les colonies de peuplement et les voies de circulation les desservant. La Cour estime que la construction du mur et le régime qui lui est associé créent sur le terrain un «fait accompli» qui pourrait fort bien devenir permanent, auquel cas, et nonobstant la description officielle qu'Israël donne du mur, la construction de celui-ci équivaudrait à une annexion *de facto*.

122. La Cour rappelle par ailleurs que, d'après le rapport du Secrétaire général, le tracé projeté incorporerait dans la zone comprise entre la Ligne verte et le mur plus de 16% du territoire de la Cisjordanie. Environ 80% des colons installés dans le territoire palestinien occupé, soit 320 000 personnes, vivraient dans cette zone. Y vivraient également 237 000 Palestiniens. En outre, du fait de la construction du mur, 160 000 autres Palestiniens environ résideraient dans des agglomérations presque totalement encerclées (voir paragraphes 84, 85 et 119 ci-dessus).

En d'autres termes, le tracé choisi pour le mur consacre sur le terrain les mesures illégales prises par Israël et déplorées par le Conseil de sécurité (voir paragraphes 75 et 120 ci-dessus) en ce qui concerne Jérusalem et les colonies de peuplement. La construction du mur risque également de conduire à de nouvelles modifications dans la composition démographique du territoire palestinien occupé, dans la mesure où elle occasionne le départ de populations palestiniennes de certaines zones, comme il sera expliqué au paragraphe 133 ci-après. Cette construction, s'ajoutant aux mesures prises antérieurement, dresse ainsi un obstacle grave à l'exercice par le peuple palestinien de son droit à l'autodétermination et viole de ce fait l'obligation incombant à Israël de respecter ce droit.

*

123. La construction du mur pose en outre plusieurs problèmes au

> and, in particular, not to transfer parts of its own civilian population into the occupied Arab territories" (resolution 446 (1979) of 22 March 1979).

The Council reaffirmed its position in resolutions 452 (1979) of 20 July 1979 and 465 (1980) of 1 March 1980. Indeed, in the latter case it described "Israel's policy and practices of settling parts of its population and new immigrants in [the occupied] territories" as a "flagrant violation" of the Fourth Geneva Convention.

The Court concludes that the Israeli settlements in the Occupied Palestinian Territory (including East Jerusalem) have been established in breach of international law.

121. Whilst the Court notes the assurance given by Israel that the construction of the wall does not amount to annexation and that the wall is of a temporary nature (see paragraph 116 above), it nevertheless cannot remain indifferent to certain fears expressed to it that the route of the wall will prejudge the future frontier between Israel and Palestine, and the fear that Israel may integrate the settlements and their means of access. The Court considers that the construction of the wall and its associated régime create a "fait accompli" on the ground that could well become permanent, in which case, and notwithstanding the formal characterization of the wall by Israel, it would be tantamount to *de facto* annexation.

122. The Court recalls moreover that, according to the report of the Secretary-General, the planned route would incorporate in the area between the Green Line and the wall more than 16 per cent of the territory of the West Bank. Around 80 per cent of the settlers living in the Occupied Palestinian Territory, that is 320,000 individuals, would reside in that area, as well as 237,000 Palestinians. Moreover, as a result of the construction of the wall, around 160,000 other Palestinians would reside in almost completely encircled communities (see paragraphs 84, 85 and 119 above).

In other terms, the route chosen for the wall gives expression *in loco* to the illegal measures taken by Israel with regard to Jerusalem and the settlements, as deplored by the Security Council (see paragraphs 75 and 120 above). There is also a risk of further alterations to the demographic composition of the Occupied Palestinian Territory resulting from the construction of the wall inasmuch as it is contributing, as will be further explained in paragraph 133 below, to the departure of Palestinian populations from certain areas. That construction, along with measures taken previously, thus severely impedes the exercise by the Palestinian people of its right to self-determination, and is therefore a breach of Israel's obligation to respect that right.

*

123. The construction of the wall also raises a number of issues in rela-

regard des dispositions pertinentes du droit international humanitaire et des conventions relatives aux droits de l'homme.

124. S'agissant du règlement de La Haye de 1907, la Cour rappellera que ce dernier traite dans sa section II des hostilités et notamment des «moyens de nuire à l'ennemi, des sièges et des bombardements». Il traite dans sa section III de l'autorité militaire dans les territoires occupés. Seule la section III est à l'heure actuelle applicable en Cisjordanie et l'article 23 *g)* du règlement qui figure dans la section II n'est donc pas pertinent.

La section III du règlement de La Haye inclut notamment les articles 43, 46 et 52, applicables dans le territoire palestinien occupé. L'article 43 donne à l'occupant le devoir de prendre «toutes les mesures qui dépendent de lui en vue de rétablir et d'assurer, autant qu'il est possible, l'ordre et la vie publics en respectant, sauf empêchement absolu, les lois en vigueur dans le pays». L'article 46 ajoute que la propriété privée doit être «respecté[e]» et «ne peut pas être confisquée». Enfin, l'article 52 autorise dans certaines limites les réquisitions en nature et des services pour les besoins de l'armée d'occupation.

125. La quatrième convention de Genève distingue, elle aussi, entre les dispositions applicables lors des opérations militaires ayant conduit à l'occupation et celles qui demeurent applicables pendant toute la durée de l'occupation. Elle dispose en effet dans son article 6:

> «La présente convention s'appliquera dès le début de tout conflit ou occupation mentionnés à l'article 2.
>
> Sur le territoire des parties au conflit, l'application de la convention cessera à la fin générale des opérations militaires.
>
> En territoire occupé, l'application de la présente convention cessera un an après la fin générale des opérations militaires; néanmoins, la puissance occupante sera liée pour la durée de l'occupation — pour autant que cette puissance exerce les fonctions de gouvernement dans le territoire en question — par les dispositions des articles suivants de la présente convention: 1 à 12, 27, 29 à 34, 47, 49, 51, 52, 53, 59, 61 à 77 et 143.
>
> Les personnes protégées, dont la libération, le rapatriement ou l'établissement auront lieu après ces délais resteront dans l'intervalle au bénéfice de la présente convention.»

Les opérations militaires qui conduisirent en 1967 à l'occupation de la Cisjordanie ayant pris fin depuis longtemps, seuls les articles de la quatrième convention de Genève visés au troisième alinéa de l'article 6 demeurent applicables dans ce territoire occupé.

126. Figurent parmi ces dispositions les articles 47, 49, 52, 53 et 59 de la quatrième convention de Genève.

D'après l'article 47:

> «Les personnes protégées qui se trouvent dans un territoire occupé

tion to the relevant provisions of international humanitarian law and of human rights instruments.

124. With regard to the Hague Regulations of 1907, the Court would recall that these deal, in Section II, with hostilities and in particular with "means of injuring the enemy, sieges, and bombardments". Section III deals with military authority in occupied territories. Only Section III is currently applicable in the West Bank and Article 23 *(g)* of the Regulations, in Section II, is thus not pertinent.

Section III of the Hague Regulations includes Articles 43, 46 and 52, which are applicable in the Occupied Palestinian Territory. Article 43 imposes a duty on the occupant to "take all measures within his power to restore, and, as far as possible, to insure public order and life, respecting the laws in force in the country". Article 46 adds that private property must be "respected" and that it cannot "be confiscated". Lastly, Article 52 authorizes, within certain limits, requisitions in kind and services for the needs of the army of occupation.

125. A distinction is also made in the Fourth Geneva Convention between provisions applying during military operations leading to occupation and those that remain applicable throughout the entire period of occupation. It thus states in Article 6:

> "The present Convention shall apply from the outset of any conflict or occupation mentioned in Article 2.
>
> In the territory of Parties to the conflict, the application of the present Convention shall cease on the general close of military operations.
>
> In the case of occupied territory, the application of the present Convention shall cease one year after the general close of military operations; however, the Occupying Power shall be bound, for the duration of the occupation, to the extent that such Power exercises the functions of government in such territory, by the provisions of the following Articles of the present Convention: 1 to 12, 27, 29 to 34, 47, 49, 51, 52, 53, 59, 61 to 77, 143.
>
> Protected persons whose release, repatriation or re-establishment may take place after such dates shall meanwhile continue to benefit by the present Convention."

Since the military operations leading to the occupation of the West Bank in 1967 ended a long time ago, only those Articles of the Fourth Geneva Convention referred to in Article 6, paragraph 3, remain applicable in that occupied territory.

126. These provisions include Articles 47, 49, 52, 53 and 59 of the Fourth Geneva Convention.

According to Article 47:

> "Protected persons who are in occupied territory shall not be

ne seront privées, en aucun cas ni d'aucune manière, du bénéfice de la présente convention, soit en vertu d'un changement quelconque intervenu du fait de l'occupation dans les institutions ou le gouvernement du territoire en question, soit par un accord passé entre les autorités du territoire occupé et la puissance occupante, soit encore en raison de l'annexion par cette dernière de tout ou partie du territoire occupé.»

L'article 49 se lit comme suit:

«Les transferts forcés, en masse ou individuels, ainsi que les déportations de personnes protégées hors du territoire occupé dans le territoire de la puissance occupante ou dans celui de tout autre Etat, occupé ou non, sont interdits, quel qu'en soit le motif.

Toutefois, la puissance occupante pourra procéder à l'évacuation totale ou partielle d'une région occupée déterminée, si la sécurité de la population ou d'impérieuses raisons militaires l'exigent. Les évacuations ne pourront entraîner le déplacement de personnes protégées qu'à l'intérieur du territoire occupé, sauf en cas d'impossibilité matérielle. La population ainsi évacuée sera ramenée dans ses foyers aussitôt que les hostilités dans ce secteur auront pris fin.

La puissance occupante, en procédant à ces transferts ou à ces évacuations, devra faire en sorte, dans toute la mesure du possible, que les personnes protégées soient accueillies dans des installations convenables, que les déplacements soient effectués dans des conditions satisfaisantes de salubrité, d'hygiène, de sécurité et d'alimentation et que les membres d'une même famille ne soient pas séparés les uns des autres.

La puissance protectrice sera informée des transferts et évacuations dès qu'ils auront eu lieu.

La puissance occupante ne pourra retenir les personnes protégées dans une région particulièrement exposée aux dangers de la guerre, sauf si la sécurité de la population ou d'impérieuses raisons militaires l'exigent.

La puissance occupante ne pourra procéder à la déportation ou au transfert d'une partie de sa propre population civile dans le territoire occupé par elle.»

D'après l'article 52:

«Aucun contrat, accord ou règlement ne pourra porter atteinte au droit de chaque travailleur, volontaire ou non, où qu'il se trouve, de s'adresser aux représentants de la puissance protectrice pour demander l'intervention de celle-ci.

Toute mesure tendant à provoquer le chômage ou à restreindre les possibilités de travail des travailleurs d'un pays occupé, en vue de les amener à travailler pour la puissance occupante, est interdite.»

deprived, in any case or in any manner whatsoever, of the benefits of the present Convention by any change introduced, as the result of the occupation of a territory, into the institutions or government of the said territory, nor by any agreement concluded between the authorities of the occupied territories and the Occupying Power, nor by any annexation by the latter of the whole or part of the occupied territory."

Article 49 reads as follows:

"Individual or mass forcible transfers, as well as deportations of protected persons from occupied territory to the territory of the Occupying Power or to that of any other country, occupied or not, are prohibited, regardless of their motive.

Nevertheless, the Occupying Power may undertake total or partial evacuation of a given area if the security of the population or imperative military reasons so demand. Such evacuations may not involve the displacement of protected persons outside the bounds of the occupied territory except when for material reasons it is impossible to avoid such displacement. Persons thus evacuated shall be transferred back to their homes as soon as hostilities in the area in question have ceased.

The Occupying Power undertaking such transfers or evacuations shall ensure, to the greatest practicable extent, that proper accommodation is provided to receive the protected persons, that the removals are effected in satisfactory conditions of hygiene, health, safety and nutrition, and that members of the same family are not separated.

The Protecting Power shall be informed of any transfers and evacuations as soon as they have taken place.

The Occupying Power shall not detain protected persons in an area particularly exposed to the dangers of war unless the security of the population or imperative military reasons so demand.

The Occupying Power shall not deport or transfer parts of its own civilian population into the territory it occupies."

According to Article 52:

"No contract, agreement or regulation shall impair the right of any worker, whether voluntary or not and wherever he may be, to apply to the representatives of the Protecting Power in order to request the said Power's intervention.

All measures aiming at creating unemployment or at restricting the opportunities offered to workers in an occupied territory, in order to induce them to work for the Occupying Power, are prohibited."

L'article 53 prévoit ce qui suit:

> «Il est interdit à la puissance occupante de détruire des biens mobiliers ou immobiliers, appartenant individuellement ou collectivement à des personnes privées, à l'Etat ou à des collectivités publiques, à des organisations sociales et coopératives, sauf dans les cas où ces destructions seraient rendues absolument nécessaires par les opérations militaires.»

Aux termes enfin de l'article 59:

> «Lorsque la population d'un territoire occupé ou une partie de celle-ci est insuffisamment approvisionnée, la puissance occupante acceptera les actions de secours faites en faveur de cette population et les facilitera dans toute la mesure de ses moyens.
>
> Ces actions, qui pourront être entreprises soit par des Etats, soit par un organisme humanitaire impartial, tel que le Comité international de la Croix-Rouge, consisteront notamment en des envois de vivres, produits médicaux et vêtements.
>
> Tous les Etats contractants devront autoriser le libre passage de ces envois et en assurer la protection.
>
> Une puissance accordant le libre passage d'envois destinés à un territoire occupé par une partie adverse au conflit aura toutefois le droit de vérifier les envois, de réglementer leur passage selon des horaires et itinéraires prescrits, et d'obtenir de la puissance protectrice une assurance suffisante que ces envois sont destinés à secourir la population dans le besoin, et ne sont pas utilisés au profit de la puissance occupante.»

127. Le pacte international relatif aux droits civils et politiques comporte, lui aussi, plusieurs dispositions pertinentes. Avant d'examiner ces dispositions, la Cour observera que l'article 4 du pacte permet sous diverses conditions de déroger à certaines dispositions de cet instrument. Israël a usé du droit de dérogation qu'il tient de cet article en adressant le 3 octobre 1991 au Secrétaire général des Nations Unies la communication suivante:

> «Depuis sa création, l'Etat d'Israël a été victime de menaces et d'attaques qui n'ont cessé d'être portées contre son existence même ainsi que contre la vie et les biens de ses citoyens.
>
> Ces actes ont pris la forme de menaces de guerre, d'attaques armées réelles et de campagnes de terrorisme à la suite desquelles des êtres humains ont été tués et blessés.
>
> Etant donné ce qui précède, l'état d'urgence qui a été proclamé en mai 1948 est resté en vigueur depuis lors. Cette situation constitue un danger public exceptionnel au sens du paragraphe 1 de l'article 4 du pacte.
>
> Le Gouvernement israélien a donc jugé nécessaire, conformément à ce même article 4, de prendre, dans la stricte mesure où la situation l'exige, des mesures visant à assurer la défense de l'Etat et la protec-

Article 53 provides that:

> "Any destruction by the Occupying Power of real or personal property belonging individually or collectively to private persons, or to the State, or to other public authorities, or to social or co-operative organizations, is prohibited, except where such destruction is rendered absolutely necessary by military operations."

Lastly, according to Article 59:

> "If the whole or part of the population of an occupied territory is inadequately supplied, the Occupying Power shall agree to relief schemes on behalf of the said population, and shall facilitate them by all the means at its disposal.
>
> Such schemes, which may be undertaken either by States or by impartial humanitarian organizations such as the International Committee of the Red Cross, shall consist, in particular, of the provision of consignments of foodstuffs, medical supplies and clothing.
>
> All Contracting Parties shall permit the free passage of these consignments and shall guarantee their protection.
>
> A Power granting free passage to consignments on their way to territory occupied by an adverse Party to the conflict shall, however, have the right to search the consignments, to regulate their passage according to prescribed times and routes, and to be reasonably satisfied through the Protecting Power that these consignments are to be used for the relief of the needy population and are not to be used for the benefit of the Occupying Power."

127. The International Covenant on Civil and Political Rights also contains several relevant provisions. Before further examining these, the Court will observe that Article 4 of the Covenant allows for derogation to be made, under various conditions, to certain provisions of that instrument. Israel made use of its right of derogation under this Article by addressing the following communication to the Secretary-General of the United Nations on 3 October 1991:

> "Since its establishment, the State of Israel has been the victim of continuous threats and attacks on its very existence as well as on the life and property of its citizens.
>
> These have taken the form of threats of war, of actual armed attacks, and campaigns of terrorism resulting in the murder of and injury to human beings.
>
> In view of the above, the State of Emergency which was proclaimed in May 1948 has remained in force ever since. This situation constitutes a public emergency within the meaning of article 4 (1) of the Covenant.
>
> The Government of Israel has therefore found it necessary, in accordance with the said article 4, to take measures to the extent strictly required by the exigencies of the situation, for the defence of

tion de la vie et des biens de ses citoyens, y compris l'exercice de pouvoirs d'arrestation et de détention.

Pour autant que l'une quelconque de ces mesures soit incompatible avec l'article 9 du pacte, Israël déroge ainsi à ses obligations au titre de cette disposition.»

La Cour constate que la dérogation ainsi notifiée ne vise que l'article 9 du pacte international relatif aux droits civils et politiques proclamant le droit à la liberté et à la sécurité de la personne et fixant les règles applicables en cas d'arrestation et de détention. Les autres articles du pacte demeurent donc applicables non seulement sur le territoire d'Israël, mais encore dans le territoire palestinien occupé.

128. Parmi ceux-ci doit être cité l'article 17, dont le paragraphe 1 se lit comme suit: «Nul ne sera l'objet d'immixtions arbitraires ou illégales dans sa vie privée, sa famille, son domicile ou sa correspondance, ni d'atteintes illégales à son honneur et à sa réputation.»

Doit également être mentionné le paragraphe 1 de l'article 12 selon lequel «[q]uiconque se trouve légalement sur le territoire d'un Etat a le droit d'y circuler librement et d'y choisir librement sa résidence».

129. Aux garanties générales fournies par l'article 12 du pacte international relatif aux droits civils et politiques en ce qui concerne la liberté de circulation s'ajoutent des garanties particulières d'accès dans le cas des Lieux saints chrétiens, juifs et musulmans. Le statut des Lieux saints chrétiens au sein de l'Empire ottoman est extrêmement ancien. Les dernières dispositions les concernant avaient été incorporées à l'article 62 du traité de Berlin du 13 juillet 1878. Le mandat pour la Palestine donné au Gouvernement britannique le 24 juillet 1922 comportait un article 13 selon lequel:

«Tout en maintenant l'ordre et la bienséance publics, le mandataire assume toute responsabilité au sujet des Lieux saints, des édifices et des sites religieux en Palestine, y compris celle de préserver les droits existants, d'assurer le libre accès des Lieux saints, des édifices et des sites religieux, et le libre exercice du culte.»

L'article 13 ajoutait ce qui suit: «Rien dans le présent mandat ne pourra être interprété comme ... autorisant à toucher aux immeubles ou à intervenir dans l'administration des sanctuaires purement musulmans, dont les privilèges sont garantis.»

Au lendemain de la seconde guerre mondiale, l'Assemblée générale, lorsqu'elle adopta la résolution 181 (II) sur le gouvernement futur de la Palestine, consacra un chapitre entier du plan de partage aux Lieux saints, édifices et sites religieux. L'article 2 de ce chapitre disposait qu'en ce qui concerne les Lieux saints

«la liberté d'accès, de visite et de transit sera[it] garantie, conformément aux droits existants, à tous les résidents ou citoyens [de l'Etat the State and for the protection of life and property, including the exercise of powers of arrest and detention.

In so far as any of these measures are inconsistent with article 9 of the Covenant, Israel thereby derogates from its obligations under that provision."

The Court notes that the derogation so notified concerns only Article 9 of the International Covenant on Civil and Political Rights, which deals with the right to liberty and security of person and lays down the rules applicable in cases of arrest or detention. The other Articles of the Covenant therefore remain applicable not only on Israeli territory, but also on the Occupied Palestinian Territory.

128. Among these mention must be made of Article 17, paragraph 1 of which reads as follows: "No one shall be subjected to arbitrary or unlawful interference with his privacy, family, home or correspondence, nor to unlawful attacks on his honour and reputation."

Mention must also be made of Article 12, paragraph 1, which provides: "Everyone lawfully within the territory of a State shall, within that territory, have the right to liberty of movement and freedom to choose his residence."

129. In addition to the general guarantees of freedom of movement under Article 12 of the International Covenant on Civil and Political Rights, account must also be taken of specific guarantees of access to the Christian, Jewish and Islamic Holy Places. The status of the Christian Holy Places in the Ottoman Empire dates far back in time, the latest provisions relating thereto having been incorporated into Article 62 of the Treaty of Berlin of 13 July 1878. The Mandate for Palestine given to the British Government on 24 July 1922 included an Article 13, under which:

"All responsibility in connection with the Holy Places and religious buildings or sites in Palestine, including that of preserving existing rights and of securing free access to the Holy Places, religious buildings and sites and the free exercise of worship, while ensuring the requirements of public order and decorum, is assumed by the Mandatory . . ."

Article 13 further stated: "nothing in this mandate shall be construed as conferring . . . authority to interfere with the fabric or the management of purely Moslem sacred shrines, the immunities of which are guaranteed".

In the aftermath of the Second World War, the General Assembly, in adopting resolution 181 (II) on the future government of Palestine, devoted an entire chapter of the Plan of Partition to the Holy Places, religious buildings and sites. Article 2 of this Chapter provided, in so far as the Holy Places were concerned:

"the liberty of access, visit and transit shall be guaranteed, in conformity with existing rights, to all residents and citizens [of the Arab

> arabe, de l'Etat juif] et de la ville de Jérusalem, ainsi qu'aux étrangers, sans distinction de nationalité, sous réserve de considérations de sécurité nationale et de maintien de l'ordre public et de la bienséance».

Puis, au lendemain du conflit armé de 1948, la convention générale d'armistice de 1949 entre la Jordanie et Israël prévit, en son article VIII, la constitution d'un comité spécial «chargé d'établir des plans et arrangements concernant les questions que l'une ou l'autre partie pourra[it] lui soumettre» en vue d'étendre la portée de la convention et d'en améliorer la mise en œuvre. Parmi ces questions, sur lesquelles un accord de principe avait déjà été réalisé, figurait «la liberté d'accès aux Lieux saints».

L'engagement ainsi pris concernait pour l'essentiel les Lieux saints situés à l'est de la Ligne verte. Toutefois, certains Lieux saints se trouvaient à l'ouest de la même ligne. Il en était ainsi, sur le mont Sion, du Cénacle et du tombeau de David. Israël comme la Jordanie s'étaient donc engagés, en concluant la convention générale d'armistice, à assurer la liberté d'accès aux Lieux saints. La Cour considère que cet engagement d'Israël est demeuré valable pour les Lieux saints passés sous son contrôle en 1967. Ledit engagement a en outre été confirmé par le paragraphe 1 de l'article 9 du traité de paix de 1994 entre Israël et la Jordanie, selon lequel, de manière plus générale, «[c]hacune des deux parties contractantes donnera la liberté d'accès aux sites ayant une signification religieuse et historique».

130. Quant au pacte international relatif aux droits économiques, sociaux et culturels, il comporte plusieurs dispositions pertinentes concernant le droit au travail (art. 6 et 7); la protection et l'assistance accordées à la famille et aux enfants et adolescents (art. 10); le droit à un niveau de vie suffisant, y compris la nourriture, le vêtement et le logement, et le droit «d'être à l'abri de la faim» (art. 11); le droit à la santé (art. 12) et le droit à l'éducation (art. 13 et 14).

131. Enfin, la convention des Nations Unies relative aux droits de l'enfant du 20 novembre 1989 comporte des dispositions analogues en ses articles 16, 24, 27 et 28.

*

132. Il ressort des informations fournies à la Cour et notamment du rapport du Secrétaire général que la construction du mur a entraîné la destruction ou la réquisition de propriétés dans des conditions contraires aux prescriptions des articles 46 et 52 du règlement de La Haye de 1907 et de l'article 53 de la quatrième convention de Genève.

133. Cette construction, la création d'une zone fermée entre la Ligne verte et le mur, et la constitution d'enclaves ont par ailleurs apporté des restrictions importantes à la liberté de circulation des habitants du territoire palestinien occupé (à l'exception des ressortissants israéliens et assi-

> State, of the Jewish State] and of the City of Jerusalem, as well as to aliens, without distinction as to nationality, subject to requirements of national security, public order and decorum".

Subsequently, in the aftermath of the armed conflict of 1948, the 1949 General Armistice Agreement between Jordan and Israel provided in Article VIII for the establishment of a special committee for "the formulation of agreed plans and arrangements for such matters as either Party may submit to it" for the purpose of enlarging the scope of the Agreement and of effecting improvement in its application. Such matters, on which an agreement of principle had already been concluded, included "free access to the Holy Places".

This commitment concerned mainly the Holy Places located to the east of the Green Line. However, some Holy Places were located west of that Line. This was the case of the Room of the Last Supper and the Tomb of David, on Mount Zion. In signing the General Armistice Agreement, Israel thus undertook, as did Jordan, to guarantee freedom of access to the Holy Places. The Court considers that this undertaking by Israel has remained valid for the Holy Places which came under its control in 1967. This undertaking has further been confirmed by Article 9, paragraph 1, of the 1994 Peace Treaty between Israel and Jordan, by virtue of which, in more general terms, "Each party will provide freedom of access to places of religious and historical significance."

130. As regards the International Covenant on Economic, Social and Cultural Rights, that instrument includes a number of relevant provisions, namely: the right to work (Arts. 6 and 7); protection and assistance accorded to the family and to children and young persons (Art. 10); the right to an adequate standard of living, including adequate food, clothing and housing, and the right "to be free from hunger" (Art. 11); the right to health (Art. 12); the right to education (Arts. 13 and 14).

131. Lastly, the United Nations Convention on the Rights of the Child of 20 November 1989 includes similar provisions in Articles 16, 24, 27 and 28.

*

132. From the information submitted to the Court, particularly the report of the Secretary-General, it appears that the construction of the wall has led to the destruction or requisition of properties under conditions which contravene the requirements of Articles 46 and 52 of the Hague Regulations of 1907 and of Article 53 of the Fourth Geneva Convention.

133. That construction, the establishment of a closed area between the Green Line and the wall itself and the creation of enclaves have moreover imposed substantial restrictions on the freedom of movement of the inhabitants of the Occupied Palestinian Territory (with the exception of

milés). Ces restrictions sont particulièrement sensibles dans des zones urbaines, telles que l'enclave de Qalqiliya ou la ville de Jérusalem et ses banlieues. Elles sont aggravées du fait que les portes d'accès sont dans certains secteurs en nombre réduit et que leurs horaires d'ouverture paraissent limités et appliqués de manière irrégulière. Par exemple, selon le rapporteur spécial de la Commission des droits de l'homme sur la situation des droits de l'homme dans les territoires palestiniens occupés par Israël depuis 1967, «[l]a ville de [Qalqiliya], qui compte 40000 habitants, est complètement entourée par le mur, et ses habitants ne peuvent y entrer ou en sortir que par un poste de contrôle militaire ouvert de 7 heures du matin à 7 heures du soir» (rapport du rapporteur spécial de la Commission des droits de l'homme, M. John Dugard, sur la situation des droits de l'homme dans les territoires palestiniens occupés par Israël depuis 1967, soumis conformément à la résolution 1993/2 A de la Commission intitulée «Question de la violation des droits de l'homme dans les territoires arabes occupés, y compris la Palestine», E/CN.4/2004/6, 8 septembre 2003, par. 9).

Il en est aussi résulté de sérieuses répercussions pour la production agricole, comme cela est attesté par plusieurs sources. Selon le Comité spécial chargé d'enquêter sur les pratiques israéliennes affectant les droits de l'homme du peuple palestinien et des autres Arabes des territoires occupés, il est

> «estim[é] que 100000 dounams [environ 10000 hectares] des terres agricoles les plus fertiles de la Cisjordanie, confisquées par les forces d'occupation israéliennes, ont été détruites pendant la première phase de construction du mur, entraînant la disparition de très nombreux biens, notamment de terres agricoles, d'oliviers, de puits, d'agrumeraies et de serres, dont des dizaines de milliers de Palestiniens étaient tributaires pour leur survie» (rapport du Comité spécial chargé d'enquêter sur les pratiques israéliennes affectant les droits de l'homme du peuple palestinien et des autres Arabes des territoires occupés, A/58/311, 22 août 2003, par. 26).

Le rapporteur spécial sur la situation des droits de l'homme dans les territoires palestiniens occupés par Israël depuis 1967 indique pour sa part que «[l]a plupart des terres palestiniennes se trouvant du côté israélien du mur sont des terres agricoles fertiles et [que l']on y trouve certains des puits les plus importants de la région»; il ajoute que «[d]e nombreux arbres fruitiers et oliviers ont été arrachés lors de sa construction» (E/CN.4/2004/6, 8 septembre 2003, par. 9). Quant au rapporteur spécial sur le droit à l'alimentation de la Commission des droits de l'homme des Nations Unies, il constate que la construction du mur «coupe les Palestiniens de leurs terres agricoles, de leurs puits et de leurs moyens de subsistance» (rapport du rapporteur spécial de la Commission des droits de l'homme, M. Jean Ziegler, «Le droit à l'alimentation», additif, mission dans les territoires palestiniens occupés, E/CN.4/2004/10/Add.2, 31 octobre 2003, par. 49). Dans une enquête récente du Programme alimentaire

Israeli citizens and those assimilated thereto). Such restrictions are most marked in urban areas, such as the Qalqiliya enclave or the City of Jerusalem and its suburbs. They are aggravated by the fact that the access gates are few in number in certain sectors and opening hours appear to be restricted and unpredictably applied. For example, according to the Special Rapporteur of the Commission on Human Rights on the situation of human rights in the Palestinian territories occupied by Israel since 1967, "Qalqiliya, a city with a population of 40,000, is completely surrounded by the Wall and residents can only enter and leave through a single military checkpoint open from 7 a.m. to 7 p.m." (Report of the Special Rapporteur of the Commission on Human Rights, John Dugard, on the situation of human rights in the Palestinian territories occupied by Israel since 1967, submitted in accordance with Commission resolution 1993/2 A and entitled "Question of the Violation of Human Rights in the Occupied Arab Territories, including Palestine", E/CN.4/2004/6, 8 September 2003, para. 9.)

There have also been serious repercussions for agricultural production, as is attested by a number of sources. According to the Special Committee to Investigate Israeli Practices Affecting the Human Rights of the Palestinian People and Other Arabs of the Occupied Territories

> "an estimated 100,000 dunums [approximately 10,000 hectares] of the West Bank's most fertile agricultural land, confiscated by the Israeli Occupation Forces, have been destroyed during the first phase of the wall construction, which involves the disappearance of vast amounts of property, notably private agricultural land and olive trees, wells, citrus grows and hothouses upon which tens of thousands of Palestinians rely for their survival" (Report of the Special Committee to Investigate Israeli Practices Affecting the Human Rights of the Palestinian People and Other Arabs of the Occupied Territories, A/58/311, 22 August 2003, para. 26).

Further, the Special Rapporteur on the situation of human rights in the Palestinian territories occupied by Israel since 1967 states that "Much of the Palestinian land on the Israeli side of the Wall consists of fertile agricultural land and some of the most important water wells in the region" and adds that "Many fruit and olive trees had been destroyed in the course of building the barrier" (E/CN.4/2004/6, 8 September 2003, para. 9). The Special Rapporteur on the Right to Food of the United Nations Commission on Human Rights states that construction of the wall "cuts off Palestinians from their agricultural lands, wells and means of subsistence" (Report by the Special Rapporteur of the United Nations Commission on Human Rights, Jean Ziegler, "The Right to Food", Addendum, Mission to the Occupied Palestinian Territories, E/CN.4/2004/10/Add.2, 31 October 2003, para. 49). In a recent survey conducted by the World Food Programme, it is stated that the situation has aggramondial, il est précisé que cette situation a aggravé l'insécurité alimentaire dans la région, qui compterait 25 000 nouveaux bénéficiaires d'aide alimentaire (rapport du Secrétaire général, par. 25).

Il en résulte en outre, pour les populations concernées, des difficultés croissantes d'accès aux services de santé, ainsi qu'aux établissements scolaires et à l'approvisionnement primaire en eau, constat également corroboré par diverses sources d'information. Le rapport du Secrétaire général mentionne ainsi de manière générale que, «[s]elon le Bureau central de statistique palestinien, la barrière a, à ce jour, coupé 30 localités des services de santé, 22 des établissements scolaires, 8 des sources primaires d'eau et 3 du réseau électrique» (rapport du Secrétaire général, par. 23). Le rapporteur spécial de la Commission des droits de l'homme sur la situation des droits de l'homme dans les territoires palestiniens occupés par Israël depuis 1967 indique quant à lui que «[l]es Palestiniens qui habitent entre le mur et la Ligne verte ne pourront plus accéder à leurs terres ni à leur lieu de travail, aux écoles, aux hôpitaux et autres services sociaux» (E/CN.4/2004/6, 8 septembre 2003, par. 9). Concernant plus particulièrement l'accès aux ressources en eau, le rapporteur spécial sur le droit à l'alimentation de la Commission des droits de l'homme relève que, «[e]n construisant la clôture, Israël annexera aussi de fait la plus grande partie de la nappe phréatique occidentale (qui fournit 51% des ressources en eau de la Cisjordanie)» (E/CN.4/2004/10/Add.2, 31 octobre 2003, par. 51). De même, en ce qui concerne l'accès aux services de santé, il a été indiqué que, du fait de la constitution de l'enclave de Qalqiliya, un hôpital des Nations Unies situé dans cette ville a connu une baisse de fréquentation de 40% (rapport du Secrétaire général, par. 24).

A Qalqiliya, selon des rapports fournis aux Nations Unies, environ 600 négoces ou entreprises ont dû fermer leurs portes et 6000 à 8000 personnes ont déjà quitté la région (E/CN.4/2004/6, 8 septembre 2003, par. 10; E/CN.4/2004/10/Add.2, 31 octobre 2003, par. 51). Le rapporteur spécial sur le droit à l'alimentation de la Commission des droits de l'homme a relevé en outre que, «[l]a clôture/le mur coupant les communautés de leurs terres et de leur eau sans leur donner d'autres moyens de subsistance, nombreux sont les Palestiniens habitant dans ces régions qui seront obligés de partir» (E/CN.4/2004/10/Add.2, 31 octobre 2003, par. 51). A cet égard également, la construction du mur priverait en fait un nombre significatif de Palestiniens de leur droit de «choisir librement [leur] résidence». Par ailleurs, de l'avis de la Cour, puisque la construction du mur et le régime qui lui est associé ont déjà obligé un nombre significatif de Palestiniens à quitter certaines zones — processus qui se poursuivra avec l'édification de nouveaux tronçons du mur —, cette construction, combinée à l'établissement des colonies de peuplement mentionné au paragraphe 120 ci-dessus, tend à modifier la composition démographique du territoire palestinien occupé.

134. Au total, de l'avis de la Cour, la construction du mur et le régime qui lui est associé entravent la liberté de circulation des habitants du territoire palestinien occupé (à l'exception des ressortissants israéliens et

vated food insecurity in the region, which reportedly numbers 25,000 new beneficiaries of food aid (report of the Secretary-General, para. 25).

It has further led to increasing difficulties for the population concerned regarding access to health services, educational establishments and primary sources of water. This is also attested by a number of different information sources. Thus the report of the Secretary-General states generally that "According to the Palestinian Central Bureau of Statistics, so far the Barrier has separated 30 localities from health services, 22 from schools, 8 from primary water sources and 3 from electricity networks." (Report of the Secretary-General, para. 23.) The Special Rapporteur of the United Nations Commission on Human Rights on the situation of human rights in the Palestinian territories occupied by Israel since 1967 states that "Palestinians between the Wall and Green Line will effectively be cut off from their land and workplaces, schools, health clinics and other social services." (E/CN.4/2004/6, 8 September 2003, para. 9.) In relation specifically to water resources, the Special Rapporteur on the Right to Food of the United Nations Commission on Human Rights observes that "By constructing the fence Israel will also effectively annex most of the western aquifer system (which provides 51 per cent of the West Bank's water resources)." (E/CN.4/2004/10/Add.2, 31 October 2003, para. 51.) Similarly, in regard to access to health services, it has been stated that, as a result of the enclosure of Qalqiliya, a United Nations hospital in that town has recorded a 40 per cent decrease in its caseload (report of the Secretary-General, para. 24).

At Qalqiliya, according to reports furnished to the United Nations, some 600 shops or businesses have shut down, and 6,000 to 8,000 people have already left the region (E/CN.4/2004/6, 8 September 2003, para. 10; E/CN.4/2004/10/Add.2, 31 October 2003, para. 51). The Special Rapporteur on the Right to Food of the United Nations Commission on Human Rights has also observed that "With the fence/wall cutting communities off from their land and water without other means of subsistence, many of the Palestinians living in these areas will be forced to leave." (E/CN.4/2004/10/Add.2, 31 October 2003, para. 51.) In this respect also the construction of the wall would effectively deprive a significant number of Palestinians of the "freedom to choose [their] residence". In addition, however, in the view of the Court, since a significant number of Palestinians have already been compelled by the construction of the wall and its associated régime to depart from certain areas, a process that will continue as more of the wall is built, that construction, coupled with the establishment of the Israeli settlements mentioned in paragraph 120 above, is tending to alter the demographic composition of the Occupied Palestinian Territory.

134. To sum up, the Court is of the opinion that the construction of the wall and its associated régime impede the liberty of movement of the inhabitants of the Occupied Palestinian Territory (with the exception

assimilés) telle que garantie par le paragraphe 1 de l'article 12 du pacte international relatif aux droits civils et politiques. Ils entravent également l'exercice par les intéressés des droits au travail, à la santé, à l'éducation et à un niveau de vie suffisant tels que proclamés par le pacte international relatif aux droits économiques, sociaux et culturels et la convention des Nations Unies relative aux droits de l'enfant. Enfin, la construction du mur et le régime qui lui est associé, en contribuant aux changements démographiques auxquels il est fait référence aux paragraphes 122 et 133 ci-dessus, sont contraires au sixième alinéa de l'article 49 de la quatrième convention de Genève et aux résolutions du Conseil de sécurité rapportées au paragraphe 120 ci-dessus.

135. La Cour observera cependant que le droit international humanitaire applicable comporte des dispositions permettant de tenir compte dans certains cas des impératifs militaires.

L'article 46 du règlement de La Haye de 1907 et l'article 47 de la quatrième convention de Genève ne contiennent pour leur part aucune clause de limitation de ce type. En ce qui concerne les transferts forcés de population ou les déportations prohibées par le premier alinéa de l'article 49 de la convention, le deuxième alinéa du même article réserve le cas où «la sécurité de la population ou d'impérieuses nécessités militaires l'exigent». Cette réserve ne couvre cependant pas le sixième alinéa du même article, qui interdit à la puissance occupante de «procéder à la déportation ou au transfert d'une partie de sa propre population civile dans le territoire occupé par elle». Quant à l'article 53 relatif à la destruction des biens, il prévoit une exception «dans les cas où ces destructions seraient rendues absolument nécessaires par les opérations militaires».

La Cour estime que les impératifs militaires prévus par ces textes peuvent être invoqués dans des territoires occupés même après la fin générale des opérations militaires ayant conduit à l'occupation de ces territoires. Toutefois, au vu du dossier, la Cour n'est pas convaincue que les destructions opérées contrairement à l'interdiction édictée à l'article 53 de la quatrième convention de Genève aient été rendues absolument nécessaires par des opérations militaires.

136. La Cour observera également que certaines des conventions relatives aux droits de l'homme, et en particulier le pacte international relatif aux droits civils et politiques, contiennent des clauses qui peuvent être invoquées par les Etats parties en vue de déroger, sous diverses conditions, à certaines de leurs obligations conventionnelles. A cet égard, la Cour rappellera cependant que la communication d'Israël, notifiée au Secrétaire général des Nations Unies conformément à l'article 4 du pacte international relatif aux droits civils et politiques, ne porte que sur l'article 9 du pacte concernant la liberté et la sécurité de la personne (voir paragraphe 127 ci-dessus); Israël est donc tenu au respect de toutes les autres dispositions de cet instrument.

La Cour relèvera en outre que certaines dispositions des conventions relatives aux droits de l'homme sont assorties de clauses de limitation des droits couverts par ces dispositions. Aucune clause de ce type ne figure à of Israeli citizens and those assimilated thereto) as guaranteed under Article 12, paragraph 1, of the International Covenant on Civil and Political Rights. They also impede the exercise by the persons concerned of the right to work, to health, to education and to an adequate standard of living as proclaimed in the International Covenant on Economic, Social and Cultural Rights and in the United Nations Convention on the Rights of the Child. Lastly, the construction of the wall and its associated régime, by contributing to the demographic changes referred to in paragraphs 122 and 133 above, contravene Article 49, paragraph 6, of the Fourth Geneva Convention and the Security Council resolutions cited in paragraph 120 above.

135. The Court would observe, however, that the applicable international humanitarian law contains provisions enabling account to be taken of military exigencies in certain circumstances.

Neither Article 46 of the Hague Regulations of 1907 nor Article 47 of the Fourth Geneva Convention contain any qualifying provision of this type. With regard to forcible transfers of population and deportations, which are prohibited under Article 49, paragraph 1, of the Convention, paragraph 2 of that Article provides for an exception in those cases in which "the security of the population or imperative military reasons so demand". This exception however does not apply to paragraph 6 of that Article, which prohibits the occupying Power from deporting or transferring parts of its own civilian population into the territories it occupies. As to Article 53 concerning the destruction of personal property, it provides for an exception "where such destruction is rendered absolutely necessary by military operations".

The Court considers that the military exigencies contemplated by these texts may be invoked in occupied territories even after the general close of the military operations that led to their occupation. However, on the material before it, the Court is not convinced that the destructions carried out contrary to the prohibition in Article 53 of the Fourth Geneva Convention were rendered absolutely necessary by military operations.

136. The Court would further observe that some human rights conventions, and in particular the International Covenant on Civil and Political Rights, contain provisions which States parties may invoke in order to derogate, under various conditions, from certain of their conventional obligations. In this respect, the Court would however recall that the communication notified by Israel to the Secretary-General of the United Nations under Article 4 of the International Covenant on Civil and Political Rights concerns only Article 9 of the Covenant, relating to the right to freedom and security of person (see paragraph 127 above); Israel is accordingly bound to respect all the other provisions of that instrument.

The Court would note, moreover, that certain provisions of human rights conventions contain clauses qualifying the rights covered by those provisions. There is no clause of this kind in Article 17 of the Internal'article 17 du pacte international relatif aux droits civils et politiques. En revanche, le paragraphe 3 de l'article 12 de cet instrument dispose que la liberté de circulation telle que garantie par ledit article

> «ne [peut] être l'objet de restrictions que si celles-ci sont prévues par la loi, nécessaires pour protéger la sécurité nationale, l'ordre public, la santé ou la moralité publiques ou les droits et libertés d'autrui et compatibles avec les autres droits reconnus par le présent pacte».

Pour sa part, le pacte international relatif aux droits économiques, sociaux et culturels contient en son article 4 une disposition générale ainsi libellée:

> «Les Etats parties au présent pacte reconnaissent que, dans la jouissance des droits assurés par l'Etat conformément au présent pacte, l'Etat ne peut soumettre ces droits qu'aux limitations établies par la loi, dans la seule mesure compatible avec la nature de ces droits et exclusivement en vue de favoriser le bien-être général dans une société démocratique.»

La Cour observera que, aux termes mêmes du paragraphe 3 de l'article 12 du pacte international relatif aux droits civils et politiques, les restrictions envisagées par ce paragraphe constituent des exceptions au droit à la liberté de circulation garanti au paragraphe 1. En outre, ces restrictions doivent non seulement servir les buts autorisés, mais encore être nécessaires pour atteindre ces buts. Pour reprendre la formulation retenue par le Comité des droits de l'homme, elles «doivent être conformes au principe de la proportionnalité» et «doivent constituer le moyen le moins perturbateur parmi ceux qui pourraient permettre d'obtenir le résultat recherché» (CCPR/C/21/Rev.1/Add.9, observation générale n° 27, par. 14). Au vu des informations dont elle dispose, la Cour estime que ces conditions ne sont pas remplies en l'espèce.

La Cour fera également observer que les restrictions à la jouissance par les Palestiniens habitant dans le territoire occupé par Israël de leurs droits économiques, sociaux et culturels, telles qu'elles résultent de la construction du mur par cet Etat, ne répondent pas à une condition posée par l'article 4 du pacte international relatif aux droits économiques, sociaux et culturels, à savoir qu'elles doivent être établies «exclusivement en vue de favoriser le bien-être général dans une société démocratique».

137. Au total, la Cour, au vu du dossier, n'est pas convaincue que la poursuite des objectifs de sécurité avancés par Israël nécessitait l'adoption du tracé choisi pour le mur. Le mur tel que tracé et le régime qui lui est associé portent atteinte de manière grave à de nombreux droits des Palestiniens habitant dans le territoire occupé par Israël sans que les atteintes résultant de ce tracé puissent être justifiées par des impératifs militaires ou des nécessités de sécurité nationale ou d'ordre public. La construction d'un tel mur constitue dès lors une violation par Israël de

tional Covenant on Civil and Political Rights. On the other hand, Article 12, paragraph 3, of that instrument provides that restrictions on liberty of movement as guaranteed under that Article

> "shall not be subject to any restrictions except those which are provided by law, are necessary to protect national security, public order *(ordre public)*, public health or morals or the rights and freedoms of others, and are consistent with the other rights recognized in the present Covenant".

As for the International Covenant on Economic, Social and Cultural Rights, Article 4 thereof contains a general provision as follows:

> "The States Parties to the present Covenant recognize that, in the enjoyment of those rights provided by the State in conformity with the present Covenant, the State may subject such rights only to such limitations as are determined by law only in so far as this may be compatible with the nature of these rights and solely for the purpose of promoting the general welfare in a democratic society."

The Court would observe that the restrictions provided for under Article 12, paragraph 3, of the International Covenant on Civil and Political Rights are, by the very terms of that provision, exceptions to the right of freedom of movement contained in paragraph 1. In addition, it is not sufficient that such restrictions be directed to the ends authorized; they must also be necessary for the attainment of those ends. As the Human Rights Committee put it, they "must conform to the principle of proportionality" and "must be the least intrusive instrument amongst those which might achieve the desired result" (CCPR/C/21/Rev.1/Add.9, General Comment No. 27, para. 14). On the basis of the information available to it, the Court finds that these conditions are not met in the present instance.

The Court would further observe that the restrictions on the enjoyment by the Palestinians living in the territory occupied by Israel of their economic, social and cultural rights, resulting from Israel's construction of the wall, fail to meet a condition laid down by Article 4 of the International Covenant on Economic, Social and Cultural Rights, that is to say that their implementation must be "solely for the purpose of promoting the general welfare in a democratic society".

137. To sum up, the Court, from the material available to it, is not convinced that the specific course Israel has chosen for the wall was necessary to attain its security objectives. The wall, along the route chosen, and its associated régime gravely infringe a number of rights of Palestinians residing in the territory occupied by Israel, and the infringements resulting from that route cannot be justified by military exigencies or by the requirements of national security or public order. The construction of such a wall accordingly constitutes breaches by Israel of various

diverses obligations qui lui incombent en vertu des instruments applicables de droit international humanitaire et des droits de l'homme.

*

138. Ainsi, la Cour a conclu que la construction du mur est un acte non conforme à diverses obligations juridiques internationales incombant à Israël. A l'annexe I du rapport du Secrétaire général, il est cependant précisé que, selon Israël, «la construction du mur est conforme à l'article 51 de la Charte des Nations Unies, ainsi qu'à son droit inhérent de légitime défense et aux résolutions 1368 (2001) et 1373 (2001) du Conseil de sécurité». Plus précisément, le représentant permanent d'Israël auprès des Nations Unies a fait valoir devant l'Assemblée générale, le 20 octobre 2003, que «la barrière est une mesure tout à fait conforme au droit [de légitime défense] des Etats ... consacré par l'article 51 de la Charte»; il a ajouté que ces résolutions «ont reconnu clairement le droit des Etats au recours à la force en cas de légitime défense contre les attentats terroristes» et qu'elles reconnaissent par conséquent le droit de recourir à cette fin à des mesures n'impliquant pas l'emploi de la force (A/ES-10/PV.21, p. 6).

139. Selon l'article 51 de la Charte des Nations Unies:

> «Aucune disposition de la présente Charte ne porte atteinte au droit naturel de légitime défense, individuelle ou collective, dans le cas où un Membre des Nations Unies est l'objet d'une agression armée, jusqu'à ce que le Conseil de sécurité ait pris les mesures nécessaires pour maintenir la paix et la sécurité internationales.»

L'article 51 de la Charte reconnaît ainsi l'existence d'un droit naturel de légitime défense en cas d'agression armée par un Etat contre un autre Etat. Toutefois, Israël ne prétend pas que les violences dont il est victime soient imputables à un Etat étranger.

La Cour note par ailleurs qu'Israël exerce son contrôle sur le territoire palestinien occupé et que, comme Israël l'indique lui-même, la menace qu'il invoque pour justifier la construction du mur trouve son origine à l'intérieur de ce territoire, et non en dehors de celui-ci. Cette situation est donc différente de celle envisagée par les résolutions 1368 (2001) et 1373 (2001) du Conseil de sécurité, et de ce fait Israël ne saurait en tout état de cause invoquer ces résolutions au soutien de sa prétention à exercer un droit de légitime défense.

En conséquence, la Cour conclut que l'article 51 de la Charte est sans pertinence au cas particulier.

140. La Cour s'est cependant demandé si Israël pourrait se prévaloir d'un état de nécessité permettant d'exclure l'illicéité de la construction du mur. A cet égard, la Cour se doit de noter que certaines des conventions en cause incluent des clauses de limitation des droits garantis ou des clauses de dérogation (voir paragraphes 135 et 136 ci-dessus). Dès lors

of its obligations under the applicable international humanitarian law and human rights instruments.

*

138. The Court has thus concluded that the construction of the wall constitutes action not in conformity with various international legal obligations incumbent upon Israel. However, Annex I to the report of the Secretary-General states that, according to Israel: "the construction of the Barrier is consistent with Article 51 of the Charter of the United Nations, its inherent right to self-defence and Security Council resolutions 1368 (2001) and 1373 (2001)". More specifically, Israel's Permanent Representative to the United Nations asserted in the General Assembly on 20 October 2003 that "the fence is a measure wholly consistent with the right of States to self-defence enshrined in Article 51 of the Charter"; the Security Council resolutions referred to, he continued, "have clearly recognized the right of States to use force in self-defence against terrorist attacks", and therefore surely recognize the right to use non-forcible measures to that end (A/ES-10/PV.21, p. 6).

139. Under the terms of Article 51 of the Charter of the United Nations:

> "Nothing in the present Charter shall impair the inherent right of individual or collective self-defence if an armed attack occurs against a Member of the United Nations, until the Security Council has taken measures necessary to maintain international peace and security."

Article 51 of the Charter thus recognizes the existence of an inherent right of self-defence in the case of armed attack by one State against another State. However, Israel does not claim that the attacks against it are imputable to a foreign State.

The Court also notes that Israel exercises control in the Occupied Palestinian Territory and that, as Israel itself states, the threat which it regards as justifying the construction of the wall originates within, and not outside, that territory. The situation is thus different from that contemplated by Security Council resolutions 1368 (2001) and 1373 (2001), and therefore Israel could not in any event invoke those resolutions in support of its claim to be exercising a right of self-defence.

Consequently, the Court concludes that Article 51 of the Charter has no relevance in this case.

140. The Court has, however, considered whether Israel could rely on a state of necessity which would preclude the wrongfulness of the construction of the wall. In this regard the Court is bound to note that some of the conventions at issue in the present instance include qualifying clauses of the rights guaranteed or provisions for derogation (see para-

que ces traités font déjà place à de telles considérations dans leurs dispositions mêmes, on pourrait se demander si l'état de nécessité tel que reconnu par le droit international coutumier pourrait être invoqué en ce qui concerne ces traités comme cause excluant l'illicéité des mesures ou décisions incriminées. Mais la Cour n'aura pas à examiner cette question. Ainsi qu'elle l'a observé en l'affaire relative au *Projet Gabčíkovo-Nagymaros (Hongrie/Slovaquie)*, «l'état de nécessité constitue une cause, reconnue par le droit international coutumier», qui «ne saurait être admise qu'à titre exceptionnel»; il «ne peut être invoqué qu'à certaines conditions, strictement définies, qui doivent être cumulativement réunies; et l'Etat concerné n'est pas seul juge de la réunion de ces conditions» (*C.I.J. Recueil 1997*, p. 40, par. 51). La Cour a précisé l'une de ces conditions en reprenant les termes employés par la Commission du droit international dans un texte qui, en sa forme actuelle, prévoit que le fait incriminé doit constituer «pour l'Etat le seul moyen de protéger un intérêt essentiel contre un péril grave et imminent» (article 25 des articles de la Commission du droit international sur la responsabilité internationale de l'Etat; voir aussi l'ancien article 33 du projet d'articles sur la responsabilité internationale des Etats, dont le libellé était identique dans la version française). Au vu du dossier, la Cour n'est pas convaincue que la construction du mur selon le tracé retenu était le seul moyen de protéger les intérêts d'Israël contre le péril dont il s'est prévalu pour justifier cette construction.

141. Reste qu'Israël doit faire face à des actes de violence indiscriminés, nombreux et meurtriers, visant sa population civile. Il a le droit, et même le devoir, d'y répondre en vue de protéger la vie de ses citoyens. Les mesures prises n'en doivent pas moins demeurer conformes au droit international applicable.

142. Au total, la Cour estime qu'Israël ne saurait se prévaloir du droit de légitime défense ou de l'état de nécessité, comme excluant l'illicéité de la construction du mur qui résulte des considérations mentionnées aux paragraphes 122 et 137 ci-dessus. En conséquence, la Cour juge que la construction du mur et le régime qui lui est associé sont contraires au droit international.

* * *

143. Etant parvenue à la conclusion que, par l'édification du mur dans le territoire palestinien occupé, y compris à l'intérieur et sur le pourtour de Jérusalem-Est, et par l'adoption du régime qui lui est associé, Israël a violé diverses obligations internationales lui incombant (voir paragraphes 114 à 137 ci-dessus), la Cour doit à présent, pour répondre à la question posée par l'Assemblée générale, procéder à l'examen des conséquences de ces violations.

* *

graphs 135 and 136 above). Since those treaties already address considerations of this kind within their own provisions, it might be asked whether a state of necessity as recognized in customary international law could be invoked with regard to those treaties as a ground for precluding the wrongfulness of the measures or decisions being challenged. However, the Court will not need to consider that question. As the Court observed in the case concerning the *Gabčíkovo-Nagymaros Project (Hungary/Slovakia)*, "the state of necessity is a ground recognized by customary international law" that "can only be accepted on an exceptional basis"; it "can only be invoked under certain strictly defined conditions which must be cumulatively satisfied; and the State concerned is not the sole judge of whether those conditions have been met" (*I.C.J. Reports 1997*, p. 40, para. 51). One of those conditions was stated by the Court in terms used by the International Law Commission, in a text which in its present form requires that the act being challenged be "the only way for the State to safeguard an essential interest against a grave and imminent peril" (Article 25 of the International Law Commission's Articles on Responsibility of States for Internationally Wrongful Acts; see also former Article 33 of the Draft Articles on the International Responsibility of States, with slightly different wording in the English text). In the light of the material before it, the Court is not convinced that the construction of the wall along the route chosen was the only means to safeguard the interests of Israel against the peril which it has invoked as justification for that construction.

141. The fact remains that Israel has to face numerous indiscriminate and deadly acts of violence against its civilian population. It has the right, and indeed the duty, to respond in order to protect the life of its citizens. The measures taken are bound nonetheless to remain in conformity with applicable international law.

142. In conclusion, the Court considers that Israel cannot rely on a right of self-defence or on a state of necessity in order to preclude the wrongfulness of the construction of the wall resulting from the considerations mentioned in paragraphs 122 and 137 above. The Court accordingly finds that the construction of the wall, and its associated régime, are contrary to international law.

* * *

143. The Court having concluded that, by the construction of the wall in the Occupied Palestinian Territory, including in and around East Jerusalem, and by adopting its associated régime, Israel has violated various international obligations incumbent upon it (see paragraphs 114-137 above), it must now, in order to reply to the question posed by the General Assembly, examine the consequences of those violations.

* *

144. Dans leurs exposés écrits et oraux, de nombreux participants à la procédure devant la Cour ont soutenu que l'édification illicite par Israël de ce mur entraînait des conséquences juridiques tant pour cet Etat que pour les autres Etats et l'Organisation des Nations Unies; dans son exposé écrit, Israël, pour sa part, n'a pas présenté d'arguments en ce qui concerne les conséquences juridiques qui pourraient résulter de la construction du mur.

145. En ce qui concerne les conséquences juridiques pour Israël, il a été allégué qu'Israël avait en premier lieu l'obligation juridique de mettre fin à la situation illicite en cessant immédiatement la construction du mur dans le territoire palestinien occupé et de donner des assurances et des garanties de non-répétition appropriées.

Israël aurait en deuxième lieu l'obligation juridique de réparer les dommages occasionnés par son comportement illicite. Cette réparation devrait tout d'abord prendre la forme d'une restitution, à savoir la démolition des portions du mur construites dans le territoire palestinien occupé et l'annulation des actes juridiques liés à l'édification du mur, ainsi que la restitution des biens réquisitionnés ou expropriés aux fins de celle-ci; la réparation devrait également consister en une indemnisation appropriée des personnes dont les habitations ou exploitations agricoles ont été détruites.

Il a encore été affirmé qu'Israël avait le devoir permanent d'exécuter toutes les obligations internationales auxquelles il a contrevenu du fait de la construction du mur dans le territoire palestinien occupé et du régime qui lui est associé; et il a par ailleurs été soutenu que, aux termes de la quatrième convention de Genève, Israël avait l'obligation de rechercher et de traduire devant ses tribunaux les personnes dont il est allégué qu'elles ont commis, ou qu'elles ont ordonné que soient commis, de graves manquements au droit international humanitaire découlant de la planification, de l'édification et de l'utilisation du mur.

146. En ce qui concerne les conséquences juridiques pour les Etats autres qu'Israël, il a été exposé devant la Cour que tous les Etats avaient l'obligation de ne pas reconnaître la situation illicite résultant de la construction du mur, de ne pas prêter aide ou assistance au maintien de cette situation et de coopérer en vue de mettre un terme aux violations alléguées et de s'assurer qu'elles donneront lieu à réparation.

Certains participants à la procédure devant la Cour ont également relevé que les Etats parties à la quatrième convention de Genève avaient l'obligation de prendre des mesures visant à assurer le respect de la convention et que, dans la mesure où la construction et le maintien du mur dans le territoire palestinien occupé seraient constitutifs d'infractions graves à cette convention, les Etats parties à celle-ci avaient l'obligation d'en poursuivre les auteurs ou de les extrader. Il a par ailleurs été relevé que

> «le Conseil de sécurité des Nations Unies devrait examiner les violations flagrantes et systématiques des règles et principes de droit

144. In their written and oral observations, many participants in the proceedings before the Court contended that Israel's action in illegally constructing this wall has legal consequences not only for Israel itself, but also for other States and for the United Nations; in its Written Statement, Israel, for its part, presented no arguments regarding the possible legal consequences of the construction of the wall.

145. As regards the legal consequences for Israel, it was contended that Israel has, first, a legal obligation to bring the illegal situation to an end by ceasing forthwith the construction of the wall in the Occupied Palestinian Territory, and to give appropriate assurances and guarantees of non-repetition.

It was argued that, secondly, Israel is under a legal obligation to make reparation for the damage arising from its unlawful conduct. It was submitted that such reparation should first of all take the form of restitution, namely demolition of those portions of the wall constructed in the Occupied Palestinian Territory and annulment of the legal acts associated with its construction and the restoration of property requisitioned or expropriated for that purpose; reparation should also include appropriate compensation for individuals whose homes or agricultural holdings have been destroyed.

It was further contended that Israel is under a continuing duty to comply with all of the international obligations violated by it as a result of the construction of the wall in the Occupied Palestinian Territory and of the associated régime. It was also argued that, under the terms of the Fourth Geneva Convention, Israel is under an obligation to search for and bring before its courts persons alleged to have committed, or to have ordered to be committed, grave breaches of international humanitarian law flowing from the planning, construction and use of the wall.

146. As regards the legal consequences for States other than Israel, it was contended before the Court that all States are under an obligation not to recognize the illegal situation arising from the construction of the wall, not to render aid or assistance in maintaining that situation and to co-operate with a view to putting an end to the alleged violations and to ensuring that reparation will be made therefor.

Certain participants in the proceedings further contended that the States parties to the Fourth Geneva Convention are obliged to take measures to ensure compliance with the Convention and that, inasmuch as the construction and maintenance of the wall in the Occupied Palestinian Territory constitutes grave breaches of that Convention, the States parties to that Convention are under an obligation to prosecute or extradite the authors of such breaches. It was further observed that

> "the United Nations Security Council should consider flagrant and systematic violation of international law norm[s] and principles by

> international, en particulier de droit international humanitaire, commises par Israël, et prendre toutes les mesures nécessaires pour y mettre fin»,

et que le Conseil de sécurité et l'Assemblée générale avaient l'obligation de tenir dûment compte de l'avis consultatif que la Cour rendrait.

* *

147. La Cour ayant constaté que l'édification du mur dans le territoire palestinien occupé, y compris à l'intérieur et sur le pourtour de Jérusalem-Est, et le régime qui lui est associé étaient contraires à diverses obligations internationales d'Israël, il s'ensuit que la responsabilité de cet Etat est engagée selon le droit international.

148. La Cour examinera maintenant les conséquences juridiques qui résultent des violations du droit international par Israël en opérant une distinction entre, d'une part, celles qui en découlent pour cet Etat et, d'autre part, celles qui en découlent pour les autres Etats et, le cas échéant, pour l'Organisation des Nations Unies. La Cour se penchera en premier lieu sur les conséquences juridiques de ces violations en ce qui concerne Israël.

*

149. La Cour note qu'Israël est tout d'abord tenu de respecter les obligations internationales auxquelles il a contrevenu par la construction du mur en territoire palestinien occupé (voir paragraphes 114 à 137 ci-dessus). En conséquence, Israël doit observer l'obligation qui lui incombe de respecter le droit à l'autodétermination du peuple palestinien et les obligations auxquelles il est tenu en vertu du droit international humanitaire et du droit international relatif aux droits de l'homme. Par ailleurs, il doit assurer la liberté d'accès aux Lieux saints passés sous son contrôle à la suite du conflit de 1967 (voir paragraphe 129 ci-dessus).

150. La Cour observe qu'Israël a également l'obligation de mettre un terme à la violation de ses obligations internationales, telle qu'elle résulte de la construction du mur en territoire palestinien occupé. L'obligation d'un Etat responsable d'un fait internationalement illicite de mettre fin à celui-ci est bien fondée en droit international général et la Cour a, à diverses reprises, confirmé l'existence de cette obligation (*Activités militaires et paramilitaires au Nicaragua et contre celui-ci (Nicaragua c. Etats-Unis d'Amérique), fond, arrêt, C.I.J. Recueil 1986*, p. 149; *Personnel diplomatique et consulaire des Etats-Unis à Téhéran, arrêt, C.I.J. Recueil 1980*, p. 44, par. 95; *Haya de la Torre, arrêt, C.I.J. Recueil 1951*, p. 82).

151. Israël a en conséquence l'obligation de cesser immédiatement les travaux d'édification du mur qu'il est en train de construire dans le territoire palestinien occupé, y compris à l'intérieur et sur le pourtour de Jérusalem-Est. Par ailleurs, la Cour ayant indiqué plus haut (voir para-

> Israel, particularly . . . international humanitarian law, and take all necessary measures to put an end [to] these violations",

and that the Security Council and the General Assembly must take due account of the advisory opinion to be given by the Court.

* *

147. Since the Court has concluded that the construction of the wall in the Occupied Palestinian Territory, including in and around East Jerusalem, and its associated régime, are contrary to various of Israel's international obligations, it follows that the responsibility of that State is engaged under international law.

148. The Court will now examine the legal consequences resulting from the violations of international law by Israel by distinguishing between, on the one hand, those arising for Israel and, on the other, those arising for other States and, where appropriate, for the United Nations. The Court will begin by examining the legal consequences of those violations for Israel.

*

149. The Court notes that Israel is first obliged to comply with the international obligations it has breached by the construction of the wall in the Occupied Palestinian Territory (see paragraphs 114-137 above). Consequently, Israel is bound to comply with its obligation to respect the right of the Palestinian people to self-determination and its obligations under international humanitarian law and international human rights law. Furthermore, it must ensure freedom of access to the Holy Places that came under its control following the 1967 War (see paragraph 129 above).

150. The Court observes that Israel also has an obligation to put an end to the violation of its international obligations flowing from the construction of the wall in the Occupied Palestinian Territory. The obligation of a State responsible for an internationally wrongful act to put an end to that act is well established in general international law, and the Court has on a number of occasions confirmed the existence of that obligation (*Military and Paramilitary Activities in and against Nicaragua (Nicaragua* v. *United States of America), Merits, Judgment, I.C.J. Reports 1986*, p. 149; *United States Diplomatic and Consular Staff in Tehran, Judgment, I.C.J. Reports 1980*, p. 44, para. 95; *Haya de la Torre, Judgment, I.C.J. Reports 1951*, p. 82).

151. Israel accordingly has the obligation to cease forthwith the works of construction of the wall being built by it in the Occupied Palestinian Territory, including in and around East Jerusalem. Moreover, in view of the Court's finding (see paragraph 143 above) that Israel's violations of

graphe 143 ci-dessus) que les violations par Israël de ses obligations internationales résultaient de l'édification du mur et du régime juridique qui lui est associé, la cessation de ces violations implique le démantèlement immédiat des portions de cet ouvrage situées dans le territoire palestinien occupé, y compris à l'intérieur et sur le pourtour de Jérusalem-Est. L'ensemble des actes législatifs et réglementaires adoptés en vue de son édification et de la mise en place du régime qui lui est associé doivent immédiatement être abrogés ou privés d'effet, sauf dans la mesure où de tels actes, en ayant ouvert droit à indemnisation ou à d'autres formes de réparation au profit de la population palestinienne, demeurent pertinents dans le contexte du respect, par Israël, des obligations visées au paragraphe 153 ci-dessous.

152. Au demeurant, la construction du mur dans le territoire palestinien occupé ayant notamment nécessité la réquisition et la destruction d'habitations, de commerces ainsi que d'exploitations agricoles, la Cour constate aussi qu'Israël a l'obligation de réparer tous les dommages causés à toutes les personnes physiques ou morales concernées. La Cour rappellera que les modalités essentielles de la réparation en droit coutumier ont été formulées comme suit par la Cour permanente de Justice internationale:

> «Le principe essentiel, qui découle de la notion même d'acte illicite et qui semble se dégager de la pratique internationale, notamment de la jurisprudence des tribunaux arbitraux, est que la réparation doit, autant que possible, effacer toutes les conséquences de l'acte illicite et rétablir l'état qui aurait vraisemblablement existé si ledit acte n'avait pas été commis. Restitution en nature, ou, si elle n'est pas possible, paiement d'une somme correspondant à la valeur qu'aurait la restitution en nature; allocation, s'il y a lieu, de dommages-intérêts pour les pertes subies et qui ne seraient pas couvertes par la restitution en nature ou le paiement qui en prend la place; tels sont les principes desquels doit s'inspirer la détermination du montant de l'indemnité due à cause d'un fait contraire au droit international.» (*Usine de Chorzów, fond, arrêt n° 13, 1928, C.P.J.I. série A n° 17*, p. 47.)

153. Israël est en conséquence tenu de restituer les terres, les vergers, les oliveraies et les autres biens immobiliers saisis à toute personne physique ou morale en vue de l'édification du mur dans le territoire palestinien occupé. Au cas où une telle restitution s'avérerait matériellement impossible, Israël serait tenu de procéder à l'indemnisation des personnes en question pour le préjudice subi par elles. De l'avis de la Cour, Israël est également tenu d'indemniser, conformément aux règles du droit international applicables en la matière, toutes les personnes physiques ou morales qui auraient subi un préjudice matériel quelconque du fait de la construction de ce mur.

*

its international obligations stem from the construction of the wall and from its associated régime, cessation of those violations entails the dismantling forthwith of those parts of that structure situated within the Occupied Palestinian Territory, including in and around East Jerusalem. All legislative and regulatory acts adopted with a view to its construction, and to the establishment of its associated régime, must forthwith be repealed or rendered ineffective, except in so far as such acts, by providing for compensation or other forms of reparation for the Palestinian population, may continue to be relevant for compliance by Israel with the obligations referred to in paragraph 153 below.

152. Moreover, given that the construction of the wall in the Occupied Palestinian Territory has, *inter alia*, entailed the requisition and destruction of homes, businesses and agricultural holdings, the Court finds further that Israel has the obligation to make reparation for the damage caused to all the natural or legal persons concerned. The Court would recall that the essential forms of reparation in customary law were laid down by the Permanent Court of International Justice in the following terms:

> "The essential principle contained in the actual notion of an illegal act — a principle which seems to be established by international practice and in particular by the decisions of arbitral tribunals — is that reparation must, as far as possible, wipe out all the consequences of the illegal act and reestablish the situation which would, in all probability, have existed if that act had not been committed. Restitution in kind, or, if this is not possible, payment of a sum corresponding to the value which a restitution in kind would bear; the award, if need be, of damages for loss sustained which would not be covered by restitution in kind or payment in place of it — such are the principles which should serve to determine the amount of compensation due for an act contrary to international law." (*Factory at Chorzów, Merits, Judgment No. 13, 1928, P.C.I.J., Series A, No. 17*, p. 47.)

153. Israel is accordingly under an obligation to return the land, orchards, olive groves and other immovable property seized from any natural or legal person for purposes of construction of the wall in the Occupied Palestinian Territory. In the event that such restitution should prove to be materially impossible, Israel has an obligation to compensate the persons in question for the damage suffered. The Court considers that Israel also has an obligation to compensate, in accordance with the applicable rules of international law, all natural or legal persons having suffered any form of material damage as a result of the wall's construction.

*

154. La Cour en arrive maintenant à l'examen des conséquences juridiques des faits internationalement illicites résultant de la construction du mur par Israël en ce qui concerne les Etats autres que ce dernier.

155. La Cour observera à cet égard qu'au rang des obligations internationales violées par Israël figurent des obligations *erga omnes*. Comme la Cour l'a précisé dans l'affaire de la *Barcelona Traction*, de telles obligations, par leur nature même, «concernent tous les Etats» et, «[v]u l'importance des droits en cause, tous les Etats peuvent être considérés comme ayant un intérêt juridique à ce que ces droits soient protégés» (*Barcelona Traction, Light and Power Company, Limited, deuxième phase, arrêt, C.I.J. Recueil 1970*, p. 32, par. 33). Les obligations *erga omnes* violées par Israël sont l'obligation de respecter le droit du peuple palestinien à l'autodétermination ainsi que certaines des obligations qui sont les siennes en vertu du droit international humanitaire.

156. S'agissant de la première de ces obligations, la Cour a déjà rappelé (voir paragraphe 88 ci-dessus) que, dans l'affaire du *Timor oriental*, elle avait estimé qu'il n'y avait «rien à redire» à l'affirmation selon laquelle «le droit des peuples à disposer d'eux-mêmes, tel qu'il s'est développé à partir de la Charte et de la pratique de l'Organisation des Nations Unies, est un droit opposable *erga omnes*» (*C.I.J. Recueil 1995*, p. 102, par. 29). La Cour relèvera également qu'aux termes de la résolution 2625 (XXV) de l'Assemblée générale, à laquelle il a déjà été fait référence (voir paragraphe 88 ci-dessus),

> «[t]out Etat a le devoir de favoriser, conjointement avec d'autres Etats ou séparément, la réalisation du principe de l'égalité de droits des peuples et de leur droit à disposer d'eux-mêmes, conformément aux dispositions de la Charte, et d'aider l'Organisation des Nations Unies à s'acquitter des responsabilités que lui a conférées la Charte en ce qui concerne l'application de ce principe...».

157. En ce qui concerne le droit international humanitaire, la Cour rappellera que, dans son avis consultatif sur la *Licéité de la menace ou de l'emploi d'armes nucléaires*, elle a indiqué qu'«un grand nombre de règles du droit humanitaire applicable dans les conflits armés sont si fondamentales pour le respect de la personne humaine et pour des «considérations élémentaires d'humanité»...», qu'elles «s'imposent ... à tous les Etats, qu'ils aient ou non ratifié les instruments conventionnels qui les expriment, parce qu'elles constituent des principes intransgressibles du droit international coutumier» (*C.I.J. Recueil 1996 (I)*, p. 257, par. 79). De l'avis de la Cour, les règles en question incorporent des obligations revêtant par essence un caractère *erga omnes*.

158. La Cour soulignera par ailleurs qu'aux termes de l'article 1er de la quatrième convention de Genève, disposition commune aux quatre conventions de Genève, «[l]es Hautes Parties contractantes s'engagent à respecter et à faire respecter la présente convention en toutes circonstances». Il résulte de cette disposition l'obligation de chaque Etat partie

154. The Court will now consider the legal consequences of the internationally wrongful acts flowing from Israel's construction of the wall as regards other States.

155. The Court would observe that the obligations violated by Israel include certain obligations *erga omnes*. As the Court indicated in the *Barcelona Traction* case, such obligations are by their very nature "the concern of all States" and, "In view of the importance of the rights involved, all States can be held to have a legal interest in their protection" (*Barcelona Traction, Light and Power Company, Limited, Second Phase, Judgment, I.C.J. Reports 1970*, p. 32, para. 33). The obligations *erga omnes* violated by Israel are the obligation to respect the right of the Palestinian people to self-determination, and certain of its obligations under international humanitarian law.

156. As regards the first of these, the Court has already observed (paragraph 88 above) that in the *East Timor* case, it described as "irreproachable" the assertion that "the right of peoples to self-determination, as it evolved from the Charter and from United Nations practice, has an *erga omnes* character" (*I.C.J. Reports 1995*, p. 102, para. 29). The Court would also recall that under the terms of General Assembly resolution 2625 (XXV), already mentioned above (see paragraph 88),

> "Every State has the duty to promote, through joint and separate action, realization of the principle of equal rights and self-determination of peoples, in accordance with the provisions of the Charter, and to render assistance to the United Nations in carrying out the responsibilities entrusted to it by the Charter regarding the implementation of the principle . . ."

157. With regard to international humanitarian law, the Court recalls that in its Advisory Opinion on the *Legality of the Threat or Use of Nuclear Weapons* it stated that "a great many rules of humanitarian law applicable in armed conflict are so fundamental to the respect of the human person and 'elementary considerations of humanity' . . .", that they are "to be observed by all States whether or not they have ratified the conventions that contain them, because they constitute intransgressible principles of international customary law" (*I.C.J. Reports 1996 (I)*, p. 257, para. 79). In the Court's view, these rules incorporate obligations which are essentially of an *erga omnes* character.

158. The Court would also emphasize that Article 1 of the Fourth Geneva Convention, a provision common to the four Geneva Conventions, provides that "The High Contracting Parties undertake to respect and to ensure respect for the present Convention in all circumstances." It follows from that provision that every State party to that Convention, whether or

à cette convention, qu'il soit partie ou non à un conflit déterminé, de faire respecter les prescriptions des instruments concernés.

159. Vu la nature et l'importance des droits et obligations en cause, la Cour est d'avis que tous les Etats sont dans l'obligation de ne pas reconnaître la situation illicite découlant de la construction du mur dans le territoire palestinien occupé, y compris à l'intérieur et sur le pourtour de Jérusalem-Est. Ils sont également dans l'obligation de ne pas prêter aide ou assistance au maintien de la situation créée par cette construction. Il appartient par ailleurs à tous les Etats de veiller, dans le respect de la Charte des Nations Unies et du droit international, à ce qu'il soit mis fin aux entraves, résultant de la construction du mur, à l'exercice par le peuple palestinien de son droit à l'autodétermination. En outre, tous les Etats parties à la convention de Genève relative à la protection des personnes civiles en temps de guerre, du 12 août 1949, ont l'obligation, dans le respect de la Charte des Nations Unies et du droit international, de faire respecter par Israël le droit international humanitaire incorporé dans cette convention.

160. La Cour est enfin d'avis que l'Organisation des Nations Unies, et spécialement l'Assemblée générale et le Conseil de sécurité, doivent, en tenant dûment compte du présent avis consultatif, examiner quelles nouvelles mesures doivent être prises afin de mettre un terme à la situation illicite découlant de la construction du mur et du régime qui lui est associé.

* * *

161. La Cour, soucieuse d'apporter son soutien aux buts et principes inscrits dans la Charte des Nations Unies, en particulier le maintien de la paix et de la sécurité internationales et le règlement pacifique des différends, tient à souligner la nécessité urgente que l'Organisation des Nations Unies dans son ensemble redouble ses efforts en vue de mettre rapidement un terme au conflit israélo-palestinen, qui continue de poser une menace à la paix et à la sécurité internationales, et d'établir ainsi une paix juste et durable dans la région.

162. La Cour a abouti à la conclusion que la construction du mur par Israël dans le territoire palestinien occupé est contraire au droit international et a précisé les conséquences juridiques qu'il convient de tirer de cette illicéité. Elle croit devoir ajouter que cette construction doit être replacée dans un contexte plus général. Depuis 1947, année de l'adoption de la résolution 181 (II) de l'Assemblée générale et de la fin du mandat pour la Palestine, se sont multipliés sur le territoire de l'ancien mandat les conflits armés, les actes de violence indiscriminés et les mesures de répression. La Cour relèvera qu'aussi bien Israël que la Palestine ont l'obligation de respecter de manière scrupuleuse le droit international humanitaire, dont l'un des buts principaux est de protéger la vie des personnes civiles. Des actions illicites ont été menées et des décisions unilatérales ont été prises par les uns et par les autres alors que, de l'avis de la Cour,

not it is a party to a specific conflict, is under an obligation to ensure that the requirements of the instruments in question are complied with.

159. Given the character and the importance of the rights and obligations involved, the Court is of the view that all States are under an obligation not to recognize the illegal situation resulting from the construction of the wall in the Occupied Palestinian Territory, including in and around East Jerusalem. They are also under an obligation not to render aid or assistance in maintaining the situation created by such construction. It is also for all States, while respecting the United Nations Charter and international law, to see to it that any impediment, resulting from the construction of the wall, to the exercise by the Palestinian people of its right to self-determination is brought to an end. In addition, all the States parties to the Geneva Convention relative to the Protection of Civilian Persons in Time of War of 12 August 1949 are under an obligation, while respecting the United Nations Charter and international law, to ensure compliance by Israel with international humanitarian law as embodied in that Convention.

160. Finally, the Court is of the view that the United Nations, and especially the General Assembly and the Security Council, should consider what further action is required to bring to an end the illegal situation resulting from the construction of the wall and the associated régime, taking due account of the present Advisory Opinion.

* * *

161. The Court, being concerned to lend its support to the purposes and principles laid down in the United Nations Charter, in particular the maintenance of international peace and security and the peaceful settlement of disputes, would emphasize the urgent necessity for the United Nations as a whole to redouble its efforts to bring the Israeli-Palestinian conflict, which continues to pose a threat to international peace and security, to a speedy conclusion, thereby establishing a just and lasting peace in the region.

162. The Court has reached the conclusion that the construction of the wall by Israel in the Occupied Palestinian Territory is contrary to international law and has stated the legal consequences that are to be drawn from that illegality. The Court considers itself bound to add that this construction must be placed in a more general context. Since 1947, the year when General Assembly resolution 181 (II) was adopted and the Mandate for Palestine was terminated, there has been a succession of armed conflicts, acts of indiscriminate violence and repressive measures on the former mandated territory. The Court would emphasize that both Israel and Palestine are under an obligation scrupulously to observe the rules of international humanitarian law, one of the paramount purposes of which is to protect civilian life. Illegal actions and unilateral decisions have been taken on all sides, whereas, in the Court's view, this tragic

seule la mise en œuvre de bonne foi de toutes les résolutions pertinentes du Conseil de sécurité, en particulier les résolutions 242 (1967) et 338 (1973), est susceptible de mettre un terme à cette situation tragique. La «feuille de route» approuvée par la résolution 1515 (2003) du Conseil de sécurité constitue l'effort le plus récent en vue de provoquer des négociations à cette fin. La Cour croit de son devoir d'appeler l'attention de l'Assemblée générale, à laquelle cet avis est destiné, sur la nécessité d'encourager ces efforts en vue d'aboutir le plus tôt possible, sur la base du droit international, à une solution négociée des problèmes pendants et à la constitution d'un Etat palestinien vivant côte à côte avec Israël et ses autres voisins, et d'assurer à chacun dans la région paix et sécurité.

* * *

163. Par ces motifs,

LA COUR,

1) A l'unanimité,

Dit qu'elle est compétente pour répondre à la demande d'avis consultatif;

2) Par quatorze voix contre une,

Décide de donner suite à la demande d'avis consultatif;

POUR: M. Shi, *président*; M. Ranjeva, *vice-président*; MM. Guillaume, Koroma, Vereshchetin, Mme Higgins, MM. Parra-Aranguren, Kooijmans, Rezek, Al-Khasawneh, Elaraby, Owada, Simma, Tomka, *juges*;

CONTRE: M. Buergenthal, *juge*;

3) *Répond* de la manière suivante à la question posée par l'Assemblée générale:

A. Par quatorze voix contre une,

L'édification du mur qu'Israël, puissance occupante, est en train de construire dans le territoire palestinien occupé, y compris à l'intérieur et sur le pourtour de Jérusalem-Est, et le régime qui lui est associé sont contraires au droit international;

POUR: M. Shi, *président*; M. Ranjeva, *vice-président*; MM. Guillaume, Koroma, Vereshchetin, Mme Higgins, MM. Parra-Aranguren, Kooijmans, Rezek, Al-Khasawneh, Elaraby, Owada, Simma, Tomka, *juges*;

CONTRE: M. Buergenthal, *juge*;

B. Par quatorze voix contre une,

Israël est dans l'obligation de mettre un terme aux violations du droit international dont il est l'auteur; il est tenu de cesser immédiatement les travaux d'édification du mur qu'il est en train de construire dans le territoire palestinien occupé, y compris à l'intérieur et sur le pourtour de Jérusalem-Est, de démanteler immédiatement l'ouvrage situé dans ce ter-situation can be brought to an end only through implementation in good faith of all relevant Security Council resolutions, in particular resolutions 242 (1967) and 338 (1973). The "Roadmap" approved by Security Council resolution 1515 (2003) represents the most recent of efforts to initiate negotiations to this end. The Court considers that it has a duty to draw the attention of the General Assembly, to which the present Opinion is addressed, to the need for these efforts to be encouraged with a view to achieving as soon as possible, on the basis of international law, a negotiated solution to the outstanding problems and the establishment of a Palestinian State, existing side by side with Israel and its other neighbours, with peace and security for all in the region.

* * *

163. For these reasons,

THE COURT,

(1) Unanimously,

Finds that it has jurisdiction to give the advisory opinion requested;

(2) By fourteen votes to one,

Decides to comply with the request for an advisory opinion;

IN FAVOUR: *President* Shi; *Vice-President* Ranjeva; *Judges* Guillaume, Koroma, Vereshchetin, Higgins, Parra-Aranguren, Kooijmans, Rezek, Al-Khasawneh, Elaraby, Owada, Simma, Tomka;

AGAINST: *Judge* Buergenthal;

(3) *Replies* in the following manner to the question put by the General Assembly:

A. By fourteen votes to one,

The construction of the wall being built by Israel, the occupying Power, in the Occupied Palestinian Territory, including in and around East Jerusalem, and its associated régime, are contrary to international law;

IN FAVOUR: *President* Shi; *Vice-President* Ranjeva; *Judges* Guillaume, Koroma, Vereshchetin, Higgins, Parra-Aranguren, Kooijmans, Rezek, Al-Khasawneh, Elaraby, Owada, Simma, Tomka;

AGAINST: *Judge* Buergenthal;

B. By fourteen votes to one,

Israel is under an obligation to terminate its breaches of international law; it is under an obligation to cease forthwith the works of construction of the wall being built in the Occupied Palestinian Territory, including in and around East Jerusalem, to dismantle forthwith the structure therein situated, and to repeal or render ineffective forthwith ritoire et d'abroger immédiatement ou de priver immédiatement d'effet l'ensemble des actes législatifs et réglementaires qui s'y rapportent, conformément au paragraphe 151 du présent avis;

POUR: M. Shi, *président*; M. Ranjeva, *vice-président*; MM. Guillaume, Koroma, Vereshchetin, Mme Higgins, MM. Parra-Aranguren, Kooijmans, Rezek, Al-Khasawneh, Elaraby, Owada, Simma, Tomka, *juges*;

CONTRE: M. Buergenthal, *juge*;

C. Par quatorze voix contre une,

Israël est dans l'obligation de réparer tous les dommages causés par la construction du mur dans le territoire palestinien occupé, y compris à l'intérieur et sur le pourtour de Jérusalem-Est;

POUR: M. Shi, *président*; M. Ranjeva, *vice-président*; MM. Guillaume, Koroma, Vereshchetin, Mme Higgins, MM. Parra-Aranguren, Kooijmans, Rezek, Al-Khasawneh, Elaraby, Owada, Simma, Tomka, *juges*;

CONTRE: M. Buergenthal, *juge*;

D. Par treize voix contre deux,

Tous les Etats sont dans l'obligation de ne pas reconnaître la situation illicite découlant de la construction du mur et de ne pas prêter aide ou assistance au maintien de la situation créée par cette construction; tous les Etats parties à la quatrième convention de Genève relative à la protection des personnes civiles en temps de guerre, du 12 août 1949, ont en outre l'obligation, dans le respect de la Charte des Nations Unies et du droit international, de faire respecter par Israël le droit international humanitaire incorporé dans cette convention;

POUR: M. Shi, *président*; M. Ranjeva, *vice-président*; MM. Guillaume, Koroma, Vereshchetin, Mme Higgins, MM. Parra-Aranguren, Rezek, Al-Khasawneh, Elaraby, Owada, Simma, Tomka, *juges*;

CONTRE: MM. Kooijmans, Buergenthal, *juges*;

E. Par quatorze voix contre une,

L'Organisation des Nations Unies, et spécialement l'Assemblée générale et le Conseil de sécurité, doit, en tenant dûment compte du présent avis consultatif, examiner quelles nouvelles mesures doivent être prises afin de mettre un terme à la situation illicite découlant de la construction du mur et du régime qui lui est associé.

POUR: M. Shi, *président*; M. Ranjeva, *vice-président*; MM. Guillaume, Koroma, Vereshchetin, Mme Higgins, MM. Parra-Aranguren, Kooijmans, Rezek, Al-Khasawneh, Elaraby, Owada, Simma, Tomka, *juges*;

CONTRE: M. Buergenthal, *juge*.

Fait en français et en anglais, le texte français faisant foi, au Palais de la Paix, à La Haye, le neuf juillet deux mille quatre, en deux exemplaires, all legislative and regulatory acts relating thereto, in accordance with paragraph 151 of this Opinion;

IN FAVOUR: *President* Shi; *Vice-President* Ranjeva; *Judges* Guillaume, Koroma, Vereshchetin, Higgins, Parra-Aranguren, Kooijmans, Rezek, Al-Khasawneh, Elaraby, Owada, Simma, Tomka;

AGAINST: *Judge* Buergenthal;

C. By fourteen votes to one,

Israel is under an obligation to make reparation for all damage caused by the construction of the wall in the Occupied Palestinian Territory, including in and around East Jerusalem;

IN FAVOUR: *President* Shi; *Vice-President* Ranjeva; *Judges* Guillaume, Koroma, Vereshchetin, Higgins, Parra-Aranguren, Kooijmans, Rezek, Al-Khasawneh, Elaraby, Owada, Simma, Tomka;

AGAINST: *Judge* Buergenthal;

D. By thirteen votes to two,

All States are under an obligation not to recognize the illegal situation resulting from the construction of the wall and not to render aid or assistance in maintaining the situation created by such construction; all States parties to the Fourth Geneva Convention relative to the Protection of Civilian Persons in Time of War of 12 August 1949 have in addition the obligation, while respecting the United Nations Charter and international law, to ensure compliance by Israel with international humanitarian law as embodied in that Convention;

IN FAVOUR: *President* Shi; *Vice-President* Ranjeva; *Judges* Guillaume, Koroma, Vereshchetin, Higgins, Parra-Aranguren, Rezek, Al-Khasawneh, Elaraby, Owada, Simma, Tomka;

AGAINST: *Judges* Kooijmans, Buergenthal;

E. By fourteen votes to one,

The United Nations, and especially the General Assembly and the Security Council, should consider what further action is required to bring to an end the illegal situation resulting from the construction of the wall and the associated régime, taking due account of the present Advisory Opinion.

IN FAVOUR: *President* Shi; *Vice-President* Ranjeva; *Judges* Guillaume, Koroma, Vereshchetin, Higgins, Parra-Aranguren, Kooijmans, Rezek, Al-Khasawneh, Elaraby, Owada, Simma, Tomka;

AGAINST: *Judge* Buergenthal.

Done in French and in English, the French text being authoritative, at the Peace Palace, The Hague, this ninth day of July, two thousand and dont l'un restera déposé aux archives de la Cour et l'autre sera transmis au Secrétaire général de l'Organisation des Nations Unies.

Le président,
(Signé) SHI Jiuyong.

Le greffier,
(Signé) Philippe COUVREUR.

M. le juge KOROMA, Mme le juge HIGGINS et MM. les juges KOOIJMANS et AL-KHASAWNEH joignent à l'avis consultatif les exposés de leur opinion individuelle; M. le juge BUERGENTHAL joint une déclaration à l'avis consultatif; MM. les juges ELARABY et OWADA joignent à l'avis consultatif les exposés de leur opinion individuelle.

(Paraphé) J.Y.S.
(Paraphé) Ph.C.

four, in two copies, one of which will be placed in the archives of the Court and the other transmitted to the Secretary-General of the United Nations.

(Signed) SHI Jiuyong,
President.

(Signed) Philippe COUVREUR,
Registrar.

Judges KOROMA, HIGGINS, KOOIJMANS and AL-KHASAWNEH append separate opinions to the Advisory Opinion of the Court; Judge BUERGENTHAL appends a declaration to the Advisory Opinion of the Court; Judges ELARABY and OWADA append separate opinions to the Advisory Opinion of the Court.

(Initialled) J.Y.S.
(Initialled) Ph.C.

9 789058 871565
13W68999/ T15/ 9789058871565